DARK FIGURES IN THE
DESIRED COUNTRY

GERDA S. NORVIG

DARK FIGURES IN THE DESIRED COUNTRY

Blake's Illustrations to *The Pilgrim's Progress*

UNIVERSITY OF CALIFORNIA PRESS

Berkeley   Los Angeles   Oxford

Frontispiece: Blake, *Christian Reading in His Book*.

This work is published with the assistance of The J. Paul Getty Trust.

The publisher also acknowledges a grant from the University of Colorado at Boulder.

University of California Press
Berkeley and Los Angeles, California
University of California Press, Ltd.
Oxford, England
© 1993 by
The Regents of the University of California
Printed in the United States of America
9 8 7 6 5 4 3 2 1

Library of Congress Cataloging-in-Publication Data

Norvig, Gerda S.
    Dark figures in the desired country : Blake's illustrations
to The pilgrim's progress / Gerda S. Norvig.
        p.   cm.
    Includes bibliographical references (p.   ) and index.
    ISBN 0-520-04471-1 (alk. paper)
    1. Blake, William, 1757–1827—Criticism and interpretation.
2. Bunyan, John, 1628–1688.   Pilgrim's progress—Illustrations.
I. Blake, William, 1757–1827.   II. Title.
NC978.5.B55N67   1992
759.2—dc20   91-20400

William Blake's twenty-eight watercolor illustrations for Bunyan's *The Pilgrim's Progress* were first reproduced in *Pilgrim's Progress*, edited by Sir Geoffrey Keynes, © 1941 by The Limited Editions Club, renewed in 1969 by The George Macy Companies, Inc., New York. The original watercolors reside in The Frick Collection, New York, and are used with permission.

The paper used in this publication meets the minimum requirements of American National Standard for Information Sciences—Permanence of Paper for Printed Library Materials, ANSI Z39.48-1984. ⊗

To Gregory Jordan and Gerda Goldfrank Stein:

Two who kept vision in time of trouble

CONTENTS

LIST OF ILLUSTRATIONS

FIGURES

APPENDIX FIGURES

KEY TO REFERENCES

Except for an occasional citation from *The Notebook of William Blake: A Photographic and Typographic Facsimile,* ed. David V. Erdman, all quotations of Blake's writings are from *The Complete Poetry and Prose of William Blake,* ed. David V. Erdman, designated as E. The Oxford Standard Authors edition of *Blake's Complete Writings,* ed. Geoffrey Keynes, remains a necessary tool for scholarship (because the Blake *Concordance,* ed. David V. Erdman, is cued to it); I have therefore cited it as well, designating it as K. Thus, whenever a text is referred to by its typography and place in E, its place in K is also given. Many references, however, are listed only by the title and plate number of Blake's works, which are abbreviated as follows:

ARO   *All Religions Are One*
DC   *A Descriptive Catalogue*
FR   *The French Revolution*
FZ   *Vala, or the Four Zoas*
Gates   *The Gates of Paradise* (both versions)
J   *Jerusalem* (alternative page numbers in brackets)
M   *Milton, a Poem*
MHH   *The Marriage of Heaven and Hell*
VLJ   "A Vision of the Last Judgment"

Note that in the cases of *Milton* and *Jerusalem* I offer variant page numberings (separated by a slash) when referring to plates whose positions shifted in alternate copies.

References to Bunyan's work are from the following two texts: *The Pilgrim's Progress from This World to That Which Is To Come,* ed. James Blanton Wharey, 2d ed. rev. Roger Sharrock (Oxford: Clarendon Press, 1960), abbreviated as *PP;* and *Grace Abounding to the Chief of Sinners,* ed. Roger Sharrock (Oxford: Clarendon Press, 1962), abbreviated as *GA.*

PREFACE AND ACKNOWLEDGMENTS

Nearly two decades ago, during the mid-1970s, when I began to explore the material from which this book has since grown, I approached the task with a missionary faith and zeal common to the critical standard of that day. I was convinced that a right reading of Blake's illustrations to *The Pilgrim's Progress* existed, that it was a symbolic reading, that it conformed to Blake's intention, and that it could be made applicable to each viewer's experience by means of a detailed psycho-aesthetic analysis. Furthermore, I presumed that the latent meaning of the designs was itself a psycho-aesthetic myth—or, to put it another way, that through his revisionary pictorial narrative of Bunyan's dream-vision, Blake was drawing up and drawing out a new map of the creative psyche and its self-interpreting vicissitudes.

Today, many years later, especially in the light of postmodern questioning of the constructs of signification and objective meaning, the dogmatism of those initial opinions seems both quaint and naive. Yet most of my primary insights about the range and focus of Blake's project remain virtually the same; for example, I still believe that a psychological reading of *Blake's* psychological exploration of Bunyan's text is valid and revealing. What has changed during the book's long gestation is rather the shape of the inquiry. Instead of beginning with the assumption that Blake's work has a singular, totalizing purpose, I have become more concerned to show the ways in which it sometimes shrewdly, sometimes inadvertently, makes problematic the quest for such a goal.

My shift from a position of assurance to one of questioning, in other words, is something I now see paralleled in the complex contextualizations of the *Progress* designs themselves. For the eye altering truly does alter all, as Blake tells us in a poem about such mental traveling.[1] In this case, my view of things has altered "all" in a literal sense as well. For it is the very status of "all," the very vision of completeness I originally attributed to his art, that I now find Blake actively deconstructing and reconstructing in order to exemplify the "continual building and destroying" of imagination in and by imagination (*J* 88) which he seems to have valued, in fact, above "all."[2]

The way I came to my subject is part of the tale of the development of my critical response to it, and as such it may shed light on some of my procedures in the chapters that follow. I had been very much involved with the depth psychology of C. G. Jung when I stumbled across an interpretation of *The Pilgrim's Progress* by the Jungian analyst Esther Harding.[3] This book, *Journey into Self,* adopted the somewhat reductive format followed by most Jungian treatments of literary texts in that it read the story monolithically as a confessional allegory of the individuation process of its author. Further, Harding's focus was doctrinal: she sought to abstract, interpret, and amplify examples of Jungian psychodynamics found in the symbolism of Bunyan's dream-vision by comparing them with interpretations of contemporary clinical case histories. From the point of view of the literary critic, that approach left glaring gaps. Reading the *Progress* as the spontaneous expression of the unconscious, Harding summarily dismissed the book's "writerly" effects and ignored as well most of the cultural contexts that helped shape its idiom.[4] Thus no attention was paid to Bunyan's strategic control over his material, and no validity given to his deliberate didacticism, his adoption of Puritan hermeneutical techniques, his topical satire, or his profound biblical traditionalism. Furthermore, his subtle irony, his intertextual gamesmanship, the variety and complexity of his narratological invention, his polymorphous and sometimes ideologically subversive handling of metaphor and metonymy—indeed, almost all of his playful tropings and unique uses of formal devices—were virtually ignored in Harding's reading. It is as if she somehow forgot the fact that the psyche speaks, and so must be represented as speaking, through rhetoric and the narrative manipulations of discourse as much as through imagery and myth.

Nevertheless, while these drawbacks caused her work to misrepresent and even trivialize Bunyan's creative achievement, Harding's psychoanalytic examination accomplished two very important things for me. First, it signaled that there was more to Bunyan's dream-vision format than mere literary convention, since his particular handling of the genre defamiliarized it in a way that made it mimetic of real psychodynamic fantasy activity. In fact, puzzling places in the *Progress* that over the centuries have been regarded by readers as critical cruxes can almost always be interpreted without strain when their inconsistencies are reenvisioned as purposeful dream rhetoric.[5] Second, through Harding's clinical insights and my own experience of depth psychology I came to appreciate the accuracy of the mental states that Bunyan's Puritan figurations projected. Harding's interpretation of those emblems of the inner life, in short, made them startlingly applicable to each of our own modern "journeys into self."

Soon after, when I encountered Blake's illustrations to the *Progress,* I was struck by the fact that his pictorial critique mirrored many aspects of Harding's polemical reading of Bunyan. Like the Jungian, Blake focused on the archetypal components of the original dream-vision and seemed to dismiss the more topical, sociopolitical scenes and allusions. (That this was a convention of the illustrative tradition of Bunyan's work—a tradition begun as early as 1682—I did not recognize until later.) Also, many of Blake's designs invoked the sort of psychosexual imagery congenial to the mythic dimensions of Jungian (rather than Freudian) analysis. Finally, the peculiar narrative reapportionment of events in Blake's graphic sequence gave centrality to just the episodes singled out by Harding as key turning points in the individuation process of the narrator/dreamer's psyche. The question was, where could this discovery of a link between the Jungian and the Blakean view of Bunyan's myth lead? I had no interest in contributing further to the literature of Jungian apologetics at either Blake's or Bunyan's expense. Instead I hoped to show how Blake's dynamic concept of the imagination, itself a sort of depth psychology, allowed him to perceive a cognate vision operating in Bunyan's *Progress*. The Jungian framework, with its archetypal emphasis, simply gave me some tools for appraising how Blake's representations of the psyche actually functioned in the composition, iconography, and narrative structure of his interpretive *Progress* drawings. It also provided a vocabulary for explaining Blake's focus on Bunyan's fable as an expression of how consciousness transforms itself from within by vision, producing its own signifiers and images of transformation to mark the way.

In the course of time, and under the influence of contemporary critical theory with its drive to awaken hard-line "new-critical" readers from the dogmatic slumber of their hidden ideological biases, my own biases began to alter. I could not help doubting the value of my original attempt to fit Blake's work into the procrustean bed of interpretive assumptions about aesthetic coherence, intentionality, master tropes, symbolic action, hierarchical value systems, and the like. Concurrently, my allegiance to the totalistic structures of orthodox Jungian thought also began to waver. In essence, I had become more of a Blakean than a Jungian. I therefore tried to practice a form of visionary Blakean hermeneutics and open my own criticism to the imaginative process of "striving with systems to deliver individuals [and their works] from systems" (*J* 11) rather than to read things through the veil of a basically monotheistic depth psychology. Blake's focus on the polymorphic and polysemic structures of imagination provided an example that itself suggested a qualified critique of the Jungian project. What was wanted, it seemed, was a psychological perspective that maintained Jung's fearless, nonpositivistic prioritizing of the psyche's self-referential typologies without succumbing to a nineteenth-century ideology of heroic progress toward a fixed goal called "spiritual wholeness."

As it happened, a similar revisionist critique was being articulated in Jungian circles by the phenomenological theorist James Hillman and his followers. These archetypal psychologists, as they call themselves, focus their inquiry and treatment methods on psychic imagery as it unfolds within the economy of its own rhetoric, its own semiosis. They see the semiotic structure of the psyche as innately polytheistic, a pantheon of primordial fantasies or gods (or "zoas," as Blake named them) that contains as one of its members—but not one that axiomatically regulates the others—the self-styled archetype of dominant monotheism, essentialism, logocentrism, and so on. In practice, they regard the function of all such images and fantasy structures as autonomous. They thus firmly eschew denaturing an image by equating it with its supposed symbolic meaning. Indeed, the very term *symbol,* so prevalent in orthodox Jungian writings, is almost entirely replaced in their vocabulary by the less encumbered, less analytical, less abstract *image*—a strategy I too have adopted in this book, for closely allied reasons. That is, I find everywhere in Blake a pressure to confront the concrete forms of imagination manifested in the verbal and visual images of his texts on their own grounds, as a chain of prolific, sliding signifiers rather than as a cluster of latent, all-too-readily appropriated signifieds.[6]

In line with their concentration on the mental image as the primary datum of psychic reality, the neo-Jungian psychologists have privileged a cognate word that I adopt as well: *imaginal*. This locution was coined by Jung's friend, the Islamic scholar Henry Corbin, to stand as a neutral term free of the dismissive (and sometimes actively pejorative) connotations popularly attached to the adjectives *imaginative* and *imaginary*. Initially Corbin employed it to describe the Sufi notion of an ontological state (the *mundus imaginalis*) that is deemed to exist in its own transpersonal domain midway between the material and the absolute, the mundane and the heavenly, the empirical and the spiritual. This imaginal world is thought to be a sort of collective unconscious independent of direct human agency, existing with something like the autonomy granted by the ancients to the macrocosmic force they named the *anima mundi,* or world soul. According to Sufi wisdom, the *mundus imaginalis* is composed of networks of self-originating archetypal images that, to borrow Lacan's tag, are "structured like a language" and that prefigure and indeed determine the basic mythic patterns of our lives.

For Hillman the concept is attractive because it expresses his view of the psyche as a determining construct or genre—the "poetic basis of mind"[7]—that is itself constitutive rather than derivative of the individual (and subjective) imagination. "The imaginal," then, as a term describing the very medium (rather than a mere faculty) of mental life, gives primacy to imagination as a cognitive matrix, "a distinct field of imaginal realities" that needs to be approached by "methods and perceptual faculties" that are native to it.[8] For the neo-Jungians, imaginal psychology thus works like a poetics of the psyche and involves a method bearing a close relation to the processes of an interpretive structuring principle that I call Blake's visionary hermeneutics. What I intend to bring into focus by applying this term *imaginal* to Blake, therefore, is an appreciation of how the psychopoetics operating in his oeuvre teaches the language required to perceive, understand, honor, and indeed resurrect that which he figures as "the eternal body" of imagination lying dormant within reader and text, spectator and image.

In addition to adopting in this study some terms and points of view that are not an accepted part of the heritage of Blake criticism, I also reject on principle a few tactics that are. In particular, I resist the prevalent practice of assuming that any single series of designs can and must be read in the context of all Blake's other designs, with the critic making inferences of iconographic meaning and identity on the basis of likenesses drawn from across the pictorial canon. My objection to such an analytical method is twofold. In the first place, reading meanings in this atomistic fashion tends to obviate the fact that design elements within individual plates of a series draw their significance—and make their necessary and sufficient impact on the viewer—*intra*textually, as part of a singular ongoing pictorial narrative. Indeed, it is the self-reflexive interdependency of both iconographic and compositional motifs within a particular series of grouped plates that constitutes the linchpin of Blake's implied visionary hermeneutics, a point I demonstrate at some length in the central discussions of this book.

Thus, although comparing iconographic likenesses culled from disparate places in the vast corpus of Blake's visual art may prove interesting in its own right, such cross-referencing rarely illuminates the contextual function of any specific occurrence of the image so cited. In other words, Blake hardly ever makes meaningful allusions to his own former work in precisely that way. So while it is true, for instance, that Blake's figures of despair share common gestures and a stock pose, as Janet Warner has so clearly documented,[9] and knowledge of that fact may enhance our understanding of an especially obscure design, normally, as with the figure of the Man in the Iron Cage of despair in the *Progress* illustrations (Plate 12), this sort of identification is implicit in both the literary and graphic context of the design itself and needs no reference to Blake's other work.

Second, it can often be interpretively misleading to play the game of matching figures from Blake's illustrations of other poets, on the one hand, with those of his own illuminated works, on the other, concluding from these pairings that the contents of the illuminated texts can function as an adequate gloss, a "key" to the hidden meanings of the interpretive illustrations. This is to limit Blake's aesthetic enterprise to the propogandizing of set doctrines that supposedly retain a fixed iconology and an invariantly defined vocabulary of images. As indicated earlier, that does not seem to be the way things work in Blake's graphic narratives. He did have a finite vocabulary, of course, both of word and of image; but one of his most salient procedures was to let the meanings of those terms expand and transform typologically within individual works, not to mention change radically from work to work. As others have pointed out in defense of a fluid, polysemous reading of Blake's visuals, every old man represented by Blake is not a Urizen, every young one not an Orc. Certainly Blake's agenda as an interpretive illustrator never entailed a demand that viewers master the mythologies of his own privately distributed illuminated poetry in order to read his graphic critiques of Dante, Spenser, Chaucer, Milton, Gray, and so on, not to mention Bunyan. On the contrary, aside from the sort of intratextual interpretive requirements mentioned above, Blake seems to have assumed a very different and more public set of contexts, expecting his viewers to respond to his drawings on the basis of familiarity with (a) the texts and reputation of the texts illustrated, (b) other illustrators of the same texts, and (c) traditional—not private—cultural/artistic iconography. We will miss the profound relation his drawings have to the works they revision if we regard them as mainly a rehash of the poetry and designs Blake himself wrote or as a crude imposition of his eccentric philosophy on inhospitable sources. These drawings, in short, are a serious species of literary criticism and not a self-indulgent exercise on Blake's part in assimilating the Other to his own system.

Another related and also questionable practice frequently adopted by commentators on Blake's interpretive designs is to treat his graphic readings as moral correctives of their sources. It is true that Blake does take obvious liberties at times with the literal images or with the story line of the works he illustrates, and in so doing he may imply that a value represented one way by the author has an additional, even opposite, connotation worth considering. (We will see several instances of this critical strategy operating in the *Pilgrim's Progress* drawings.) But I believe we unnecessarily distort the peculiar analytical power and supple dialogic focus of Blake's revisionary process when we reduce our readings of his graphic criticism to an exposé of the "corrective" over the "appreciative" elements of his interpretations.[10] The division of labor is never so simple as that. Usually when Blake seems to be "correcting" an author's ideological biases he is actually extending subtexts that exert their influence, however unconsciously, in the originary text itself. In this way, Blake's illustrations invite the careful reader to reassess (often deconstructively) the urtext and thus broaden his or her conception both of it and of Blake's latter-day pictorial critique of it. For example, *The Pilgrim's Progress* is no longer the book that it was for me before studying Blake's illustrative treatment of it. When I go back to it now, I see in it first and foremost all those elements that Blake's designs so powerfully emulate and uncover: its modern/postmodern contents and procedures, its narratological complexities, its subversions and self-subversions, its psychological explorations of subjectivity and the imaginal, and, most of all, its call to the reader to honor the unfolding of her own imaginative, visionary hermeneutics as both product and cause of her private pilgrimage through the received text.

My own journey through still another text—the book that follows—has not been accomplished in such solitary fashion. Rather, it has been supported, encouraged, and helpfully critiqued by more people and organizations than I have the space to name, and possibly more than I remember, too. But whether they are cited here or not, I am grateful to them all. In the earliest stages of the work, the kind and careful mentorship of Aileen Ward and Benjamin B. Hoover sustained me and pushed me on to attempt a deeper intellectual vision. In those years I also relied shamelessly on the steady stream of positive comments and exhortations offered by my friend and colleague Jane Lilienfeld, who thought better of me than I deserved. Victor Harris, Suzanne Hoover, Allen Grossman, and Irene Tayler were additional advocates of the enterprise at that time, and for their attentive readings, critiques, and reassurances I remain thankful.

Later, welcome encouragement came from numerous generous colleagues and students at the University of Colorado. I have been most fortunate in the companionable and often inspired research assistance of Robert Wells, Mark Scott, Joseph Hogan, Paul Butler, Roberta Martin, and Curtis Westberg. And for challenging responses to portions of the manuscript-in-process I owe a fond debt of gratitude to Elizabeth Nelson, John Murphy, Martin Bickman, Joan Burbick, James Kincaid, and especially the hundreds of hours of fruitful discussion unstintingly proffered by my longtime friend, associate, and erstwhile department chair, Jeffrey Robinson.

In the extended community of Blake scholars I have also been lucky enough to meet a range of highly stimulating critics whose work and remarks I have drawn strong sustenance from, in many cases more powerfully and personally than they themselves may have realized. From among this group I single out particularly Joseph Wittreich, Morton Paley, Anne Mellor, Sir Geoffrey Keynes, Leslie Tannenbaum, Robert Gleckner, Jean Hagstrum, Robert Essick, Mary Lynn Johnson, John Grant, John Wright, Morris Eaves, Nelson Hilton, Alicia Ostriker, Donald Ault, David Erdman, and Hazard Adams.

But my thanks for significant support does not stop with individuals. The still wider world of academic and cultural institutions has also offered invaluable assistance. This backing has sometimes come in monetary form, as in the case of generous publication grants issued by the Getty Foundation and the University of Colorado; and sometimes it has simply been by way of making resources available often in ideal conditions such as the ones scholars famously revel in at the Huntington Library in San Marino, California. Most of the museums and libraries to which I extend grateful acknowledgments of this kind are mentioned in the credits of my list of illustrations.

In a completely different vein is another "institution" to which I owe more than can be conveyed even by the most heartfelt expressions of thanks. This is the institution of deep friendship mixed with intellectual companionship and practical, everyday nurturance—a loving network of support that I have happily taken part in with two outstanding and unusual women scholars, Elizabeth Robertson and Dana Cuff. As fellow laborers in the never-ending struggle to write with suitable flair precisely what one thinks and means, these two have empowered both me and my work. From the clear and clarifying eye of Dana, who has inherited her mother's talent first to discern and then warmly to promote exactly what is best in others, I learned how to shape and reshape germane ideas I might otherwise have abandoned. By her spirited honoring of the individuality of my project, she helped make things happen whenever furtherance seemed in jeopardy. Similarly, I have benefited beyond measure from the energy of Beth's optimism and unflagging willingness to scold me into greater effort, greater thought. Without her magical knack for locating trouble spots in the flow of an argument, and without the wit, the caring, and the loyal persistence of her attention to such matters, many key passages in this book would never have been formulated.

Finally I would like to acknowledge family, friends, and editors whose patient reassurance and goodwill often far exceeded what I had any right to expect. So to Peter, Marc, and Laura Norvig, to Myra Glazer-Schotz, Shoshana Benjamin, Dani Siena, Schuyler Hoffman, Barbara Hartmann, Gordon Nelson, Deborah Marrow, Susan Rennie, Caroline Hinkley, Doris Kretschmer, and Barbara Ras, many thanks.

The
Pilgrim's Progress
From
This World
To
That which is to come [is]
Delivered under the Similitude of a
DREAM
Wherein is Discovered,
The Manner of his setting out,
His Dangerous Journey,
And
Safe Arrival at the Desired Countrey.

JOHN BUNYAN

May I not write in such a stile as this?
In such a method too, and yet not miss
Mine end, thy good? why may not it be done?
Dark Clouds bring Waters, when the bright bring none;

. . . .

[and] holy Writ,
Which for its Stile, and Phrase, puts down all Wit,
Is every where so full of all these things,
(Dark Figures, Allegories,) yet there springs
From that same Book that lustre, and those rayes
Of light, that turns our darkest nights to days.

JOHN BUNYAN

ORIGINAL
DERIVATION

The Jewish & Christian Testaments are An original
derivation from the Poetic Genius. this is necessary
from the confined nature of bodily sensations.

BLAKE, *All Religions Are One*

In the middle of Bunhill Fields, the small Dissenters' burial ground on the margins of the old City of London, an impressive monument to John Bunyan holds the place of honor. It shows a larger-than-life statue of the writer and preacher at rest on top of a high stone catafalque. One has to look up to see the figure of the man; but at eye level with the viewer, relief sculptures representing key episodes from Bunyan's *Pilgrim's Progress* animate the catafalque walls. What this juxtaposition of writer-in-effigy with narrative-in-effigy most clearly aims to convey is that Bunyan in death has become the pilgrim of his own dream allegory. Like Christian, the work's protagonist, he has undergone all the vicissitudes of the familiar hero's journey "from this world to that which is to come" and has presumably enacted the apotheosis only glimpsed in the last pages of the text.

This is the primary message. But the monument has other implications too, some of which would have interested William Blake, himself buried nearby in an unknown grave while a conspicuously bare headstone commemorating his death faces Bunyan's statue at a distance of only a dozen or so yards. That very situation, in fact, captures an aspect of a larger issue about the agency of the image in the work of both men. For it is ironic that Blake the graphic artist, Blake the indefatigable illustrator of so many culturally significant works, including Bunyan's *Progress,* should be represented in death by a virtually imageless graveyard marker when Bunyan, a visualizer through words alone, ends up with both his personality and his work memorialized graphically. At the same time, the foregrounding of the *Progress* images in this scene testifies to the unusual iconographic power of Bunyan's text, which seeks pictorial realization outside itself in a way that makes the producers of its imagery—artist and writer alike—seem supplementary to it rather than the reverse.

It is precisely this iconic imperative, responded to by illustrators of the text from the fifth edition onward, that interested Blake in Bunyan's work to begin with. Or to put it another way, Blake was attracted to what he called the visionary (and what we might call the archetypal or imaginal) aspects of the book's otherwise strictly allegorical structure.[1] Indeed, for him the *Progress* served as a test case that by its liminal nature demonstrated the technical difference he saw between transpersonal iconography ("vision") on the one hand and the deliberate metaphors of controlled propaganda ("allegory") on the other. The curious part of *this* visionary imagery, however, is that while it transcends and in a sense displaces the authorial, which is taken up and taken in by it, it simultaneously depends on the trope of the autobiographical, wherein author and text are identified or at least are seen to implicate each other. Such figurative appropriation of the relation between the producer and the produced has to do, of course, with the particular nature of Bunyan's narrative, which itself continually probes the dialectic of text-as-psyche/psyche-as-text in strikingly postmodern ways—ways it was the business of Blake to treat in the designs that my study explores.

This book, then, has a double focus. First, it offers a thorough case study of Blake's *Progress* illustrations along with an analysis of his changing relationship to Bunyan's persona, Bunyan's ideology, and Bunyan's poetics over a period of more than thirty years. Second, it argues for a way of reading Blake's designs that is both responsive to the concerns of contemporary critical thought and congruent with a process that his own art routinely results from, exemplifies, and teaches. I call that process visionary hermeneutics and claim for it a cornerstone position in the structure of Blake's larger artistic program.

Normally, hermeneutics refers to a set of predetermined interpretive strategies that a reader brings to and imposes on a work for one or more ulterior purposes, that is, either to critique and deconstruct or to amplify and valorize what is taken to be the text's consciously intended meaning (Paul Ricoeur calls these contrary approaches the "hermeneutics of suspicion" versus the "hermeneutics of faith").[2] My application of the term, however, extends this definition in two ways having to do with the linkage Blake makes in theory and practice between the concept of vision and the concept of interpretation. First, a hermeneutics that is visionary, when considered as a method of extrinsic interpretation (Blake's reading of Bunyan's *Progress,* for instance), charts a middle course between the Scylla of antithetical criticism and the Charybdis of appreciative exegesis. Less parasitic than either of these strategies, visionary hermeneutics aims neither to undermine nor shore up the originary text by providing a "secondary revision" (this is Freud's phrase for the distortion of dream experience perpetrated by the dreamer through the final assemblage and telling, that is, the remembering and translation into words, of the dream).[3] Rather it attempts, oxymoronically, a "primary revision"—what Blake calls elsewhere (in a phrase I have chosen as the title of this chapter) an "original derivation" (*ARO,* E1/K98). This goal of visionary hermeneutics is possible to achieve because in Blake's view there is no significant distinction between vision and re-vision: both are "derivative," in unique and hence original ways, of one and the same inexhaustible source, that "faculty of knowing" that Blake variously called "the human imagination," "the poetic genius," "spiritual sensation," "intellectual [as opposed to corporeal] understanding," "Existence itself," and so on. In this respect, Blake shares with poststructuralist theorists the conviction that all utterances are virtual texts and that texts (especially, in Blake's case, "visionary" texts) are always simultaneously supplementary and sui generis.

The second way my sense of the term "visionary hermeneutics" departs from ordinary usage is that I treat hermeneutics itself as an intratextual as well as an intertextual maneuver. By this I mean that I focus on the manner in which figures and images internal to the text "read" and are "read by" their later typological recurrences. A simple example familiar to most students of Blake would be the antiphonal way "The Lamb" and "The Tyger" (or indeed any of the obviously paired poems from the *Songs of Innocence and of Experience*) call to and interpret each other across the pastoral landscape of the *Songs*. This one-on-one codependency of meaning, however—often termed by critics the principle of dialectics in Blake's early work—is only part of the story. For visionary hermeneutics is not limited to dialectical processes: far from it. Even in the *Songs* itself a much more intricate pattern of mutual commentary, plotted by the progressive permutations of repeated verbal and pictorial motifs shown in changing contexts throughout the song cycle, emerges to enrich the reader's experience of the work as a sort of primer of visionary literacy. Instead of a moral message or a totalizing myth *about* "the two contrary states of the human soul," the *Songs* (following the propaedeutic function of primers) teaches a supple method of reading that actually sets as well as "shews" these imagined states of the soul in motion. Thus the very structure of the book (along with the demands of its genre as a self-styled children's reader) "rouzes the [hermeneutical] faculties to act" (E702/K793), and it does so in a fashion that surpasses and indeed critiques reliance on the binary codings of a simple doctrine of contraries. In this sense, the *Songs,* like so much of Blake's work, is "hermeneutic in the further sense . . . of containing a circular reflection on its own condition."[4]

Finally, although it is hard to generalize about Blake's development (he deliberately frustrates and explicitly denounces the attempt),[5] I think it is fair to say that his own focus on visionary hermeneutics, not only as a method but also as a subject for graphic and poetic expression, intensifies over the span of his artistic life. Of course, interpretive questions are thematized from the start, as for instance in the early *Religion* tracts (1788) and, again, in the *Songs* (1789–94), where "The Fly," "A Dream," and "The Tyger" may serve as representative examples. But only with the ripening of Blake's prophetic style in his longer poems, and especially in his graphic narratives illustrating long poems by others, does the concept of hermeneutic action come to dominate as a central image that itself reflects and requires a "visionary" interpretation. It is as if, in the explicitly interpretive project of revisioning the work of other writers through pictorial representation, Blake more and more forced interpretation into image and image into interpretation, thereby inciting the hermeneutical consciousness of the reader, like the represented consciousness of the text, to "catch itself in its own act."[6]

I have been speaking of visionary hermeneutics as a process that depends less on rules of interpretation than on an imaginative perspective, meaning both a perspective we learn to take toward the image and a perspective the imagination gradually gains on itself. As such it may be described as a reach for an outlook that is simultaneously an inlook, a sort of mental Möbius strip—making that entails a stance of consciousness which Blake embodies, discusses, solicits, and employs throughout the range of his poetic and graphic canon.[7] Yet nowhere does he address the process more directly than in his pictorial interpretation of Bunyan's dream allegory—a text that, for its part, already concerns a relentless investigation of the dynamic interplay between hermeneutics and visionary experience, visionary expression.

THE DRAWINGS

Blake's *Progress* illustrations themselves form a set of twenty-eight watercolor drawings with an extra design existing outside the series, most likely as an alternate for one included in the final grouping.[8] Each drawing measures approximately five by seven inches, a size appropriate for placement in a standard quarto volume. And while there is nothing to indicate that Blake intended them as material for inclusion in any real or imagined edition of Bunyan's text, their bookish dimension does imply that they can be thought of as constituting a parallel or competing "readable" text of their own, an answering volume with a distinct narrative ordering arranged to draw out and displace elements of the original.

It should be noted that among the twenty-eight designs, several remain in an unfinished state, with two still in the preliminary stages of composition and a handful more lacking full color and outline. Far from being a detriment to evaluation or analysis, however, the status of the series as something of a work-in-progress adds to its interest in many respects, for it gives us the opportunity to see Blake's method of adaptation and change—his own pilgrimage through the process of creating a pictorial intertext—in a clearer light. We can observe, for example, that the sketchiest design (Plate 27) is also the one most slavishly indebted to the popular tradition of *Progress* illustrations, as if it were an undeveloped transplant still awaiting transformation of its "minute particulars" by Blake's considered, revisionary hand and eye. Conversely, the drawings most worked up by Blake are the ones that carry original iconographic motifs that resonate throughout the graphic narrative to give it its unique interpretive codings and thematic structure.[9]

Of course, in the absence of any external evidence as to the artist's explicit intentions in this work (neither the precise circumstances of its production nor the reasons for its abandonment are known),[10] both the incompleteness of the series and the charge by some art historians that various designs have been touched up by a hand other than Blake's require of the reader a certain critical caution.[11] My policy has been to avoid making claims dependent on the resolution of these problems, because in my view there is a preeminent value in treating the designs just as they appear, regarding them as a received text with a telling "chain of signifiers" deserving attention on its own merit. Therefore, while the conundrums surrounding production questions play an important role in critically assessing (or agreeing to leave unassessed) certain aspects of the artist's intention, they remain subordinate to my project of interpreting the phenomena before us. At the same time, I have not hesitated to speculate on contextual matters or to see in this series significant formal trends that show Blake energetically advancing the potentialities of the genre of interpretive graphic narrative beyond the limits he had already so successfully mastered.

Blake's decision to treat *The Pilgrim's Progress* graphically came toward the end of his career, in approximately 1824, just three years before his death. He had by that time been practicing the art of interpretive illustration as a form of literary criticism for over a quarter of a century. The past subjects of his major pictorial commentaries were the poetic texts of such then canonical writers as Edward Young, Thomas Gray, Robert Blair, Milton, Shakespeare, Spenser, and Chaucer, resulting in a body of work that included well over 750 drawings and engravings.[12] Moreover, he was poised in 1824 between two of his greatest ventures in this line: the 100 illustrations to Dante's *Divine Comedy,* which were still to come, and the revised designs for the 21 engravings of the Book of Job, just completed. Thus he was at the height of his powers as an interpretive illustrator when he took on the Bunyan project, a fact that alone should alert us to the critical value of looking more closely than has been done to date at the structure and function of the *Progress* designs.

Indeed, given the importance of the place of these drawings in Blake's career, along with the relevance of Bunyan as a figure for Blake in his statements about poetics, it is surprising that they have received so little analytical attention from either art or literary critics. In part this relative neglect of the Bunyan designs is due to the fact that the watercolors themselves, currently among the holdings of the Frick Collection in New York City, have been on general view only four times since their arrival in the United States during World War II, and before that, in England, only once. The availability of copies of the complete series has similarly been much restricted, although since Martin Butlin's 1981 *catalogue raisonné* of Blake's paintings and drawings we do now have a source in which black-and-white reproductions of all the water-colors can be seen together.[13] Still, a way of approaching the designs analytically is not suggested by Butlin's work, which is concerned only with presenting full descriptive and bibliographic information.

Such has been the fate of almost all discussion of this series from the beginning. In 1941, for instance, Sir Geoffrey Keynes, one of the most eminent Blake scholar-collectors of this century, introduced color reproductions of the drawings to a select readership in a Limited Editions publication of Bunyan's text.[14] To this fit-audience-though-few he told the history of the drawings, speculating on the impetus for their creation and charting their early consignment to obscurity, their rediscovery in the possession of Lord Crewe, and their eventual rescue from public oblivion by Keynes himself in the late 1930s. His annotations to the plates, however, are almost mechanically descriptive and tantalizingly brief. He seems to have had no curiosity about the value of the pictorial enterprise as an interpretive commentary on Bunyan's dream-vision, and even less does his discussion deal with the series as a gestalt or as a problematic narrative statement with a telling mythos of its own to impart. Thus, despite the service Keynes rendered by identifying the drawings, reproducing them in color, and detailing their provenance, much remained to be done with respect to critiquing the contextual and intertextual implications of the sequence, analyzing its internal dynamics, and evaluating its relative importance in the total range of Blake's artistic canon. Yet in the nearly fifty years since Keynes's work on these illustrations, no full critical study of the series has been published. It is this lacuna that the present work aims to mend.[15]

CRITICAL METHODOLOGY

In treating this series of designs, my purpose has been to understand its revisionary motives and to elucidate the intentionality of its images in their contexts. While I examine the formative pressures on the work of biography, history, ideology, genre, and the conditions of production, my reading of the drawings themselves remains largely phenomenological. Not only do Blake's *Progress* drawings yield to such a criticism focused on the image, but they also are *about* such an approach—a coincidence of subject and interpretive strategy that in my view is a plus for the process of understanding.

However, in the current upsurge of ideological warfare among schools of literary theorists, many take the contrary position. Influential New Historicists and Cultural Materialists like Jerome McGann and Clifford Siskin, for example, argue that attempting to match one's own critical method with the method or values of the text under investigation is an essentially acritical, if not anticritical, maneuver.[16] Such deliberately constructed "resemblances between interpretation and that which is interpreted" (Siskin, 5) obfuscate, it is charged, the salient otherness of the text, including the culture-specific significance of its discursive methodology. What is wanted, these theorists insist, is first of all a self-consciously antithetical criticism, one that systematically *devalorizes* the techniques and underlying assumptions operating within the work in question. But of equal importance is the use of an *extrinsic* approach (what anthropologists call an "etic" versus an "emic" investigation) that keeps its historical and rhetorical distance from the text under study. Therefore, for these extrinsic-devalorizing methodologists, an *intrinsic* approach, no matter how antithetical, is not enough. Because although the act of "piercing Apollyon with his own bow" (*J* 12) can deconstruct and devalorize, it neither enables us "to see our object of inquiry in terms other than its own" (McGann, 41) nor keeps us from being "trapped in the discourse" of the Other's "desire" (Siskin, 28). The extrinsic-devalorizer's main caution here is against the perils of a devouring unconscious subjectivism associated with ahistorical Romantic conceptualizations on the one hand and regarded as a threat to individual critical autonomy on the other. So the importance attached by extrinsic-devalorizers to seeing the "object" *qua* object can be understood as part of a second-order program of disidentification and differentiation allied to the positivistic values that dominate contemporary Western culture. In sum, what the newer sociohistoric literary theorists especially deplore in Romantic studies is the potentially sterile solipsism of those intrinsic critical practices, which, by their "uncritical employment of Romanticism's self-representing concepts" (McGann, 41), land up being "authorized by the very writing they sought to analyze" (Siskin, 5). (Of course, critics who rely wholly on extrinsic-devalorizing procedures have themselves been called solipsistic inasmuch as, by adopting an etic approach to the text, they impose their objectivist ideology on the material and so remake that text in their own images.)[17]

While this call for a vigorous, extrinsically determined "hermeneutics of suspicion" is very compelling—especially as an antidote to the hagiographic reification of Romanticist tenets that often prevails in specific readings of specific Romantic authors and artists—the practice has its own set of limitations and consequences which bear looking into.

In the first place, the skeptical perspective of extrinsic-devalorizing critiques tends to keep faith with the ideology of Cartesian dualism, depending on an axiomatic subject/object split that denies (or anyhow brackets out) the complex and complicitous relations existing between what the critic sees and how she sees it. To put it another way, antithetical criticism of the "etic" variety is not set up to account for the determining role its methodology plays in shaping either the meaning or the "otherness" of the "object" it analyzes. Rather, the strictly objectivist stance of its investigative agenda protects it from the necessity of such a self-reflexive step: it does not have to consider the effective and affective distortions of its own projective mechanisms because the epistemological innocence (or naiveté) of its theoretical presuppositions denies the relevance of such matters. Indeed, in these writings the issue of personal bias is often considered to be no more than yet another product of the quintessentially ahistorical Romantic myth they name (with pejorative emphasis) "psychologism." Thus, while critics of this school readily invoke the caveat implied by Blake's adage "as the eye sees, so its object" in order to uncover the restrictive, subtextual ideologies operating in the work of the authors they study (that is, in the "object"), they rarely apply the same criteria in any but the most perfunctory sense to their own writing. In this way they sidestep a range of semantic issues that relate to the transference occurring between the reader and the work in the process of reading. Slighted, therefore, are not only specific reader-response elements in the text, but also the question of how such heuristic procedures function as an organizing principle of our experience of a work and what this tells us about the formal, imaginal intention of that work.

Another and related limitation of the extrinsic-devalorizing methodology in criticism, at least as it is practiced by many contemporary neo-Romanticists, is that it operates on exclusionary premises that deny validity to what it regards as competing (but I would call complementary) methods. In particular, by attempting to avoid "absorption in Romanticism's own self-representations" (McGann, 137), these new critics rule out adoption of virtually all critical procedures that seem to them to be outgrowths of the tenets of Romantic theory, even though many such procedures take on a very different meaning today, in their postmodern dress, than they did in the early nineteenth century. The problem with this stance is that, although motivated by historicist sympathies, it actually becomes proscriptively ahistorical insofar as it identifies and conflates specific methodologies with the varying ideological uses they are put to in varying historical circumstances. For while every method functions within an ideological framework and carries ideological implications, these ideologies and implications shift over time. That is, the ideological component of the method is what is culture-specific, not necessarily the method itself. Thus, the method does not belong to, nor should it automatically be stigmatized by its use in, any given period or cultural context. Its historic significance wants acknowledging, of course, but *it* does not thereby need to be abandoned: at least it deserves evaluation on a basis other than simple guilt by association. Besides, were we successfully to eschew every procedure that reflects, extends, or is analogous to a methodology favored by the Romantics themselves, we might well find ourselves speechless—or anyhow at a loss to understand the emotional shape and impact of their discourse. Without employing some of their own "coinages," as Freud put it (speaking of ways to approach the psyche), we would be so far outside their system of expression that we could not decipher it.[18] Or we would be deciphering it with such a foreign code that we would be even more likely to distort it beyond its own cultural context than would the so-called ahistorical, intrinsic critics. Finally, by turning away from what Jonathan Culler fancifully calls, after Lacan, the "mirror stage" of Romanticist critical thinking, extrinsic-devalorizers inevitably embrace a dichotomous, objectivist language of response especially appropriate to the "Name" and "symbolic order" of "the Father."[19]

This is the last significant consequence of an exclusionary extrinsic approach to Romantic writers: it tends for better or worse toward the patriarchal. For even though the critics I have been talking about use their methodological program to puncture the ideological "false consciousnesses" of the writings they study so as to stand outside and therefore buck the assumed values of the status quo, their antithetical postures and "etic" forms of analysis actually derive from and in that sense underwrite the status quo. By refusing to adopt the subject's point of view and guarding against being caught in the "discourse" of the Other's "desire," they inadvertently dismiss an empathic and relational model of knowledge that today carries the values of feminism and other marginal ideologies—points of view which can be said to represent the neglected energies of the culture's unconscious. In this way, instead of uncovering the full range of a work's cultural implications, they explore only the half that can be seen with the hierarchical eye. And as spokespersons of the structure (though not the content) of hierarchy, they become hegemonic discourse-makers who create not only a privileged but also, by default, a forbidden discourse in their wake.

My view is that as critics we can benefit from deliberately reinstating some of the values and methods of this forbidden discourse (which borrows and revisions notions native to Romanticism) even when—or rather, especially when—we are reading Romantic works themselves. But the key word here is *deliberately,* for the very real pitfalls that Siskin, McGann, and others find in certain romantic readings of Romantic texts stem largely from the degree of unconsciousness with which many traditional critics ape the shibboleths of Romanticism's own literary theories, all the while believing themselves to be methodologically neutral. They assume, in short, that they are working outside a hermeneutic circle that in fact they unwittingly, and so, as it were, indescribably, in- and de-scribe. Such Romanticized Romantic criticism, then, because it is unaware of its ideological allegiance and unreflective about its sympathic process, rather negates than exemplifies a true intrinsic-valorizing method. The complaint is really not that writers of this stripe go too far in adopting methods endemic of the works they analyze; instead it is (or ought to be) that they do not go far enough. Because they borrow only the dogma and not the critical self-consciousness of the Romantic tradition, they wind up without a methodological position of any kind, much less an intrinsic-valorizing position. Thus they are critiquing the products of Romantic irony without employing—rather than by expressly employing—the proper sort of Romantic irony that always acknowledges its own belatedness, its own necessarily deconstructive relation to its source.

By consciously utilizing an intrinsic-valorizing approach, however, and fully recognizing that this approach is itself a legacy of key Romantic assumptions, the writer on Romantic texts gains the advantage of probing, from within, the affective details of richly self-critical constructs whose experiential power and complexities are often a mere blur to the far-sighted extrinsic eye. We can, in other words, apprehend certain imaginal structures only if we see by means of them. The result is that such a critic accepts the inevitability of staying inside the hermeneutic circle, thereby retaining "a positive possibility of the most primordial kind of knowing" without sacrificing access to the cultural cues and codes that shape those texts.[20] Because Romantic theories usually value and rely on inclusionary rather than exclusionary principles, the critic who works within these models of interpretation is mandated to admit the complementary relevance of the extrinsic in a way the extrinsic denies to the intrinsic. Awareness thus can turn the intrinsic method itself into a quasi-extrinsic approach satisfying the critical need to establish a flexible range of contexts in which to operate. Blake's helpful distinction between a "negation" (that which defensively hinders or represses another) and a "contrary" (that which confronts or relates to another) is applicable here.[21] In his terms, the inclusionary model of Romantic intrinsic criticism, by recognizing the integrity (even when disputing the ideological motive) of approaches that appear alien both to itself and to the text being interpreted, has the capacity to transform a negation into a contrary and hence to broaden as well as enhance the dynamism of its field of reference. At the same time, the admission of contraries, with their separate but equal claim on the dialectical discourse of criticism, has a political consequence in that it fosters a relational rather than a hierarchical paradigm and so remains receptive to views that have been culturally or institutionally marginalized.

Insofar as I have just invoked Blake to authorize a particular approach to the readings of his own and other Romantic works, the above discussion has in effect offered a small demonstration of the method it seeks to justify. Let me now give another, more salient example of how a Romantic critical notion can both endorse and become the historicized subject of an intrinsic-valorizing analysis. The notion I want briefly to examine, call on, and then adapt to my own critical project is the idea held by many Romantic writers that successful transactions between audience and text evoke and require a particular intersubjectivity, often referred to as "sympathetic identification." Sympathetic identification in this sense is of course an ideal rather than a necessary condition of response (there can be *un*successful transactions that do *not* manage to evoke it), although most Romantic theorizers argue for its naturalness as a reflex of the healthy creative imagination. Clifford Siskin gives us a compelling account of how this works among Romanticists as well as Romantics in his treatment of what he sees as the anachronistic resemblance between the Yale school of deconstructive criticism on the one hand and Romantic ideologies on the other. Examining the pitfalls of Geoffrey Hartman's discussion in *Criticism in the Wilderness* about his own "creative criticism" as a function of an "absolute theory of reading" (49), Siskin points out that

> Hartman is following Wordsworth in premising his author-reader relationship upon a reciprocity between the author's creative imagination and the "co-operating *power* in the mind of the reader" ["Essay Supplementary to the Preface," *Prose* 3:81]. The creative text thus demands, to borrow Wordsworth's phrase, that the reader be "prompt/In sympathy" (1805 *Prelude*, I.645–646). James Beattie's 1778 dictum that "the philosophy of sympathy ought always to form a part of the science of Criticism" [*Essays on Poetry and Music as They Affect the Mind*, 2d ed. (Edinburgh, 1778)] . . . clarifies the generic interrelations at issue. The literary appropriations of philosophical discussions of the "mind" psychologized the acts of reading and writing, thereby redirecting authorial strategy towards consideration of individual emotional response. Thus Coleridge and Wordsworth's initial conversations during the first year of their friendship (1797) turned upon, in Coleridge's words, "the power of exciting the sympathy of the reader" [*Biographia Literaria*, ed. John Shawcross (Oxford, 1907), 2:5–6]. (Siskin, 50)

For Siskin this displacement of a difference in kind (writer versus reader, poet versus critic) onto a difference of degree (more creative poet/less creative reader-critic) is built into the notion of sympathetic identification, which for its part leads on to an insufferable elitism perpetrated by poets and poet-interpreters on the victimized reader. While I concur that such elitism underlies what Siskin calls "the politics of creativity" (53) informing many Romantic dicta (Wordsworth's hierarchical way of privileging the sensitivity of the poet over the duller responses of ordinary "men" in the "Preface" to the *Lyrical Ballads* is a case in point, as Siskin notes), I do not agree that concern for the processes of sympathetic identification is the culprit.[22]

On the contrary, sympathetic identification, taken as a cognitive function operating in the human physiology of author and audience alike (rather than as an emotional allegiance demanded of the subject reader by the lordly fiat of poet or critic), refers to a mental capacity independent of cultural categorizations or value rankings of any sort. It is one of the things the imagination empircally *does* when it wants to understand the experiential reality of the Other, and the sociopolitical use to which that understanding is later put is a separate matter altogether. In fact, the exercise of sympathetic identification—or empathy, as the contemporary self-psychologists currently term it[23]—tends in the act to undermine hegemonic power politics. That is why Keats called it "negative capability" (the ability to let go temporarily of conceptual paradigms of distinction) and why its practice by therapists is often recommended as a way of breaking down some of the authoritarian structures in traditional psychoanalysis that function as bars to emotional knowledge of another's psychic reality.

The endorsed practices of sympathetic identification, empathy, negative capability, and a criticism prone to intrinsic-valorizing procedures all have one thing in common: they each underwrite the insight that understanding operates *within,* and not just *on,* a system of relations. According to this "emic" point of view, unless one willingly enters into that system of relations to some degree (momentarily risking merger with it), its subjective-phenomenological dimensions cannot be accurately perceived, much less assessed, and its experiential impact will be deadened. Furthermore, to characterize that momentary merger negatively as an *entrapment* in the "discourse of the other's desire" is itself a way of getting trapped—but trapped, in this case, in a fantasy of conceptual objectivity and autonomy (Keats might call it a "positive capability") that ignores the role played by intersubjectivity in the processes of reading and understanding. Blake characterizes the dilemma succinctly in a line from his final epic *Jerusalem* where he has the Divine Voice (a voice that by definition divines otherness) explain how to come into relation with the unknown. The unknown in this case is what the Voice calls "The Reactor," a Satanic figure for the repressed who "hath hid himself thro envy." "I behold him," says the Voice; "But you cannot behold him till he be reveald *in his System*" (*J* 29, italics added).

What Blake suggests here is that we need to make the imaginative leap into the system of the other before the Other can even be made visible. There is no critiquing until there is beholding, and there is no beholding until there is appreciation of the contextual system shared by beholder and beheld alike. Applying this notion to a theory of critical reading, as Blake clearly does elsewhere, is to emphasize once more that to be situated within the hermeneutic circle is an inevitable condition of understanding;[24] and to accept rather than to foreclose that fact is to allow that criticism itself functions first and foremost as a displacement of the reading text, not a mastery of or over it. To put it another way, extrinsic-devalorizers imagine that they can break out of the hermeneutic circle, while intrinsic-valorizers imagine that the way out is the way in. Thus it is that Blake invites us to "Enter into" the "Images of wonder" depicted in his work and to do so "on the Fiery Chariot" of "Contemplative Thought":

> If the Spectator could Enter into these Images in his Imagination approaching them on the Fiery Chariot of his Contemplative Thought if he could Enter into Noahs Rainbow or into his bosom or could make a Friend & Companion of one of these Images of wonder which always intreats him to leave mortal things as he must know then would he arise from his Grave then would he meet the Lord in the Air & then he would be happy. (VLJ, E560/K611)

More important than the general hortatory invitation to the reader/critic to step inward, though, is the question of what sort of inwardness Blake is here proposing. For in this passage there is a distinct and seemingly purposeful ambiguity as to whether Blake refers to images existing in the objective work (the manifest "text" of his painting of the Last Judgment) or whether he is alluding to a primarily latent and subjective order of mental images evoked *by* his painting, images that are enterable only to the degree that they already reside "in [the spectator's] Imagination." Blake, it seems to me, would like to have it both ways, not only to emphasize that an empathic reading by definition entails a deliberate mingling of subject and object, but also to indicate that the psyche itself is a world of images that is "wondrous" precisely because it has the dual ontological status of being simultaneously objective and subjective. So when he writes, "If the Spectator could Enter into these Images *in his Imagination*" (italics added), he suggests that the imagination is on the one hand a place of origination (modifying the noun *Images*) and on the other a vehicle of transformation (modifying the verb *Enter*). But whether site or agency, objective or subjective reality, the imaginal world unfolds for Blake's hypothetical "Spectator" only by way of the process of sympathetic identification—a process reflective of the autonomous psyche's own dynamic activity and hence doubly "sympathic."

Part of what I have been trying to establish in the foregoing defense of method is the right to read Blake psychologically without automatically incurring thereby the charge of reductionism. The reason I propose such a critical psychological reading is that any intrinsic-valorizing approach to Blake must be willing to respond imaginatively to Blake's own prioritizing of psychic reality—his unequivocal assertion that "Mental Things are alone Real," for example (VLJ, E565/K617)[25]—and his relentless probing of the generic forms and functions of the psyche's imaginal language—its "ever Existent Images" (VLJ, E555/K605), which continually seek renewed and revisioned embodiment.

What I am focusing on, therefore, is as much Blake's psychologizing of the imaginative material at his disposal as my own psychologizing of Blake; particularly, in terms of this study, I want to chart and explicate the psychopoetic reading that his *Progress* drawings give to the archetypal dimensions of Bunyan's narrative. There can be little doubt that Blake *does* intentionally psychologize Bunyan's text in these drawings. But of course the sense in which I use the word *psychologize* here differs radically from the pejorative way the term has come to be applied by theorists dismissive of the reductive goals of much traditional psychoanalytic literary criticism. Usually the complaint of "psychologizing" is leveled against the writer who treats a work of art in any of the following ways. (1) He or she may take that work to be a symptom of its author's psychopathology and so read it, à la Freud, as a manifest text distorting a personalized latent meaning; (2) he or she may act as if the aim of the work were to present (in the case of fiction) a clinical picture of the interpersonal and developmental problems of one or more of its story's characters; and finally (3), he or she may discuss the text as if its contents served exclusively to represent extrinsic notions posed by a particular school of psychodynamic thought. In practice, what is most often common to all three of these approaches is a more or less sweeping disregard for the integral meaning of the work relative, on the one hand, to its social and historical contexts and, on the other hand, to its rhetorical strategies, its structural complexity, and its conscious manipulation of allusions, sources, generic conventions, and received ideas.

Blake's critical psychologizing, like the one I attempt to apply, is of another sort. First, he never ignores the cultural contexts that shape the vision of the text he reads; but he does place the cultural information itself in a psychological perspective, viewing historical events plus the socially constructed attitudes that determine or reflect them as "original derivations" of recurrent fantasy structures. Further, he attributes to these fantasy structures a privileged ontological status and a transpersonal life of their own in the human imagination. One could say, then, that what Blake's psychological vision uncovers is a sort of cultural immaterialism—a way of reading social vicissitudes as epiphenomena that are responsive to the self-generating, self-signifying activity of an objective psyche operating uniquely on and within each of us. "Eternity," as one of his proverbs of Hell proclaims, "is in love with the productions of time" (*MHH* 7).

Second, Blake's psychologizing remains critical rather than reductionist insofar as he is always concerned with the text as subject rather than merely with the subjects in the text or with the subjects responsible for its creation. Thus he honors the integrity of the work he critiques and deals with its rhetorical dominants as the principal signifiers of its conscious and unconscious expression. When I in my turn critique *Blake's* critique, I keep the same psychological frame of reference. This means that I pay close interpretive attention to those compositional and other formal devices in his *Progress* drawings which "copy Imagination" ("Public Address," E574/K594) and hence represent not only a plot of images but also the unconscious psyche's structural and dynamic methods of signification: its visual language and its visual speech, its medium and its messages. Such a focus is particularly appropriate to any commentary on *The Pilgrim's Progress* which takes seriously the fact that Bunyan's text, like Blake's revisionist treatment of it, is couched "in the similitude of a dream." For dreams, as we have known since Freud's designation of them as the *via regia* to a knowledge of the unconscious, offer us the most direct translations we have of the native imaginal discourse of the psyche.

When in the following chapters I explore Blake's psychologizing of Bunyan's myth, I draw often, as mentioned in the preface, on the vocabulary of Jungian and post-Jungian theory to articulate some of Blake's most characteristic moves. What has led me to choose the Jungian perspectives of analytical and archetypal psychology for this task is that the central vision of these approaches so clearly echoes the conception of the imagination dominating Blake's every word and every stroke of graphic expression. James Hillman, the chief spokesperson of Jungian revisionism, even claims Blake as a forerunner, a sort of archetypal psychologist *avant la lettre* who understood and demonstrated that the "Images in . . . imagination" (VLJ) were both the prime data and the radical "transformers" of psychic life.[26] Such an appreciation of Blake's insistence on the archetypal agency of the image highlights the equation so often made in Blake's work between psychic reality and what he calls imagination—that grand epistemic matrix constituting the very medium that makes every other human experience, action, and cognitive process possible. In other words, for both Blake and the Jungians, "imagination is not a state" (*M* 32, E132/K522), nor is it just one of the many faculties of the mind; rather, it is the root capacity conditioning all mental functioning. It is "the only uncontrovertible reality, directly presented, immediately felt" (Hillman, *Revisioning,* 50); "it is the Human Existence itself" (*M* 32). "Consciousness," as Hillman would have it, "rests upon a self-sustaining and imagining substrate" whose "images are both the raw materials and finished products of psyche" (*Revisioning*, x, xi). In fact he goes on to say regarding these images that "we can never be certain whether we imagine them or they imagine us" (*Revisioning*, 151). And it is this turn in Jung's thought as in Blake's that serves radically to deconstruct the cause-and-effect relationship usually deemed to exist between the individual personality and "his" or "her" unconscious. From the Jungian standpoint, the psyche cannot be regarded as a personal possession, nor can its contents be reduced to something created from repressed events by the desire of the subject. Indeed, in the eyes of the archetypal psychologist, if we wish to claim credit for inventing the images coming to us from the unconscious we must allow that we invent them only "according to the patterns they themselves lay down" (*Revisioning*, 151). For while "the psychic world is experienced empirically as inside us . . . yet it encompasses us with images" (*Revisioning*, 23) that exist "within their own field of relations, undetermined by personal psychodynamics" (Hillman, *Archetypal Psychology*, 7). In short, "not only is psyche in us as a set of dynamisms, but we are in the psyche," since in itself, "psyche is both immanent in persons, and between persons, and also transcends persons" (*Revisioning*, 133, 151), having a measure of irreducible autonomy in what Blake would call an "eternal" realm of its own.

If we replace the word *psyche* in this last quotation with the word *imagination*, we have a fair description of Blake's axiomatic view of the world of imaginal reality. For him, too, the archetypal structures, functions, fictions, and images of the human imagination have both primacy over and ontological independence from the psychodynamics of any individual person's case history. Thus, his statement that "The Eternal Body of Man is the IMAGINATION that is God himself The Divine Body . . . JESUS we are his Members" (*Laocoön*, E273/K776) creates a picture of the psyche as larger than the body and life of the individual subjects who articulate it.[27]

Among other things, this superordinate view of the imaginal has the effect of problematizing the role of subjectivity in psychological experience. From the archetypal perspective, subjectivity is a compelling fiction elaborated by what Blake would call "the poetic genius" from an innate image or archetype of the personal that in itself is non- or trans-personal.[28] Hence individual identity may be thought of as (again) an "original derivation" of a primordial image that ultimately decenters and deconstructs the subjective nature of the self even while it personalizes the otherwise impersonal objective psyche. Nowhere is this more evident than in the forms of dreaming, and in the corollary genre of dream-vision so often (as in the case of the *Progress* drawings) adopted by Blake, wherein the dreamer is figured as a character in his or her own psychic production. "For it is in the dream," as Hillman observes, "that the dreamer himself performs as one image among others and where it can legitimately be shown that the dreamer is in the image rather than the image in the dreamer" (*Archetypal Psychology*, 6; *Revisioning*, 175).

Blake's exploration of the psychological slippages that occur in and around the relations of identity and image, subject and object, ego and archetype, is matched by his concern with the metaphoric and metonymic ties existing among three key aspects of the imagination: its structure, its contents, and its rhetorical processes. Here, too, the signifier of one category frequently slides over into another in Blake's work—not perversely, but in accordance with the way of the imaginal itself, where every thing is potentially bound by tropes and polysemic overdetermination to every other thing. Jungian and archetypal psychologies offer a way to discuss such semantic slidings and slippages, since they assume with Blake that the psyche is structured on the basis of a system of images (rather than, as in Lacan's view, like a verbal language) that creates meaning both through difference and through its chain of contextual associations and metaphoric identities.[29]

Yet within the field of Jungian investigation it is not the orthodox branch but rather the neo-Jungians who welcome the challenges of postmodern thought with its distrust of absolutist, monotheistic, logocentric formulations. And so it is neo-Jungians who most aggressively address the question of categorical overlaps in what they regard as a decentering and polyvalent imagination. Several times in several different places, for example, James Hillman stresses that archetypal content and archetypal process must be thought of as radically convergent, insofar as the "stuff" of the psyche—its fund of nonreferential images—is at once that which one sees and that by which one sees.[30] Here Hillman is drawing on Jung's own provocative comment that "every psychic process is an image and an 'imagining,' otherwise no consciousness could exist."[31] Jung implies, in other words, that the mental activity that allows us to process experience is a component part—a synecdoche—of the image of that experience. Thus in this metapsychological version of the hermeneutic circle, "the means by which the world is imagined and . . . the modes by which all knowledge, all experiences whatsoever become possible" (*Archetypal Psychology*, 12) are themselves held to be images identical to those variable "archetypal epistemes" (*Revisioning*, 132) that structure and fill the individual psyche.

To sum up, the Jungian tradition emulates Blake in promoting a tropological understanding of imaginal events and, further, in regarding the tropological perspective itself as an adequation (that is, a trope) of the psychological. This is in part a question of "psychological faith," which, like Coleridge's idea of poetic faith, demands a willing suspension of disbelief in, and an imaginative openness toward, the reality of each of the undecidable, polysemic identities (Coleridge calls them "shadows") presented to/by/in the imagination.[32] With this faith, single-visioned, totalizing, reductive readings of the psyche (for example, the voice in Coleridge that chose the word *shadows* to describe its content) are themselves read not as objective descriptions of that psyche but rather as one of its own products, one of its own multivalent figurings.

In a recent critical article, Hazard Adams has proposed that Blake's psychological attitude toward tropes and troping generates an artistic and poetic method with profound ethical implications for the relations of self and other.[33] He then goes on to name the trope of tropes responsible as "radical synecdoche"—a figure for the progressive interinvolvement of part and whole existing not just in rhetoric but in the psyche and in the world. "For in the very fabric of synecdoche," he writes, " . . . there lies everywhere the principal ethical pattern we constitute from Blake's work: the need for annihilation of the selfhood, for sympathetic expansive identity to include the other" (Adams, 69). Adams's focus here on the moral significance of Blake's figural choices, like Morris Eaves's insight into the holistic implications of what he calls Blake's "metaphors of identity," highlights the fact that aesthetic and rhetorical strategy in Blake has a crucial psychosocial dimension that cannot be ignored if either his stylistics or his cultural vision are to be understood. The formal intentionality of his work, in other words, is not simply formal: it is *transformal,* having a larger telos or goal embedded in its representational modality. Moreover, this embedded goal is one that is itself transformational. That is, like Ezekiel's actions in *The Marriage of Heaven and Hell,* Blake's expressive forms embody the prophetic "desire of raising other men [and women] into a perception of the infinite" (*MHH* 12).[34] The structures he favors, for example, force a recognition of the fearful symmetries we tend to repress in ourselves as well as those that exist between ourselves and others. At the same time, they require a visionary hermeneutic that depends on openness to polysemic identities and an attitude of mutual forgiveness toward and among dialectical elements of the work's rhetorical design.

Thus every device has a consciousness-raising significance, and every adequate response to that device a consciousness-raising result. Adapting Wordsworth's claim for the renovative power of his own poetry, we might say that Blake's work creates not only the "taste" but also the visionary literacy by which it and the world it illumines can be perennially comprehended, revisioned, and "enjoyed."[35] As Adams (71) remarks, there is a special urgency to Blake's aim of generating in text and reader alike the sort of metaphorical eco-consciousness that shapes and experiences reality as "an endlessly exfoliating potentiality of identities." For such desire makes of art a radical teaching and a radical therapy, one in which the audience learns through formal necessity to admit its link with the full spectrum of the imaginal world depicted and hence to envision (and perhaps to covet) the scope of the human potential as yet unrealized, as yet actively thwarted by defensive structures in both individuals and society.

The many means by which Blake introduces us to such liberating motions of the imaginal in the ongoing "intellectual allegory" that is his life's work cannot be adequately charted here. But the way some of these themes and methods take center stage in his paradigmatic manipulation of the Bunyan material over more than a quarter of a century is the subject of the chapters that follow.

In Chapter 1 I set out the contexts and examine some of the particulars of Blake's and Bunyan's shared obsession with the role of interpretation in the imaginative life. First I look at Blake, for whom acts of interpretation are part of the creative process, involving continual aesthetic and psychic revisionings that function like repeated passings of a biblical Last Judgment. Shifts in perspective cause and are themselves caused by such revelatory firings of the imagination, and they have emotional, moral, and spiritual consequences. From Blake's theoretical standpoint, every revisionary interpretation holds the seed of a perceptual conversion capable of transforming not only the object interpreted but also the interpreter herself. The example I use to explore Blake's ideas about interpretation and revision is the commentary he wrote on his own much revised painting of the Judgment scene of *Revelation*. This text, "A vision of the Last Judgment," is a hermeneutic exercise in a multiple sense. First it describes Blake's pictorial representation—itself an interpretation—of a visionary event from the New Testament. Next it interprets that interpretation, providing, as it were, a vision of a vision of a vision. And finally it raises to the thematic level the critical question of interpretation itself. The text is key not only because its focus on visionary hermeneutics and on the psychology of eschatological perspectives parallels the themes of *The Pilgrim's Progress,* but also because it is the site of Blake's most provocative comment on the *Progress:* for it is there that he marks Bunyan's allegory as a paradigm of failed vision— one full of the imaginative quality that liberates but which flounders on what he regards as the generic misuse of formal, ideological, and interpretive strategies. In short, Blake singles out the *Progress* along with several classical texts to exemplify how the dogmatism of allegory and didactic fable literally deforms the visionary potential of these genres, incidentally making them all the more attractive as targets of revisionary rescue. "A vision of the Last Judgment," then, assumes the status of a kind of preface to Blake's own pictorial treatment of the *Progress* and clues us into some of the deconstructive and visionary motives operating in the full series of watercolor designs discussed at length in Chapter 3.

The second part of Chapter 1 compares Blake's psycho-aesthetic theories of reading with Bunyan's spiritual view of the function of interpretation. I explore especially the seventeenth-century Calvinistic desire (prevalent in Bunyan as well as in some of his fictional characters) to achieve certainty of salvation through a strenuous, revisionary hermeneutics of the self. Bunyan's complex attitude toward the Puritan doctrine of predestination is then shown to have rhetorical implications that share much more with Blake's ideal conception of "Everexistent Images" and "identical form" than one might suspect (especially given Blake's stated contempt for predestinarian principles as expressed in his "Annotations to Swedenborg's *Divine Providence*).[36] I thus treat the dissenting tradition out of which both men rose in terms of its effect on their formal handling of metaphor, emblem, and myth; and as an example I show how the Puritan practice of "heavenly meditation" (drawn on so strongly by Bunyan in the *Progress*) is structurally reflected in Blake's portrayals of the redemptive function of the visionary imagination. My aim is to illuminate the underlying bonds between the different imaginative styles of Blake and Bunyan and so suggest what it was that Blake sought to honor when, despite the evident quarrel he had with Bunyan's dogmatics, he lovingly came to illustrate the text of the *Progress* late in his life.

Chapter 2 charts Blake's overt indebtedness to the example of Bunyan, demonstrating how first the figures in the *Progress* and then the figure of the author of the *Progress* functioned more and more as a clear type for Blake of the imaginative mental traveler struggling through psychic states on the path of individuation. I start out by pinpointing the conscious allusions to Bunyan's themes, images, and aesthetic procedures that abound in Blake's art and writings from a fairly early date (1793). In the process I show how the character of Blake's engagement with Bunyan shifts over time, becoming less and less parodic and antithetical as his identification with the visionary aspects of Bunyan's work and creative persona increases. It is as if he gradually evolved along a line of critical thinking, with respect to Bunyan, that began with an extrinsic-devalorizing approach and ended with an intrinsic-valorizing one. I stress that he was led to make this move on two important counts. First, there was the goading of his patron, William Hayley, a belle-lettrist who subtly disparaged what he called Blake's "extravagant" imagination by comparing it to Bunyan's "mad enthusiasm." But lumping Blake and Bunyan together in this derogatory way only fostered in Blake a defensive reaction, causing Blake covertly to prize his supposed link with his misunderstood precursor. This sense of brotherhood in turn made Blake look for the unique imaginal strengths of Bunyan's work—strengths that lay below the surface threatening rhetorical orthodoxy and disturbing the claims of Bunyan's Puritan polemics. Second, the shift from an extrinsic-devalorizing to an intrinsic-valorizing reading of the *Progress* carried with it a certain poetic justice inasmuch as that is one of the hermeneutic lessons thematized in the book itself. Moreover, it is just this interpretive theme that Blake was later to highlight in the illustrations I analyze in Chapter 3.

The rest of Chapter 2 deals with the crucial role Bunyan's imagery played in

Blake's developing concepts of "Sublime Allegory," "States and Individuals," and "Mutual Forgiveness." I end by illustrating how these quasi-aesthetic, quasi-psychological "doctrines" exert pressure on Blake's revisions of his emblem book, *The Gates of Paradise,* which he drastically altered twenty-five years after its initial publication. The changes he made amount to a recontextualization of the original images by means of a reworked title and many additions, including an epilogue and tailpiece based on the figure of Bunyan's dream protagonist in the *Progress.* My reading of the epilogue and tailpiece then invites a rereading of the whole work such that all the emblems in the book are seen to compose the mosaic of a single emblem: the narrator's dream of the developing relation between "states" and individuals and his intrinsic-valorizing interpretation of that dream.

Recognizing how Blake refashioned the *Gates* along the lines of a Bunyanesque dream-vision sets the stage for my final chapter, a close reading of the full series of his *Progress* watercolors. I focus on the way these designs constitute a literary critique of Bunyan's work and also a critique of the psychology and culture of interpretive criticism itself. To make this critical aspect of the designs clear, I discuss Blake's debt to the previous tradition of Bunyan illustration, I examine his deliberate iconographic and compositional departures from that tradition, and I provide a picture-by-picture analysis of the structural dynamics that shape the completed sequence considered as a pictorial narrative in its own right.

In the course of this analysis I pay particular attention to two striking features of Blake's redactive treatment of the text. The first is his amalgamation of the roles of dreamer and protagonist (roles assiduously kept separate by Bunyan); the second concerns his notable reapportionment of Bunyan's narrative time, duration, and plotting. Each of these narratological manipulations serves a heuristic purpose, affecting in intimate ways the visionary education required of both the dreamer dreaming the pictured dream and the reader-viewer interpreting it. Moreover, as the journey through the drawings proceeds, this synecdochic relation between the imaginal development of reader and dreamer gathers strength until in the last design Blake rewards the visionary hermeneut with an emblem of mutual identity that completes even as it expands the very hermeneutic circle his "Images of wonder" initially enticed us to penetrate. Thus by way of conclusion the book recapitulates the themes of tropological and psychological individuation that are themselves brought together in the final plate of the series, a traditional apotheosis-scene transformed into an ongoing transumptive event of the imagination.

CHAPTER ONE

INTERPRETATION
AND DISSENT

The story of how Blake came to be revered as a prophetic teacher in the closing years of his life, albeit by an offbeat group of struggling young artists, is well known.[1] These painters, classed today as Blake's "disciples," convened during the 1820s in an avant-garde mood. Aspiring to a sort of Romantic brotherhood, they called themselves the "Ancients," in one sense a glaring misnomer since most of them were hardly more than boys in their teens at the time. The sort of ancientness they coveted, however, had nothing to do with age and everything to do with the ideal of a lost order replete with originary powers of heart, mind, and eye.[2] As with the "Primitifs" and the "Nazarenes," contemporary aesthetic movements in France and Germany, their beliefs "centered around the revolutionary desire to break away from what they considered the corruption of the present and to create a completely new art based on the purest sources."[3] For them as for many creative artists like them throughout the century, the only real path forward was an apparent step backward, from decadence to the emulation of earlier, simpler modes more in touch, they thought, with primordial essences. They therefore tried in a minor way to generate a healing "cult of primitivism" and latched on to Blake as a paradigm of the true, spiritual artist who consciously invoked the deepest strata of psychic reality to express truths ignored by current fashions in literature, art, and religion. A slogan from one of Blake's own aesthetic manifestos written over a decade earlier mirrors their stance and even their very name, indicating the aptness of their choice of the older man as master: "The Nature of my Work," Blake's motto declares, "is Visionary or Imaginative it is an Endeavour to Restore what the Ancients calld the Golden Age" (VLJ, E555/ K605).

It was not his art alone that entranced these young followers of Blake. They saw in his entire personality the archetype of visionary wisdom. His ceaseless quest as a painter, as a poet, and as a man to illuminate mental forms and display the inner identity of all phenomena gave him special status as a seer and teacher in their eyes. One of their number compared being in his presence to "walking with the Prophet Isaiah,"[4] another experienced him as "a new kind of man, wholly original and in all things,"[5] while a third likened him to "one of the Antique patriarchs" and to "energy itself"—a sunlike source who "shed around him a kindling influence; an atmosphere of life, full of the ideal."[6] It was in this spirit that the neophyte painters dubbed Blake "the Interpreter" and called his London quarters "the House of the Interpreter," alluding to the numinous guide in Bunyan's *Pilgrim's Progress* who taught men the hermeneutic skills of allegorical understanding by leading them through room after room of surreal and symbolic scenes, each one staged as a living emblem of the imagination.

To give Blake the title of Bunyan's "Interpreter" on these grounds was in a way an emblematic event in its own right, since it focused on so much that was basic to his entire practice and theory. In the first place, it epitomized his lifelong habit of blending acts of interpretation with acts of art. Second, it underlined the increasing importance that themes of critical exegesis and prophetic explication came to play in his work. As mentioned in the introduction, his mature poems, paintings, and illustrations are often about interpretive issues, just as his expressive structures tend more and more at the culmination of his career to demonstrate, and simultaneously to require, the use of a new style of interpretation, which I have called visionary hermeneutics.[7] Finally, the honorific title the Ancients gave to Blake points up an affinity between him and Bunyan that throws light on the goals and procedures of both artists in unexpected ways. This is an affinity that Blake himself revises and extends—out-interpreting the Interpreter, as it were—in the twenty-eight illustrations to *The Pilgrim's Progress* that are the ultimate concern of this study.

HERMENEUTICS AND THE
REVISIONARY IMAGINATION

To remark that Blake had a lifelong habit of combining acts of interpretation with acts of art is true as far as it goes. Left out of consideration, however, is the depth, the vitality, and the pervasiveness of his commitment to the double procedure, for in one way or another, everything he ever wrote or designed involved this pairing. His very idea of art as an "Intellectual Thing" (*J* 52; E202/K683)—that is, as something conceptual that carries ideational and imaginal significance capable of awakening us—is based on it, and his avowed aim of teasing an exegetical response from reader or viewer compounds it. About this tendency in the poetry, Northrop Frye writes:

Blake is one of the poets who believe that, as Wallace Stevens says, the only subject of poetry is poetry itself, and that the writing of a poem is itself a theory of poetry. He interests a critic because he removes the barriers between poetry and criticism. He defines the greatest poetry as "allegory addressed to the intellectual powers," and defends the practice of not being too explicit on the ground that it "rouzes the faculties to act." His language in his later prophecies is almost deliberately colloquial and "unpoetic," as though he intended his poetry to be also a work of criticism, just as he expected the critic's response to be also a creative one.[8]

But the most famous claim for the didactic value of Blake's art comes from his own public boast, in a passage already referred to, about the heuristic properties of one of his major paintings (now lost) called "A Vision of the Last Judgment." The passage is part of a long notebook jotting (also titled "A Vision of the Last Judgment") composed as a catalog entry, which unhappily was never printed.

Often regarded as Blake's aesthetic manifesto, the text of "A Vision" is full of polemical declarations about the nature of "Vision or Imagination" (E554/ K604) and the role played by "Visions *of* Imagination" (E554/K604–5; italics added) in artist, artwork, and audience alike. It is a tract about the value of maintaining an archetypal perspective on "All that Exists" (E554/K604), and it demonstrates a method of doing so by instructing us how to approach the images in the painting presumably before us. But it is not simply the content of Blake's critical ideas on this point that carries the message and "rouzes" the imaginal faculties to act; the form of his statements does so as well. The theoretical assumptions and the rhetorical format of the paragraph in question are both fairly typical in this regard and give us a good example of Blake's full-blown critical temper at work. Thus, addressing the would-be viewer of his "Last Judgment" canvas, he suddenly breaks off his descriptive commentary with the quasi-evangelical advertisement quoted in my introduction:

> If the Spectator could Enter into these Images in his Imagination approaching them on the Fiery Chariot of his Contemplative Thought if he could Enter into Noahs Rainbow or into his bosom or could make a Friend & Companion of one of these Images of wonder which always intreats him to leave mortal things as he must know then would he arise from his Grave then would he meet the Lord in the Air & then he would be happy. (VLJ, E560/K611)

On one level this passage is simply a promise or prophecy about the effects of interpreting and so experiencing another prophecy (Blake's painted vision of the rising up of dead souls) correctly. Grammatically, it is a provisional prediction in the subjunctive mood that hedges its promissory intent through the use of a sentence structure called the "ideal conditional": "if he could . . . then he would." There is a subtle enticement to the twofold contingency here. That is, the *if* sets up one qualification, the *could* another, creating an overload of qualifiers unsettling to the listener, who then naturally desires to resolve at least one of them. What is appealed to by this structure is an imaginative impulse to make the future-less-vivid (an alternate name for the ideal conditional) *more* vivid, to turn the speculative "if he could . . . then he would" into the stronger and more prophetic claim of a "when he does . . . then he will." The statement "If the Spectator could Enter into these Images" is thus a sort of double dare that challenges the reader-viewer to engage "his" prophetic powers both linguistically and imagistically. Although it may seem pedantic to give a syntactic form the high-sounding name of prophecy, we have a sufficient precedent for doing so in Blake's distinctly unpedantic statement that "Every honest man is a Prophet he utters his opinion both of private & public matters/Thus/If you go on So/the result is So/He never says/such a thing shall happen let you do what you will" ("Annotations to Watson's *Apology for the Bible*," E617/K392).

Blake's linguistic tactics in this instance (as in so many others) conform to his larger artistic strategy of performative revelation. By "performative revelation" I mean simply an art of action, like those attributed to the prophets Ezekiel and Isaiah in the *Marriage,* that teaches by doing the very thing it causes its audience to learn by doing. So in the "Vision" passage, Blake is using the bait of prophecy *about* prophetic vision to lure the potential viewer, as reader of the commentary, into the prophetic frame of mind; for Blake knows that neither reader nor viewer can rightly comprehend or even recognize "Vision" without employing it. We have here an instance, then, of that method mentioned in the introduction wherein the artist creates the hermeneutic by which he is to be understood. There is a catch, though: in this case, the prophetic vision in question (Blake's picture) is already an interpretation of a prophetic vision (the Last Judgment of the Apocalypse), making the commentary that Blake wrote to elucidate the picture an interpretation of an interpretation of a vision.

One might suspect that the energy of thought and the interest in direct visionary experience would rapidly diminish down the line of these ever-recessive revisionings. But somehow or other this does not happen in Blake, perhaps because all his visions retain the central form of a Last Judgment. That is, by their synecdochic relation to a primordial image of ultimate evaluation, they all simultaneously anticipate and resist a prophetic closure, they all both use and deconstruct the very process of aesthetic judgment. Furthermore, since the figure who judges in John's vision of the Apocalypse (that is, the "Saviour" Jesus) is for Blake not an extrinsic power but rather the archetype of

"The Human Imagination" (E555/K604), any vision drawn in this pattern will retain the imaginative urgency of the psyche watching itself "Coming to Judgment" (E555/K604) in all possible roles: judge, plaintiff, audience, and imaginer.

Let us clarify by taking a closer look at the psychological implications of the passage in question. Although the grammatical structure of the sentence on the fate awaiting the visionary spectator apes a dispassionate statement in logic (if A, then B), its tone is remarkably subjective, passionate, present, even personal—like a psychic reading or evangelical pep talk supporting the individual's inner aspiration. You, too, he is saying, can rise like Noah and be an image of wonder. Through the rhetoric of diction and imagery Blake thus seems to be wooing the reader, asking him to become a sort of specular lover whose gaze will then "Enter into" an actualization and justification, not of the written, but of the pictorial text. The scene of actualization, however, is to take place beyond the canvas in the viewer's own imagination, a place described earlier in the same essay as one where the "ever Existent Images" already live "Really & Unchangeably" (VLJ, E554/K604), though in a latent state, requiring only the "seed of Contemplative Thought" (E555/K605) to be renewed:

> The Nature of Visionary Fancy or Imagination is very little Known & the Eternal nature & permanence of its ever Existent Images is considered as less permanent than the things of Vegetative & Generative Nature yet the Oak dies as well as the Lettuce but its Eternal Image & Individuality never dies. but renews by its seed. just so the Imaginative Image returns by the seed of Contemplative Thought.

Blake's conception here is of a transpersonal psyche more or less equivalent both to Jung's notion of the collective unconscious and to what the neo-Jungians think of as the archetypal substrate of all mental life. This *mundus imaginalis* is not just an eternal world, one timeless organization of forms among many, but is rather the "World of Eternity" itself (E555/K604).[9] It is, in other words, the imaginative perspective from which archetypal images appear to be the "Permanent Realities of Every Thing which we see reflected" (E555/K605) in the finite, natural universe of "mortal things" (E560/K611) and ordinary consciousness. With such a view of the visionary imagination, the role of artist takes on an educative rather than a godlike cast. Instead of functioning as a creator ex nihilo, therefore, Blake works as a guide whose artistic productions are an illustrated tour book of the psyche dedicated to making the original "Images of wonder" within his own mind and the mind of the reader-viewer accessible.[10]

Were the viewer to focus full imaginative attention on these illustrated images, Blake suggests, she would find them preexistently alive within her. As discussed in the introduction, the idea of discovering *with* imagination that what is "out there" is already *in* imagination is the burden of meaning carried by the prepositional ambiguities of the statement "If the Spectator could Enter into these *Images in his Imagination*." But the difficulty of the task of so discovering (the doubtfulness of which accomplishment is expressed by Blake's choice of the word *could* rather than *would* in the phrase "If the Spectator could") comes from the fact that the method of "entering" demands heightened abilities of identification, empathy, visualization—just those tools of imagining that one expects the visionary realm to yield, not require. In other words, envisioning presumes the very thing it promises.

It takes a hardy Spectator to overcome this bind. She must first feel that her powers of inward perception are inherently vigorous and capable of rapid expansion. That is why at this point in the text the image of "Contemplative Thought" is no longer presented as a mere "seed," as it was earlier in the commentary when Blake was comparing "Visionary Fancy" to "Generative Nature," asserting that "the Imaginative Image returns by the seed of Contemplative Thought." It is now pictured instead as something much more potent and volatile: a "Fiery Chariot," the prophetic vehicle par excellence. It is as if, at the threshold of delving into the vision of the Last Judgment, in the strenuous "operation bootstrap" of reviving the imagination *by* imagination, Blake realized that an extra spurt of energy and encouragement was needed. And he supplies it by his strong evocation of the contemplative faculty as a highly charged carrier of heavenly, archetypal values. In effect, the adoption of this new metaphor prefigures the process of awakening entailed in witnessing a Last Judgment because its imagery has already obeyed the entreaty "to leave mortal things" (the seed) and to seek immortal ones (the divine chariot).

In the commentary, once Blake establishes the fiery chariot of contemplative thought as the vehicle on which the spectator might best approach the pictorial images, his verbal images also become more fiery and contemplative, which is to say more radically synecdochic (to use Hazard Adams's phrase). They thus require a stronger metaphoric consciousness and greater visionary hermeneutics from the reader. For Blake speaks next of the desirability of "Enter[ing] into Noahs Rainbow or into his bosom," but what this means metaphorically, and why identifying with exactly this figure might aid the would-be visionary, is explained only by reference to an earlier hermeneutic portion of the descriptive text:

> The Persons who ascend to Meet the Lord coming in the Clouds with power &
> great Glory. are representations of those States described in the Bible under the
> Names of the Fathers before & after the Flood Noah is seen in the Midst of these
> Canopied by a Rainbow. on his right hand Shem & on his Left Japhet these three

Persons represent Poetry Painting & Music the three Powers in Man of conversing with Paradise which the flood did not Sweep away. (VLJ, E559/K610)

By this account, Noah is placed in the design among those closest to the goal of meeting the Lord. He holds a crucial and central position there, as a type of the creative visionary, set off and haloed by his overarching rainbow.[11] Given that earlier in this text the Lord is defined by Blake as representing the complete structure of the "Human Imagination"[12] and that Noah evidently stands for the special function of visual thinking required by human imaginers who are painters and seers of paintings, the esoteric meaning of the figure becomes clear.[13] Noah is our own submerged remnant of the "Divine Vision" *qua* vision. He is the capacity latent in us for picturing and interpreting things transcendentally (including his own place in Blake's painting and Blake's painting as a whole). He thus both activates and represents the visionary hermeneutic we must employ to recognize him. Noah, then, is the missing link that we as spectators not only need but also can acquire by deliberately identifying with his image. Again, a seamless web of interaction is being proposed here, because the process of willed identification with a visual image—a process that psychotherapists today call creative fantasy, active imagination, heightened awareness, structured meditation, and so on[14]—is itself a replica of Noah's power. The viewer's stance is thus, *pace* Lacan, rather like that of someone looking into a mirror not in order to see oneself, but to see oneself looking at oneself.

The ultimate result of this fearful symmetry between beholder and beheld is (or should be, in Blake's view) a revision of the spectator's aesthetic understanding regarding the inner form of the Last Judgment. Furthermore, this revision is to be experienced by "him" not just intellectually but imagistically and metaphorically, in terms of the Judgment's *outer* form: "then would he arise from his Grave then would he meet the Lord in the Air & then he would be happy." No longer divided from the object of his contemplation, the spectator and the figures on view arise in unison, Blake implies, from the grave, or death trap, of false knowledge about the creative process. It is also clear that the happiness reached thereby is precisely the happiness of correct interpretation. For as Blake reminds us a little further on, "whenever any Individual Rejects Error & Embraces Truth a Last Judgment passes upon that Individual" (E562/K613).[15]

The commentary we have been considering is a case in which the responsibility of interpretation shifts subtly from author to audience as its own subject of instruction is gradually inwardized. But taken together with the design it refers to, the work exists as well in an external context of richly informing revisions and allusions. We can cite as one still largely neglected example its complex, dialectical relation to Michelangelo's Judgment fresco in the Sistine Chapel.[16] The point, however, is not to enumerate specific instances. Instead I wish to focus on some aspects of the fundamental principle of revisionism itself, since it is just the radically revisionary nature of Blake's inspiration as an artist that best characterizes his critical impulse and his interpreter role.

Basically, Blake was a revisionist because by temperament he had an exceptionally retentive attitude toward form. This may sound paradoxical, but in fact it is not. It only means that Blake's concept of form was archetypal, allowing for the idea of an essential pattern with infinite variation as the norm. As he explained early on in his first work of illuminated printing, even the *human* form expresses itself through individuals who are at once alike and "infinitely various" (*ARO*, E2/K98), being in his view self-reflexive products of the living psyche (he called it there "the Poetic Genius"), which as a virtual form in its own right inevitably seeks the individuation and identity that comes only from continual self-revisioning. Such an archetypal view of form and variation is also reflected, as has often been pointed out, in Blake's original illuminated method of printing his work from engravings, in which the fixed form of the image on the copper plate is repeatedly renewed and revised in the print not only by ever-changing styles of inking and pressure during the printing process, but also by Blake's individualized postprinting applications of color and ink, which cause in many cases a substantively altered design.

For Blake, then, the "Eternal Identity" (VLJ, E556/K607) of any form or shape of the imagination was a value to be honored, preserved, and recycled through "original derivations." Thus, while he never swerved from his ultraliberal stand on the need for sweeping societal and personal change, he nonetheless remained an archconservative where the idea of the image was concerned. "His art is to find form, and to keep it," he announced proudly of himself, contrasting his classical linear drawing style with the painterly experiments of the most influential chiaroscurists of his era (*DC*, E538/K573). But the issue went deeper than the question of choosing a representational technique. For Blake's addiction to the "bounding outline" of linear abstraction,[17] like his penchant for the definite and his repeated caveats that so-called universal truths existed only in minutely particularized acts and images,[18] was part and parcel of his experience of the mental world as one in which individuality and "eternal existence" were synonymous. Thus it was not only his own conceptions that he sought to "find" and to "keep" in the manner Yeats regarded as that of a "too literal realist of imagination";[19] he had the same conservative feelings about the work of other creative visionaries.

To put it most simply, Blake held sacred the shapes of myths and inner images—their iconography and morphology—because he felt they came from the deepest part of the psyche, namely the divine or transpersonal part. One could not willy-nilly obliterate authentic vestiges of an imagination one recognized as holy and immortal. Furthermore, these organized contents of the objective psyche, whether they figured in dreams, "poetic tales" (*MHH* 11), "Visionary Fancy" (E555/K605), or the productions of the greatest artists, were understood by Blake to have the function of transformers in a giant energy system.[20] As metaphors of imaginal states, they seemed to him to carry over (that is, literally to "meta-phor") creative value from a world of eternal identities already lodged within. In his own work, Blake therefore naturally strove to preserve these structures and coincidentally to teach others the methods of preserving as well as using them. To do otherwise, to turn one's back on them, was to risk cutting oneself off from the very sources of personal and suprapersonal imaginal power. That way lay the sleep of death, truncation of the human potential progressing by degrees from mild dissociation (the malaise of everyday life) to extreme perturbation and insanity.[21]

But while Blake clung to the quasi-Platonic idea of preexistent mental forms,[22] holding that these forms were fittingly recapitulated in the images of visionary art and fable, he also wanted to promote release from conventional modes of viewing art and fable. The fact that visionary images *were* for him belated emblems of primal and permanent identity would be recognized, he felt, only if they were somehow wrenched from their normal contexts (doctrinal and perceptual) and made to be seen afresh. At the same time, enough of the old context had to be kept intact that the new departure from it would be experienced consciously as a transfiguration. This meant that Blake had to develop aesthetic tactics that both contained and liberated the forms of precedent visions in a strong dialectic of revisioning. He had the goal of transfiguring by this method not only the thing seen, but also our acts of vision, demonstrating and facilitating an alteration in the perception of forms such that the "stubborn structure" (*J* 40, E183/K668) remaining could open to its own "infinite which was hid" (*MHH* 14).[23]

The conservation of form thus turns out to be a sort of visionary law for Blake, comparable in some ways to the natural law of conservation of matter and energy in physics. Like the physical principle, it provides for both coherence and change within its system, making revision the supreme strategy of creative organization.[24] In the process, the revisionist, situated in a middle position between the poles of the coherence-and-change continuum, becomes at once an antithetical critic, a generator of new configurations, and a syncretic, or prophetic, interpreter of form. Actions of this sort, then, share with the typological processes of visionary hermeneutics a way of moving through transformational networks to recover transformation itself as both the controlling theme and "central form" of imaginal understanding.

BUNYAN, BLAKE, AND THE
TRADITION OF DISSENT

So far we have dealt only with the general relevance of naming Blake "the Interpreter" and calling his meager quarters at Fountain Court "the House of the Interpreter." But the scenes in *The Pilgrim's Progress* from which those titles derive contain specific aesthetic implications that make the allusion even more apt. Broadly speaking, these implications involve two issues: on the one hand, the peculiar function of the Interpreter as an agent of symbolic awareness in Bunyan's fictive process and, on the other, the special nature of the visions this figure presents and explicates.

Both points, which we will assess in our discussion of the drawings in Chapter 3, need to be looked at in the context of the affinities linking Bunyan and Blake, affinities stemming in part from the background of Protestant dissent that the two men shared. Bunyan was a Calvinist Baptist, and Blake grew up among Nonconformists of unrecorded denomination;[25] still, all sects within the dissenting tradition stressed the right and necessity of individual interpretation of Scripture and taught methods of interpreting as the primary propaedeutic to a life of spiritual grace and understanding. What took place for Catholics and Anglicans within the framework of an ecclesiastical order, in other words, occurred for dissenters in the dialectical relation each believer established between him or herself and the biblical Word of God. In short, for orthodox dissenters, Scripture itself became a kind of mother church. Without a secondary authority to validate their readings or provide external sanctions for their behavior, the faithful remained tied to the testamentary Word in an urgent familial bond. One can observe some of this displaced maternalistic feeling being evoked by Bunyan's Interpreter in the *Progress* when he describes the indwelling biblical guide—and, by transference, the whole sense of Scripture—as an androgynous figure who "can beget Children, Travel in birth with Children, and Nurse them himself when they are borne."[26] This feeling that the ground of being and the source of nourishment lay in the relating of person to text gave the role of exegetical interpretation the magnified importance of a basic survival tactic. All instruction, all practical advice, all connection with one's destiny in the life to come, all knowledge of identity and "Eternal Truth," came to men and women through acts of scriptural inference. Scriptural inference then, in its turn, received a sublimated status equal to that of God's Word, as is explained in plain terms by one Puritan divine: "*Scripture-Inference is Scripture; that is to say, That which may be inferr'd from Scripture by natural, and necessary consequence, is to be received as the Scripture itself.* The word of God, *rightly interpreted,* is the word of God."[27]

But it wasn't only the Bible that was read with interpretive fervor by hard-line dissenters. The exegetical bent extended to the habit of learning to read one's life aright as well—not in order to change it, but simply to evaluate it. The pressure to evaluate the self and ferret out evidences of one's permanent identity was enormous, because the Calvinist legacy, with its doctrine of predestined election or damnation, allowed men creative scope as participants in their own salvation *only* as interpreters of their private circumstances, feelings, and conduct. They became ingenious hunters for signs in the text of their daily lives, telltale signs that would hint of a fate they understood to be certain, even if pure *knowledge* of it was unascertainable. For the *certitudo salutis* could not in fact be reached from a temporal perspective, within the life being read; rather, confirmation of election awaited transumption of the individual to a time outside time, beyond the final events of Death and Judgment. As with Scripture, however, one could meanwhile infer, and the inference could then be treated as at least partial proof. This state of affairs made self-analytical revisionists of every would-be saint, for the power to create meaning out of one's life rested almost entirely with the ability to revise and reconceive it according to the fears and desires of its imagined denouement.[28]

The power lay that way, but also the trauma of personal doubt. So much was always riding on these critical analyses that they could not afford to be too loosely construed. In the interpretive readings that an individual believer made, then, whether of his life story or of Scripture, the crying need was for unambiguous, rational, and authoritative explications. Jacob's nightlong struggle to secure a blessing from the Angel of the Lord was not more imperative in the eyes of these Puritan Christians than the effort to seize straightforward meaning and concrete advice from even the darkest passage of the Bible and of experience. Surety of instruction from these sources (mostly on how to receive and keep the faith *as if* elected) was an absolutely essential compensation for those who saw themselves living in a world fraught with sinful disharmonies between man and God, in which human redemption was arbitrary and God's all-embracing determinism undecipherable.[29]

The hermeneutical imperative was a thorny issue, though, because private textual interpretation—one's own or another man's—might well turn out to be the product of a reprobate imagination; yet there was no way of judging the truth of faith except by such interpretations. In these circumstances one can easily sympathize with Christian at the beginning of *The Pilgrim's Progress* when he throws up his hands in despair as a result of his Bible reading and cries out almost petulantly, but also with fear and trembling, like St. Paul in Acts 9:6, "What shall I do?" It is significant that this question modulates its note of panic only when, upon recapitulation some paragraphs later, it is transformed to harmonize with a second Pauline conversion text in Acts 16:31 that reads,

"What shall I do *to be saved?*" (italics added). The suggestion is that one can cope most effectively with personal confusion and uncertainty as to faith by relying fully on the letter of Scripture.

Literalism of this sort had a calming influence capable of combating the threat of "Nervous Fear" (E708/K799) or incipient paranoia, which was a feature of most of the dissenting faiths. For the pattern of self-scrutiny fostered by Calvinism was structured on the model of a schizophrenic suspiciousness not unlike that "Two Horned Reasoning, Cloven Fiction / In Doubt which is Self contradiction" which Blake railed against in the revised *Gates of Paradise* (E26/K770). The resultant psychological perils were quite real, and the devout who wished to remain stable and functioning had to build strong defenses against the virtual psychoses of uncertainty latent in these beliefs. Puritan hermeneutic practice met that challenge by adopting various self-imposed strictures on the form and manner of exegetical exposition. First, it courted a plain style, easily understood. In the minds of influential Puritan divines, nothing too figurative, fanciful, or syntactically convoluted was thought appropriate to expository truth, nor did they welcome overdetermined or abstruse symbolism. Such things were termed, scornfully, "men's devises" and were shunned.[30] Second, exegetes looked for a clear and logical consistency in the propounding of places in Scripture (as of places in the narrative of people's lives), with the expectation that all readings would conform to a dogmatic model and coincide with what was called the "proportion of faith." This way, the Bible or a person's spiritual biography could be regarded as a unified collection of commands and examples that were on the one hand reducible to doctrine and on the other faithful to the literal or surface meaning of the Word. An allegorizing tendency that sifted through biblical narrative for dogma, continually distilling mythos to logos, was thus matched by the opposing mode of amplifying rhetorical tropes into narrative moral exempla or homilies. But in both cases—the homiletic and amplifying as well as the allegoric and reductive—the goal was to satisfy what U. Milo Kaufmann calls "the insatiate appetite of the Puritan for doctrine."[31]

What were some of the aesthetic effects of these methods of reading reality and the Word? A passage from the pronouncement of a Puritan minister explaining the dogma of the "one sense" of Scripture will help elucidate. He is differentiating Puritan method from Anglican and Catholic practice, which imputed a fourfold meaning to each place in the Testaments, offering four essentially unrelated levels of interpretation:

> We concede such things as allegory, anagoge, and tropology in scripture; but meanwhile we deny that there are many and various senses. We affirm that there is but one true, proper and genuine sense of scripture, arising from the words

rightly understood, which we call the literal: and we contend that allegories, tropologies, and anagoges are not various senses, but various collections from one sense, or various applications and accommodations of that one meaning.[32]

The critical implication of such a view of biblical decorum is that it sees all the parts of the testamentary canon forming an absolute aesthetic unity, as if every book and genre, every figure and story, every chapter and verse therein were the necessarily concordant exfoliations of a single designing consciousness. Since each unit of Scripture was taken to have an intentional harmony with the whole system of faith, and since all of it came "from the same spring of divine inspiration," it was regarded as being "in all things perfectly consistent with itself."[33] In other words, the seamless integrity of the created artifact and the integrity of its creator were held to be synonymous. Blake's assertion that the Old and New Testaments were the "Great Code of Art" (*Laocoön,* E274/K777) stems from a similar appreciation. At the same time (and in contrast to Blake's view), the nature of scriptural coherence thus insisted upon by the Puritans is essentially static. Readers facing the text with the assumptions outlined above admitted structural parallelism, amplification, typology, symmetry, and logical accumulation of meaning—but not paradigm shifts, not process, not symbolic overdetermination, not polysemy.

The reason for this rigidity was that there was no sanction for interpreting episodes in Scripture as dynamic myth or vision; quite the reverse. Many influential tracts warned readers not to "raise their contemplations by fancy and imagination above Scripture revelation" lest they "dark[en] counsel without knowledge, uttering things which they understood not, which have no substance or spiritual food of faith in them."[34] Blake's conception that the purpose of scriptural prophecy, like that of art, was "to open the immortal Eyes/Of Man inwards into the Worlds of Thought: into Eternity/Ever expanding" (*J* 5, E147/K623) would have seemed anathema to the Puritan exegete of Bunyan's day. The inner worlds of thought were simply not felt to be trustworthy enough regions in which to find truth, and the idea of expanding into eternity would have terrified men and women who sought definitive boundaries to clarify a shaky divine identity and to keep them safely focused on the straight and narrow. Even more to the point, in the Puritan view men did not possess "immortal Eyes." If there was a sanctified organ in the human form at all, it was the ear, the receptor of Logos delivered in the revealed Word. Thus not only the action of the imagination, but visual imagery itself was generally discredited: without the clarifying assertion of God's voice speaking through the Word, even St. John's visions of the world's Last Things were thought unreliable vehicles of divine enlightenment. For a message from God to man to be helpful and possess eternal validity it had to arrive aurally, it had to be addressed to the reasoning intellect, and it had to be delivered loud and clear. Kaufmann sums it up this way:

> "If the trumpet give an uncertain sound," Paul the Apostle asks, "who shall prepare himself to the battle?" Bunyan's Christian trod his way in armor. The Christian battle was a grim reality, and the soldier had to be able to read his fighting orders unambiguously in the revealed Word. When the Puritan Christian went to the Scripture, he was looking for transparent rather than translucent revelation. He wanted no half-silvered surfaces that let his gaze only partially penetrate to spiritual truths while they reflected the fancies of his own mind, but authoritative words of counsel and promise.[35]

This is the hermeneutic convention out of which both Bunyan and Blake evolved. For each artist, the emphasis on the role of interpretation as a structuring principle of experience remained paramount, but both resisted strongly the restraints imposed on visionary perception and expression. Blake's rejection of a code of knowledge that preferred transparent to translucent revelation is, of course, implied on every page of his poetic and polemical work,[36] and it even frequently becomes the explicit subject of his prophetic discourse as, for example, when he proclaims in *Jerusalem:*

> What is Above is Within, for every-thing in Eternity is translucent:
> The Circumference is Within: Without, is formed the Selfish Center
> And the Circumference still expands going forward to Eternity.
> And the Center has Eternal States! . . .
>   . . . in your own Bosom you bear your Heaven
> And Earth, & all you behold, tho it appears Without it is Within
> In your Imagination of which this World of Mortality is but a Shadow.
>   (*J* 71, E225/K709)

Here Blake testifies that he believes in an aesthetic of objective inwardness (or we might better say "inside-outness") and that he is the declared adversary of those who would divide our individual consciousness from its own imaginative processes. Bunyan, in contrast, makes no such declaration. His rebellion against the Puritan mistrust of vision is much less overt than Blake's, and the dynamics of it are complicated by the fact that in his conscious life he was himself a dedicated preacher of the very faith whose rationalistic tradition his creative instincts nevertheless tended to subvert.[37] When he takes a stand on the issues, as in the verse apology prefacing *The Pilgrim's Progress,* he can really do no more than inventively equivocate about the values he unconsciously deconstructs, producing a masterpiece of rhetorical contradictions and reversals that manages at once to contain and to undercut all the going Puritan dictates against the use of "Dark Figures" as agents of revelation.[38] The apology, like the dream-fable proper, thus becomes an occasion for Bunyan to weave in and out of the sensibility of primary process-thinking, now using evocative images and metaphors to draw us elliptically away from the center of allegorical argument, now providing a dialectical commentary on those metaphoric terms—all in the form of a sort of psychodramatic dialogue staged between the personified voices of his own ambivalent attitudes.

Consciously, logically, Bunyan followed the logos orientation of his peers. He observed its laws in his analytical attitude toward truth and showed his fictive characters observing it too. On this level of experience, every emblematic event created by him or encountered by his characters functioned simply as a setup for the interpretations abstracted from it, "as Cabinets inclose the Gold."[39] But intuitively and emotionally, Bunyan embraced the psyche's imaginal method of symbolic expression for its own sake, and situated the figures of his allegory in a context—the dream state—that feeds on and produces mythic knowledge. He therefore evolved an aesthetic of double and reflexive motives by which he continually transformed the doctrines derived *from* vision back *into* vision, while at the same time he submitted his own allegorical procedure to the dogmatic scrutiny of characters operating within its rules.

Although in the *Progress* he obviously felt constrained to defend the less orthodox parts of his visionary method in a reasoned apology, Bunyan's turn toward mythos and his practice of creating mental landscapes out of the inner logic of metaphor were not in fact totally heretical. One confined area of Puritan devotional custom—the convention of heavenly meditation—not only sanctioned but actually encouraged such imaginative exercises. Heavenly meditation consisted in constructing, through fantasy, scenarios of the afterlife, and it served the vital function of renewing in the heart of the faithful an active appetite for eternity. By its practice, the values of creative imagination were reinstated and deemed consonant with divine values. The importance of this convention as a loophole in the Puritan system of strictly rational interpretation cannot be overstressed, and its inheritance in Blake is the key to the parallels between his vision and Bunyan's.

As employed by the Puritans of Bunyan's time, heavenly meditation had two branches, both of which called on the rhetoric of imaginal expression. The first involved rousing the faculties of what Blake called "Spiritual Sensation" by the practice of referring all naturals to their supernaturals, that is, regarding the pleasures of the senses afforded us here-and-now in the visible, tangible, physical universe as little "prophecies" of spiritual pleasures to come.[40] We may justly conjure up the beauty and sensual enjoyment of an earthly rose, for example, so long as we see it primarily as constituting a clue to the much greater beauty and enjoyment of its counterpart in the life beyond. Blake calls this view of nature "holy Generation, Image of regeneration" (*J* 7, E150/K626) and sees it as a poetic stance validating natural things by way of their imaginal counterparts and causes in an eternal dimension that exists *now*. For the Puritans, the emphasis was reversed: the linkage of things visible to things unseen was designed not to reconcile us with the expansive potential of present experience but to whet our lust for futurity and stimulate us to reach with a clearer purpose for the wholly other transcendent goal. Still, in both cases the natural object is endowed with symbolic, imaginal possibilities and can function as a visionary emblem.

The second branch of heavenly meditation entailed imagining the end of one's pilgrimage through life in seductively utopian terms, picturing paradise with as many lavish details as was consistent with the hints given in Scripture. Puritans regarded the ascetic measures they endured in this world as necessary prerequisites for the reversed fate of lasting enjoyments in the hereafter. In their heavenly meditations they were thus expected to cultivate visions of their final rewards such as would entice them to increase their ascetic piety and prove themselves deserving of those eternal benefits. As has been demonstrated by prisoners of war in recent times, people can put up with a lot of deprivation if they hold a vivid image of release in mind; and Blake provides a classical emblem of this psychology in one of the songs from *Songs of Innocence,* "The Chimney Sweeper," where Tom Dacre renews himself and his faith by "[keeping] the Divine Vision in time of trouble" (*J* 44/30, E193/K655) through the medium of a dream that is structured exactly like a heavenly meditation.

The pattern of heavenly meditation is in fact a crucial aspect of the prototypical pattern discussed earlier in regard to Blake's apocalyptic poetics announced in "A Vision of the Last Judgment." Indeed, Reverend Sibbes, a Puritan divine who did much to regularize this form of meditational practice, makes a statement about its purpose that seems to anticipate the hermeneutical thrust of Blake's entreaty to the spectator of "A Vision." "If we have interest in Christ, who is in glory 'at the right hand of God,'" he explains, then our souls will be raised to heaven "in our affections before we be there in our bodies."[41] Like Blake, Sibbes suggests here that the very act of entering into the image through empathic contemplation (Blake's "Fiery Chariot of Contemplative Thought") effects and affects the results depicted, which are themselves imaginatively regenerative.

Although Bunyan's visionary modality cannot be defined solely on the basis of its similarity to the convention of heavenly meditation, two places in the *Progress* that had a significant effect on Blake owe their impact to the free adaptation of this practice. The first such episode is the one describing "Beulah":

Now I saw in my Dream, that by this time the Pilgrims were got over the Inchanted Ground, and entering into the Country of *Beulah*, whose Air was very sweet and pleasant, the way lying directly through it, they solaced themselves there for a season. Yea, here they heard continually the singing of Birds, and saw every day the flowers appear in the earth: and heard the voice of the Turtle in the Land. In this Countrey the Sun shineth night and day; wherefore this was beyond the Valley of the *shadow of death*, and also out of the reach of Giant *Despair*; neither could they from this place so much as see *Doubting-Castle*. Here they were within sight of the City they were going to: also here met them some of the Inhabitants thereof. For in this Land the shining Ones commonly walked, because it was upon the Borders of Heaven. In this Land also the contract between the Bride and the Bridegroom was renewed: Yea here, *as the Bridegroom rejoyceth over the Bride, so did their God rejoyce over them.* Here they had no want of Corn and Wine; for in this place they met with abundance of what they had sought for in all their Pilgrimage. Here they heard voices from out of the City, loud voices, saying, *Say ye to the daughter of* Zion, *Behold thy Salvation cometh, behold his reward is with him.* Here all the Inhabitants of the Countrey called them, *The holy People, the redeemed of the Lord, Sought out, &c.* (PP 154–55)

This interlude is associated with two scriptural sources: Isaiah 62:4, where the name Beulah is named; and the Song of Songs, where the imagery of sensual longing is thought by most Christian exegetes to be an allegory of the spirit of the covenant. In Isaiah 62, Beulah is intoned in passing as the future name and condition of the redeemed land of Israel—Israel in its "eternal identity"—and the surrounding biblical text at that point is itself a sort of "heavenly meditation." Bunyan, taking off from that hint, created a myth of the foretaste of salvation that was entirely his own. For such is the meaning of the Beulah passage as far as the pilgrims in the *Progress* are concerned: both the passage itself and the characters' narrative time there function as a lead-in to the anticipated moment of their entry into heaven, which occurs less than ten pages later. Bunyan's account of Beulah-land, then, added the lush, libidinal details missing from Isaiah's description—details that derived from the imagery of the Song of Songs and were intended to underscore Isaiah's provocative metaphor of the divine covenant as a marriage ("Beulah," as the narrator of Isaiah explicates, *means* "married"). So with that combination of erotic desire and spiritual anticipation of salvation, Bunyan's narrative made the land of Beulah represent the conditional grounding of a subsequent breakthrough to paradise.

Blake's response to this maneuver on Bunyan's part began to show up in his prophetic epics in the late 1790s and early 1800s, about twenty years before he thought of illustrating the full text of the *Progress*. In the revised portions of *The Four Zoas,* in *Milton,* and in *Jerusalem,* Blake honored Bunyan's evocation of the biblical Beulah by incorporating the name and state it represented into his own extended mythography.[42] In Blake, too, it becomes an expression of the psychic borderland between eternity and time, between the state of "Eden" and the state of "Generation," the place where "Contrarieties are equally True" (*M* 30, E129/K518). Like Bunyan, Blake exploits the libidinal potential of the marriage symbolism inherent in the name, defining *his* Beulah in terms of a "moony" and luxuriant, feminine sexuality. More particularly, he builds on an element of Bunyan's Beulah narrative that is not even hinted at by the biblical sources: the description of the active sleep undergone in that land by the pilgrims. In the *Progress,* this element is introduced as follows:

> So the Gardiner had them into the Vineyards, and bid them refresh themselves with the Dainties; he also shewed them *there* the Kings Walks and the *Arbors* where he delighted to be: And here they tarried and slept.
>
> Now I beheld in my Dream, that they talked more in their sleep at this time, then ever they did in all their Journey; and being in a muse there-about, the Gardiner said even to me, Wherefore musest thou at the matter? It is the nature of the fruit of the Grapes of these Vineyards to go down so sweetly, as to cause the lips of them that are asleep to speak. (*PP* 155–56)

Blake's Beulah likewise becomes the place of sleep, of dreams, but for him it takes on the uncanny and ambivalent value of the self-created personal unconscious—a realm of the psyche that harbors defenses and illusions as well as prophetic thought, painful as well as joyous memories, latent as well as manifest meanings, strategies of evil as well as strategies of good. Further, the Beulah of Blake's epics functions not simply as a one-way route to eternity, but as a gateway back, too, into the distorting light of the everday where Blake saw lurking the delusive forms of material generation. For Blake, then, Beulah was a threshold state, a place of rest and renewal for the imagination, yet one where through fantasies and dreams individuals blurred the boundaries between what Lacan calls the imaginary and the symbolic registers, experiencing their attachment to both in an unconscious and sometimes inflexibly literalistic way.[43]

Given the importance of Beulah in the imaginative schemes of Blake's own poetry, it is something of a mystery why he never sought to make its source in Bunyan the main subject of any of the designs he invented to illustrate the *Progress.* Perhaps he considered the "Beulah function," if I may coin a phrase, to have been subsumed by his depictions of other episodes of Bunyan's text, or even by the dream as a whole.[44] One reason for believing this to be the case is that the very quality of sleep-talking, a characteristic of the vineyards of Bunyan's Beulah, demonstrates the possibility of lucid dreaming and self-interpreting, which Blake's full series of designs already emphasizes at the very start and, recurrently, throughout.[45] Also, the crucially interactive role played by *Bunyan's* narrator in the Beulah scene merely amplifies a function that *Blake* already gave to other representatives of the narrator/dreamer's psyche who intervene at earlier stages in the action of the dream.[46]

An example (which is, coincidentally, the *Progress's* second most important use of heavenly meditation insofar as a reading of Blake is concerned) is the episode inside the House of the Interpreter, where Christian meets the Man Who Dreamed of the Day of Judgment. There, the figure of the Interpreter is presented by Blake as a type of the self-interpreting capacity of the dreamer (Plate 13; see also my discussion in Chapter 3), and he in turn presents to Christian the warning example of the imaginatively stunted dreamer *within* the dream. That dreamer-within-the-dream goes through his paces in the style of a cautionary figure from a *tableau vivant,* or like one of Blake's "Visionary forms dramatic" (*J* 98, E257/K746), and his role is to awake continually from a nightmare version of heavenly meditation in which he anticipates not his release, but rather his doom at the scene of the Last Judgment.[47]

As in the land of Beulah according to Blake, where "Contrarieties are equally True," and as in the land of Beulah according to Bunyan, where the grapes of Christ's blood cause the pilgrims to fall into an active, Logos-centered sleep, so here in the House of the Interpreter another type of the pilgrim shows us how our relation to all our dreams—including the dream format of *The Pilgrim's Progress* itself—can both follow and subvert the pattern of heavenly meditation. The redemptive power of vision, this episode declares, is in the last analysis a function of the psychic state and imaginal attitude of the perceiver. Our Man Who Dreamed of the Last Judgment is indisposed by self-doubt and cannot therefore enter into the positive aspects of his vision of Judgment. Instead, judging ill of himself, he projects that judgment onto eternal fate and associates to its negative connotations. Both Blake and Bunyan wished a better imaginative destiny for their audiences. Indeed, if we follow Blake's entreaty to the spectator of his Last Judgment picture and apply that rule to our readings of his Bunyan designs, we will be responding to his pictorial commentary on Bunyan the way Bunyan hoped his readers would respond to the original text. In that way we can complete a circuit of interpretation and empathy that illuminates the relations between creator, reader-viewer, dreamer, self, and work of art. For Bunyan winds up his introductory verses to *The Pilgrim's Progress* as follows:

> *This book will make a Travailer of thee,*
> *If by its Counsel thou wilt ruled be;*
> *It will direct thee to the Holy Land,*
> *If thou wilt its Directions understand:*

Yea, it will make the sloathful, active be;
The Blind also, delightful things to see.
   Art thou for something rare, and profitable?
Wouldest thou see a Truth within a Fable?

. . . .

   Wouldst thou divert thy self from Melancholly?
Would'st thou be pleasant, yet be far from folly?
Would'st thou read Riddles, and their Explanation,
Or else be drownded in thy Contemplation?
Dost thou love picking-meat? or would'st thou see
A man i' th Clouds, and hear him speak to thee?
Would'st thou be in a Dream, and yet not sleep?
Or would'st thou in a moment Laugh and Weep?
Wouldest thou loose thy self, and catch no harm?
And find thy self again without a charm?
Would'st read thy self, and read thou know'st not what
And yet know whether thou art blest or not,
By reading the same lines? O then come hither,
And lay my Book, thy Head and Heart together.

(PP 6–7)

Here speaking in one of his many (often contradictory) authorial voices, Bunyan claims for *his* visions what Blake later attributes to the whole genre of "Sublime Allegory." Thus in the lines "Would'st read thy self, and read thou knows't what/And yet know whether thou art blest or not,/By reading the same lines?" the *Progress* is presented as a story that is "addressd to the Intellectual powers while it is altogether hidden from the Corporeal Understanding" ("Letters," E730/K825). Then, too, when Bunyan promises that his book will bring spiritual results to the correctly attuned reader, which happen synchronistically to match those gradually acquired through the course of the dream-narrative by the protagonist ("It will direct thee to the Holy Land/If thou wilt its Directions understand"), we recognize that this enticement to a hermeneutics of reader-response is practically the same lure Blake extends to the Spectator of "A Vision of the Last Judgment" in the passage already analyzed. In both these cases, the underlying assumption is that a meaningful coincidence, indeed a fearful symmetry, can and should occur between the audience and the work through the very act of reading imaginatively and interpretively. Moreover, a third term enters the symmetric overlap in the eyes of both Blake and Bunyan when the audience understands that the work objectifies an inner reality that exists simultaneously in and through its creator. "Or would'st thou see/A man i' th Clouds, and hear him speak to thee?" says Bunyan, announcing that behind every allegorical figure, or "cloud," stands a human-form-divine (himself at one level, Christ as paradigm of the Self at another) speaking out of his own psychological experience, his own immediate spiritual knowledge.[48] (Blake's declaration that his "Grand Poem"—the epic *Milton*—is a transmuted spiritual autobiography of his "three years slumber on the banks of the ocean" is a parallel occasion.)[49]

Finally, it is the confluence of all these factors that permits both Bunyan and Blake to regard fable (Blake comes to prefer the generic term *vision*) as the carrier of *ineffable, imaginal truths. The Pilgrim's Progress* is recommended by Bunyan specifically to those who would "see a Truth within a Fable," and Blake goes so far as to claim that the truths within his Last Judgment picture are understood only when it is seen that *every* turning toward truth is symbolically a Last Judgment.[50] If we generalize from those examples, we may say that the truth to be found within a fable about personal transcendence is itself transcendent and consonant with the hermeneutic act of finding it. To read Bunyan's allegory in depth, then, and to "read" the illustrations that make up Blake's interpretive and visionary response to it, is to gain a rich knowledge of how each of these "Images of wonder" constantly reveals itself to be one of those images of truth about which Blake's devil in the *Marriage* remarks: "Every thing possible to be believ'd is an image of truth" (*MHH* 8).

CHAPTER TWO

BLAKE'S BUNYAN

Blake's interest in restoring a mythopoetic integrity to the visual representation of Bunyan's text was a late development in the history of his relationship to *The Pilgrim's Progress*. Earlier in his career, he exhibited a markedly critical attitude to the repressive, Puritan theology of Bunyan's story. As a staunch member of the "Devil's Party," he tended to take ironic potshots at the pietistic emblems and the homiletic allegorizing of Christian's dream journey—when he referred to it at all. But in the active days of the Lambeth period (1790–1800, when Blake lived at 13 Hercules Building, Lambeth), absorbed in the dynamic relations and counterposes of his own prophetic art to the orthodox energies of Milton's religious poetics, Blake evidently did not consider Bunyan a bardic compatriot or rival worthy of systematic attention. He sometimes drew on Bunyanesque imagery, but normally in a rather casual way, and even then he seemed to regard the *Progress* as a merely "negative source."[1] Such scattered allusions as we can trace were made in order to exemplify the perceptual limitations of Bunyan's hard-line Calvinisms. Their aim is invariably corrective, their manner ironic, and they exist mainly as foils, or points of departure, for expansive themes in his own poetry and designs.

Gradually, however, when Blake's concept of the creative ego's role as an artist-interpreter of the personality began to take root in an aesthetic of redemption, he experienced a change of heart toward the visionary function of Bunyan's fable. By the time he had developed a style of serial illustration adequate to handle literary critiques that were, simultaneously, visions of individuation, he was ready to turn to the hermeneutic complexity of the *Progress* and give it the innovative treatment I will be examining in Chapter 3.

INTERPRETING THE INTERPRETER'S PARLOR: METHODICAL PARODY, PROPHETIC CRITIQUE

Before we analyze in detail these drawings fashioned during the high point of his late career, a closer look at the history and development of Blake's confrontations with Bunyan is in order. It is important to recognize that it was not just the encouragement of the Ancients in 1824 that stimulated him to interpret Bunyan's allegory in pictorial terms. In fact, the most substantial preliminary attempt seems to have occurred approximately thirty years earlier, when he engraved a representation of the second lesson in the House of the Interpreter: that episode from the *Progress* in which Christian witnesses the living emblem of the Man Sweeping the Interpreter's Parlor.[2]

This was clearly a subject of more than routine interest for Blake, since it is likely that he used the design as a vehicle for his first experiment with a new (or at least newly described) printmaking process: the "woodcut on pewter" method he speaks of in his *Notebook*.[3] Blake's sensitivity to the metaphoric and epistemological overtones of each medium he worked in ensured that the choice of motif for a composition designed to break new technical ground would not have been accidental or unconsidered.[4] Rather, the iconography, theme, and style would be likely to bear a meaningful analogy to the shift in formal process and materials. In the case of the pewter engraving of ca. 1794, the conformation between illustrative method and theme—a theme itself concerned with method—is indeed meaningful. One need simply examine Blake's description of the "woodcut" technique he used and match it against the contents of the episode in Bunyan's text to see the links that piqued his interest and contributed to the formulation of the design.

The memorandum in question appears on page four of the *Notebook* and reads as follows:

> To Woodcut on Pewter: lay a ground on the Plate & smoke it as for Etching; then trace your outlines, and beginning with the spots of light on each object with an oval pointed needle scrape off the ground as a direction for your graver; then proceed to graving with the ground on the plate, being as careful as possible not to hurt the ground, because it, being black, will shew perfectly what is wanted. (Deletions omitted; punctuation added)

This minitreatise is sandwiched between two other descriptions of print processes. In that context, it seeks on the one hand to distinguish preparations for intaglio engraving from preparations for woodcut, when the plate in both instances is made of pewter;[5] on the other hand, in conjunction with the "woodcut on copper" note that follows, it highlights the differences between approaches to the two metals, copper and pewter. (Pewter is soft enough for carving larger areas, as in woodcut proper; comparable copper surfaces need to be bitten away.)

What is isolated in the statement quoted, then, is the white-line aesthetic of woodcut and the pliant property of pewter. Both of these features bear a relation not only to the moral of the Interpreter's emblem, but also to the defense of the allegorical method of the book as a whole, as that defense is articulated by Bunyan in his verse "Apology." Championing the heuristic value of the "dark . . . allegor[y]" that "finds the light" through the reader's "digging" among its images even though the narrative may appear to "want solidness" (*PP* 4.1, 4.18, 5.20, 4.20), Bunyan brings us to the very crux of his stubborn stance against the constraints of the approved Puritan plain-style. Coincidentally, this part of his apology describes what occurs in woodcut on pewter when, after laying a dark, smoked ground, the oval needle begins locating the "spots of light" and then proceeds to "scrape off" the ground, directing the "graver" to carve out the main areas of the design in the (relatively) unsolid metal. The program of discovery, as it were, is the same for both.

But the issues raised by method go deeper than mutual analogy and involve a troubling metaphysic of discontinuity on Bunyan's part that Blake firmly rejected, procedural similitudes notwithstanding. That metaphysic, part and parcel of the divided Puritan consciousness, led Bunyan to regard figuration as a veil placed over another more valuable reality, and he claimed that the form of *The Pilgrim's Progress* "curtained" a truth that was a discrete and separable "substance."[6] As we have seen, such a notion was anathema to Blake, for whom the prevailing dictum, in art as in life, was "to find form, and to keep it" (*DC*, E538/K573). For him, the image, so long as its creation coincided with a process of mental discovery, itself could be trusted to embody truth and to convey it. Thus, "*Every thing* possible to be believ'd is an image of truth" (*MHH* 8; italics added)—and that Proverb of Hell applies equally to the material creation of the world and to the formal creation of art.[7]

Bunyan, in contrast, was ever ambivalent in his feelings about the efficacy of "finding form." This made it possible for him to defend a rousing metaphorical style in his verse apology, as we have seen, and at the same time to undercut the reliability of the process. "Digging" among his dark figures was a hermeneutical exercise he recommended to the reader for its moral worth. But the outcome of such digging was not guaranteed, since parables and metaphors were understood, according to the Puritan doctrine of accommodation, as a sort of sugarcoating that pandered to human appetites but that masked a grimly distant and difficult truth. Just as the individual's spiritual identity was always in doubt while in the body, so the visionary value of form was considered questionable in the Calvinistic picture of things.[8]

In *The Pilgrim's Progress,* then, theological anxiety and artistic strategy become completely intertwined. Like certitude of election, the truths of fictive formulations are presented as elusive, and evidences of both need constantly to be "grop'd for" or "snared" or wrested from "dark and cloudy" emblems of experience, even though normally the truths behind the evidence often may "not be catch'd *what e're you do*" (PP 3.13, 3.10, 3.21, 2.34, 4.24. 3.14). In this way, the message that gets communicated by the text is that an eternal antinomy exists between the events that life offers on its surface and the Way of Christ, a right path forever being established on the other side of some gate, barrier, or challenging bodily confrontation. We live here in the flesh with hints and promises; but truth, security, and the reality of "spiritual sensation" are always elsewhere, in endless and infinite retreat. Similarly, we must fear yet not experience God's wrathful judgment, since it cannot be successfully embodied or imagined as a present reality but remains perpetually "to come" (PP 10).

It is a strange aesthetic that results from this deep distrust of manifestation, and two of its major tactics, as its major themes, are postponement of visionary fulfillment and displacement of the image by the foregrounding of interpretation—tactics that match the engraving technique of visual recession employed in the fashioning of a pewter woodcut. That is, instead of eating away "apparent surfaces" to let the "infinite and holy" image stand out bodily like raised type from the plate, as in Blake's "infernal" relief-etching process described in the *Marriage,* plate 14, woodcut on pewter requires that the defining lines of the image be recessed in the metal while the design's surrounding negative space is physically foregrounded. In the "Interpreter's Parlor" print, Blake uses this method with conscious irony. Piercing Apollyon with his own bow (*J* 12), he thus exposes the paradox at the heart of a self-doubting psyche's search for an answerable style.

The incident depicted occurs in the *Progress* just after the first lesson in the House of the Interpreter. In that lesson, Christian had been shown and had heard the Interpreter's explication of an emblematic portrait of a figure who seems in some way to be a stand-in for the Gospel texts themselves, representing the transmittance of the Good News of Christ.[9] The most striking aspect of this initial emblem, however, is that it is inactive and not, like all the ensuing lessons, a "visionary form dramatic" (*J* 100). The archetypal Evangelist, in other words (if that is what the portrait represents), is really only prefigured there, rather than actually presented; for in a mute and inert picture—something between a frontispiece and a religious icon[10]—his graphic image hangs on a recessed wall that is itself closeted behind a door, and in this concealed compartment acts as both a mediating factor and a reminder of the gap between vision and imminent reality.

So at the opening of the pilgrim's exploration of things interior, in his neophyte status, he finds not the Man (his appointed guide to Christ), but only the multiply recessed and static likeness of the Man.[11] This condition of essential absence parallels the paradoxical revelation, necessary to every pilgrimage, that a key ingredient required for progress and development is missing from consciousness. Entailed once again is the Puritan double bind. Without the thing-that-is-wanting, one cannot begin the journey, even though the journey's sole purpose is to get that thing. On its hopeful side, however, the situation expresses the premises of the old homeopathic paradox: like cures like, and lack (or awareness of lack) cures lack.

In the text, the Interpreter hammers the point of absence home by a syntactical device, his rhetorical doubling of the locution "the Man whose picture this is," a phrase insistent on the fact that although the picture is there, the man is not. "*The Man whose picture this is,* is one of a thousand," the Interpreter begins; and some lines later in homiletic summation he goes on to explain: "I have shewed thee this Picture first, because *the Man whose Picture this is,* is the only Man, whom the Lord of the Place whither thou art going, hath Authorized, to be thy Guide in all difficult places thou mayest meet with in the way" (*PP* 29; italics added). By relegating the tangible, visible object of contemplation (the picture) to the secondary position of a possessive relative clause and making the absent "Man" the principal subject of the telltale phrase, the Interpreter plays on the poignant distinction between the static, available, but subordinate image and the dynamic, unavailable, ideal.

It is as a complement to this experience of numinous distance and present inactivity that Christian is then led by the Interpreter

> into a very large *Parlour* that was full of dust, because never swept; the which, after he had reviewed a little while, the *Interpreter* called for a man to *sweep:* Now when he began to sweep, the dust began so abundantly to fly about, that *Christian* had almost therewith been choaked: Then said the *Interpreter* to a *Damsel* that stood by, Bring hither Water, and sprinkle the Room; which when she had done, was swept and cleansed with pleasure. (*PP* 29–30)

This is the little morality play that underlies Blake's emblematic print (Fig. 1).[12] We cannot say that Blake has engraved the scene itself, however, because the design does not depict "a very large *Parlour*," nor does it show either Christian's participation or the Interpreter's. Perhaps Blake is consciously opposing in this way the work of an earlier Bunyan illustrator, the popular Dutch engraver Jan Luiken, who focuses on the realistic details of the parlor

FIG. 1 Blake, *The Man Sweeping the Interpreter's Parlor*

FIG. 2 Jan Luiken, *The Man Sweeping the Interpreter's Parlor*

scene in the only known treatment of this subject before Blake's (Fig. 2). In any case, just as Bunyan's text deliberately eliminated the presence of the archetypal Evangelist in the first lesson, so Blake's print makes a point of ignoring the literal level of Christian's experience in this second emblematic encounter. Instead he offers a visual commentary on the ensuing *exegesis* of the event. That is, by a species of subtle graphic parody, Blake manages to criticize the Interpreter's doctrinal "comparison" of the above episode at the same time as he illustrates its exemplary components.[13]

The Interpreter evaluates the scene as follows:

> This Parlor, is the heart of a Man that was never sanctified by the sweet Grace of the Gospel: the *dust*, is his Original Sin, and inward Corruptions that have defiled the whole Man. He that began to sweep at first, is the Law; but She that brought water, and did sprinkle it, is the Gospel: Now, whereas thou sawest that so soon as the first began to sweep, the dust did so fly about, that the Room by him could not be cleansed, but that thou wast almost choaked therewith, this is to shew thee, that the Law, instead of cleansing the heart (by its working) from sin, doth revive, put strength into, and increase it in the soul, even as it doth discover and forbid it, for it doth not give power to subdue.
>
> Again, as thou sawest the *Damsel* sprinkle the Room with Water, upon which it was cleansed with pleasure: This is to shew thee, that when the Gospel comes in the sweet and precious influences thereof to the heart, then I say, even as thou sawest the Damsel lay the dust by sprinkling the Floor with Water, so is sin vanquished and subdued, and the soul made clean, through the Faith of it; and consequently fit for the King of Glory to inhabit. (*PP* 30)

Blake's composition nicely adumbrates the balanced structure of the third statement in this exposition, where the figures of the Man and the Damsel are compared as separate but equal representatives of the two biblical dispensations. Each personified character occupies its own domain in its own half of the plate, with some overlap in the middle properly faced and integrated only by the Damsel-Gospel. The pictorial scene has the distributive weight of a similar adage in "A Vision of the Last Judgment" on the differences between the methods of the heavenly Father and the heavenly Son: "First God Almighty comes with a Thump on the Head Then Jesus Christ comes with a balm to heal it" (VLJ, E565/K617). In Blake's pewter cut, the right side of the print depicts the allegorized Law not as a house servant but as a naked, bat-winged man with a beard, who energetically sweeps the soul's "inward Corruptions" up in a dark funnel of dust that forms a thick cloud around him. The left side of the engraving is given over to the figure of the Gospel, here no mere domestic, but rather a white-robed angel complete with folded wings. She is shown descending a short flight of stairs, indicating that her entrance to the parlor is in process, and she carries a bowl in her right hand, while from her left there flows a sprinkling of water.

So far so good, as far as faithfulness to the spirit of the text is concerned. The nature of the liberties Blake has taken here with Bunyan's images, transforming the Damsel-Gospel into an angel and the servant-Law into a devil, does not negate but only exaggerates the polarity that the Interpreter himself expresses between the helpful effect of the Gospel and the deleterious influence of the letter of the Law. It is true that the Interpreter equivocates on this point, never claiming anything like a Manichaean antagonism between the two personified testaments. Indeed, he carefully avoids imputing evil to the holy content of the Law, which in his account only "by its working," and not by its message, increases the very sin it "doth discover and forbid." To that extent, Blake's gift of Apollyonic bat wings to the figure of the sweeper is a critical, evaluative measure, signifying the artist's conviction that an entity in a state of such deep ambivalence and imaginative contradiction needs to be shown to be spectrous in his own person as well as in his effect. But the iconographic addition is still in the category of an embellishment or an adaptation of a meaning already implied by Bunyan.

The same is *not* true of the little creatures Blake portrays cluttering the floor and swirling in the dust cloud. The only justification for their presence on the basis of an antecedent in the text is the phrase "inward Corruptions," in the verbal comparison explaining that "the *dust*, is his Original sin, and inward Corruptions that have defiled the whole Man." Because a certain flavor of personification enriches the rhetoric of the passage and animates the definition of the dust, it is understandable that the inward corruptions might be represented as humanized motes of dust. But Blake has not drawn a corresponding crew of autonomous miniature evils existing as hypostatized representatives of dust and defilement. On the contrary, he has distinguished the small figures from the dusty system of Original Sin, showing *it* to be an agent that disturbs and in fact violently transforms *them*. Thus originally, the "inward Corruptions" as Blake sees them are evidently not corrupt, for in the foreground, in their mostly uncontaminated condition, some tiny shapes appear to be souls with butterfly wings.[14]

Aside from an amorphous heap of them huddled on the floor at the feet of the Gospel, three of these figures stand out. One flounders as if stepped on by the Law's foot; one is swept in the air by his broom; and a third, with wing clipped and altered, seems to be escaping from a hole higher up in the dust swirl. But other more demonic forms that have been enfolded in the cloud of choking sin mimic the face of their devilish "benefactor," the sweeping Mosaic Law. More pointedly, these apparitions are *only* face. The first, wearing a beard that merges with the dust at the sweeper's feet, exhibits an agonized expression suitable to proponents of the doctrine of original sin. Another, possessed of electrified hair that exaggerates the fright-afflicted appearance of the face of the Law, peers out on the right side of the plate, just above the broom. And the last such demon emerges from the top left of the dust cloud, a dark sun breaking through the storm, doubling the facial attitude of the sweeper and sporting its own developed bat wing.

The grouping of these six children of light and darkness tells us that they bear a personalized relationship to one another: each fairy soul is counterpoised and reacted to by one of the dark faces. It is not clear, however, whether they are meant to be natural contraries, or whether the frightened faces in the cloud of dust represent the negations (in Blake's sense) of the fairy energies once the heart of man becomes embroiled in the very concept of inward corruption. Clearly Blake engraved the sweeper's half of the plate such that the cloud of dust (Original Sin) looks like a creation and inevitable extension of the man's wings and not a wholly other aspect that the stony Law "doth discover and forbid." We are thus permitted to see how dogmatic morality generates both a faulty method and the condition that method is insufficient to subdue.

This mannerism of having the clouds around a figure appear, through affinity of shape and lineation, as an integral part of the mood or mentality of that figure occurs frequently in Blake and is worth noting as a significant rhetorical device that we will meet again in the full Bunyan series. One of its purposes is to objectify the subjective reality created by the limited vision of the figures depicted and at the same time to involve the believing consciousness of the viewer in that reality. In this respect, the device becomes another way of rendering Blake's notion that man's total environment is human. As mentioned earlier, the so-called phenomenal world, "this Vegetable Glass of Nature" (VLJ, E555/K605), is normally treated by Blake as if it were essentially *epi*phenomenal, deriving what we think of as its formal properties from the inner needs, drives, mind-set of each individual perceiver, who thus becomes an agent at its center. External nature is therefore often pictured anthropomorphically in Blake's art. Sometimes this feat is accomplished by the visual personification of natural forms and forces, in the mode of literary fable, allegory, and epithet. The pastoral landscape of the *Songs,* of *Thel,* and of Blake's early illustrations to Gray and Young are full of such peopled flowers, humanized elements, and "animated . . . sensible objects" (*MHH* 11). Other times, as here in the "Interpreter's Parlor" print, when the question of the relation between man and manifestation is itself regarded as a clouded issue, the material world is presented as a clear and literal projection of the human form dominating the scene. The cloud is simultaneously an element of the "outward Creation" (VLJ, E565/K617) and one of those "Mental Things" that "are alone Real" (VLJ, E565/K617). Its presence portrays an event of con-

FIG. 3   Blake, *Satan Smiting Job with Sore Boils*

FIG. 4   Blake, *Satan Smiting Job with Sore Boils*

sciousness which precedes those motions of imaginative behavior that permit us, for good and ill, to react to external stimuli and to become what we behold.

Both acts of the mind—the cumulative creation and the magnetic beholding of projected psychic contents—are key themes of Blake's art, and his iconic representations of them are intended to convey a knowledge of the complex function of psychological projection in our mental lives. An instructive example, showing the wider application of the principle involved, is plate 6 of the *Job* series, usually called *Satan Smiting Job with Sore Boils* (Fig. 3). Here, moreover, we can see the visual expression of the concept developing through several versions done over the years.[15] When the design reached the engraving stage, Blake made Satan's menacing background cloud take a dark-winged, cruciform shape, complete with halo, that distinctly duplicates the fallen angel's body stance. At the same time, it retained its identity and its autonomy as a storm cloud. The result is a pictural rendering (that is, a literal portrayal in visual terms)[16] of the concept of psychological influence—what is called "emotional vibrations" in the modern, secular idiom, and "emanation" or "aura" in religious traditions. Job's Satan is, of course, giving off a *deadly* feeling tone, trailing clouds of spectrally perverted glory as he comes. And Blake's parodic allusion, through structural likeness, to the conventional aureole surrounding divine figures in Christian art only intensifies our recognition of the distorting function Satan has in Job's psychic revolution. On the one hand we witness Job experiencing Satan as an evil influence visited on him from the environment; in this sense the design is an emblem of dissociation. On the other hand, the pictorial reminders of a Christly incarnation emphasize the broader view of Satan's role as a heaven-sent neurosis: a critical but often necessary stage in the growth of spiritual consciousness, a *felix malefactum* with method in its madness.

A year or so later, when this same composition was turned into a small tempera painting (Fig. 4), the greater part of the cloud had ceased to be pictured as an atmospheric emanation. Instead it became incorporated into Satan's own outline, sprouting from his back in the form of a huge pair of orange bat wings. The projection of the Satanic state has become rooted and attached to the evildoer in this rendition and indicates a significant shift in psychological perspective.[17]

The implications of such a shift will be examined in our discussion of the way background works in the complete series of the *Pilgrim's Progress* drawings. At this point it is enough to note that the "Interpreter's Parlor" engraving employs both methods of representing the negative influence of the state of evil, utilizing the symbolism of cloud and bat wing. It is as if Bunyan's very concept of a divided self as it is reflected in a divisive morality—a notion given scope in this emblem—urged Blake on to a visual grammar of double negatives that might better alert the viewer to the traps of such "two horned reasoning" (*Gates* 1818, E268/K770).

Two final instances of Blake's ironic intent in his pictorial treatment of Bunyan's emblem may be mentioned. First, and most important, is the way the figure of the Damsel is presented here. She comes from the left, pushed by a flood of light, along a diagonal that repeats the line of effort embodied by the Man's broom. This is the fundamental evidence of a resemblance between them, reifying the text's assurance that they are both engaged in the same propaedeutic act of cleansing the sinful heart. That resemblance has different connotations in Blake's version than it does in the Bunyan account, however, because in the print, rather than parlor maid and manservant, it is angel and devil who are pictured as boon companions in the work: odd bedfellows in any traditional scheme of moral leadership. Behind this graphic maneuver, of course, is the fact that for Blake the primary belief that the heart was inherently sinful was itself a falsehood that needed exposing. So *his* devilishly angelic Damsel is shown spilling her water on the nascent mass of barely defined, barely emerged creatures grouped on the very edge of the dust cloud of Original Sin. Is she damping down sin? Or is she drowning the genesis of new potentialities in the soul?[18] Through iconographic ambiguities, Blake leaves these questions deliberately unanswered. By so doing, his print evokes a questioning and critical response in us, and we find ourselves reacting to the balance of visual motifs as signs of the complicity of the two doctrines of Grace and the Law, each of which here sees the energies of the souls as sins, each of which joins in the common goal of repression. One dampens and one be-clouds, but both attempt to vanquish and subdue.

Second, there is an element of caricature in the portrayal of these figures which is enhanced by the fact that their sanctified status seems to be a satiric embellishment of a specific allusion. As we mentioned earlier, Bunyan's text

FIG. 5 Anton Wierix, *Jesu Cor Expurgans*

lends itself to a sort of cartoon rendering, because the *tableau vivant* style of presentation, and the emblematic mode, bear within them an expectation of conceptual excess and figural exaggeration. In this case, though, Bunyan's version of the parable is itself already a partial caricature of a previous emblem originally engraved by Anton Wierix and entitled *Jesu Cor Expurgans* (Fig. 5).[19] In this picture the infant Jesus, broom in hand, sweeps a pile of snakes, vermin, and other unidentifiable detritus out of a large, heart-shaped chamber that is suspended in the heavens. Jesus himself stands on a cloud reminiscent of the Law's dust cloud, and his broom sends the wormlike sins of the heart plummeting into the abyss below. Iconographically, his pose suggests the stance of Christ at the beginning of time when he routed the rebel angels out of heaven, and Blake borrowed that pose for his representation of the Interpreter's Mosaic Law. It might have seemed a specially noteworthy irony to Blake that Bunyan made Christian's Interpreter preempt Jesus from the room of the heart, replacing him with the servile representatives of two error-provoking "sacred codes" (*MHH* 4).[20] And if he did know the earlier print—a plausible conjecture given the frequent reuse and widespread availability of such popular illustrations in Blake's day[21]—his autonomous creatures of the dust, venemous and cherubic alike, could be intended as allusions to the lost religion of Jesus that Wierix's model of the devout heart tried to embody. Thus the design of Blake's engraving becomes an attempt to restore, by ironic revision, a sense of the heart's virile, imaginative integrity.

We began this section with a question of motivation: what spurred Blake on to address the lesson of the Man sweeping the Interpreter's Parlor in a metal-cut technique new to his artistic practice? No precise biographical answer can be given. But if we recall that in the 1790s Blake was busy creating his "Bible of Hell" expressly to counter the dominance of "angelic" interpretations of Jesus' message and Jesus' acts (*MHH*), we can appreciate his interest in parodying the Interpreter's domesticated presentation of the role of the Gospel. And if we remember, also, that in one of the books of this Bible of Hell Blake pours scorn on religious systems that enslave humanity with the promise of an Eternal Life "in an *allegorical* abode where Existence hath never come" (*Europe* 5; italics added), we can get a feeling for his impatience with the ideological and imaginative perversions of the allegorizing mode per se. Already he was using the term *allegory* in a pejorative sense (a sense he later defined with specific reference to the aesthetic limitations of the *Progress*).[22] For him it signified a method of fixed comparison dependent on a mechanical frame of mind that valued the image only as a counter or code for an abstract precept. He seems to have felt that moral allegory of this sort both bred and was nurtured by a reductive dualism inimical to imaginative health. Its blindered pursuit of a single authoritarian meaning dulled the senses and the intellect. As a tool of tyrannical religious systems, it went hand in hand with the arts of repression, which capitalized on the capacity for dissociation in the psyche and sanctioned the divorce of form and latent content. By its very intention to substitute a spiritual tenor for a literal vehicle of meaning, it emphasized the mind-body and soul-body splits that kept individuals from a "perception of the infinite" (*MHH* 13) in their ordinary lives. And like the imposition of the Puritan worldview, the operations of allegory implicated man in a psychology of doubt and postponement, of secrecy and restraint.

The opposite psychology, part and parcel of an opposite aesthetic, is given expression by Blake in the famous passage from the *Marriage* (pl. 14) where he announces his own program for sweeping clean the whole sensorium of fallen man.[23] The "allegorical abode where Existence hath never come" proves in this account to be life as the caverned man tends to experience it here and now, thanks to doctrines like that of Original Sin which make things present seem "finite & corrupt." But life as it *is* here and now can be known with certainty to be "infinite and holy" as soon as distinctions between body and soul, medium and message, "sensual enjoyment" and spiritual understanding, are recognized as expendable. Achieving such a visionary perspective is clearly not a matter of wresting a precept from an image. On the contrary, Blake's whole effort is spent encouraging trust in the immanent wisdom of observable form. For him, things seen are literally "metaphors" of vision, designed to "carry over" the imaginal archetypes they embody and express. One's attitude *toward* things, as toward the processes of embodiment and ensouling, may need correction; but the problem is perceptual and not ontological. So the "infernal method" of etching on copper is intended to exemplify and to involve the participant in a process of sudden apprehension of surface truth, an apprehension that carries the certitude of revelation and needs no "corporeal" explication. Just the reverse of Bunyan's formal strategy of recession, it reflects a coming-forth procedure. Every encounter with Blake's acid-forged forms is meant as a mutual epiphany, a friendship through the eye on the plane of appearance, between the deep structures of the spectator's psyche and the content displayed. The pun on the word *apparent,* in the phrase "melting apparent surfaces away," tells the story. For Blake, real surfaces were made apparent (visible) by the elimination of apparent (seeming) surfaces. But the images of truth do not hide as ideas *behind* a false appearance in his conception, nor do they exist in *contradiction* to "apparent surfaces." Rather, Blake makes his visions of the infinite lift out of the everyday by emphatically affirming their concrete substantiality. Through the "infernal method," his printed language of forms—visual and verbal combined—a spiritual body is literally raised. There is a concept of redemption here, both of the spirit and of the body, both of the form and of the inward meaning—the "infernal sense"[24]—of the form.

We have already noted how different Bunyan's method of dealing with the eternal and infinite is. But one more look at the hermeneutic of the *Progress* may serve to bring the contrast into greater relief. I cite a paradigmatic passage that by precept and formal organization exemplifies the "rule of interpretation" that the reader of Bunyan's dream must apply to the book as a whole.[25] "*Then I perceive,*" says Christian, in reference to one of his experiences in the Interpreter's House, " *'tis not best to covet things that are* now, *but to wait for things to* come." And the Interpreter responds:

> You say the Truth, *For the things that are seen, are* Temporal; *but the things that are not seen, are* Eternal: But though this be so, yet since things present, and our fleshly appetite, *are such near Neighbours one to another;* and again, because things to come, and carnal sense, are such strangers one to another: therefore it is, that the first of these so suddenly fall into *amity,* and that *distance* is so continued between the second. (*PP* 32)

Strangeness and distance, given here as the qualities of a relationship to the eternal, are the very attributes of a dark and cloudy metaphorical style according to Bunyan; and they match up nicely as contraries to the qualities that Blake, in later years, demands of his spectators when he begs them to "make a Friend & Companion" of some of his "Images of wonder" (VLJ, E560/K611). Blake chose to alter the expectation of enmity and distance between outward form and spiritual or symbolic content in his illuminated canon by designing iconic counterexamples that surfaced the Forms Eternal. His relief-etching process was thus a way of accepting "Things present and our fleshly appetites" as "near neighbours" not merely to each other, but also to those "things to come," which could then enter into an expanded presence.

When it came to offering a critical opinion on the work of another writer through a mode of direct visual commentary such as the "Interpreter's Parlor" print, however, employing the "salutary" medicine of his "infernal method" was not the tactic Blake felt to be appropriate. Here was not occasion for mobilizing an alternate system. Rather, to show the insufficiency of the Interpreter's Puritan methodology, Blake chose to adopt the approach of caricature implicit in it, correcting by hyperbole the underlying assumptions of Bunyan's distancing psychology. This he did, in part, by printing in what might ironically be termed the "celestial method" of pewter woodcut.

In sum, we can see Blake delighting in the multiple ploy of interpreting the interpretation of the emblem of the Man sweeping the Interpreter's heart by a technique that mimics and stirs up the errors of the sweepers. Like the Man, Blake "scrapes off the ground," and then, like his accomplice, Bunyan's Gospel-Damsel, he subdues and recesses the images of truth, "being as careful as possible not to hurt the ground, because it, being black, will shew prefectly what is wanted." In this last phase, the work of the graver symbolically adumbrates the work of the visual satire, leaving untouched, and in relief for all to see, the blackhearted concept that the ground of our present being is inherently black.

EMBLEM AND ALLEGORY: BLAKE'S USE OF BUNYAN BEFORE 1800

Although there is no other instance in which *The Pilgrim's Progress* is the direct target of Blake's pictorial commentary before 1824, Bunyan did exert a visible influence on Blake's mental imagery through the years, and references to him often lurk in the background of the wide-ranging context of allusions from which individual poems, designs, and commentaries by Blake take their prophetic departure.

In the 1790s, for example, the pressure of Bunyan can be felt making its mark on Blake's experimental attitude toward the emblem, on the one hand, and toward the uses of satiric visual allegory, on the other. The clearest documented case of this double influence is that described by David Erdman in *Prophet Against Empire,* where Erdman shows how Blake's design no. 9 of the *Gates of Paradise* (Fig. 6) takes off from a 1793 political cartoon by the celebrated caricaturist James Gillray.[26] Gillray's satiric print, entitled *The Slough of Despond; Vide the Patriot's Progress* (Fig. 7), casts Charles Fox, the head of the Whig opposition party, in the role of a pilgrim vainly struggling toward the "Straight Gate or the way to the Patriot's Paradise." In this manner, Gillray ridicules in one fell swoop both the despair mentality of Bunyan's allegory and the futile expectations of the English Patriots whose Jacobin dreams of a free society were proving more and more chimerical.

Gillray juxtaposes two separate *Progress* episodes to satirize Fox's political predicament: Christian's sinking in the Slough of Despond and his arrival several scenes later at the Wicket Gate. Fox, as Christian, is shown bemired up to his shoulders. He has dropped his Bible, the "Gospel of Liberty by the four Evangelists St. Paine, St. Price, St. Priestly, and St. Petion," and cries for help from a more reliable source. But the burden on his back, labeled "French Gold/French Loyalty/French Daggers/And/Crimes more numerous/than the sands upon/the Ocean's shore," overwhelms him and presses him down. "I shall Rise no more!" he moans. "I am lost for ever, & shall never see the Promis'd Land!!" In the background, the gateway to paradise is revealed as a mere façade: nothing is behind it except a short ladder ludicrously inadequate to the task of reaching the only promised land in view: the fool's paradise of a crescent moon. As Erdman points out, Blake's response is to contradict Gillray's cynical attitude toward the desire for freedom by including in his emblem "an extension of the ladder long enough to reach the moon and a youthful pilgrim energetic enough to climb it."[27] Yet when Blake adopts and adapts the ladder imagery, he is not only attacking Gillray; he is also, and perhaps more importantly, defending Bunyan by stressing the value (and problems) of a thematic concern for human aspiration, which is at the root of the *Progress.* So it is the nihilistic bent of Gillray's deliberate distortion of Bunyan's purpose, as much as the debunking quality of the Tory politics of the cartoon, that Blake is reacting to. At that level, then, we can read an intent to correct Gillray's implicit literary criticism of Bunyan in the way Blake manipulates this image.[28]

But Blake's "correction" is itself a critical response to the episode in the *Progress* that is its source, and it certainly does not imply an unreserved endorsement of the Puritan fable of striving. Taken by itself, it is possible to regard the climber in *Gates* 9 as a positive personification of the faculty of

FIG. 6   Blake, *I Want! I Want!*

FIG. 7   James Gillray, *The Slough of Despond; Vide the Patriot's Progress*

imaginative yearning. He has his extension ladder—his libido—attached to a celestial goal that will bring him to a higher state, above sublunary things. But in the context of the emblems that come before and follow, this hieroglyph contains a warning and seems to refer to the pitfalls inherent in a "puritanical" sublimation of unfulfilled desire. For the climbing act, paired and contrasted with the requited love of the couple standing on the ground beside the pilgrim,

FIG. 8 Blake, *Help! Help!*

FIG. 9 Blake, *My Son! My Son!*

has disastrous consequences in the next emblem, which shows a man drowning (*Gates* 10; Fig. 8). These two representations, seen in a series with the previous episode, the father–son–defiance design (*Gates* 8; Fig. 9), tell a story like that of Icarus. One might even say that the pilgrim of emblem no. 9 is playing out a "lunatic" myth of displaced aspiration, shooting for the moon instead of winging for the sun as Icarus does. Supporting this view is Blake's own poetic comment on the event, in his revised version of the *Gates* retitled *For the Sexes: The Gates of Paradise* and published twenty-five years later, where "The Keys of the Gates" describe the pilgrim as "Climbing thro Nights highest noon" (E268/K771), that is, toward a substitute sun risen to its zenith at night, in the unconscious, where we dream our lives away.

The notion that our Bunyanesque climber is a malformation and mask of the real Icarian hero of the soul is further suggested by emblem no. 11 (Fig. 10). There the soul, having gone through the purgatorial drowning of design no. 10, appears afresh as a boy with wings, consciously approaching a conscious sun, only to be thwarted by "Aged Ignorance." The ironic reversals mount in this final reference to the Icarus legend; for the moral intention of the Greek myth is to condemn the excess hubris of youthful folly, not to defend it against the nearsighted, wing-clipping spirit of hoary experience as Blake has it here. But by blending the truth of Icarus with the truth of the aspiring pilgrim, the tonality of Blake's message is clear: division between sensual and spiritual

FIG. 10 Blake, *Aged Ignorance*

desires is a self-negating mechanism that brings puritanical souls (like Bunyan and his protagonist, Christian) repeatedly to the brink of melancholic despondency.

What makes the ladder image of projected unconscious desire refer specifically to *Bunyan's* view of Christian in despair, and not just to topical Fox or mythical Icarus, is that it leads to that sinking state (design no. 10) from which, as in Christian's case, Help is called upon to draw one out. Yet by placing the emblem inscribed "Help! Help!" *after* the Gillray-inspired design, Blake is deliberately reversing the relations of cause and effect laid out in the narrative of the *Progress*. For if "Help! Help!" does emphatically point to the situation of Christian in the Slough of Despond (and it seems to do so, again, by way of Gillray's cartoon),[29] then the ladder-climbing incident ought to *follow* the rescue from that despair. After all, the ladder image, via Gillray, alludes to the theme of ascent attainable only on the other side of the gate, passage through which is the reward of the pilgrim who progresses through the bog and whose cry of help is answered. Blake's emblematic vision of human psychological development in *his* version of the boundary issues implied by the imagery of the gate (which the title of the *Gates* reifies) is, in this respect, an inverse analogue of Bunyan's rendering of the spiritual journey—and makes its point partly by the wit of that inversion. The point itself is in fact quite central and deserves some elaboration.

From Blake's view, the process that both Gillray and Bunyan misconstrue (however differently) is the process we noted earlier as fundamental to his art: the psychological dynamic of symbolic projection.[30] To project one's desires through the strait gate of the "cavernd senses" onto a distant object in the outer world, such as the moon, is a necessary first step toward engagement with the unrealized potential those desires hold. To drown in the disappointed recognition that the object, so conceived, is out of reach and that the projected value must be withdrawn from it—a painful business—is the next critical stage in integration of the whole man. Both phases, projection and withdrawal of projection, though fraught with their own emotional dangers, are essential for the liberation of the "human form divine" within. But the first implies the second, and not vice versa.

This progression from "I want! I want!" to "Help! Help!" describes the evolution of a consciousness that is running the wanderer's course between the manic-depressive Scylla and Charybdis of "infinite desire," as that course is charted in the second series of *There Is No Natural Religion,* written five years before the first *Gates* series. There Blake compresses into propositions V and VI the dilemma of the seeker for personal salvation, whether Lockean empiricist or Puritan Calvinist. (It is perhaps noteworthy that these tracts, composed in a spirit of contention with deistic materialism, serve equally well to illuminate the problems of self-doubt on which the Puritan quest is based.) " . . . More! More! is the cry of a mistaken soul, less than All cannot satisfy Man," says proposition V (E2/K97), logically requiring an expanded definition of "All" that transcends "number, weight & measure" (*MHH* 7) and leaves behind the world of countable, clippable, sublunary things. This dismissal of the values of a quantified universe would correspond to a leap *beyond* the moon, outside the categories of space and time, such as is not yet envisioned by the ladder climber in emblem no. 9 of the *Gates.* Blake's moon-struck pilgrim further betrays his kinship with the "mistaken soul" of proposition V by his very diction, for "I want! I want!" is simply a personalized, ego-oriented transformation of the earlier undifferentiated phrase "More! More!"[31]

There is an important difference, however, between our experience of the objectified "mistaken soul" and the subjective traveler. The readers of proposition V have two alternatives presented to them: they can choose the way of the mistaken soul or they can opt for "All." The pilgrim of the *Gates,* however, as an experiencing ego, must commit his error of yearning and cannot at that juncture reverse it for the fuller, more satisfying aspiration of a redefined "All." Therefore he is destined to fulfill the negative prophecy of proposition VI: "If any could desire what he is incapable of possessing, despair must be his eternal lot" (E2/K96). And so in emblem no. 10 we see him fallen and immersed in the very element of despair, a state and element imaged by Bunyan, and by Gillray after him, as a watery bog but by Blake as a lonely sea. When in "The Keys of the Gates" Blake later named this element "Time's Ocean" (E268/K771), he refined the story further and made it clear that such despair consisted in the drowning concept of life as timebound. One's "eternal" lot was despair only so long as eternity was pitted against time in the mind that believed time and space to be real categories capable of alienating a man from his rightful *certitudo salutis* in eternity.

By switching here the sequential order of the themes of ascent and despair, Blake comments simultaneously on Bunyan and Gillray, as we have seen. Yet he makes a distinction in his criticism of the two allegorists when, in design no. 10, he supports and amplifies Bunyan's imagery while opposing Gillray's parody of it. That is, instead of dwelling on the hopelessness of his pilgrim's plight (as Gillray dwells on Christian/Fox's imminent drowning), Blake depicts the fervor and energy of the call for help and hints that it is in itself a natural, positive transformation of his fallen man's misplaced desire. Before, he wanted the moon; now he seeks a human hand. Just so, "I want! I want!"— a repetitive exclamation of the selfhood—modulates into "Help! Help!"—a repetitive prayer too urgent for personal pronouns.

The felt urgency is further portrayed by Blake's having drawn the drowning man with his left arm fully extended upward, whereas Gillray presents Fox sinking without resistance in the slough, his two hands effetely spread out at water level. Finally, Blake's protagonist flounders in his Ocean of Despond with what looks like the tip of a flotation device (perhaps inflatable water wings) bobbing in the waves with him.[32] This addition to the iconography of Gillray's caricature returns the emblem all the more strongly to the trusting, self-regulatory psychology of a religious outlook, in contrast to the satiric motives of the political cartoon. For although it is barely perceived, and apparently unused, the safety float ensures the fallen soul's survival, and its presence thus has a function which corresponds to the placement of hidden stepping stones in Bunyan's dangerous bog, the stairs that are glossed in the margins of the *Progress* text as "The Promises of forgiveness and acceptance to life by Faith in Christ." These are spoken of by Help when he tells the dreamer of the *Progress* about the nature of the slough, explaining at the very end of his discourse that

> there are by direction of the Law-giver, certain good and substantiall steps, placed even through the very midst of this *Slough;* but at such time as this place doth much spue out its filth, as it doth against change of weather, these steps are hardly seen; or if they be, Men through the diziness of their Heads, step besides; and then they are bemired to purpose, notwithstanding the steps be there. (*PP* 16)

It seems once again that Blake and Bunyan are allied in their assessment of the rescue aids available to a soul who will, through breadth and clarity of vision, discover them.

In sum, it can be said that two characteristic aesthetic attitudes are at work in the way Blake juggled the claims of Bunyan's allegory with the wit of Gillray's spoof. First, Blake disallowed Gillray's methodical deflation of the mythic dimension of Christian's experience in the *Progress.* Attacking both the foibles of current political action *and* the archetypal integrity of the underlying image on which the political analogy was based was a species of overkill Blake rarely stooped to. He would invert or correct, but he would not deride or destroy, for the sheer sport, structures that held mythic content. Second, Blake strove to preserve, by serial treatment, a psychodynamic feature of Bunyan's work that Gillray's single shot of "The Patriot's Progress" perforce ignored, namely, the quality of entelechal unfolding. In fiction, that quality requires the formal properties of a narrative context and relies on scenes of figuration and fulfillment. But any sequence of tropes permits motives of development to be played out with the aid of doublings and inversions of images—just the sort of symbolic transformations that occur within the allegoric dream genre and are the stock in trade of serial illustrators and epic poets alike. In the present instance, we see Blake raising to high seriousness the topical and literary slander of Gillray, by retaining Gillray's pictorial imagery and re-embedding it in its original context: the Bunyanesque idiom of a psychic journey through time. One could say Blake has rescued Bunyan from Gillray in these emblems as he rescued the vision of Wierix from Bunyan in the "Interpreter's Parlor" print.

As a general tactic, this reactionary trend, which makes Blake jump to the defense of an originating formulation at the expense of later reductive interpretations, is familiar to us from his stylistic and thematic concern with "what the Ancients calld the Golden Age" (VLJ, E555/K605). But more than that conservative impulse is at stake here. Rather, the whole strategy of giving current issues an objective and far-ranging psychic reference is involved.

Fundamentally, Blake's use of pictorial caricature as a tool of political commentary was the reverse of Gillray's. Gillray demythologized contemporary events by linking them with what he took to be quaint, or controversial, imaginative models whose mythic validity was equally the subject of ridicule. The Fox/Bunyan parody is one example. Another example, even more familiar to students of Blake, is Gillray's "Sin, Death, and the Devil" print, which makes fun of the supposedly "unskilful allegory" in Milton's *Paradise Lost* even as it mocks Pitt's sin-born, anti-jacobin antics.[33] In this way, lacking a real dialectic, Gillray's work slashes both sides of the metaphoric equation, canceling out one's trust in the ability of the signifying form or image to carry reliable meaning. Blake's effort, however, was in the other direction. He highlighted the prophetic, psychological purport of eighteenth-century political activity by stationing allusions to it in the mythic context of "poetic tales" (*MHH* 11) already told. The very fact that current events could be so linked, by metaphor, to powerful imaginative symbols was for Blake an omen of their apocalyptic dignity—even when those events were clearly negative and fit into satanic molds. The method Blake used was just as satiric, just as allegorical, and just as emblematic as Gillray's, but his intent was invariably to save the appearance and the ontological status of the primordial images involved, not to debunk them. Put somewhat differently, parody in Blake is always pushing toward parable to create a symbolic symbiosis that renders *neither* side of the metaphoric equation expendable. The literary allusions in which political allusions nest operate as "mythological envelopes" (to use Erdman's phrase)[34] nourishing our awareness of the psychological meaning of the event. Indeed, every mythic form or image found by creative thought had, for Blake, the eternal value of a "state" constructed by imagination for the sake of helping individuals pass through it. No state, as such, was dismissable, and no clear image of a state could be deemed so either: as mental travelers who rest in contemporary events and places, we need the images of art to perceive and experience our own archetypal morphology.

The visionary integrity of established poetic tales were thus deliberately conserved in those Blakean political allegories that used literary or pictorial sources. This method had the heuristic function of apprising individuals how they, their political leaders, and their period of history were all in fact caught in recognizably symbolic states of passage. Presumably such a recognition could lead to an apocalypse. For to know that one is following the psychic patterns of created fiction makes it easier to disidentify from them and cast them off, either as "error" (VLJ) or as objective truth, like the books in the libraries of the sixth chamber of Blake's "Printing house in Hell" (*MHH* 15).

A case in point is the further use Blake made of the components of Gillray's Bunyan/Fox parody when he affected "the reappearance of the pilgrim in a political guise in *Europe*."[35] There in the first "Preludium" plate (Fig. 11), the pictorial allusion to Bunyan's Christian as a burdened traveler wearing contemporary dress—"the buff and blue of George Washington adopted by the Foxite Whigs of the 1790s"[36]—shows an appreciation of the Jacobin situation as part of the theme of pilgrimage through a dream of history, for that is the poetic context in which the figure appears. Bunyan's root metaphor is thus restored here to its full propaedeutic vigor, initiating a bildungsroman motif that swells to prophetic proportions. Blake emphasizes the fact of personal psychological endurance and change that such motifs imply, by reintroducing this pilgrim protagonist in the illustration of *Europe*'s plate 13 (Fig. 12), where Enitharmon's dream is ended. The character has played no part in either the intervening narrative or the intervening pictorial designs, but now suddenly he returns, in the image of a man suffering through a state that has clear iconographic reference (via a design of Flaxman's, Fig. 13) to Christian's imprisonment in Doubting Castle.[37] Why? Because for Blake the figure of Bunyan's dream-hero is more than a Foxite Whig aiming futilely for liber-

FIG. 11 Blake, *Preludium:* plate 1 of *Europe*

FIG. 12 Blake, Plate 13 of *Europe*

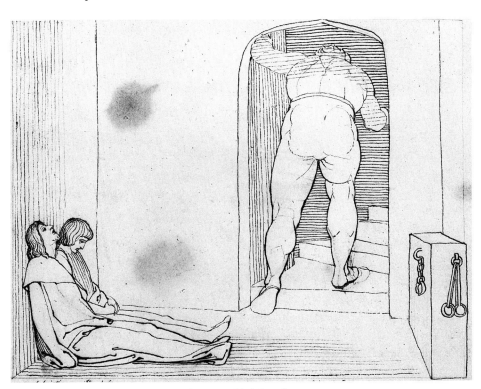

FIG. 13 John Flaxman, *At This They Trembled Greatly*

tarian political solutions. He is also a type of the psyche of the historical individual, a mental traveler who started his progress with a dream of salvation that has evolved disastrously through eighteen centuries of Western Christian history. And now he wakes up *from* the nightmare of it, *into* the nightmare of it: a jailed condition of the imagination that locks him in a dungeon of doubt and despair.

Blake is anxious to use the traditional metaphoric associations that Bunyan's protagonist calls up, in order to state his case about the plight of modern people. But more important even than the imagery of specific moments in Christian's journey is the function of the mythic journey itself. The political allegory has true prophetic bite only in the context of an overarching concept of eschatological development toward a Last Judgment (such as *Europe* initiates on plate 13 with Newton's Trump of Doom).[38] Eschatological development, moreover, requires a vehicle of change. Plot is such a vehicle. Thus Blake insists on presenting the imagery of the pilgrim traveler *serially,* within a visual narrative that charts its own transformations through time—the reader's time. In a sense, he gives mythic integrity to Bunyan's text simply by taking the fact of its mythos seriously. Instead of being content with a quick-tag reference to the symbolic idea, or logos, of a Christian pilgrim, Blake makes the journeying figure actually journey, from one plate to another, in a system of rhetorical sequence and consequence. The system in question is transposed (from Bunyan's verbal to Blake's visual medium, for one thing), but it is still a process. In fact, it is a "progress" that takes the reader through changes of response, making him or her the perceptual traveler who thereby mirrors, or becomes the very image (in the colloquial sense) of, Bunyan's dreamer.

This motif, of a self who is both spectator and protagonist seeking to experience salvation through displacement of the symbolic forms of self, is frequently underlined in Blake by the device of doubling a standard image or giving two contrary versions of a subject in sequel. Already in emblems no. 9 and 10 of the *Gates* we noted how Blake spread the content of Gillray's Bunyan allusion over two plates. The same technique of expansion will become a key dynamic of the aesthetics of the later *Pilgrim's Progress* illustrations, and it is intimately tied to the hermeneutics of self-realization, which Blake more and more saw Bunyan's fable typifying, as we shall see.

Other individual emblems in the *Gates of Paradise* that were linked to themes from the *Progress* were handled with the same doubling, spillover aims. For example, Erdman notes that plate 14, showing a "Traveller" hasting in the evening, seems based on Stothard's idiom in an illustration for the 1792 edition of Bunyan's text; and he suggests that the design of plate 15, the hasting traveler's counterpart at death's door, derived some of its iconographic detail from the same volume (Figs. 14 and 15).[39] Clearly, the idea of an emblematic

FIG. 14 Blake, *The Traveller Hasteth in the Evening*

FIG. 15 Blake, *Death's Door*

progress, Bunyan-style, *is* being imagistically distilled here, at the same time as its structural and functional dynamics are epitomized by the transpositions that occur in the passage from design no. 14 to no. 15. It is significant, I believe, that the image of the journeying pilgrim finally presents itself in this pure form only at the *end* of the reader's journey through the *Gates*—an inversion of Bunyan's dream rhetoric. One might say its crystallization is a sort of reward for the wanderings of the perceiving eye that has come that far through the book and can recognize its own principle of movement in this emblem. This would tally with Blake's conviction that an unclouded vision of one's state of passage is enough to precipitate a disengagement from its traps and snares.

The iconic representation of an operating "doctrine of contraries" (without which there is no progression)[40] is also given in pure form at this juncture, for no two sequential plates in the series as a whole are so obviously paired as opposites as are these traveler emblems, their countercompositional thrusts making up a near-perfect symmetry of antithetical leanings. In design no. 14, the figure of the traveler moves energetically forward, from left to right (the direction in which our eyes advance as we read), only to lead us to the closure of the whole circuit of evolvement in design no. 15. There the visual vector of the pilgrimage is reversed; there the mental traveller has become a beggar, old, attracted by some wind force (note his hair and swirling garment) back toward the "sinister" left. Together these complementary presentations of the soul nearing the fulfillment of its aim to reenter Eden exemplify the mutual attraction and repulsion of contraries "necessary for Human existence" (*MHH* 3). They attract each other by the energy of their implied movement toward each other, and they repulse by the opposition of their attitudes—psychological and figural—regarding the ultimate goal. They form in this way a visual paren-thesis (a closed system that is itself an emblem of completeness), summing up the dialectical principle of alteration that has ruled the foregoing "narrative." Emblems of expansion and emblems of contraction are placed in juxtaposition from the first design onward, but up to this point in the series they do not *face* each other. Doing so at the penultimate moment in the story when the pilgrimage theme clearly enunciates itself makes the vision of peregrination a gateway to the final image of release from life-as-a-dream-of-the-devouring-mother (emblem no. 16).[41]

It would be a mistake to stress too heavily the role of Bunyan's fable as an influence on motifs in the *Gates*. These emblems are not about *The Pilgrim's Progress* per se, and the unraveling of conflated allusions leads just as insistently to other literary "sources." For example, emblem no. 12 renders a scene from Dante's narrative of Ugolino in the *Inferno;* the inscriptions to the frontispiece and to design no. 16 refer to the Book of Job; design no. 8 is associated with the story of Absalom from 2 Samuel; and a line from Dryden's version of Chau-cer's Palamon and Arcite legend in "The Knight's Tale" is quoted as the motto for design no. 6. Nevertheless, for the purpose of this study, which is to trace Blake's changing conception of the visionary content of the *Progress,* it is interesting to note the subliminal references to Bunyan's dreamer that appear in emblems other than those already discussed. Certainly the passage in Chris-tian's story dramatizing his departure from the House of the Interpreter con-tributes to the context of emblem no. 13. At least the inscription of that design for the *Gates*—"Fear & Hope are—Vision"[42]—echoes the following summa-tive advice of the Interpreter at the point in the book when Christian begins "to gird up his loins, and to address himself to his journey":

> Then said the *Interpreter to Christian, Hast thou considered all these things?*
> *Chri.* Yes, and they put me in *hope* and *fear.*
> *Inter.* Well, keep all things so in thy mind, that they may be as a *Goad* in thy sides, to prick thee forward in the way thou must go. (*PP* 37)

In Bunyan's text, this interchange marks a stasis—a period of backward and forward glancing that amounts to a critique of the "Visionary forms dramatic" that Christian and the reader have just been experiencing. Emblems such as those we have passed through that evoke hope and fear, implies the Inter-preter, are vision; and, like Los's "Divine Vision" (*J* 30), they can profitably be "kept" in time of trouble.

A parallel situation exists in Blake's *Gates* series at the moment in the visual narrative that we meet design no. 13. The design depicts a deathbed scene in

FIG. 16 Blake, *Fear & Hope Are—*
Vision

which a mother and her children watch the soul of the expired father lift off, as
it were, with a cautionary gesture heavenward (Fig. 16). One of the many
ways to read this crucial emblem is to see the risen spirit of the dead man as a
sort of Interpreter of the house of the body who is also an interpreter of the
narrative, speaking in his own person the words of the inscription. The words
are then a prophecy uttered to two separate audiences simultaneously. First,
the spirit is addressing the gathered family members who, along with the
corpse, represent his five bodily senses. To them he is affirming his own
psychic reality, a reality reflected in their startled reactions, which measure the
emotions that fuel the faculties of imaginative perception. In this respect he is a
seer *of* self appearing *to* self and demonstrating by that performance the nature
and value of "spiritual sensation" (E703/K794). Second, and on a different
level of discourse, this spokesman of the sixth sense addresses us, his viewers,
to remind us that the entire emblematic journey, insofar as it has depicted
scenes arousing us to hope and fear, has served to train us in the visionary
capacity that alone can propel man through the gates of paradise. In both the
Progress and the *Gates,* then, emblems of fear and hope are defined as visionary
tools at a point just before the traveler consciously "addresses himself to his
journey." In Blake's case, the interpreting spirit actually directs the viewer with
the index finger of his right hand to the following emblem of the hasting
traveler, while with the other hand he points to the traditional location of
paradise.[43] It is as if the very subject of visionary hermeneutics called for this
reminder that the "paradise within" is translocatable and can be pictured
"above"[44] as well as in the images on the next pages of the *Gates.*

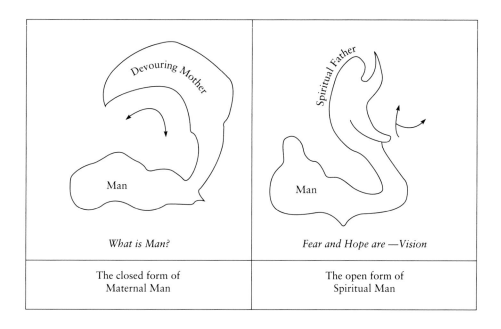

What is Man?	*Fear and Hope are —Vision*
The closed form of Maternal Man	The open form of Spiritual Man

FIG. 17   Diagram of Figs. 16 and 18

FIG. 18   Blake, *What Is Man?*

Finally, a structural symmetry between the formal arrangement of this spirit-speaking design and the layout of the frontispiece tells us in yet another way that an important gestalt is reaching a conclusion with emblem no. 13 (Fig. 17).[45] "What is Man?" asks the motto of the frontispiece (Fig. 18). "Fear & Hope are—Vision," answers the plate depicting the risen spirit. After that, there is nothing else but to gird up one's loins, like Christian in the *Progress,* and rush to embrace the life of the spirit, the life of the imaginal.

Later we will see how Blake extends the reference to Christian's archetypal voyage in the *Progress* when he revises the *Gates* in 1818, adding an epilogue and tailpiece. The tailpiece, illustrating Blake's description of Satan as "The lost Travellers Dream under the Hill," clearly evokes that moment in Christian's story when the hero falls asleep in the Arbor on Hill Difficulty and loses his certificate of Eternal Identity.[46] But no such comprehensive symbolic allusion to the *Progress* was in the works during the 1790s. In fact, scrutinizing the subject matter of single emblems contributes less to an understanding of Blake's deliberate reliance on Bunyan than does the question of the genre as a whole.

Bunyan, after all, was popular as an author not only of *The Pilgrim's Progress,* but also of "the first emblem book written expressly for children," as Rosemary Freeman reminds us in her standard study of English emblem books.[47] This primerlike collection, which in Blake's day came to be called *Divine Emblems,* "has a certain historical importance for it directed the convention into the channel in which it was ultimately to survive."[48] Given Blake's habit of returning to the strong originals of whatever formal conventions he considered diluted by contemporary fashion, it is plausible to assume that one of his major models for a series of emblems entitled "For Children" would have been Bunyan's *Book for Boys and Girls; or, Temporal Things Spiritualized.*[49] At the same time, Bunyan's "first" in this category grew out of an older, vigorous context of serious emblem literature, in which it occupies a declining phase. Freeman calls her chapter on Bunyan's treatment of emblems "The End of a Tradition" and shows ways in which both *The Pilgrim's Progress* and *Divine Emblems* represent a weakening of the allegoric expansiveness that earlier emblem artists brought to the form.

We have already studied Blake's deliberate correction of such a weakened metaphoric emblem in the *Progress*—the case of the "Interpreter's Parlor" print, where Blake reverted to elements of Wierix's design to invigorate Bunyan's domesticated images of the Gospel, the Law, and the sinful heart. But now we will see that this essentially neoclassical tendency to restore the lost vitality of an earlier aesthetic, an earlier mode of envisioning reality through word and design, permeates Blake's entire approach to the emblem during this period.[50] Indeed, the dynamics of Blake's artistic response to

Bunyan remains for a long time deeply bound up with his desire to redefine and extend the potentials of emblematic and allegoric expression against the derivative, Protestant norm set by Bunyan's example.

The place where this desire first begins to be worked out is, of course, the *Notebook*. There, from about 1788 to 1793, Blake drew a series of sixty-four designs grouped to follow under what appears to have been their intended title, "Ideas of Good & Evil."[51] With the "religion" tracts and the *Songs of Innocence* completed (all relatively small publications), it would seem Blake planned a larger work to enrich and strive with the entire emblem-book tradition. The three "religion" tractates had been his first experiment in illuminated relief printing, his first series of engraved plates arranged to form a developing argument. Verbally, the logic of the progression in these pamphlets was straight out of propositional, philosophic discourse. Visually, the unifying principle of each sequence remained less tied to an evident concept of teleological growth. But the designs for the individual tracts were certainly not just incidental "illustrations." In terms of composition, the plates seemed to be matched off in static, symmetric pairs (a leftward-facing design followed by a rightward-facing design, and so on),[52] while thematically they advanced according to a loosely Hegelian scheme of dialectical continuance.

Next, in the *Songs of Innocence,* Blake took an immense technical and conceptual step forward by turning his focus on the intricate intraplate relationship of verbal and visual emblem. The units of expression were now separable songs (covering one or two plates), each of which had its own integrity as a singular, complex, mixed-media statement.[53] Thus the serial arrangement of plates in this book had a new function, affecting the meaning of the whole song cycle in a much subtler, but at the same time more suggestive, way. The regulation of the ordering of the plates, furthermore, was not a fixed aspect of the macrostructure of the *Songs of Innocence* but rather one of its most deliberately exploited variables. Like a director controlling the performance of a play, Blake manipulated this semantic element of the text differently almost every time he issued it. Virtually each copy of *Songs of Innocence* was in this respect a new production, indicating that its central form retained, for Blake, the flexibility of a movable mythos.[54]

Not so the *Notebook* emblems. In these, Blake was apparently searching for a permanent arrangement of mostly pictorial statements that would transform the idea of an emblem "collection" into an instrument of prophetic narrative. The plot was to be constructed thematically on the basis of the iconographic content of sixty-four emblems with their associations and literary allusions; but the brunt of the cognitive message was to be carried by the graphic sequence-and-consequence of one plate upon the next. As each emblem integrated into the succeeding emblem, they were to tell a connected story and yet to represent an allegorized progression of opposing human motives—a sort of phenomenology of soul-making. As we know from repeated erasures and emendations in the numbering of these emblems, Blake spent much energy trying to find the exactly appropriate order for them to express his understanding of the psychology of spiritual growth.[55] Only later, when the concept of a sequel to *Songs of Innocence* began to take shape as a suitable vehicle for the amplified display of contrary states, did he bifurcate his efforts and extract from the original *Notebook* series the seventeen emblems of the *Gates* and nine of the designs for the *Songs of Experience*.[56]

Thus the emblem work of the *Notebook* holds the seeds of Blake's evolving visionary hermeneutics, by which he in fact revolutionizes both the psychological and figurative method of individual poetic emblems and the very idea of an anthology of related, symbolic illustrations. It would be too much to say that Bunyan's influence was responsible for Blake's venture in this line, but clearly the controlling metaphor of the Puritan traveler, placed in the context of the children's-book format, owes something to Blake's contact with Bunyan's two most popular texts and their familiar illustrations.[57] Indeed, the innovation of Blake's notebook series is just this superimposition of the integrating bildungsroman theme upon the normally eclectic and, as it were, picaresque mode of most emblem collections for children as well as for adults.[58]

The *Notebook*, in its turn, seemed to serve in a minor way as a source for Blake's own work on the *Pilgrim's Progress* illustrations almost thirty years later. An example is the emblem on page 41 of the *Notebook*, showing a reversed prototype of Blake's eleventh *Progress* design, "Christian received by Good-will" (see Plate 11), complete with Gothic doorway and oversized welcomer.[59] Another is the figure of the chained man on page N85 (Fig. 19)—a motif that has many analogues in the corpus of Blake's work, not the least among them being drawing no. 12 of the *Progress* set, where the Man in the Iron Cage is depicted agonizing in the House of the Interpreter for Christian's benefit (see Plate 12).

Not only these emblems, but the songs, too, sometimes show an affinity for Bunyanesque themes, whether they derive from the period of the *Notebook* or not. The poem "Infant Joy," for instance, addresses itself to the problem of naming in a way that recalls Bunyan's focus on this issue. In Blake's verse, the nature of the relationship between Joy's individual identity and his/her personified quality, or *virtu*, is seen from two perspectives, dramatized by the dialogue format of the poem. The mother figure never quite seems to trust the inherent joyfulness of joy, and feels the necessity of importuning an exterior power to shed joy *on* Joy and so ensure the continuance of the state in which the

FIG. 19 Blake, *Whose Changeless Brow*

being temporarily rests. The baby Joy itself, however, in all innocence, abjures the implied distinction between attribute and essence: "I happy am/Joy is my name." Joy *is* joyful because the identity of the so-called abstraction with the individuated living form is the very given of that climate—Innocence—where distinctions between ideas and human acts are absent.

In the *Progress,* Bunyan sees the same problem but handles it differently—more like Joy's mother. For he clearly differentiates between archetypal figures with substantival names, who are personifications like Good-will, and the more "realistic," exemplary characters called by adjectival names that "hint at attribute(s)" but do not embody them[60]—for example, Faithful. In *The Pilgrim's Progress, Part II,* one of these exemplary figures himself notes the distinction and, in a manner exactly opposed to that of Blake's Infant Joy, refuses to identify with and so transfigure an impersonal quality of mind. This occurs in the incident in which Great Heart salutes the character Honest as "Old Honesty"; and Honest, true to form, immediately demures, insisting that "Not Honesty in the *Abstract,* but *Honest* is my Name, and I wish that my *Nature* shall agree to what I am called" (*PP* 247).

Part II may have been in Blake's mind also as a context of the lyric "The Fly." For although that poem has stronger and more direct connections with other literary treatments of its "venerable topos comparing man's fate with the fly's fate,"[61] there is between its mythos, on the one hand, and the incident of

Christiana and the spider in the House of the Interpreter, on the other, a distinct morphological similarity. In any case, the episode in Bunyan represents a moment of mutual valuation and forgiveness between insect and man that Blake might well have approved; and it seems to have had other reverberations in his canonical imagery, as we shall see in a moment. The passage in question takes place just after the Interpreter leads Christiana and her entourage into "the very best Room in the house" (*PP* 200.) There he asks them to "see if they could find anything profitable." Mercy responds first:

> . . . Here is not anything, but an *ugly Spider,* who hangs by her Hands upon the Wall. Then said [the Interpreter], Is there but one *Spider* in all this spacious Room? Then the water stood in *Christiana's* Eyes, for she was a Woman quick of apprehension: and she said, Yes Lord, there is more here than one. Yea, and *Spiders* whose Venom is far more destructive than that which is in her. The *Interpreter* then looked pleasantly upon her, and said, Thou hast said the Truth. This made *Mercie* blush, and the Boys to cover their Faces. For they all began now understand the Riddle.
>
> Then said the *Interpreter* again, *The Spider taketh hold with her hands, as you see, and is in Kings Pallaces.* And wherefore is this recorded; but to show you, that how full of the Venome of Sin soever you be, yet you may by the hand of Faith lay hold of, and dwell in the best Room that belongs to the Kings House above?
>
> *Chris.* I thought, said *Christiana,* of something of this; but I could not imagin it all. I thought that we were like *Spiders,* and that we looked like ugly Creatures, in what fine Room soever we were: But that by this *Spider,* this venomous and ill favored Creature, we were to learn *how to act Faith,* that came not into my mind. And yet she has taken hold with her hands as I see, and dwells in the best Room in the House. God has made nothing in vain. (*PP,* 200–201)

Bunyan put a good deal of stock in this metaphor amplified from Scripture (Proverbs 30:28), repeating it in his book of emblems for children and elsewhere.[62] As U. Milo Kaufmann points out, the trope itself was a commonplace of seventeenth-century Puritan conduct books, which offered suggestions for "occasional meditations."[63] There, the emphasis was put on the happy benefits of contemplative thought itself, by which "even the spider could be made to yield spiritual meanings."[64] A similar emphasis is felt in Blake's riddle poem "The Fly," where the speaker discovers that his very capacity and desire to compare himself to the insect involves forgiveness and constitutes in its own right a lesson in divine hermeneutics. The objective analogy of man and fly is unimportant compared to the subjective process of finding and entering into the analogy—an imaginative feat that has permanent rewards: "Then Am I/A happy fly,/If I live,/Or if I die." It is, then, this process of empathic identity that is being celebrated alike in Blake's poem and Bunyan's literary emblem.[65]

It is significant, however, that these themes in the *Songs,* which are analogous to issues articulated in Part II of the *Progress,* are recognizably Bunyanesque only in their verbal emblems.[66] By contrast, the design elements of the plates for "Infant Joy" and "The Fly" have visual meanings in their contexts that are definitely not allusive to the Bunyan tradition.

Blake's addiction to the pictural aspects of verbal emblems and to the eidetic quality of linguistic metaphors has been studied by almost every critic seeking to define and account for the poet's peculiar rhetorical power. Although Yeats, as noted earlier, thought this addiction made Blake "a too literal realist of imagination," latter-day students of allegory, emblem, and Blake's particular focus on the infinite/definite dynamic of the polysemous play of signifiers have appreciated how he "modified emblematic art to symbolic purposes" in his poetic as well as his pictorial emblems.[67] Blake's devotion and fidelity to the imagistic rhetoric of the psyche ("Men think they can Copy Nature as Correctly as I copy Imagination this they will find Impossible" ["Public Address," E574/K594]) places his work in what Angus Fletcher calls a "borderland" between the Romantic critical notions of "allegory" and "symbol"—a borderland that Bunyan's fable, for its own syncretic motives, also inhabits.[68]

Blake, of course, called this type of artistic endeavour "visionary." Further on, we will explore his critical assessment of Bunyan's questionable fealty to the same apocalytic muse; here I would simply stress that the properties of verbal emblems served both writers as parables of psychic processes, and this was the link between them that Blake early exploited. In *The French Revolution,* for instance, the seven allegorical towers of imprisonment share at least a parodic resemblance to the seven rooms visited by Christian in the House of the Interpreter (though they evoke, as well, more essential models, particularly the seven seals in the Book of Revelation).[69] Blake even provided the king of France with the personification of a gruesome, intrapsychic figure resembling a pathological version of Christian's Interpreter to lead him through the dens and their allegoric tableaux:

> . . . in his soul stood the purple plague,
> Tugging his iron manacles, and piercing through the seven towers dark and
> sickly,
> Panting over the prisoners like a wolf gorg'd.
>
> (*FR* 1:24–26, E287/K135)

As for the occupants of the Bastille towers themselves, they have traits that correspond to the emblematic characters in the House of the Interpreter only in the case of the last two: the den of Destiny and the tower of God, reflective of the inhabitants of Bunyan's last two rooms. In the den of Destiny, a "strong man" is manacled to face an image of despair, reminding us of Bunyan's Man in the Iron Cage of despair. Indeed, Blake's emblem design in the *Notebook*, which I claim as a prototype for his later illustration of the Man in the Iron Cage (see Fig. 19 and Plate 12), is seen by Erdman to be related to this very episode in *The French Revolution*.[70] Finally, the seventh tower, "nam'd the tower of God," houses a madman "fed with hopes year by year":

>   . . . he pined
> For liberty; vain hopes: his reason decay'd, and the world of attraction in his
>   bosom
> Center'd, and the rushing of chaos overwhelm'd his dark soul.
>
> (*FR* 1:48–50, E288/K136)

This figure of insanity who longs for liberty but is inundated by stormy chaos compares interestingly to the frightened dreamer of the Last Judgment, the subject of Bunyan's seventh tableau in *his* House of Interpretation. The hint of a conscious debt to Bunyan in these passages of Blake is especially noteworthy, because the same two tableaux from the *Progress* as are evoked here are the only ones Blake chose to make designs for in his set of watercolor drawings in 1824.

Needless to say, the parallels of the situations of "France" and of Christian highlight not only their similarities, but also their more important differences. For the King of France is really a demonic counterpart to the salvation-seeking Pilgrim; and the dens of tyranny's tower reveal the horrors of crimes already committed, while the Interpreter's rooms contain proleptic visions of steps in a pilgrimage to come. In both cases, however, the trip through the seven rooms of instruction leads to acts of expansion and release. As William Halloran points out, when Blake's narrative moves on from the tower of God, the prisoners of France immediately "look up and laugh at the jailor's light, [and] we feel a power rising from below to consume the King in the hell he has created."[71] At the matching juncture in the *Progress*, Christian experiences a comparable triumph as he meets the figure of Christ for the first time and his burden automatically drops from his back.

Evidently this theme of an emblematic journey through a house of development is an important one for Blake, and it never quite loses a flavor of the Bunyanesque in his mind. For example, in *The Marriage of Heaven and Hell*, the description of the chambers of the Printing house in Hell cast an ironic reflection on the cumulative imagery presented to Christian by the Interpreter. But this is not surprising when we remember that one of the major aims of the *Marriage* was to extend the concept of Christian hermeneutics beyond the low-church, Protestant models—especially the Calvinist and Swedenborgian versions; hence its contrary allusions to a variety of paradigmatic achievements in that vein, from Milton to Bunyan.

In any case, whether we suppose intentional, point-by-point displacement on Blake's part or not, instructive ironies abound as we set "the method in which knowledge is transmitted from generation to generation" in Blake's Printing house "Fancy" (*MHH* 15) against the educational tactics of Bunyan's Interpreter. For the Printing house plate is a parable of a creative, artistic process, the symbolic energies of which subsume the critical and interpretive modes of knowing and explicating. Passage through the chambers of *this* house permits no pauses for homiletic edification of the "corporeal understanding." Instead, the progress of Blake's imagery carries its own hermeneutic on the model of evolutionary development: from Dragon to Man to symbolic Man (or book).[72] In the Interpreter's house, by contrast, the steps are if anything iconically retrogressive, descending from the figurative vision of Evangel—the man who will act as psychopomp—to a confrontation with a mistaken soul dreaming negative visions of the Last Judgment.

There is a still more telling point of imaginative interaction between the depictions of these two "houses." It comes up in Blake's chronicle of the first printing-house chamber, where his narrator reports: "In the first chamber was a Dragon-Man, clearing away the rubbish from a caves mouth; within, a number of Dragons were hollowing the cave" (*MHH* 15). If we compare this image with *Man Sweeping the Interpreter's Parlor* (a subject quite possibly engraved by Blake, we will recall, very shortly after the publication of the *Marriage*), we can perhaps feel the vigor of Blake's contention with Bunyan's orthodox assumptions about divine inspiration and the proper housekeeping of the soul. Both scenes are, after all, emblems of the birth of creative power in the conscious, inner life of man; both picture the process as one of clearing. Yet whereas Bunyan looks at the event in religious terms as a visitation by Grace, Blake regards it psychologically as the freeing of libido. In Bunyan's emblem, the agents are watered-down versions of divine dispensations who have their own, autonomous *psychomachia* to work out in the manner of servants squabbling below-stairs. The soul itself is not changed by their rival methods, though it is tidied up, at last, through the services of the clever parlor maid, God's Grace.

As we noted earlier, there is something pinched and reductive about this homely analogy, something alien to the aesthetic of "sublime allegory" in which Blake's imagination felt at home. Blake thus envisions the process begun by the personification of a "ruling passion": a single, commanding force who is fabulous in character, primitive in connotation, and who functions as a mythical representative of the instinctual life. The Dragon-man, coming from below with the power of a chthonic archetype, has no wish to tame, or to adopt a domestic form. In his authoritative persona he carries a significance closer to the picture of Evangel in the *Progress*. Indeed, these two figures have a parallel propaedeutic function, since they are each the occupants of the first chambers in their respective houses and so are meant to symbolize aspects of the method and the way to come. But the Dragon-man is active and not, like Evangel, an emblem of "passive good" ("Annotations to Lavater's *Aphorisms on Man*," E592/K77; *MHH* 3). Also, in his activity he performs a dual role— first as a principal agent of creative transmission, and second as what might be called an anti-interpreter. If, that is, we understand the "rubbish" at the "cave's mouth" to signify excess verbalization (the offal of Rational Man pandering to his own "corporeal understanding"),[73] then the Dragon-man's clearing away of that rubbish indicates that he will not tolerate doctrinal garbage getting in the way of direct, visionary experience.[74] He is opposed to the use of language as a defense against the spontaneity of emotional response (the opening of the inner cave of man), and so he provides no hermeneutic, no moral commentary, no totalizing conceptualization of his own. One suspects this dragon, like Blake, would regard the exegetical function of Bunyan's Interpreter in a similarly negative light—as a piling up of debris before the organs of perception and expression.

In the Printing house, mouth-clearing is indeed a propaedeutic and results in the actual widening of the caverned soul so that it may produce a book that is "the Image of God."[75] By comparison, the meaning of Bunyan's emblem about the sinful heart seems as tame as its imagery. Whereas the Interpreter's parlor gets genteelly cleaned by two domestic servants, the Dragon-man's cave is restructured from within by *many* untamed animal helpers. In sum, the radical contrast between cultivated parlor and primordial cave, between the dust of Original Sin and the rubbish of moral doctrines, between the act of sweeping clean and the work of hollowing out, between a voluble Interpreter and a dumb Dragon-man—all these contrasts are provocative and meaningful, whether they are intended to be read as an intertextual debate or not. Add to this the fact that the Printing house "fancy" contains a dimension of allegory that refers to the "infernal method" in which it is itself engraved, and we understand how thoroughly Blake's "hellish" hermeneutic (emblematized in this passage) counters the "heavenly" norm of Swedenborg, first, and Bunyan, second.[76]

Insofar as *The Pilgrim's Progress* does function as an intertext for the Printing house allegory, it operates almost entirely as a "negative source." Only later on in the *Marriage,* in the "memorable fancy" of plates 17–20, does the echo of Bunyan's fable provide a positive context. There, the Angel and the narrator compare "eternal lots" and discover that although they pass through the same psychic territory, their experiences and their conceptions of that territory differ. In the metaphysical belief-structure of the Angel, the "infinite Abyss" is "fiery as the smoke of a burning city," and it contains devilish "Powers of the air," which are "in the most terrific shapes of animals sprung from corruption." Its "nether deep" grows "black as a sea" and rolls "with a terrible noise"—and finally produces a terrifying, though gorgeously colored, Leviathan. Yet to the narrator's eyes, uncomplicated by the outlook of his friend the Angel, the abyss is a pastoral landscape productive of transformative poetry "sung to the harp."

Bunyan uses a similar device to unsettle and stretch the understanding of the reader when he has Faithful and Christian converse about their recent, separate, journeys through the valleys of Humiliation and of the Shadow of Death. For Christian, the Valley of the Shadow of Death was like Blake's Angel's infinite abyss. It contained the "mouth of hell," from which "the flame and smoke [came] out in such abundance, with sparks and hideous noises," and from which "a company of fiends," like Powers of the Air, came forward to attack him (*PP* 63). Faithful, however, "had Sun-shine" all the way through this same landscape (*PP* 74). The effect of these recountings in *The Pilgrim's Progress* is to make the reader understand that the stages of the pilgrimage are not fixed, but rather alter to suit the personality of the pilgrim. Christian at this point becomes only *a* Christian, and the sense of shifting possibilities for imaginative journeyings increases. The suggestion is, of course, that events conform to the individual's powers and deficiencies, needs and preconceptions, rather than to "One Law for the Lion & Ox" (*MHH* 24); and the revelation of that very fact itself alters the nature of the reader's relation to the text, as it affects the quality of his or her notions about salvation's path.

That Blake found this incident to be a significant turning in Bunyan's narrative in later years is attested by his choosing it as a subject for one of the key designs (Plate 21) in the 1824 series of illustrations. In 1793, however, we can only speculate that it was alive in his mind as one of the many referents informing the shape and rhetoric of the *Marriage*'s penultimate "fancy." Faithful and Christian "impose on one another" (*MHH* 20) in friendlier and more accepting ways than the Angel and the narrator of the *Marriage,* and their opposite experiences are of temporary states safely passed, rather than of imagined "eternal lots"; but the motif of an exchange of vision, accompanied by conversational diction and dialogue, and the device of presenting the reader with a pair of radically diverse views of "the Shadow of Death," are major elements common to both texts. Furthermore, by recalling Bunyan as a generic model in this passage, which at the same time makes fun of the limited vision of Swedenborg's writings, Blake is implicitly imputing a greater flexibility to Bunyan than to the New Church doctrines. He thereby declares the new religion of the Swedenborg movement to be more restrictive and puritanical than even Christian's anxiety-ridden weltangschauung, which was the standard popular example of Calvinist excess in Blake's day.[77] As he said in his annotations to *The Angelic Wisdom of Divine Providence,* where Swedenborg's deterministic attitude toward the individual's "eternal lot" repeatedly roused Blake to a pitch of prophetic wrath, "Predestination after this Life is more Abominable than Calvins & Swedenborg is Such a Spiritual Predestinarian . . . Cursed Folly!" (E610/K133). In comparison, Bunyan's motif of progress and positive mutability may well have stood out as redemptive and therefore useful as a generic backdrop for Blake's own reversal of the Swedenborgian idiom.

THE PERSONAL REFERENCE: BUNYAN, CHRISTIAN, COWPER, ROSE, AND HAYLEY'S ANXIOUS ENTHUSIAST

The narrative exchange between Faithful and Christian in the *Progress* was an emblem of "true Friendship" (*MHH* 20) suitable to the message of the *Marriage*. But the states of passage referred to in that exchange—especially Christian's journey through the two dark valleys (the Valley of Humiliation and the Valley of the Shadow of Death)—had in their own right a strong hold on Blake's imagination. Evidence of the personal significance Blake attached to these valley episodes from the *Progress* emerges during the most problematic period of his relationship with his patron, William Hayley. Thus in the last years of Blake's stay at Felpham, allusions to the blackest parts of Christian's journey crop up anew in the imagery of Blake's letters. There is no doubt that Blake felt himself, at that time, to be passing out of his own private straits of humiliation and of emotional death, by virtue of the "Spiritual Acts" of his "three years Slumber on the banks of the Ocean" (E728/K823)—namely, his contention with Hayley over the value of his "Just Right as an Artist & as a Man" (E731/K825) to follow freely his own genius, his own "leading propensity" ("Annotations to Lavatar's *Aphorisms on Man,*" E601/K88). In fact, it is in the famous letter to Butts where Blake first expresses his spiritual enmity with Hayley and announces the poem "descriptive of those Acts" that the Bunyan reference unmistakably appears.[78]

Blake is writing in the closing paragraph of this letter of April 25, 1803, about "the sore travel which has been given [him] these three years," and quotes Psalm 139 ("I am fearfully & wonderfully made") to remind himself it all has had a glorious purpose.[79] And then:

I see the face of my Heavenly Father he lays his Hand upon my Head & gives a blessing to all my works why should I be troubled why should my heart & flesh cry out. *I will go on in the Strength of the Lord through Hell will I sing forth his Praises.* that the Dragons of the Deep may praise him & that those who dwell in darkness & on the Sea coasts may be gatherd into his Kingdom. (E729/K823; italics added)

The italicized phrases above are a (mis)quotation of the outcry made by Bunyan's pilgrim in the Valley of the Shadow of Death—an exclamation that succeeded in saving Christian from the attack of the foul fiend at hell's mouth: "Yet the *Fiends* seemed to come nearer and nearer, but when they were come even almost at him, he cried out with a most vehement voice, *I will walk in the strength of the Lord God;* so they gave back, and came no further" (*PP* 63). The appositeness of this passage from the *Progress* to his own condition as a victim of Hayley's psychological assaults apparently gripped Blake anew in the later part of the Felpham era, possibly coming freshly to his attention by means of Cowper's posthumous influence.[80] For in two of Blake's letters, the Bunyan imagery is intertwined with allusions to Cowper (and of course, it must be recalled that Hayley's *Life of Cowper,* with Blake's engravings, was in preparation during the same years).[81] That Cowper, with his bouts of neurosis and manic-depressive psychosis, seemed to Blake (as he had to Hayley) to be a soul bedeviled by the potentially warping dualism of Calvinist consciousness, is evidenced by Hayley himself in a letter he wrote to Cowper's high-placed cousin, Lady Hesketh:[82]

> my Friend the anxious, enthusiastic Engraver [i.e., Blake] says, that all the Demons, who tormented our dear Cowper when living, are now labouring to impede the publication of his Life. —To which I reply that it may be so, but if it is, I am confident my two dear Angels the Bard & the Sculptor will assist us in *our Conflict* with the *powers* of *darkness,* & enable us to triumph over *all their Machinations.*[83]

With hindsight and ample knowledge of Blake's manner and method, we can read between the lines here and see the statements attributed to Blake as having come from an ironic standpoint critical of Hayley's self-serving manipulation of Cowper's literary remains[84]—but one suspects Hayley could not. He seems always to have misread the literalism of Blake's imaginal thought. In this instance, the tone of gentle but smug condescension (to which Hayley habitually subjected Blake, according to Blake's account) is clearly directed against the "anxious, enthusiastic" temper of Blake's imagination. That temperament, in its turn, associates in Hayley's mind to a typically Bunyanesque world of torment—a "Hell of terrors & horrors" (E758/K941)—which grows from a character-structure (like Cowper's) devoid of the resilience necessary for a successful adaptation to life.[85]

In Hayley's outlook generally, one senses an indiscriminate condemnation of the visionary aspects of religious enthusiasm, a tendency to lump all exuberant expression of the dark, irrational side of psychic life together and label the whole pathological. The snobbery of Hayley's aristocratic pretensions no doubt contributed to his poor opinion of the kind of fervor that swept masses of the common people up in Methodist conversions and other passionate displays of evangelical fervor. There was too much of a taint of the lowbrow about such personal effusions of the spirit for Hayley's taste; and Bunyan's *Pilgrim's Progress* was an accepted dramatic embodiment of just that crude, simple-minded, unsophisticated devotional attitude he felt to be beneath him, sentimentalist though he was.[86] Cowper himself defended against this eighteenth-century elitist view of Bunyan in the following lines praising him, half-shamedly, as a fond memory of childhood:

> O thou, whom, borne on Fancy's wing
> Back to the season of life's happy spring,
> I pleased remember, and, while memory yet
> Holds fast her office here, can ne'er forget.
> Ingenious dreamer! in whose well-told tale
> Sweet fiction and sweet truth alike prevail;
> Whose humerous vein, strong sense, and simple style,
> May teach the gayest, make the gravest smile;
> Witty, and well employ'd, and like thy Lord,
> Speaking in parables his slighted word!
> I name thee not, lest so despised a name
> Should move a sneer at thy deserved fame;
> Yet even in transitory life's late day,
>
> That mingles all my brown with sober gray,
> Revere the man, whose PILGRIM marks the road,
> And guides the PROGRESS of the soul to God.
>
> ("Tirocinium; or, A Review of Schools," 131–46)

Might Hayley have turned out to be one of the "sneerers" Cowper anticipated? Apparently Blake thought so; for his mixture of Cowperesque and Bunyanesque rhetoric, in some of his more exaggeratedly sycophantic letters to Hayley, seem to indicate that on these occasions he was deliberately modeling himself after the literary exemplars Hayley held in unconscious contempt.[87] Thus:

> I am thankful that I feel [affection and gratitude] it draws the soul towards Eternal life & conjunction with Spirits of just men made perfect by love and gratitude the two angels who stand at heavens gate ever open ever inviting guests to the marriage O foolish Philosophy! Gratitude is Heaven itself there could be no

heaven without Gratitude I feel it & I know it I thank God & Man for it & above all You My dear friend & benefactor in the Lord.

(January 14, 1804; E740/K833–34)

These "Spirits of just men made perfect" are allusive in so typically multifarious a way that the web of interwoven contexts they call up—part Bible, part Bunyan, part Cowper, and part Hayley—bears brief examination.

The biblical source is Hebrews 12:22–24 and reads as follows:

> But ye are come unto mount sion, and unto the city of the living God, the heavenly Jerusalem, and to an innumerable company of angels, / To the general assembly and church of the firstborn, which are written in heaven, and to God the Judge of all, and to the spirits of just men made perfect, / And to Jesus the mediator of the new convenant.

On its own ground, this passage from the Epistles echoes the place in Revelation where Jesus, the Lamb, stands on Mount Zion with "an hundred forty and four thousand" of the elect, confirming their position in heaven before the terrors of the Last Judgment (Revelation 14:1), and again the place where the "righteous saints" are figured as guests at the marriage of the Bride and the Lamb (Revelation 19:7–9). Like Blake in his letter of gratitude to Hayley, Bunyan routinely conflates the imagery of these scattered scriptural verses whenever he cites one of them—which he does on three strategically significant occasions in his two most popular narratives, *Grace Abounding* and the *Progress*.[88]

Grace Abounding to the Chief of Sinners, Bunyan's spiritual autobiography, has two parts: the relation of his conversion and the relation of his call to the ministry. At the end of each of these sections, Bunyan pays homage, as it were, to the use of "*Hebrews* the twelfth, about the mount *Zion*" (*GA* par. 262) as an antidote to his backslidings: "The words are these [here follow verses 22–24 of Hebrews 12, verbatim]: Thorow this blessed Sentence the Lord led me over and over, first to this word, and then to that, and shewed me wonderful glory in every one of them. These words also have oft since this time been great refreshment to my Spirit. Blessed be God for having mercy on me" (*GA*, par. 264). This paragraph concludes Part I. Then, toward the close of Part II, Bunyan praises the same text for its therapeutic effect on his spiritual condition in prison: "I have had sweet sights of the forgiveness of my sins in this place, and of my being with Jesus in another world: *O the mount Zion, the heavenly Jerusalem, the innumerable company of Angels, and God the Judge of all, and the Spirits of just men made perfect, and Jesus,* have been sweet unto me in this place" (*GA*, par. 322). When the eschatological vision of Hebrews 12 is amplified in

The Pilgrim's Progress, it appears, intermingled with the full panoply of echoes from Revelation, as a preliminary to the description of Christian's and Hopeful's entrance into heaven's gate in the afterlife:

> Now upon the bank of the River, on the other side, they saw the two shining men again, who there waited for them. Wherefore being come out of the River, they saluted them, saying, *We are ministring Spirits, sent forth to minister for those that shall be Heirs of Salvation.* . . . They therefore went up through the Regions of the Air, sweetly talking as they went, being comforted, because they safely got over the River, and had such glorious Companions to attend them.
>
> The talk that they had with the shining Ones, was about the glory of the place, who told them, that the beauty, and glory of it was inexpressible. There, said they, is the Mount *Sion,* the heavenly *Jerusalem,* the innumerable company of Angels, and the Spirits of Just Men made perfect: You are going now, said they, to the Paradice of God, wherein you shall see the Tree of Life, and eat the never-fading fruits thereof: And when you come there, you shall have white Robes given you, and your walk and talk shall be every day with the King, even all the days of eternity. (*PP,* 158–59)

In each of these instances, the scripture from Hebrews serves, in effect, as an envoi; so in their places, these passages are literally last (or almost last) visions as well as visions of Last Things. Blake adopts this usage in *his* reference to the biblical image at the close of his letter to Hayley. But notably, Hebrews has now become thoroughly admixed with details taken from its derivative in the *Progress* as well as from Revelation, for the "two angels" of love and gratitude operate in Blake's figure the way the shining ones do in the passage from Bunyan. Blake, however, is also playing in a deferential way on Hayley's own rhetorical use of the same scriptural topos as it is presented in the final pages of the *Life of Cowper* (1st ed.), viz.: "In composing this cordial tribute to a man, whose history is so universally interesting, my chief ambition has been to deserve the approbation of his pure Spirit, who appeared to me on earth among the most amiable of earthly friends, and whom I cherish a lively hope of beholding in a state of happier existence, with the Spirit of 'just men made perfect.' "[89] The "two angels" that Bunyan and Blake added to the source in Hebrews are absent from the scene as Hayley figures it here in the *Life.* But they made a conspicuous public appearance in a notorious episode of the *real* life of Cowper, as engineered by Hayley in 1797. Hayley had invented a tall story, a sort of travesty of the biblical myth of converse with spirits, starring Hayley and Cowper and their two dead mothers. He claimed the content of the story had descended on him in the form of an authentic, "ecstatic vision." The purpose of the maneuver was to impress Cowper with God's partiality toward him (Cowper) and thus coax him out of a severe depression. The ruse of the dream-fable's having a heaven-sent authority was therefore deemed essential. Hayley wrote of it to Cowper thus:

> I beheld the throne of God, whose splendour, though in excess, did not strike me blind, but left me power to discern on the steps of it two kneeling, angelic forms. A kind seraph seemed to whisper to me that these heavenly petitioners were your lovely mother and my own. . . . I sprang eagerly forward to enquire your destiny of your mother. Turning towards me with a look of seraphic benignity, she smiled upon me and said: "Warmest of earthly friends! Moderate the anxiety of thy zeal, lest it distract thy declining faculties, and know that as a reward for thy kindness my son shall be restored to himself and to friendship."[90]

The letter then goes on to quote the "Maternal Spirit's" prophecy that Cowper would receive an influx of accolades from earthly authorities as a sign of divine favor—accolades Hayley intended to wrest from government officials, judges, bishops, and even the king, through his own wheeling and dealing. Blake's response to this deliberate, though well-intentioned, attempt on Hayley's part to play the role of a false prophet and visionary must have been strong and complex. Surely he knew of the scheme (it had become general knowledge among Cowper's relatives and was advertised by Hayley himself),[91] and I believe we are warranted in sensing a covert, ironical reference to it in the metaphor of the angels of love and gratitude.

In any event, the amalgamation of motifs, readily associated with Scripture as interpreted by Bunyan and Cowper, makes its own statement. It is Blake's way of both defying and deferring to Hayley's classification of him as an unstable dreamer of the enthusiast stamp.[92]

The letter in which Blake most overtly plays on Hayley's reductive interpretation of both Bunyan's worth and his own, though, is one of December 4, 1804, where he concludes:

> —Hope in a few days to send Proofs of Plates which I must say are far beyond Any thing I have ever done. For O happiness never enough to be grateful for! I have lost my Confusion of Thought while at work & am as much myself when I take the Pencil or Graver into my hand as I used to be in my Youth I have indeed fought thro a Hell of terrors & horrors (which none could know but myself.) in a Divided Existence now no longer Divided. nor at war with myself I shall travel on in the Strength of the Lord God as Poor Pilgrim says. (E758/K941)

"Poor Pilgrim" is, of course, Christian, and the scene evoked is again that perilous pathway through Bunyan's Valley of the Shadow of Death. In the letter to Thomas Butts quoted earlier, we saw Blake use the identical episode as an emblem of his struggle to maintain his own integrity under Hayley's regime of insidious, contrary pressures. He also made it quite plain, in an earlier paragraph from that same letter, that the person whom he saw as responsible for his "Confusion of Thought" was none other than Hayley, the "enemy" of Blake's spiritual life:

> Now I may say to you what perhaps I should not dare to say to anyone else. That I can alone carry on my visionary studies in London unannoyd & that I may converse with my friends in Eternity. See Visions, Dream Dreams, & prophecy & speak Parables unobserv'd & at liberty from the Doubts of other Mortals. perhaps Doubts proceeding from Kindness. but Doubts are always pernicious Especially when we Doubt our Friends Christ is very decided on this Point. "He who is Not With Me is Against Me" There is no Medium or Middle state & if a Man is the Enemy of my Spiritual Life while he pretends to be the Friend of my Corporeal. he is a Real Enemy—but the Man may be the friend of my Spiritual Life while he seems the Enemy of my Corporeal but Not Vice Versa. (E728/K822)

That was in April 1803. Now, in December 1804, the Bunyan reference is carried over. Christian's cry in the dark valley is requoted, and the vision of hell's mouth is conjured up afresh. But the identification of Hayley as hell's archfiend is, naturally, not articulated, since the letter is addressed *to* Hayley; the ostensible signification of the whole Bunyan passage is therefore subtly altered. Here, the hell is a "Divided Existence," and the cause of the condition is a vague psychological distress, a state of inner warfare that goes unnamed but is such as professors of enthusiast religions customarily experienced and confessed to. Blake thus paints the picture Hayley wants to see. But the words, seen from a different and less gullible standpoint, have a dimension of veiled satire, and can be read as a secret reproach by Blake against the agent of his torment and Division—Hayley, with his pernicious "Doubts."

The ambiguity of attitude expressed here is not a matter of simple irony, however, for both standpoints are equally true and both are held by Blake with full sincerity. The phrase that tells us he is writing from a truly double perspective is the parenthetical qualifier, "which none could know but myself." This is the giveaway notation of a relativistic psychology—a view of events that permits acceptance of contrary formulations and promotes "mutual forgiveness." Blake is acknowledging in this remark that his hell, like Christian's and Faithful's in the *Progress,* is subjective and hidden in its particulars from other men. Implicit is the idea that such a hell belongs to, and is in fact created by, the personality that suffers it. In this respect, Hayley's function as a satanic tyrant is not admissable as a sufficient cause or target of blame:

> . . . You know Satans mildness and his self-imposition,
> Seeming a brother, being a tyrant, even thinking himself a brother
> While he is murdering the just; prophetic I behold

His future course thro' darkness and despair to eternal death
But we must not be tyrants also! . . .

. . . .

How should he he know the duties of another?

(*M* 7)

This is the way Blake puts the matter in lines from his mythic epic *Milton* (engraved at least in part during the same year as the letter in question), where Hayley figures as Satan. And in a different, subsequent letter to Butts (August 16, 1803), he summed up the situation in the following manner: "I have been very much degraded & injuriously treated. but if it all arise from my own fault I ought to blame myself" (E733/K828). That Blake is admitting his hell was a private ordeal of his own making is one point; that he also regards it able to be correctly *perceived* only from a subjective angle is another. For he had "indeed fought thro' a hell of terrors & horrors" in a psychological reality that none *could* know but himself, and thus Hayley's *false* knowledge of that reality was a predictable part of the bargain. Blake's knowledge of his own existential reality was ipso facto superior to Hayley's, and in this letter he is educating Hayley on that point, using the Bunyan allusion to suggest that not only every man's hell, but also "Every Man's Wisdom is peculiar to his own Individuality" (*M* 4). For of course, this wisdom *about* Wisdom recapitulates that moment in *The Pilgrim's Progress* already discussed, where Christian and Faithful discover the nature of limited vision by sharing their opposite experiences of the soul's advance over apparently identical ground: the states of humiliation and hell. Bunyan's comprehensive presentation of the Valley of the Shadow of Death thus embodies the concept that individual perceptions vary according to the perceiver's altering eye.

The poetic justice involved in Blake's calling up Bunyan to stress this point is really a case of "piercing Apollyon with his own bow" (*J* 12), since Hayley saw Bunyan the way Apollyon professed to see Christian in the passage alluded to: as a personified type of that "too apprehensive Spirit" which sent men like Cowper and Blake into fits of "nervous infirmity."[93] This distortion of "Poor Pilgrim"'s inner reality begged for the demonstrative defense that Bunyan and Blake, in their respective places, willingly supplied.

Less combative in its imagery, but just as rife with hidden ironies, is an earlier part of this same letter of December 1804, where the Bunyan-Blake comparison is directly voiced and worked over. The question at issue is a project to print and have Blake illustrate Hayley's backlog of unpublished material under the supervision of Flaxman—an overlordship that Blake was not eager to accept: "—I was about to have written to you to express my wish that two so unequal labourers might not be yoked to the same Plow & to desire you if you could to get Flaxman to do the whole because I thought it would be

(to say the best of myself) like putting John Milton with John Bunyan."
Considering that Flaxman had actually illustrated Bunyan, not Milton, while
Blake was busy both illustrating and radically reinterpreting Milton at around
this time, it is likely that the reverse type-castings are meant to be at least
hyperbolically deferential, at most facetious.[94] Not, of course, to Hayley's way
of thinking, though. Again, it is Hayley's conventional opinion of Bunyan as
the rude man's John Milton that Blake is assuming here. But knowing that
Blake did not in fact consider himself, in his artistic identity, to be so easily and
derogatorily classed as a rude man's John Flaxman, we can perhaps read back
into the equation and infer a similar dissenting (that is, more positive) evaluation of Bunyan—at least to the extent of Blake's coming into a new appreciation of the depths and complexities of Bunyan's "prophetic character" in the
early 1800s. In a sense, his own work, considered as one "Grand poem" about
the integration and transformation of the prophetic character, grows as much
out of the spirit of exemplary Puritan autobiography ennobled by Bunyan as it
does from the traditions of Miltonic epic, apocalypse, and "Sublime Allegory." The poem *Milton* could thus be construed as a triumphant experiment
of mixed genres equal to that "putting John Milton with John Bunyan" which
Blake so obsequiously, but ironically, abjures in the letter.[95]

The final reference to the Bunyan-Cowper-Hayley association in the chronology of Blake's correspondence occurs in another letter to Hayley, mailed
three weeks later on the occasion of Samuel Rose's death. Rose, Blake's lawyer
at his famous Chichester court trial for sedition, was a friend of both Hayley
and Cowper and in fact had agreed to serve Blake as defense attorney on
Hayley's account.[96] Blake's rhetorical flight acknowledging the passing of his
"Generous Advocate" plugs right into the Cowper-Bunyan identification—
indeed, so patently that one senses the establishment among them of a set of
habitual associations, amounting to a tacit family myth, that typed them all
according to the *Progress* allegory at least since the time of the trial.[97] Perhaps
the trial itself, being based on malicious charges, was associated by the parties
concerned with the trial of Faithful and Christian at Vanity Fair. Certainly a
consent to see the tribulations of Cowper, Bunyan, Christian, Blake, and now
Rose as mutually analogous is implied in Blake's aside to Rose's spirit, replete
as that apostrophe is with the imagery and vocabulary of Hebrews 12 and the
last pages of *The Pilgrim's Progress*: "Farewell Sweet Rose thou hast got before
me into the Celestial City. I also have but a few more Mountains to pass. for I
hear the bells ring & the trumpets sound to welcome thy arrival among
Cowpers Glorified Band of Spirits of Just Men made Perfect" (E759/K854).[98]

The mountains Blake conjures up here are probably meant to signify the
Delectable Mountains that Bunyan places within view of the Celestial City:

Now there was on the tops of these Mountains, Shepherds feeding their flocks, and they stood by the high-way side. The Pilgrims therefore went to them, and leaning upon their staves, (as is common with weary Pilgrims, when they stand to talk with any by the way,) they asked, *Whose delectable Mountains are these? and whose be the sheep that feed upon them?*

Shep. These Mountains are *Immanuels Land,* and they are within sight of his City, and the sheep also are his, and he laid down his life for them.

Chr. Is this the way to the Celestial City?

Shep. You are just in your way.

Chr. How far is it thither?

Shep. Too far for any, but those that *shall* get thither indeed. (*PP* 119)

Certainly the bell ringing and the trumpeting that Blake mentions are calculated to recall the joyful apotheosis of Christian and Hopeful, who, "while they were thus drawing towards the Gate," beheld a "company of the heavenly host" coming to meet them with "several of the King's Trumpeters" (*PP* 160). The vision of the two pilgrims as Bunyan describes it is different from its model in Revelation and Hebrews 12, especially with respect to the sound of the bells—the very detail Blake picks up on.[99] Bunyan writes:

Thus therefore they walked on together, and as they walked, ever and anon, these Trumpeters, even, with joyful sound, would, by mixing their Musick, with looks and gestures, still signifie to *Christian* and his Brother, how welcome they were into their company, and with what gladness they came to meet them: And now were these two men, as 'twere, in Heaven, before they came at it; being swallowed up with the sight of Angels, and with hearing of their melodious notes. Here also they had the City it self in view, and they thought they heard all the Bells therein to ring, to welcome them thereto. (*PP* 160–61)

Having thus tolled Rose's passing in a Bunyanesque manner appropriate to the circumstances (and to the lawyer's own enthusiast, religious temper), Blake's letter goes on: "Now My Dear Sir I will thank you for the transmission of ten Pounds to the Dreamer over his own Fortunes. for I certainly am that Dreamer, but tho I dream over my own Fortunes I ought not to Dream over those of other Men." This passage reads as though it were based on a previous exchange, and one wonders: could the "Dreamer over his own Fortunes" be an epithet Hayley had dubbed Blake with earlier, in playful allusion to the stance of the narrator/dreamer of Bunyan's *Progress?* Clearly, from Hayley's viewpoint, this sort of dreaming in real life is a self-indulgence, a detraction from practical affairs, an "Abstract folly" (E716/K809) that gets the individual nowhere, though his fantasy may make an entertaining pilgrimage. Blake, however, seems to be accepting the doubtful designation almost proudly. "Certainly I am that Dreamer," he says, affirming his identification with the "prophetic character" of those who "See Visions Dream Dreams & prophecy & speak Parables unobserv'd & at liberty from the Doubts of other Mortals." Whether the antecedent reference is Bunyan's dreamer or not, we catch a glimpse here of a revised attitude toward the function of dreaming that paves the way for a reevaluation of the goal and the character of Bunyan's dream-fable in Blake's mind.[100]

With this letter to Hayley about the death of Rose, all mention of Bunyan in Blake's correspondence ceases. In fact, Blake wrote only five more letters to Hayley all told (if we assume that the letters now in the public domain make up the complete record). Apparently when his contact with Hayley petered out, so did his rhetorical evocation of Bunyan-Christian as a second self. And after 1804, except for an epigram in the *Notebook* characterizing Hayley as a "Pick Thank" in epistolary exchanges (Pickthank is the name of one of the three accusers at Faithful's trial in the *Progress*),[101] the fictional figures in Bunyan's allegory were no longer put to use by Blake as representative of his personal torment.

Instead, the existential model of Bunyan as a poet-prophet concerned with the theme of pilgrimage joined others in the workshop of Blake's imagination and helped him define his crucial concept of "States" versus "Individuals." This we see from the development of that idea as it is presented in several key places in the three major incarnations of Blake's "One Grand Theme" (E728/K823)—*The Four Zoas, Milton,* and *Jerusalem*—and in his aesthetic manifesto, "A Vision of the Last Judgment." The importance of the evolved concept as a gloss to Blake's vision of *The Pilgrim's Progress* will become evident as we proceed.

BUNYAN'S VISION AND BLAKE'S DOCTRINE OF STATES

Making its first appearance as a clear assertion in *The Four Zoas* (Night 8.379–83), the doctrine of states is intoned by Los as a sort of catechism for Rahab to explain the sacramental history of the archetypal Satan-Hayley (that history, elaborated later in the "Bard's Song" of *Milton,* is given in epitome here):

> There is a State namd Satan learn distinct to know O Rahab
> The Difference between States & Individuals of those States

> The State namd Satan never can be redeemd in all Eternity
> But when Luvah in Orc became a Serpent he des[c]ended into
> That State calld Satan.

> (*FZ* 115, E380/K351)

In this formulation of the doctrine, Satan is a "State" but Luvah is not; Luvah is an "Individual." Also, the process by which an individual enters a state is imaged as a downfall, a descent: "he des[c]ended into/That State calld Satan." The paradigm is evidently the great scriptural and Miltonic image of Lucifer's fall. But it is not apparent what the ultimate fate of the individual is in relation to the state; indeed, the doctrine seems to exist here more for the sake of explaining that "states" are a metaphor for the form of a gestalt than to clarify the operation of our mortal entrance into these moods, meanings, and events. The whole matter is further confused because Luvah, though an individual in terms of his role as a unique character within the drama of *The Four Zoas,* is really something less and something more than what we ordinarily think of as an individual. He is one of the "Four Mighty Ones" who "are in Every Man" (*FZ,* E300/K264)—that is, an elemental, intrapsychic figure, an archetype, a god.

When Blake amplifies this passage in plate 32/35 of *Milton,* the concern shifts. The goal of the new speakers, identified as the "Seven Angels of the Presence," is again to instruct, but this time the pupil is a true individual pilgrim—Milton himself—who needs to know "What is Eternal & what Changeable? & what Annihilable!" (*M* 32/35, E132/K522) before he lets a part of himself become, through Blake's creation, a symbolic value—the "State about to be Created/Called Eternal Annihilation" (*M* 32/35). So the Angels advise:

> Distinguish therefore States from Individuals in those States.
> States Change: but Individual Identities never change nor cease:
> You cannot go to Eternal Death in that which can never Die.

> (*M* 32/35)

The process of differentiating a person's identity from the state he or she is in is now seen from the perspective of the individual's eternal essence, or psychic center—something a priori, like a Platonic "form," that is separable from whatever aspect the particular "Human Existence" agrees to clothe itself in. From that point of view, the states appear to change like garments (the "Linen Clothes" of Jesus are mentioned as an example, *M* 32/35.42), while the individual identity remains constant. One puts on such a garment, or enters such a state, for creative reasons. Milton, in the "State about to be Created" (*M*

32/35.26), will serve a purpose as the exemplar and the embodiment of a condition other men and women will "Dare to enter" for the sake of their own development. The concept of entrance is thus adjusted to portray a symbolic act that is the opposite of the Luciferian fall. For according to Milton's Angelic, spiritual advisor, those who dare enter "shall enter triumphant over Death/ And Hell & the Grave! States that are not, but ah! Seem to be" (*M* 32/35).

The implicit paradigm in *this* image is, of course, the Christian resurrection of the body—an apocalyptic ascent into the Celestial City. During the major action of the poem, however, Milton himself does not ascend. He—or his Shadow—*descends,* like his own image of Jesus in *Paradise Lost,* driven back to earth in this instance by the message of the Bard's Song, which inspires him to seek and redeem his neglected feminine aspects. Therefore, the psychological material of *Milton* concerns the sacrifice of the selfhood, or of personal identification with the rational ego, initiated by a "Spiritual Form" in order to integrate a repressed aspect of the psychic totality. In this regard, *Milton* deals with a transcendent function, and not with a type of earthling/mankind—except insofar as the character of Blake is involved as the beneficiary of Milton's actions. The focus is on the transformations of the once transformed and does not follow the trials and tribulations of the beginner pilgrim learning "distinct to know . . . the Difference between States & individuals of those States."

But that Blake nevertheless thought of *Milton* as a conduct book for readers embarking on such a pilgrimage is clear from the way he refers to it in a July 6, 1803, letter to Butts: "I hope that all our three years trouble Ends in Good Luck at last & shall be forgot by my affections & only rememberd by my Understanding to be a Memento in time to come & to speak to future generations by a Sublime Allegory which is now perfectly completed into a Grand Poem" (E730/K825). As a "Memento in time to come," for himself and for "future generations," his own experiences needed to be purged of their private emotional content ("forgot by my affections") and transmuted into a symbolic statement—a spiritual autobiography that was simultaneously a "Sublime Allegory." This is precisely the motivation of Christian biography and allegory from the Book of Acts (on which so many Puritan autobiographies were modeled, including Bunyan's *Grace Abounding*) to Augustine's *Confessions,* Dante's *Commedia,* and *The Pilgrim's Progress,* to name but a few examples.[102]

Seen in this context, *Milton* is the story of a conversion. That is what spiritual autobiographies are *about.* And when Blake speaks of "the Spiritual Acts" of his "three years Slumber on the banks of the Ocean" which "none can know" without reading the "long Poem descriptive of those Acts" (E728/ K823), he is perhaps aligning himself, by the insistence of the term *acts,* with the innumerable prophetic autobiographers of the preceding era who wrote about their protestant conversions in the style of chapters 9 and 22 of the Acts of the Apostles:

> The author of the Acts, whose attention to visions, voices, and spastic seizures was indefatigable and exact, devoted these passages to the rebirth, vocation, and ministry of Paul. The potential autobiographer recognized with delight his identity with Paul; and in the record of his own sensations, gifts, and acts, which a miraculous influence immediately compelled him to compose and publish, he piously imitated the history of his celebrated predecessor.[103]

Certainly *Milton* is loaded with allusions to the standard symbols, tropes, types, and metaphors of apostolic conversion, from the joke about Milton descending as a fallen star on the tarsus of Blake's left foot (recalling the blinding light that carried Jesus' words to Paul/Saul of Tarsus in Acts 9)[104] to the many echoes of the story of Exodus as a "state" or figure for the soul's turning.[105]

I stress this rather obvious element of the narrative of *Milton* because it is in the light of the experience of conversion that the doctrine of states and individuals takes on its fullest psychological relevance as a strategy for change. It is not simply a mechanism to help the epic resolve itself (although it is that). Instead, the doctrine of States becomes an exhortation—a "Dare" (*M* 32/35)—to the reader to consider a new kind of conversion, a new kind of revolution and deliverance, one that involves entering into the vortex of one's own inner images, or "states," on the "infinite plane" (*M* 15/17) of the individual psyche in a conscious act of the imagination. This means deliberately sacrificing fixed expectations ("States Change"), since fixed expectations descend from "Memory," which "is a State always," and "Reason," which "is a State/Created to be Annihilated" (*M* 32/35).

The effort of the poem, *Milton*, is to make itself such a "state" of change. It works hard to frustrate memory and reason—especially reason about both psychological and narrative conversion—and to entice us to investigate our own "eternal salvation" (*M* 2). On the pattern of the *mise-en-abîme* of the Bard's Song *within* the Bard's (Blake's) song, it is designed to become a motive and a vehicle for the reader's journey of individuation. As such, it stresses the changeability of states in contrast to the permanence of the individual identity experiencing those states. This is the opposite of the traditional Christian view, which speaks of a "new man" replacing the old. From Blake's perspective in *Milton,* man is not new after conversion, only his state is. Each of us, in other words, has an inward form—the imagination—that is "not a State: it is the Human Existence itself" (*M* 32/35), and this is incorruptible, a "soul of sweet delight" that "can never be defiled."[106]

The next time Blake articulates the doctrine of states and individuals, he presents it from the opposite point of view and emphasizes the permanence of states through which the individual (also permanent, but in a different sense) travels. "Man Passes on but States remain for Ever" (VLJ, E556/K606), he says in a central passage that we will examine fully in a moment.

The occasion for the new formulation is Blake's draft of a prose commentary on his large, symbolic picture (now lost) "A Vision of the Last Judgment." As we noted in Chapter 1, he is addressing the reader of this little tract in the reader's role as a viewer of the painting. His major concern is therefore to alert this audience to the immediate and lasting relevance—personal and transpersonal—of the minute particulars of the vision. Thus he keeps pausing in his description of the "literal" events portrayed to instruct us on how to discriminate the meanings of the forms created—that is, on how to see. In this respect, the text of "A Vision" puts us in the same student-teacher relation to Blake, our Interpreter, as Rahab was to Los in the *Four Zoas* passage cited earlier and as Milton was to the Seven Angels of the Presence in the lines quoted above from *Milton. We* now receive the hermeneutic that the characters of the epics received earlier; only our application of the doctrine is supposed to be to the experience of art in addition to all other imaginative acts. For example, at one point in the descriptive commentary Blake interrupts to make this exhortation: "It ought to be understood that the Persons Moses & Abraham are not here meant but the States signified by those Names the Individuals being representatives or Visions of those States as they were reveald to Mortal Man in the Series of Divine Revelations. as they were written in the Bible" (E556/K607).

This statement is at once a doctrine concerning imaginal art and a reminder of how, in practice, historical persons get imbued with divine values—not euhemeristically, but through a process of conflating states with individuals of those states. We project archetypal qualities on to people in real life all the time, of course; it is one of the basic motives of emotional attraction and repulsion and a major psychological mechanism enabling us to relate to our own intrapsychic aspects. For instance, in our eyes the Beloved (like the Accursed) initially carries for us much of the ineffable dynamism of the "human form divine," to use Blake's term for the supreme image of psychic centrality. When we see characteristic features of this dynamism organized, out there, in the Other, we recognize it as if for the first time and thus contact consciously a component of the psyche that was formerly unconscious. Our seeing is enlarged by this love—a fact manifested literally on the somatic level via the dilation of the pupils caused by the sight of a loved object.[107] This enlargement, in any case, is a prerequisite for slowly learning to differentiate the archetypal value from the Beloved's individual humanity, after which we can (ideally) integrate the symbolic energy of the "state" into our own psychic economy as we willingly release the Beloved from its bonds.

Jung remarks on this point that we always experience the new component of our development first in projection and that the job of distinguishing that component from the individual person or thing onto which it had been transferred is a continual process.[108] One "withdraws" the projection when the differentiation is fully experienced—when one has in fact (and not just in mind) distinguished between the state and the individual and knows "What is Eternal & what Changeable? & what Annihilable!" in terms of a given gestalt.

For Blake, striving as a poet and prophet to articulate his vision of the Last Judgment, both in picture and in word, the processes of art became identified with these stages of psychological growth. Nor were the emblems and images of art alone at issue; as we saw in Chapter 1, the very procedure of formulating and understanding these images was conceived of as a growth experience by Blake, an icon of individuation that *is* the Last Judgment.[109] It is proper to project the psychic content of states on to visions of persons in art, he says in the "aside" quoted above (E556/K607), because art, like the "Series of Divine Revelations as they were written in the Bible" (which he elsewhere identifies as "the Great Code of Art"),[110] exists for the purpose of differentiating these values.

By giving formal and thematic expression to such typical psychological conditions, complexes, and mindsets, art demonstrates the objectively permanent status of the psychic configurations involved, and thus permits the viewer, on the one hand, to disidentify and distinguish his or her subjective individuality from the fixed "States Signified by those Names" (E556/K607) and, on the other hand, to recognize the extent to which he or she is at the same time temporarily caught up in one or more of those generic gestalts of psychic experience that Blake calls collectively the "Eternal Realities as they Exist in the Human Imagination" (VLJ, E562/K613).

It is from *this* perspective, then, that Blake now envisions "states" as "permanent," though before it suited him to define them as changing. In fact, "states" can be regarded from either standpoint, according to the situation of the viewer. It is essential to an understanding of Blake's method to see that these two perspectives have absolute parity and are complementary, not contradictory. From the vantage of the process-conscious individual, states appear to change: this is the vantage of *Milton*. But "A Vision" is concerned rather with showing that "Images of Existences" (E555/K606) occupy an eternal psychic present, and that "*Every Thing* is Eternal" (E556/K606; italics added). Through the guise of explicating his own artistic intention regarding his painting of the Last Judgment, Blake entices us to view our passage through eternity from eternity's vista, as it were. From there, states appear as static patterns through which we roam, just as our eye roams over the canvas that portrays these states. The biblical figures of "A Vision" are not simply historical legends or moral allegories or holy myths, Blake insists; they are perennial archetypes, for "these States Exist now" (E556/K606). By their organization into expressive images for a cohesive work of art, they provide patterns of deliverance, describing our pathway through life, our landscape, our psychic ground:

> These States Exist now Man Passes on but States remain for Ever he passes thro them like a traveller who may as well suppose that the places he has passed thro exist no more as a Man may suppose that the States he has passed thro exist no more Every thing is Eternal
> In Eternity one Thing never Changes into another Thing. (E556/K606)

The relation of this passage to the *Progress* should be obvious. For in Bunyan's text, also, the landscape is the ground of the traveler's imaginal psychic journey, and the "places he has passed thro" are so clearly states of mind that they bear the English names of those states: the Slough of Despond, Hill Difficulty, Doubting Castle, and so forth. Of course, it cannot be proved that Blake meant to evoke *The Pilgrim's Progress* here; but the circumstantial evidence suggesting that Bunyan's mental traveler was his imaginative model at this point is very strong. "A Vision" is, after all, the place in Blake's writing where the *Progress* is evoked by name in the context of an aesthetic polemic. That is, as Blake tries to define the nature of allegorical fiction and distinguish it from the more "sublime" genre he calls Vision (that "Representation of what Eternally Exists. Really & Unchangeably" [E554/K604]), the only English writer who serves him as an edifying example of either form is Bunyan:

> Fable is Allegory but what Critics call The Fable is Vision itself The Hebrew Bible & the Gospel of Jesus are not Allegory, but Eternal Vision or Imagination of All that Exists Note here that Fable or Allegory is Seldom without some Vision Pilgrims Progress is full of it the Greek Poets the same but Allegory & Vision ought to be known as Two Distinct Things & so calld for the Sake of Eternal Life.
>
> (E554/K604–5; deletions omitted)

Here Blake formally recognizes what we today might call the mythopoetic dimension of *The Pilgrim's Progress*. The book is full of vision, he says—full of "ever Existent Images" (E555/K605) or "imagination of All that Exists" (E554/K604)—even though its genre and sectarian theology (formed, as he would put it, by the "daughters of Memory") mitigates the force of that visionary thrust. In that way, Bunyan's fiction is like the Greek Fables in

Blake's opinion, whose "Real Visions" often become "Lost & clouded in Fable & Allegory" (E555/K605). But does the *Progress* in fact have the same paradigmatic significance for Blake as the Greek tales? In the passage following the section that describes states as places passed by the individual traveler, Blake specifies further his complaint against the Greek mentality: "In Eternity one Thing never Changes into another Thing Each Identity is Eternal consequently Apuleius's Golden Ass & Ovids Metamorphosis & others of the like kind are Fable yet they contain Vision in a sublime degree being derived from real Vision in More Ancient Writings" (E556/K607). The objection to calling Ovid and Apuleius "& others of the like kind" visionary artists is made on the basis of their metaphoric distortion of the relationship between identity and subjectivity and of the individuation process. They represent change as if it entailed the loss of fundamental forms, which for Blake is a loss of identity, a loss of creative outline, a loss of life itself:[111] "How do we distinguish one face or countenance from another, but by the bounding line and its infinite inflexions and movements? . . . Leave out this l[i]ne and you leave out life itself; all is chaos again, and the line of the almighty must be drawn out upon it before man or beast can exist" (*DC*, E550/K585).

To portray man's metamorphoses from the casual viewpoint of what temporarily appears to be happening—that is, change of one thing into another thing—is, in Blake's opinion, to blur the inward process; and his quarrel with fabulists who adhere to this method is that they have been drawn into misleading "categories of metaphor"[112] that present spiritual phenomena extrinsically devalorized from the outside of imagination, that is to say from within a positivistic psychology and from a protopsychotic state of psychological dissociation. This metaphorical system, in its turn, fosters our incipient tendency to mistake "what is within" for a separate reality "now seen without" (*FZ*2.55, E314/K281) and thus to misconceive the very nature both of "Eternal Life" and of "Visionary fancy" (VLJ, E555/K605).

These are the pitfalls of allegory as handled by the Greeks, according to Blake. But *The Pilgrim's Progress* cannot be faulted for the same kind of visionary disorder, since Christian's dream-journey deals at a meta-level with an emblematics of transformation that all the while holds tenaciously on to the "Eternal Image & Individuality" of the experiencing, interpreting ego.[113] Thus the imaginal strategies of Bunyan's dream-vision tend to fulfill Blake's strictures for a spiritual aesthetic based on the deliverance of individuals from created "states." Furthermore, the progressive differentiation of the traveling subject from the places and states he passes through is imaged as occurring *within* imagination—the dream—so that the reader of the visionary matter perceives that it *is* an internal/eternal process, and not an "outward ceremony" (*Laocoön*, E274/K776). To this extent, the *Progress* embodies a method contrary to that of the Greek fable, and one that seems much closer to Blake's own artistic habit of employing a symbolic process both to represent and to comment on the archetypal aspects of that process.[114] Thus it is tempting to see Blake's point about Ovid and Apuleius as if it were intended as a displaced piece of positive literary criticism on Bunyan's work—a spliced-in definition-by-counterexample of the properly visionary aspects of the *Progress*. I say "spliced in" because the allegorical motives of the Greeks are called to account just after the Bunyanesque description of states and individuals has been plotted as evidence that states are in fact eternal and permanent and that nothing ever changes its real identity in its "wondrous journey" (*M* 15) through time and space.

Equally suggestive in locating this passage about Ovid and Apuleius as a partial answer to the puzzle of the *Progress*'s generic ambivalence is the Bunyanesque way in which Blake amplifies the subject of how to symbolize visionary transformation. As soon as he acknowledges that even *The Golden Ass* and *The Metamorphoses* "contain Vision in a sublime degree, being derived from real Vision in More ancient Writings" (thus placing these Greek poets once more on a par with Bunyan, whose allegory also was previously described as being "full of" real Vision), Blake immediately launches into an explication of the "real Vision" of Lot's wife: "Lots Wife being Changed into [a] Pillar of Salt alludes to the Mortal Body being renderd a Permanent Statue but not Changed or Transformed into Another Identity while it retains its own Individuality" (E556/K607). The figure is apt as an emblem of the metaphoric mode of representing metamorphosis. But it has as well a specific relation to the character of allegory in *The Pilgrim's Progress*, since Bunyan makes the same scriptural example appear—literally—in the following section of Christian's and Hopeful's journey:

> . . . the Pilgrims came to a place where stood an old *Monument*, hard by the High-way-side, at the sight of which they were both concerned, because of the strangeness of the form thereof; for it seemed to them as if it had been a *Woman* transformed into the shape of a Pillar: here therefore they stood looking, and looking upon it, but could not for a time tell what they should make thereof. At last *Hopeful* espied written above upon the head thereof, a Writing in an unusual hand; but he being no Scholar, called to *Christian* (for he was learned) to see if he could pick out the meaning: so he came, and after a little laying of Letters together, he found the same to be this, *Remember Lot's Wife*. So he read it to his fellow; after which, they both concluded, that that was the Pillar of Salt into which *Lot's Wife* was turned for her looking back with a *covetous heart,* when she was going from *Sodom* for safety. Which sudden and amazing sight, gave them occasion of this discourse. (*PP* 108–9)

It is interesting to note, first of all, that the pilgrims meet the vision in its self-consciously memorial guise, as an "old *Monument*" (Blake's "Permanent Statue"), and not as either a woman or a naturalistic column of salt. It is a made object, a sculpture created to contain the mystery of its woman/salt double-ness in the "strangeness of the form thereof." Also, the statue is not named "Lot's Wife"; it is named "*Remember* Lot's Wife," suggesting that in its essence it is a signifier of signification itself—a thing that is not itself but something other.[115] In the same vein, Christian remarks during the ensuing "discourse" that the apparition of the statue of the pillar of salt "is a seasonable sight" (no pun on the verb *to season* intended) which "came opportunely" to them just after they had almost committed a sin similar to that of Lot's wife. It is a "meaningful coincidence"[116] of the kind that might well occur in the unfolding of a dream narrative, where the same psychic nexus is often spread over two symbolic incidents or repeated in two different, contiguous formulations. The fact that the sight is so "sudden and amazing" and yet so opportune seems to indicate that the meaning of the event as an emblem of imaginal awakening, rather than the magical fact of a changed identity, is what has been energized here, its presence being constellated by the dream figures' motivating need to meet that meaning in effigy, as it were.

So far I have cited only those portions of Bunyan's presentation that make him seem to conform to Blake's definition of a visionary artist. In fact, however, this passage and others like it in the *Progress* have a distinctly doc-trinal-allegoric impact, mostly owing to the characters' familiar insistence on making their own moral interpretations.[117] It is evidently for this reason, more than on grounds of a false representation of things changing into other things, that Blake dubs *The Pilgrim's Progress* allegorical in the negative sense, for "Allegories are things that Relate to Moral Virtues Moral Virtues do not Exist they are Allegories & dissimulations" (E563/K614). Yet even with respect to the "Greek" error of distorting visions of change, Bunyan is not totally guiltless—a fact that shows up in the Lot's Wife episode as well as anywhere. Christian, indeed, reveals it when he remarks: "Let us take notice of what we see here, for our help for time to come: *This* woman escaped one Judgment; for she fell not by the destruction of *Sodom,* yet she was destroyed by another; as we see, she is turned into a Pillar of Salt" (*PP* 109). In the very act of identifying the pillar of salt as a symbolic statement (a statue whose significance is its use as a "sign"), Bunyan's pilgrims invest heavily in the belief that the sign *is* the woman. This is tantamount to asserting what Blake emphatically denies re-garding the biblical figure in question, that is, that the pillar "alludes to the Mortal Body being . . . Transformed into Another Identity while it retains its own Individuality."

The fact that Bunyan's characters frequently maintained toward the image both a didactically reductive attitude and a naive, concretistic approach only increased what Blake regarded as the unfortunate allegoric dimension of the *Progress*. Each attitude, in his view, represented a mode of belief that served sectarian needs and detracted from the reader's direct confrontation with the vision as an eternal state, stripped of doctrinal or historical accident.[118]

THE PILGRIMAGE AS DREAM

What redeemed the *Progress* and set it apart in Blake's eyes from all other potentially visionary fiction was its overarching metaphor of a generic Christian pilgrimage. That concept was not original with Bunyan, of course: far from it. Its lineage is as ancient as the scriptural tellings of Christ's own pattern of experience in the world, and it has functioned as the informing principle of countless allegories, romances, biographies, emblem series, epics, novels, confessions, and so forth down through the centuries.[119] But Bunyan's vivid and energetic deployment of the standard trope had some special features that made it particularly useful to Blake as a model (albeit *manqué*) of the imaginal aesthetics of intrapsychic prophecy rooted in the visionary metaphors of the Bible.

I will summarize these special features in a moment. First, however, I want to assert that I am talking here exclusively about the character of *Christian* pilgrimages. The emphasis is important, because of course the *general* metaphor of the journey as an image of man's development is a commonplace without known historic boundaries. But the incarnation and the life of Christ, together constituting a unique event, offer a paradigm of uniqueness that structures the Christian quest and is coextensive with the theme of the conscious evolution of the autonomous personality.[120] Understood in this fashion, Christianity is the religion of personality, its highest value the image of the individual human identity accepting the cross—that is, the crucial fact—of his or her own double nature.[121] Furthermore, for believers the taking on of that cross is acknowledged by the authority of Jesus as the necessary and sufficient way both to God and to the discovery of the inner self.[122] Thus, the Christian pilgrimage as a pathway that leads to personal and eternal salvation is also inevitably a deliberate, psychological journey toward expansion and integration of the personality. The "traveller thro Eternity" (*M* 15) who knowingly becomes a pilgrim advances the cause of greater consciousness by experiencing the interpenetration of God and man in the one "human form divine," of which we are all, paradoxically, only-begotten sons and daughters.[123]

Perhaps the best way to isolate the special, psycho-aesthetic value that Bunyan's dream-quest finally held for Blake is to glance briefly at *A Descriptive Catalogue*. There Blake interprets another, quite different model of Christian pilgrimage—Chaucer's Prologue to *The Canterbury Tales*—in ways that illuminate by contrast his appreciation of the imagery of states versus individuals in the *Progress*. As with "A Vision," the commentary on Chaucer takes the form of a verbal interpretation of Blake's own *pictorial* interpretation of the primary text. [124] The pictorial statement in question is Blake's painting "The Canterbury Pilgrims"; and the long entry in the *Catalogue* describing it is his first extended attempt at literary criticism in this twice-told vein. [125] The thing he wants most to convey about the painting and about Chaucer's poem is that both depict "classes of men." By this he means that the Prologue offers objectively valid information on what we, today, might call a psychology of types:

> Of Chaucer's characters, as described in his Canterbury Tales, some of the names or titles are altered by time, but the characters themselves for ever remain unaltered, and consequently they are the physiognomies or lineaments of universal human life, beyond which Nature never steps. Names alter, things never alter. I have known multitudes of those who would have been monks in the age of monkery, who in this deistical age are deists. As Newton numbered the stars, and as Linneus numbered the plants, so Chaucer numbered the classes of men.
>
> (*DC*, E532–33/K567)

Placing Chaucer on a scale of analogy with Newton and Linnaeus already tells us a good deal. For the last-named men were contemporary heroes of just the rational, quantifying, positivistic mentality that Blake so often faulted for its dangerous one-sidedness. Newton, especially, carried a dark symbolic coloration for Blake (as is well known), frequently appearing in the poems and epigrams as a sort of archfiend representing the dissociated "sleep" of scientific materialism. [126] Newton is the nadir in this respect, because his "single vision"—so inimical to spiritual wholeness—is self-enclosed, being reflected in and by his own system of thought. Is Chaucer then the zenith, the redeemer of that same intellectual faculty? A certain logic of progressive development in the manner of Blake's listing here—"As Newton numbered the stars and as Linneus numbered the plants, so Chaucer numbered the classes of men"—suggests as much. Thus, as the statement evolves from mention of Newton to Linnaeus to Chaucer, the images signaling their respective objects of numeration also evolve, bringing our mind's eye from the distant realm of cold, inanimate "stars," down to the plane of earth and its organic "plant" life, to the world of human values and the "classes of men." In this way, Blake types Chaucer himself as a classifier of external facts, but insofar as these facts are

"Visions of . . . eternal principles or characters of *human* life" (E536/K571; italics added), they serve to orient and reveal man to knowledge of his own nature. Put to use as part of a poetic act envisioning the pilgrimage of personalities through time, the differentiated classifying function does not close men and women in or alienate them from their surroundings, but opens them out, allowing them to view themselves from many angles.

Nevertheless, it is clear that Blake admires Chaucer as an anatomist of character—a phenomenologist of the conscious personality—and not as an explorer of the unconscious. This is perfectly appropriate, for to the extent that the subject of the Prologue is the classifying of characters, it will confine itself to sorting out patterns of symptomatic, adaptive behavior, which Chaucer does indeed do with great vividness and intellectual brilliance. Psychological typologies of this sort, however, can be considered a pilgrimage for what Blake saw as the permanent individual identity only in the sense that persons, "deciding" to be born, are obliged to take on the human outline and fate of one or another of these types for the period of their life span. Blake phrases it this way: "Chaucer's characters live age after age. Every age is a Canterbury Pilgrimage; we all pass on, each sustaining one or other of these characters; nor can a child be born, who is not one of these characters of Chaucer" (E536/ K570). And elsewhere in the same discussion he stresses again the eternal repetition of the forms in the ever-new costumes of successive ages: "The characters of Chaucer's Pilgrims are the characters which compose all ages and nations: as one age falls, another rises, different to mortal sight, but to immortals only the same" (E532/K567).

It is the historical era and the duration of time that constitute the condition of pilgrimage here: just the opposite of the situation in Bunyan's work, where the *spatial* interaction of characters striving in, and with, the landscape determines the nature of man's spiritual progress along the inner, psychic gradient of the Christian Way. But time and space are not themselves the defining categories that exemplify the difference between these two versions of the Christian pilgrimage. Much more central for Blake, as for modern readers, is the extraverted quality of the Chaucerian perspective versus the introverted scenario of Bunyan's story. Both are archetypal and specifically Christian in the ways I have mentioned; but from the Blakean perspective, one embodies a doctrine of personality based on individuals in relation to *classes* of men and is therefore a cultural and sociological statement, while the other enacts the phases of inner development by providing images of the ego discriminating its functions in regard to primordial psychic *states*.

In fact, Blake's effort to distinguish the archetypal nature of Chaucer's schema from the visionary aspects of the *Progress* may well be the watershed of his thinking about the differences between classes and states. For while the two terms are never really equated (though they sometimes appear to be used interchangeably),[127] only when Blake's work on the Chaucerian classification of character is complete does his idea of states achieve an adequately independent definition, free of (some might say displaced from) what might be called "class consciousness." At that point, furthermore, it does so by association with a Bunyanesque formula of pilgrimage, in the passage from "A Vision" already quoted: "These States Exist now Man Passes on but States remain for Ever he passes thro them like a traveller who may as well suppose that the places he has passed thro exist no more as a Man may suppose that the States he has passd thro exist no more" (E556/K606). Indeed, after writing this evocation of the permanence of states, in a rhetoric that utilizes the model of Bunyan's plot for its imagery, the word *class* and its cognates virtually drop out of Blake's vocabulary.[128] It is as if the very concept of categorical differences among persons is henceforward subordinated to and subsumed by what was for Blake the more dynamic, flexible vision of unique identities moving (the way Bunyan's pilgrims do) through Eternal States. In *Jerusalem,* there is even a strong suggestion that the attempt to type individuals according to their traits and conditions (or, conversely, to identify personified states with actual human beings) involves a deadly, "deistical" error, itself born of a state that "must be put off before [one] can be the Friend of Man" (*J* 52).[129]

Thus, despite an unqualified appreciation of Chaucer's genius for envisioning the timeless "characters of human life" as autonomous men and women, each the "image of a class" (E536/K571), Blake was not motivated to adopt Chaucerian methods, and *The Canterbury Tales* had, finally, less of an impact on his own visionary aesthetic than did the structure of Bunyan's dreamscapes.

How do we know this? For one thing, in his writing after this period, whenever he wants to explicate the mechanism of redemption, Blake retains the basic trope of the pilgrim as a traveler entering and leaving permanent states the way Christian passes fixed and concrete landmarks. In *Jerusalem,* for example, we find six key references to "states,"[130] and in each one this telltale dialectic of individuation is preserved. The last such instance, on plate 73, lines 44–45, reads like a two-line epitome of them all, recapitulating the very diction of the previous passage quoted:

> As the Pilgrim passes while the Country permanent remains
> So Men pass on: but States remain permanent for ever.

Even more important in establishing Bunyan's influence on Blake's later treatment of the "Grand Theme" of deliverance, however, is the evidence offered by certain additions to the revised version of *The Gates of Paradise.* The copper plates completed in 1793 for this series of emblems were suddenly taken up again by Blake around the year 1818, with their title page re-engraved to implicate "the sexes" instead of "children" and numerous other changes made.[131] One change involved the cutting of three new plates to supply a verse commentary called "The Keys of the Gates" and an epilogue entitled "To the Accuser who is The God of This World." It is the epilogue that demands our attention here, because it speaks bluntly about the shifting relation of fixed states to individuals, and its plate carries an engraved tailpiece (Fig. 20) representing an obviously mental traveler who has marked affinities with at least two dreamers of the *Progress*. The double association is important and will be explained as we proceed. First, though, we need to establish what is going on in the design itself.

The human figure depicted, though clearly a wayfarer, is unlike the other pilgrims seen traveling through the *Gates* (that is, the climber from emblem 9 and the one who "hasteth in the evening" in the design of that title [see Figs. 6 and 14 above]). To begin with, this new traveler is naked, and he is stretched out on a rock with his walking staff lying on the ground beside him. Moreover, he is asleep—apparently dreaming the dream of the devil-dunce addressed in the epilogue poem above him. This much we gather because, as Nelson Hilton has pointed out, the black, bat-winged figure with the imprint of the sun, moon, and stars on his wings is spurting from the place of the sleeper's genitals like a nocturnal emission.[132] Indeed, the picture is almost a pun on the phrase "nocturnal emission," for Satan takes the very shape of night, and he is literally being emitted from the dreaming man by the agency of his own (Satan's) right foot, which holds the place of, and has a distinct resemblance to, a serpentlike version of the dreamer's phallus.[133] To emphasize the double source (mental and sexual) of this overdetermined libidinal discharge, Blake has accentuated the line leading from the specter's left ankle to the dreamer's head—a line that simultaneously functions to describe the dreamer's neck.[134] In this way the image of the wet dream is tethered by one foot to the genitals and by the other to the breast and brain of the dreamer—for the neck, of course, is itself a bodily bridge between the seats of thinking and feeling. It is important that both these "tethers" (and the whole underside of the demon's left leg) are fully explicable as parts of the boundary of the dreamer's body, since by this device we get a further expression of the synonymity between satanic *effect* and *affect* in the imagination of the sleeping pilgrim.

The thing that makes both sleeper and pictured dream-content directly related to Bunyan's pilgrim, though, concerns an association to the last line of the poem, which identifies the satanic image as "The lost Travellers Dream under the Hill."[135] I quote the poem in full:

To The Accuser who is
The God of This World

Truly My Satan thou art but a Dunce
And dost not know the Garment from the Man
Every Harlot was a Virgin once
Nor canst thou ever change Kate into Nan

Tho thou art Worshipd by the Names Divine
Of Jesus & Jehovah: thou art still
The Son of Morn in weary Nights decline
The lost Travellers Dream under the Hill

FIG. 20 Blake, Epilogue for *Gates*

To The Accuser who is
The God of This World

Truly My Satan thou art but a Dunce
And dost not know the Garment from the Man
Every Harlot was a Virgin once
Nor canst thou ever change Kate into Nan

Tho thou art Worshipd by the Names Divine
Of Jesus & Jehovah: thou art still
The Son of Morn in weary Nights decline
The lost Travellers Dream under the Hill.

As noted earlier in this chapter, the event in the *Progress* alluded to by this final phrase is the incident where Christian falls asleep in the Arbor of Grace, halfway up Hill Difficulty. The sleep is fateful, because during it he drops his ID—his roll or scroll, "which used to relieve him, and . . . which should have been his pass into the Celestial City" (*PP* 43). There is a covert sexual nuance in Bunyan's rhetoric here (the scroll as an object of desire that "used to relieve him"), and this nuance dovetails nicely with the ejaculating dream-image Blake has designed. Similarly, the earlier description of Christian's handling of his roll and garment before sleep in the arbor has autoerotic overtones: "Then *he pull'd* his Roll out of his bosom and read therein *to his comfort;* he also now began afresh to take a review of the Coat or Garment that was given him as he stood by the Cross. *Thus pleasing himself a while,* he at last *fell into a slumber,* and thence into a fast sleep . . . and in his sleep his Roll *fell out of his hand*" (*PP* 42; italics added). The overt meaning of the text at this point, however, is plain: Christian has forfeited his entry into paradise by the error of literally forgetting himself "in the midst of difficulty" (*PP* 44). In fact, Christian's loss of contact with his eternal identity is so crucial that its expression undergoes a splitting characteristic of affect-laden events in dreams and fiction, and its meaning is carried by a twofold metaphor: the sleep and the dropping of the roll. Splitting into two, of course, also neatly epitomizes the condition of this Christian traveler lost to himself, and so the episode in the telling has a rich, iconic ring.

Although the mechanisms of self-forgetting are not spelled out in this passage, Bunyan does hint at a cause that is pertinent to the Blakean context in the *Gates*. When, just before falling asleep, as described in the passage quoted above, Christian shifts his attention from the testament of his permanent individuality (the roll) to a "review" of the outward sign of his present state of grace (the coat), it is as if he is slipping into the mentality of Blake's dunce, who "dost not know the Garment from the Man." Becoming identified with his "change of Raiment" (*PP* 38) in this way, Christian suffers what we would today call an ego inflation, which makes his discriminating functions fade like the morning star, Blake's light of Lucifer disappearing in "weary Nights decline." And this fading *is* the lost traveler's dream.

In Blake's evocation of the Bunyan incident inscribed in the *Gates* tailpiece, however, the scroll, image of Christian's eternal identity, has become a pilgrim's staff. This metamorphosis is evidenced by the fact that in the emblem it is the staff that lies forgotten by the traveler's side, where it has apparently remained unused throughout the symbolic night of the traveler's long sleep—long enough, that is, for a cobweb to have grown, or been spun, on it.[136] The amount of time elapsed since the man took up his proper function is, then, an emblematic day, something like a biblical day, one that allows a complete cycle of web building. For the sleeping pilgrim, in effect, it is an entire psychic lifetime during which he has dreamed his way from the frontispiece of the book through the sixteen gates to the epilogue, "weaving to Dreams the Sexual strife / And weeping over the Web of Life." The thread we see connecting the staff to the rock is a sign of the web, a signature of it. And the *thematic* thread that links this design to the frontispiece emblem (where the story of transformation had its embryonic beginnings) is the condition and posture of dreaming, of sleep (see Fig. 18). In that first emblem of the book we were shown a human personality assuming the form of a dormant chrysalis, a swaddled baby, with his head resting near the lower left corner of the plate. The tailpiece engraving dilates on this idea and portrays a now matured man, divested of his "garment," who yet occupies the same physical position and the same mental state of sleep. The naked figure can thus be seen as the metamorphosed imago—or adult form—of the originally cocooned butterfly-soul. The final portrait in that sense develops out of the first design.

But *develops* is a misleading term, since it signifies that the images exist in a well-ordered context of temporal cause and effect—a signification that it is the precise function of the epilogue plate to contradict. While the narrative pressure leads us to experience the last drawing as an evolution of the initial emblem (the child is father of the man), the meaning implied is that the lost traveler is a Bunyanesque dreamer-pilgrim who is himself the *originator* of the first image. In this sense the more comprehensive experience of Blake's work is that the frontispiece is a development of the tailpiece, not vice versa. If we look at the epilogue from such a standpoint, it is brought home to us that man in his complete identity creates his own gestalts, from childhood to death's door and beyond, and that the individuated consciousness is both preexistent and imaginal, seeded in our psychic structure *sub specie aeternitatis,* like a DNA of the mind.

There are many clues in the makeup of the epilogue plate to encourage a reading of this sort. The presence of a tiny butterfly hanging from the underside of the cobweb thread, for example, indicates that the motif of plate 1 (not to mention plates 6 and 15) is actually a magnification of what is only a small part of the larger picture viewed from the final perspective of unaccommodated man dreaming. It is almost as if the frontispiece were meant to be perceived as an altered detail of the epilogue's grand canvas, which (as in some art books) is not revealed until the end of a series of such fragmented "inserts." The dreamer's reality encompasses the earlier state but is not of it. He lies, as it were, outside the gates of the *Gates* and at the same time outside his identity with the traditional figure of phased transformation, the butterfly. In that extratemporal, extraterrestrial theater, the butterfly is seen to be concerned not with growth and development, but with spinning reality's *restraining* mechanism—the web of life, which ties the man's walking stick down to earth. In the earlier book, *For Children: The Gates of Paradise,* no such distinction between the trope of transformation (the butterfly forms) and man's permanent identity was made visible. In this late revision of the emblem series, however, by alluding to Christian's lost identity scroll in *The Pilgrim's Progress,* the walking stick of the epilogue plate serves to emblematize the function of the eternal personality, which is shown to be basically at odds with those states of change we enter into and out of all the time, like sleep.[137] The message is a terse development of the whole metaphysics of individuals versus states as Blake had refined it during the years since his experiences at Felpham; and it is given expression in the poem accompanying the emblem in terms of the difference between "Man" and "Garment"—a difference that Satan (our own intrapsychic Accuser aspect) has *not* learned "distinct to know."

Once again, then, we see Bunyan's image of the Christian mental traveler linked by Blake with his own system of imaginal representation and with the concept of individuation via the route of differentiating self from "state," man from garment, permanent identity from temporary condition, the "Eternal Human" from "those States or Worlds in which the Spirit travels" (*J* 49).

Two innovations that we have not yet mentioned in the treatment of the revised *Gates* are important to recognize as part of the overall expansion of the Bunyan theme and its associations in Blake's mind. The first concerns the device of the dream within the dream, and the second involves the concept of "Mutual Forgiveness." Both are what might be called psychostructural elements of the aesthetic whole, the one being a formal device to achieve the perspective required for the second. While neither is by itself new to Blake, forgiveness of sins—though implied as the necessary redemptive consequence of distinguishing individuals from states—does not receive its title and battle-cry status until this instance, and the motif of the double dreamer has no emblematic specificity until joined with the concept of mutual charity toward self and other.[138]

Let us begin by examining the overdetermination of the figure of the dream and its agent, the dreamer, within the workings of the plate itself. When we first look at the tailpiece engraving and see a picture of a man sleeping, probably dreaming (a point driven home to the eye by the furrowed brow and overwrought expression on the sleeper's face), our tendency is to assume it is meant as an illustrative gloss on the last line of the epilogue poem, the one that calls Satan's "real" identity a dream: "The lost Travellers Dream under the Hill." In this reading, the man in the picture is a character in the poem (the lost traveler) and, moreover, a character who is within the domain, one might almost say within the very *name,* of Satan. This is so because of the structure of the poem, which devotes its entire second quatrain to expressing the false— and then revealing the true—names and epithets of the devil-principle. He is not Jesus, not Jehovah—divine titles that ought to be reserved for the holy identities they signify. Rather, he is more fittingly invoked by epithet, like a Greek god or an American Indian brave: thus, The-Son-of-Morn-in-weary-Nights-decline, The-lost-Travellers-Dream-under-the-Hill. So taken, the lost traveler is an aspect of the devil. At the same time, though, because he is the dreaming agent, he has evidently *produced* the devil, who thus becomes an aspect of *him.* As dreamer, the traveler therefore creates a vision that includes himself in two guises, demon and lost-traveler-dreaming, the one named after the other in a relation of perpetual reflexivity. It is a vicious circle. But it can be cut through by a second, more inclusive view of the graphic design, a view that regards the dreamer as existing outside the poem in the same way that he exists outside the dream: as its producer.

This is an interpretation neglected so far by the critics, yet there are indications in the structure of the plate that the poem, as well as the figure of Satan, is intended as a part of the traveler's dream. For although we see the devil exuding from the pilgrim's head, side, and genitals, Satan's reality as a dream content does not end there. His seminal character is bound in or isolated by the outline of his bodily form but reacts in an intimate dialectical way with the poem inscribed above him. Indeed, just as the traveler and the satanic dream-figure form one visual gestalt, joined at the root, so Satan and the physical presence of the poem form another. Seen in this way, the Accuser, far from "vanish[ing] like a raven of dawn,"[139] is rising upward to confront the poem in a head-on embrace. The poem, correspondingly, appears to descend toward him and in terms of visual balance rests on his wings. This motion of potential congress is duplicated in the *illusional* space where verse and figure face each other, because in relation to Satan the words seem to be coming forward from a plane behind him, and the twist and foreshortening of his upper back make him appear to be leaning in as if to meet them.[140] The devil is thus positioned more or less as we are relative to the poem; that is, he is looking inward over a narrow gulf (just as we are looking into the picture plane across a space that separates reader and book) while the words of the poem answer both him and us from a contrary standpoint, in direct dialogue or antiphonal debate.

Another sign that the poem and the vision of Satan are interdependent aspects of the same dream is that they speak the same language, embodying the same style of relating: both are accusers. The verse is addressed, disapprovingly enough, to "The Accuser who is/The God of This World," but at the same time the verse is itself cast in the form of an accusation. In a sense, we have here a case of the pot calling the kettle black—an instance of mutual projection whereby the poem "becomes what it beholds," to use Blake's own refrain for this phenomenon. That is the ironic, one might almost say the satanic, way of looking at it. A more inclusive and "forgiving" view is to see in the shared methodology of these two antagonists a mutual recognition of their joint origin. This view would suggest that while these counterforces of the dreaming psyche spring from a single consciousness divided against itself, the division is a fiction entered into knowingly and for the purpose of effecting an *agnoresis,* or self-recognition: the beginning of the possibility of a reunion and integration on a "higher" plane.

The question all this leads to is, where does the *poem* come from in the psychological universe represented by the pictorial space, and who is its speaker? I contend that the poem derives from the essential nature of the man dreaming and that its speaker is an archetypal figure of the prolific inner self, who is both creator and interpreter of the identity it serves. In the Jungian schema, which I feel is especially pertinent here, the speaker would represent the Self, Satan would be a shadow-figure, and the sleeping pilgrim would signify the individuating ego—all endopsychic aspects of one personality. The Self, as an image of the center of the psychic totality, is always experienced by the ego as a numinous entity; and often it will speak in a hieratic manner, as here, where it adopts the persona of the disembodied Word of God coming from an "Above" that is also "Within."[141] That Blake represents it as emerging from a deeper plane of the picture space than that occupied by either the pilgrim-ego or the Satan-shadow is fitting in another way, too, since the self is generally agreed to manifest as a felt form—image or voice—from the innermost layers of the transpersonal psyche only after a certain amount of shadow recognition opens the gateway to the contents of the collective unconscious.

If we accept a psychological reading such as the Jungian model provides, we can better appreciate the range and purpose of the dream-within-a-dream motif with which Blake surrounds the trope of the dreamer. First, the naked dreamer is, as a metaphor, a sort of oxymoron because he represents the conscious ego in a state of *un*consciousness—a mode of temporary self-contradiction that Blake calls "lost" (following Bunyan's example, as we noted above). Second, the dreamer literally "dreams up" the solution to his situation in a vision of division that rises above him. There the unconscious is split into two personified parts reacting as opposites to each other. Unlike the original splitting between the conscious ego and its unconscious shadow, however, *this* opposition seeks relation and resolution. In the course of the interrelating, one part—the shadow or devil—is exposed by the other part—the Self or speaker of the poem—as the product of a dream capable of being cast off like the garment from the man. To evoke Satan as a dream is an interior duplication of the enveloping reality, itself a dream, and so we come to the core expression of the figure of the dream-within-the-dream. But the ripples of relation go further, because, as we saw above, the voice of the poem has adopted Satan's tactics and acknowledged the latter as belonging to him ("Truly *My* Satan"; italics added). Is the speaker then also the creator of the dream of Satan? By positing that there is a dream within a dream, the plate further suggests that there is a dreamer within the dreamer, a creative force wiser than the conscious ego but in collusion with it. It is this force that dreams the dream onward, luring the satanic aspect into a sacrificial attitude more or less equivalent to the many self-annihilation emblems placed by Blake at strategic points in other works.[142] But the sacrifice here is willingly to *become* a state (that is, a dream) so that the rest of the personality may be "delivered." The *mise-en-abîme* of the dreamer-within-the-dreamer accomplishes the release of the shadow from the state of Satan, therefore, by giving each aspect of the psychic system perceptions of itself in the act of dreaming. For example, the sleeping ego learns that Satan is such a state, such a "garment" covering his naked consciousness; and the ejaculating motif thus becomes symbolically equivalent to the casting off of that black garment before awakening.[143]

In Blake's view, the goal of every pilgrim's dream is that the dreamer awake from it—a goal best reached by including among its mental forms visions of its evolving process. That Blake saw fit to import an emblematic episode from *The Pilgrim's Progress* to reorient the message of *The Gates of Paradise* in this direction, is testimony to his deepened perception of the way Bunyan's myth paralleled the thematic concerns of his own poetics. The revised *Gates,* then, through the agency of the new Bunyanesque tailpiece, has become a kind of Hegelian epitome of "the unwitting quest of the Spirit to redeem itself by repossessing its own lost and sundered self in an ultimate recognition of its own identity whereby, as Hegel says in his concluding section, it can be 'at home with itself in its otherness.' "[144] As such, it is an emblem series that might as well have been called "The Phenomenology of the Spirit Dreaming," and it serves us well as an introduction to the next stage in Blake's treatment of this theme: his direct, pictorial commentary on the full text of *The Pilgrim's Progress.*

CHAPTER THREE

THE NEXT ROOM
OF THE DREAM

As with a dream interpreted by one still sleeping
The interpretation is only the next room of the dream.

—HOWARD NEMEROV

In the previous chapter we traced the development of Blake's affinity with Bunyan through events in Blake's personal history and through the many allusions to *The Pilgrim's Progress* that appear with increasing significance in his work from the 1790s on. Now we will turn to the drawings themselves, the series of watercolors he executed around 1824 that directly illustrate and comment on Bunyan's allegory. To appreciate fully the prophetic energy of these designs, however, both as vision and revision, it is important to see them first in the context of the history of Bunyan illustration—a history with which Blake himself was eminently familiar.[1]

THE TRADITION OF BUNYAN ILLUSTRATION

The practice of issuing copies of *The Pilgrim's Progress* with full sets of pictures began in 1680, only two years after the book was first licensed for publication.[2] By then it had gone through four editions, and when the fifth came out it carried an advertisement announcing that the project of giving pictorial representation to the story would henceforth be realized, according to public demand:

> The *Pilgrim's Progress* having found good Acceptation among the People, to the carrying off the Fourth Impression, which had many Additions, more than any preceding: And the Publisher observing that many persons desired to have it illustrated with Pictures, hath endeavoured to gratifie them therein: And besides those that are ordinarily printed to this Fifth Impression, hath provided Thirteen Copper Cuts curiously Engraven for such as desire them. (*PP* li–lii)[3]

These thirteen prints were sold unbound on individual sheets at an extra cost of a shilling per set. Though marketed primarily to interested purchasers of the book, they were also available separately;[4] thus, the designs were evidently intended to make a statement by themselves, on purely visual and self-referential grounds. They had their own summary texts appended to them, in the form of rhymed quatrains, one to an engraving; taken together, then, they told a cohesive story much in the manner of the consecutive emblem series discussed earlier. Conceived and presented as a unit, they could be enjoyed as a sort of digest or dumbshow of the fable as a whole.

In subsequent editions, woodcut copies of these same illustrations were interleaved in the printed text, appearing opposite the narrative moment (or moments) they were each meant to epitomize. The reader had then to respond to them as sporadic, graphic evocations of a linguistic enterprise, which meant that his or her experience of them as a concentrated visual narrative was greatly diluted. The purely decorative impact of the designs suffered in this way as well, because in addition to losing semantic force, their compositional relations were effectively obscured by their separations and dispersals over some two hundred–odd pages.[5]

This watering down of an originally challenging, graphic presentation by the demands of standard publishing practices continued and in fact increased as the text became more popular. In the early eighteenth century, the *Progress* often appeared in carelessly produced, pirated editions with sloppy recuts of the old prints included. Its main audience, after all, was not the sophisticated elite, but a populace used to the pictorial hackwork that turned up in frequently substandard impressions of inexpensive broadsides and chapbooks.

Later in the eighteenth century, when styles of illustrating books changed, and when some of the key episodes in Bunyan's story drew the attention of many inventive artists, there was still no adequate visual rendition of the allegory on an interpretive level. This was the fault not so much of pictorial fashion as of a general lack of analytical interest in the text of the *Progress* as a literary artifact. Its humble, evangelical roots seemed to preclude it from such scrutiny. *Paradise Lost,* to cite a counterexample, had no dearth of illustrator-interpreters to highlight its much-discussed epic content and structure. In fact, it became a source of vigorous and fairly unified graphic commentaries, many of which—like Blake's own—had a strong conceptual bent.[6] But Milton's poem, considered serious stuff, had achieved enormous status as a national masterpiece, and so the relative merits of its complex, rhetorical strategies were the subject of a lot of cultured debate. Bunyan's narrative, in contrast, was never considered to be a work worth plumbing for architectonic profundities, even by admirers of its moral and psychological "lessons." Insufficiently satisfying visual treatments of the comprehensive (and in fact psychologically complex) pattern of Christian's dream-journey therefore proliferated; and so it was a deteriorating convention that Blake fell heir to, at least from his point of view.

This slacking-off of a holistic approach to illustrating the *Progress* took place in three major ways. Looking at a panorama of examples from the earliest illustrated edition down through graphic representations accorded the text by some of Blake's contemporaries (Figs. B1–B58, Appendix B), we see, first, a gradual neglect of the concept of purely pictorial unity within each sequence of designs. Second, when changes are made in the established iconography, the new mix of subjects chosen follows an increasingly haphazard plan, blurring thematic connections between scenes, reducing the visibility of typological recurrences, and altogether diminishing the semantic potential of the serial format. Finally, with respect to individual designs, a trend toward stylistic realism in the work of later illustrators virtually emasculates the symbolic quality of the dream-images Bunyan evoked within his own half-naturalistic, half-emblematic literary mode.[7] Therefore, whether by weaknesses of composition, of iconographic invention, or of style, the run-of-the-mill *Progress* designs vitiated the organic and archetypal structure of the text. Even without Linnell and the Ancients to prod him in the ways described earlier, this discrepancy between the power of Bunyan's conception and the paucity of the illustrative tradition might well have been enough to motivate Blake's attempt at wresting for re-presentation from an allegory he increasingly deemed "full of" vision a clearer mythographic shape and content.

The declining ability of the pictorial tradition to provide readers of Bunyan's fable with an interpretive tool is already evident in the illustrations to the fourteenth edition of the *Progress* (1695). There, two sets of designs—the first English plates made for the fifth edition (1680) and a series of Dutch engravings published in a Flemish translation in 1685—were abridged and combined in a group of fourteen woodcut copies that became the standard iconographic reference for thousands of readers throughout many decades (Figs. B24–B36).[8] The random conflation of these two pictorial series, however, destroyed the not inconsiderable sequential integrity of each and resulted in a collection of visual motifs that had a very weak formal unity. Thereafter, the very idea of a well-ordered visual narrative that could make its own statement independent of the Bunyan text was fairly well eclipsed—until 1728, when a completely new set of engravings appeared in the large centennial edition of Bunyan's works (Figs. B37–B50).[9] These fresh copper-cuts were heavily influenced by the previous hodgepodge series with respect to iconographic topics. Nevertheless, the care of their designer, John Sturt, for making a complete aesthetic statement through the balance and interrelation of purely formal factors in adjacent compositions had a transformative effect both on the invention of separate plates and on the visual impact of the series as a whole. Thus, the new engravings formed a harmonious grouping with a satisfying pictorial continuity. The viewer could "read" these prints in the manner soon to be advocated by Hogarth, whose own serial illustrations so powerfully documented a quite different sort of "progress."

In the treatment of its allegorical subject matter, however, Sturt's sequence suffered from the absence of an interpretive point of view, so that the narrative development of images had finally no real conceptual significance. This did not disturb either the publishers or populace of the eighteenth century, however. The same designs were used over and over again in subsequent editions for almost fifty years, and we can be certain that Blake knew them, even admired them, because he made several "quotations" of Sturt's visual thought in his own Bunyan drawings.[10] At the same time it must be stressed once more that Blake deliberately set himself against many of the axioms of the illustrative convention established by Bunyan's publishers and carried on by the example of Sturt. Like Los, his own creative hero in the mythology of his poetic canon, for whom "Striving with Systems" (J 11) was a prophetic habit, Blake had both temperamental and didactic reasons for tampering with the old, illustrative clichés. Partly it was a natural playfulness mixed with the desire to fashion a boldly "original derivation," and partly it was a mode of serious criticism, a way of arguing with and emending the limited hermeneutical vision of his predecessors. An obvious and emblematic instance of such a change is Blake's decision to double the number of drawings customarily allotted to the plot of the *Progress:* instead of fourteen plates, Blake gives us twenty-eight. This broad advertisement of a difference between himself and his predecessors may be seen as a wry boast on Blake's part that his graphic commentary had twice the value, and twice the energy, of the work of standard illustrators bound by the fourteen-plate convention. But the doubling also made a deeper point, as we shall see later when analyzing the leitmotif of replication maintained in various ways throughout Blake's pictorial gloss of Bunyan's dream-fable.

In the 1790s, fashions in illustrating Bunyan changed markedly, as did the received opinion of the virtues of *The Pilgrim's Progress.* Honored in this era more for its scenes of homiletic naturalism than for its allegoric modality, Bunyan's story became subject to illustrators who strove to represent individual episodes in the manner of contemporary "genre paintings" or "conversation pieces." These were paintings conceived as self-contained family portraiture, stressing domestic settings and a vivid interest in local, realistic detail. Consequently, the artists operating in this idiom gave little thought to recreating a sustained, visual context for Bunyan's overall mythos. The sense that the plot of the *Progress* shaped a continuous allegory was further diluted by the "gallery" effect of editions carrying what amounted to an anthology of engravings designed and executed by many different artists working without reference to one another.[11] This conglomerate aspect of the contemporary trend was reversed by one of Blake's archrivals, Thomas Stothard, who made a set of sixteen Bunyan designs that were engraved and issued separately from the text in 1788 (Figs. B51–B58).[12] Stothard's prettified compositions were still in the genre-painting mode, however (see, for example, Fig. B51). Although they appeared as a graphic series—a little pamphlet of loose-leaf prints—the emphasis remained on the excerpted scene, not on the development of one emblematic moment into the next. Furthermore, only eight of these sixteen designs actually illustrated Part I of the *Progress*. Stothard's well-known predilection for feminine forms drew him inexorably to Bunyan's Part II, the dream sequel that deals with the fate of Christiana and her brood, leading him to give equal time to the distaff side of the quest for salvation. In this case, however, equal time meant virtually half time as far as the usual complement of fourteen plates for Part I was concerned.[13] Reducing by six the number of illustrations traditionally allotted Christian's story thus had the effect of shrinking the scope and potential of serial commentary even more. Nevertheless, Stothard's designs were very popular and influential. Few illustrators after him failed to allude to at least one of his compositions (usually the celebrated treatment of Christian fighting Apollyon; Fig. B54), and in this Blake was no exception, as we shall see.

From the French Revolution on into the middle of the nineteenth century, Bunyan's fable gained in appeal as a stock example of the problems of a developing consciousness. Because of a sharp decline in the orthodox religious focus of its new, fin-de-siècle audience, the book was dissociated from its sectarian applications and became available as an emblem of the paradigmatic quest for inner change itself. M. H. Abrams and other scholars of the period have shown us how the literary structures of Scripture and the archetypal dynamism of other standard spiritual forms were taken over piecemeal by the secular age and made to serve the new social, ideological, and psychological views of the individual's relation to culture.[14] Creating modern inversions of the old numinous images, cast in a multiplicity of fresh idioms and genres, was part of the ethos and part of the sport of the revolutionary inheritance. The story and imagery of *The Pilgrim's Progress* obeyed the common rule in this. It was versified, it was parodied, it supplied the context for political satire in prose and graphic caricature; it appeared summarized on broadsheets, was turned into a collection of hymns, became the subject of numerous literary commentaries and explanatory "keys," was mapped and then manufactured as a popular jigsaw puzzle, was translated into dozens of languages (including "words-of-one-syllable" for children), and, of course, continued to be issued in more than a score of different editions as well as in several series of prints sold, like Stothard's designs, apart from the text.[15] But with the exception of some unpublished drawings by Flaxman (a few of which had marked similarities to Blake's Bunyan-related engravings of the 1790s, as we have seen),[16] most of the contemporary *Progress* designs were tame in conception, polished in execution, and polite in overall manner. The crude but more vigorous impact achieved in the woodcut illustrations of earlier and cheaper editions of the text was now consciously disparaged and avoided. Yet when Blake set about designing his own full-fledged pictorial rendition of the Bunyan story, it was to this older aesthetic that he deliberately returned.

Few of the critics who first saw Blake's watercolors discerned the purpose of this aesthetic. William Michael Rossetti, initiating critical mention of the designs in 1863, went so far as to impute blame to the conjectured "handiwork" of Blake's wife, Catherine, for some of the very effects I will be considering as intentional, structural elements of the "Grand Theme" treated.[17] In fact, viewers and reviewers a century after Rossetti were only a little more tolerant of these same retrogressive strategies, as we can see from a commentary on the 1960 showing of the designs at the Frick Collection. The critic here is taking a censorious view of two designs in particular, Plates 6 and 12: "In 'Christian Drawn Out of The Slough By Help,' the anatomy is sadly distorted in favor of the symbolic pattern, while in 'The Man in The Iron Cage' . . . the effort at the horrendous approaches the comic."[18] Apparently the writer of this review did not consider that Blake may have intended the effects perceived, and did not see that the meaning of Plate 12, for example, depends precisely on the way "the horrendous approaches the comic."

This misunderstanding about the aim of Blake's figural distortions and of his pseudosimplistic style is today an old story that has been amply corrected by a host of art historians and literary scholars of recent years.[19] In the present instance, however, Blake's partial reliance on an earlier mode of illustrating Bunyan will be shown to have other motives as well. Visual allusion to elements of that mode plays both a symbolic and a compositional role in these designs, and it is inexorably intertwined with Blake's desire to rescue a primary hermeneutic vision from the traditional *Progress* iconography as well as from the archetypal stratum of the text itself.

A READING OF BLAKE'S
PILGRIM'S PROGRESS DESIGNS

The first thing to be noted in looking at the plotting of these watercolor drawings is a point familiar to us from our study of the emblems of the *Gates* in the previous chapter: the Bunyan series not only illustrates but *is* a narrative progress in which the act of pilgrimage belongs to the eye and mind of the viewer. This time, though, the general course of events, like stations along the way, are preset by another man's imaginative itinerary. For Blake, whose visionary powers thrived on revisionary impulses, this state of affairs had never been and was not now a deterrent to prophetic inventiveness. On the contrary, fresh from his most highly acclaimed success in this line—the contemporaneous *Job* engravings—Blake approached the task of remapping the adventures dreamed by Bunyan's narrator with a sure knowledge of the artistic strategies best suited to guide the attentive spectator through successive stages of an imaginal transformation process.

Still, the *Progress,* as a unique construct in its own right, presented new challenges to Blake's language of art, since the visual dynamics governing the relationship of elements within and between drawings had to be adapted to the special episodic character of the fictional format. Until this time, all Blake's major efforts as an interpretive illustrator had been applied to poetic texts. Even the Book of Job is more hymn and poem than prose narrative, and the incidents that carry the symbolic action forward in that scriptural work do not relate to movement through the world in the way the acts of a story or a novel do. Now, as Blake addressed himself to converting the protonovelistic structure of the *Progress* into pictorial terms, expansion and contraction of narrative time become a stylistic issue with new semantic overtones. Therefore, the choice of subjects to be depicted and the grouping of these choices in perceptible sets and subsets called on new rhetorical sensibilities, new methods, new graphic devices. Also, as we shall see, the experience of journeying from one plate to the next takes on a peculiarly iconic cast, since that very action (journeying) is simultaneously the dominant trope of the plot. Characters in the pictures point forward and backward and upward in design after design, giving road directions at once to the travelers who are the protagonists and the travelers who are the readers. Thus there is a clear congruence between the tactics of representation and the controlling imagery of the text (something that is not true of most of Blake's other great serial illustrations), and this congruence deeply affects the visionary hermeneutics of the series as a whole. As Bunyan said of this text, so Blake could say of his pictorial narrative:

> This Book will make a Travailer of thee,
> If by its Counsel thou wilt ruled be.
>
> *(PP 6)*

Bunyan's prophetic promise to the reader in the couplet just cited, which appears in the opening "apology" of the book, is balanced at the end of his narrative by verses that warn us against both over- and underinterpreting:

> *Now Reader, I have told my Dream to thee;*
> *See if thou canst Interpret it to me;*
> *Or to thy self, or Neighbour: but take heed*
> *Of mis-interpreting . . .*
>
> > *Take heed also, that thou be not extream,*
> > *In playing with the out-side of my Dream:*
> > *Nor let my figure, or similitude,*
> > *Put thee into a laughter or a feud;*
> > *Leave this for Boys and Fools; but as for thee,*
> > *Do thou the substance of my matter see.*
>
> > > *Put by the Curtains, look within my Vail;*
> > > *Turn up my Metaphors and do not fail:*
> > > *There, if thou seekest them, such things to find,*
> > > *As will be helpful to an honest mind.*
>
> > > > *What of my* dross *thou findest there, be bold*
> > > > *To throw away, but yet preserve the Gold.*
>
> > > > > (PP 164)

Bunyan hints here that his message is both hidden and deep—at once under wraps (curtained, veiled), and underground like roots or bulbs that we must "turn up," or like precious metal needing to be mined. He asks us to penetrate what Blake might have characterized as the "apparent surface" (*MHH* 14) of the "litteral expression" (*M* 42) of metaphoric and allegoric similitudes in order to witness through them the "substance."[20] Like a proto-Freudian, Bunyan cautions us, therefore, against getting stuck on the manifest level of the plot and its imagery—the outside of the dream—and entreats us instead to sacrifice all such fixations on appearance for a grasp of the latent, inner meaning, the true "gold." Yet he urges us not to "mis-interpret" through the wrong kind of allegorization, by which he seems to mean that we should not twist the text defensively or nefariously to prove a self-serving point, "for that, instead/Of doing good, will but thyself abuse:/By misinterpreting evil insues."

I believe that Blake deliberately addressed himself to all these specific commands, challenged to action especially by Bunyan's open invitation to interpret and play back to him, its author, the latent significance of the whole dream format. Blake certainly did boldly throw away the dross for the gold, eliminating from his pictorial consideration many episodes and exchanges embellishing the "outside" of Bunyan's narrative. Even more importantly, though, he took with high seriousness the seemingly conventional "figure or similitude" of the dreamer dreaming, and he made that authorial and narratorial perspective the chief and radical "substance" of *his* "matter." Thus, it was not so much the salient scenes of the story as the evolution of the consciousness creating those scenes that Blake saw to be the real visionary focus of the *Progress*. As far as he was concerned, the trouble with the book (considered apart from its illustrations) was that in it this central focus remained hopelessly "lost & clouded in Fable & Allegory" (E555/K605). At bottom the quarrel here, then, is with Bunyan's choice of genre: neither fable nor allegory will do as a medium of visionary consciousness, because in Blake's eyes they are by nature inferior semiotic structures designed to stunt and veil rather than to support and reveal the capacious exfoliations of imaginations "just and true" (*M* 1). As we saw in Chapter 1, Blake articulated this notion in 1810 when he first cited the *Progress* as a text "full of," yet generically antithetical to, "Vision": "Note here that Fable or Allegory is Seldom without some Vision Pilgrim's Progress is full of it the Greek Poets the same *but Allegory & Vision ought to be known as Two Distinct Things & so calld for the Sake of Eternal Life*" (VLJ, E554/K604–5; italics added).

This statement is strong. Cast in the prophetic terms of Christ's judgmental distinction in the Gospels between the sheep and the goats (Matthew 25:31–46), it pictures the adoption of allegory over vision as a fatal eschatological error, ruinous of the very "Eternal Life" that Bunyan's pilgrims so determinedly pursue. In other words, Blake implies that Bunyan's generic mode of fictional expression (allegory) is ontologically inimical to the vision of salvation that is the work's purported subject. His own idea of salvation thus includes deliverance from the straitjacket of Bunyan's allegorical view of salvation. The problem seems to be that allegory as a form is too much like the "single vision of Newton's sleep": it dulls perception because it reflects a mechanical mentality and builds on a code of memory that uses metaphors as if they were dead counters for abstract values. By contrast, according to Blake, images at work within any genuinely visionary structure never simply substitute as fixed vehicles for displaced and equally fixed tenors. Instead they function as complex "identities" that literally hold their own, evolving, unfolding, and yielding only to further images rendered meaningful through their interrelations and extended contextual references.[21] In particular, visionary images do not stand for or "Relate to Moral Virtues" (K614), and they therefore never sink into the reductionist format of moralized fable that Blake felt Bunyan's rendering of the *Progress* ultimately relied on.

Blake's work on these Bunyan designs, therefore, can be seen not only as a critical interpretation of the received text, but also as an expressly "formal" salvage mission: a way of restoring the book's authentic imaginal content to its appropriate aesthetic genre. For despite many patches of imagistic power, the fundamental vision of Bunyan's tale, in Blake's opinion, remained trapped and trivialized by the rigid overlay of the book's allegorizing perspective. So it was that he strove in his illustrations to recreate a structure for the *Progress* that would free it from the parochial restraints of moral dogma, that would stress the figural and typological over the doctrinal import of the dream, and that could rise above the formula of "clouded . . . Fable & Allegory" to be experienced as "Real Vision" (E555/K605).

In asserting this much, I realize that I may seem to be applying to Blake's work the same hermeneutic yardstick that I claim Blake applied to Bunyan's. But this is only partly the case, since Blake's designs need rescue only from neglect; they do not require generic restructuring in order to be understood as visionary. Nevertheless, the present analysis is in its own right an interpretation of a revisionary interpretation of a narrative of a dream *about* successive interpretations, and simply by being in this line of descent I have felt bound to observe the very caveats Bunyan requested his readers heed. In my reading of Blake's drawings, therefore, I, too, have tried to emphasize the type in the figure and the spirit in the "Litteral expression" while sticking close both to the precise images presented and to what I understand is the core of the controlling "similitude": the relation of the dreamer to the dream.

In sum, the "metaphors" and compositional devices of this series that I have been most concerned to "turn up," to use Bunyan's analogy, are the very ones I believe Blake consciously planted in order to transform, "for the Sake of Eternal Life," allegory into vision. And although in my analyses of the drawings I sometimes employ terms foreign to Blake that are largely taken from the parlance of modern depth psychology, my intent is not to re-allegorize or impose an alien system on his achievement; rather, it is to describe, in as readily answerable a metalanguage as I could find, the profoundly psychological conception of the *Progress* that Blake himself unfolds with such calculated purpose in the symbolic vocabulary of his pictorial/visionary form. As I suggest throughout this study, there is no separating the visionary or the aesthetic from the psychological in Blake's work. In fact, it is his unflagging assertion of the homologous relationship among these modes that defines and constitutes the enlarged significance of each. Thus, from Blake's perspective, unlike Bunyan's, the transcendental function of the spirit can be regarded as an integral, psycho-aesthetic component of consciousness itself. Psyche—or imagination—is its creative ground; redemption is therefore not a divine fiat passed upon us from an external source, but rather an internally generated expansion of human perception.

The result in the present case is that wherever the text of the *Progress* pictures a necessary disjunction between the divine and the human imagination (or, analogously, between dreamer and dream-content), Blake's drawings picture a necessary identity. And where Bunyan's dream-hero seeks a final deliverance *from* psychological process, Blake envisions the opposite: a therapeutic awak-

PLATES

PLATE 1 The Dreamer Dreams a Dream

PLATE 2 Christian Reading in His Book

PLATE 3   Christian Meets Evangelist

PLATE 4   Christian Pursued by Obstinate and Pliable

PLATE 5   Christian in the Slough of Despond

PLATE 6 Christian Drawn out of the Slough by Help

PLATE 7 Christian Directed by Worldly Wiseman

PLATE 8   Christian Fears the Fire from the Mountain

PLATE 9   Christian Falls at the Feet of Evangelist

PLATE 10 Christian Knocks at the Wicket Gate

PLATE 11   The Gate Is Opened by Good-will

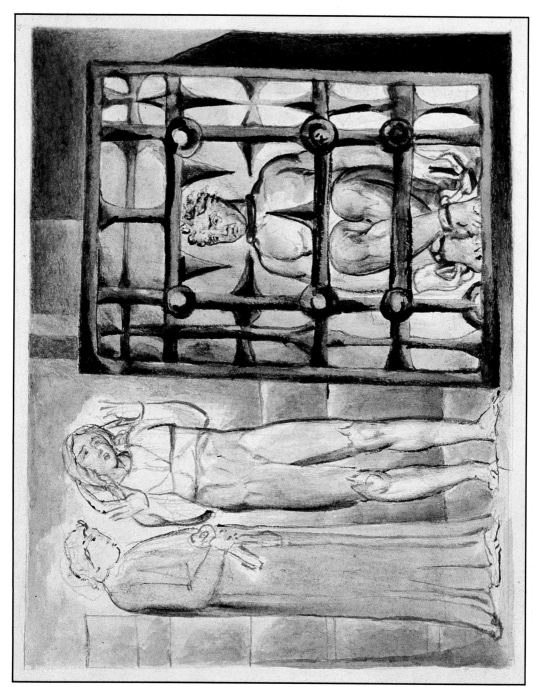

PLATE 12   The Man in the Iron Cage

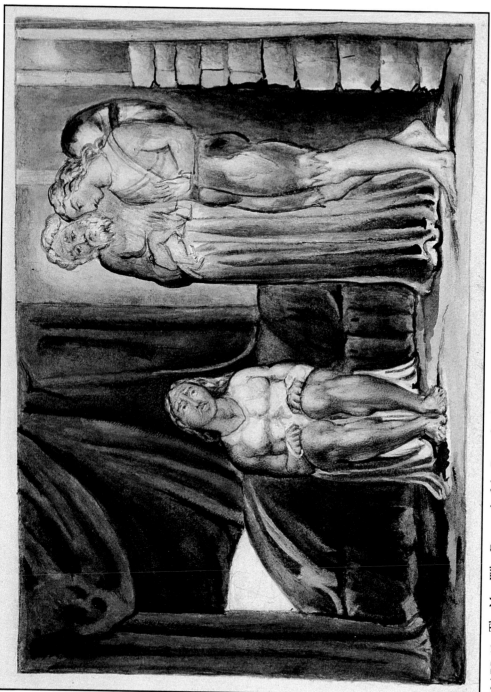

PLATE 13   The Man Who Dreamed of the Day of Judgment

PLATE 14 Christian at the Cross

PLATE 15   Christian Met by the Three Shining Ones

PLATE 16 Christian Climbs Hill Difficulty

PLATE 17 Christian at the Arbour

PLATE 18 Christian Passes the Lions

PLATE 19   Christian Goes Forth Armed

PLATE 20   Christian Fights Apollyon

PLATE 21 Christian and Faithful Conversing

PLATE 22 Vanity Fair

PLATE 23 Faithful's Martyrdom

PLATE 24 Christian and Hopeful in Doubting Castle

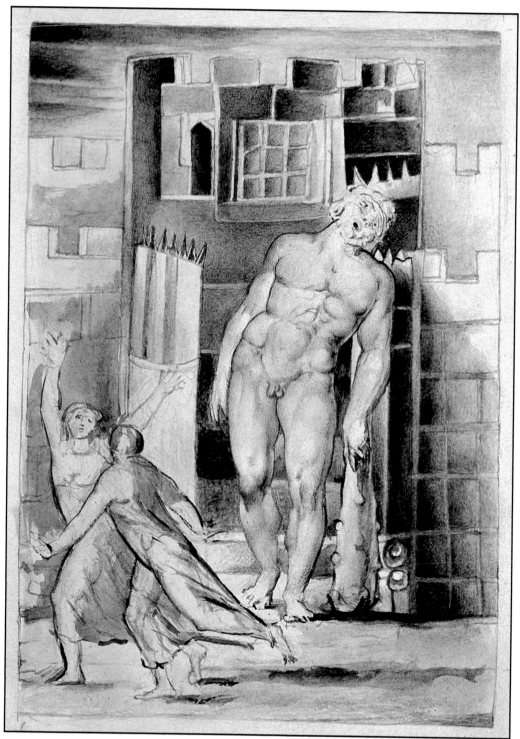

PLATE 25 Christian and Hopeful Escape Giant Despair

PLATE 26   The Shepherds of the Delectable Mountains

PLATE 27   Christian and Hopeful in the River

PLATE 28   At the Gates of Heaven

ening *into* it. In terms of the plot of the *Progress,* this meant that Blake understood the salvatory power sought by the characters of the dream to lie in the rhetorical strategies of their creator's (that is, the dreamer/narrator's) dreaming psyche. For Blake, that is, the story was largely about the visionary aim of the dreamer's unconscious to dream the dream awake, thereby exemplifying a typological process of psychological individuation. Bunyan, in contrast, virtually ignored the significance of the narrator's role as shaper of the dream. His text unfolds as a psychobiography not of the dreamer, but of Christian; and on the rare occasions when the narrator appears as an effective participant in the action of his own dream,[22] the event does not resonate with self-reflexive implications. Rather, it seems a mere by-product of his dream-hero's spiritual progress toward an external divine reality. So it is that Bunyan left in a latent state the intimations that his fable contained about the curative, self-regulatory structure of the dreamer's imaginal life. The fact that this latency now and then surfaces, as if against Bunyan's better judgment, in such formal elements as the figural patterning of the bildungsroman plot or the richness of the narrative's intradiegetic complexity, provides one of the challenges of interpreting *The Pilgrim's Progress.*

In Blake's interpretation, as we shall see, the text's predominantly single vision of spiritual development is not only doubled, it is quadrupled. His pictorial series keeps one channel open to record Christian's symbolic individuation process as hero of the dream, another to show the dreamer's connection with the mythic elements of the dream content, and a third to relay the dreamer's representational procedure as an embodiment of his deepening visionary perspective; a fourth, finally, focuses on the spectator's developing hermeneutic as part of his or her process of awareness, for these drawings, like all other designs in Blake's visual canon, are didactic in the sense that they teach and have as their goal the activation of the transforming and transformative imagination of the viewer.

My aim in the reading of the designs that follows is to forward Blake's aim as much as possible and to encourage the viewer to relate to Blake's vision the way Christian related to the visions he encountered in the House of *his* Interpreter when he sang these words:

> *Here I have seen things rare, and profitable;*
> *Thing pleasant, dreadful, things to make me stable*
> *In what I have begun to take in hand:*
> *Then let me think on them, and understand*
> *Wherefore they shewed me was, and let me be*
> *Thankful, O good Interpreter, to thee.*

> *(PP 37)*

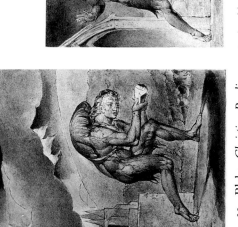

FIG. 22   Blake, *Christian Reading in His Book*

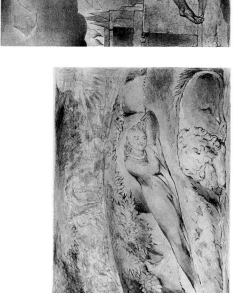

FIG. 21   Blake, *The Dreamer Dreams a Dream*

FIG. 23   Blake, *Christian Meets Evangelist*

FIG. 26   Blake, *Christian Drawn out of the Slough by Help*

FIG. 25   Blake, *Christian in the Slough of Despond*

FIG. 24   Blake, *Christian Pursued by Obstinate and Pliable*

FIG. 27　Blake, *Christian Directed by Worldly Wiseman*

FIG. 28　Blake, *Christian Fears the Fire from the Mountain*

FIG. 29　Blake, *Christian Falls at the Feet of Evangelist*

FIG. 30　Blake, *Christian Knocks at the Wicket Gate*

FIG. 31　Blake, *The Gate Is Opened by Good-will*

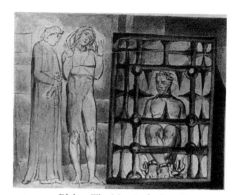

FIG. 32　Blake, *The Man in the Iron Cage*

FIG. 33　Blake, *The Man Who Dreamed of the Day of Judgment*

FIG. 36 Blake, *Christian Climbs Hill Difficulty*

FIG. 37 Blake, *Christian at the Arbour*

FIG. 38 Blake, *Christian Passes the Lions*

FIG. 35 Blake, *Christian Met by the Three Shining Ones*

FIG. 39 Blake, *Christian Goes Forth Armed*

FIG. 34 Blake, *Christian at the Cross*

FIG. 40 Blake, *Christian Fights Apollyon*

FIG. 41 Blake, *Christian and Faithful Conversing*

FIG. 42 Blake, *Vanity Fair*

FIG. 43 Blake, *Faithful's Martyrdom*

FIG. 44 Blake, *Christian and Hopeful in Doubting Castle*

FIG. 45 Blake, *Christian and Hopeful Escape Giant Despair*

FIG. 46 Blake, *The Shepherds of the Delectable Mountains*

FIG. 48 Blake, *At the Gates of Heaven*

FIG. 47 Blake, *Christian and Hopeful in the River*

DRAWING 1

As I walk'd through the wilderness of this world,
I lighted on a certain place, where was a Denn; And
I laid me down in that place to sleep: And as I slept I
dreamed a Dream. (*PP* 8)

The subject here (Plate 1, Fig. 21) relates to the Dantesque opening of Bunyan's text in which the narrator quickly situates himself inside the deepest
chamber of a nest of progressively more intimate enclosures. We move with
him through this vortex of inwardization as he tells us first that he is in the
world's wilderness, then in a den within that world, then in a sleep inside the
den, then in a dream inside the sleep. Blake picks up and develops this idea of
interior embeddedness, making it a major pictorial theme both of the present
drawing and of the series as a whole.

The plate shows a man, eyes closed, reclining on the rise of a small hill under
thick and verdant beech trees.[23] He wears a blue robe that enfolds his limbs like
a loose but full-length straitjacket, or like a shroud or a cocoon. His right foot
(incompletely drawn) protrudes from the robe at the lower left of the plate and
seems to have the characteristics of a leaf stem. By this detail is conveyed the
sense that the sleeper exists psychologically in a prehuman, vegetative state:
the natural condition of the "natural" man. The cone-shaped configuration of
his wrapped body further suggests latent organic development as it calls up
visual associations to a new leaf as yet unfolded.[24]

The man occupies the middle of three horizontal bands into which the
composition is spatially divided. Below him, in the lowest band on the right
side of the plate, a lion lies asleep. The lion and the man bear a certain
resemblance: both rest with their heads on their forearms, both have curly
manes of reddish-gold hair, and both are encapsulated in their separate spaces.
The animal's head, furthermore, is situated in a vertical line of descent directly
beneath the man's head, and his body forms the base of a triangle that reaches
completion at the apex of a smaller, internal, roughly similar triangle shaped
by the angles of the man's arms, shoulder, and head. Visually, then, the lion
seems to be an integral part of the man's reality. Apparently symbolizing a
brute and sluggish aspect of the dreamer's psyche, he faces away from the
vector of the visionary realm depicted in the arc of the rainbow above.

This rainbow segment constitutes the uppermost of the composition's three
horizontal bands. It cuts a swath through the foliage of the trees, creating a
protective dome over the two sleepers. Within its arch, moving from left to
right, are figures representative of the incidents in the dreamer's dream. They
are indistinctly drawn—indistinctly on purpose, we may suppose, to suggest
that at this stage of their presentation their visionary content is still only in

embryo.[25] None of the figures hazily formulated in this way matches exactly the figures to be shown in the ensuing set of designs, but hindsight enables us to identify these miniature scenes as different portrayals of, in order, (1) Christian leaving the City of Destruction; (2) Christian dueling with Apollyon; (3) a sojourner, possibly Christian, standing in an arbor, possibly the arbor of Beulah; and (4) light streaming from the Celestial City, which is Christian's goal. In other words, the rainbow scenario is at once a preview and a synoptic epitome of an unfolding still to come. The fact that the whole dream plot with its apotheotic close is proleptically pictured here makes this a vision that follows the Hegelian model at least insofar as it has its end in its beginning. Blake underscores that point both by including in the rainbow the light from the Heavenly City (a light that represents the story's end) and by having it bear a double visionary function in this beginning design. First, he gives it the traditional connotation of a rising sun—the dawn of consciousness—which breaks through and disperses the form of the rainbow in the upper right of the plate (although as a metaphor of the sun it can also be seen as the source of that rainbow). Second, this light is located in the climactic position along the main diagonal of the picture plane, where it caps and attracts the form of the dreamer. Visually, the figure whom we recognize as the originator of the vision is also "in" the vision to the extent that he and the sunlight imagery of his dream share a symbiotic relation analogous in both proportion and placement to the one his body shares with his head. Together the dreamer and the last segment of his dream make up a complete pictorial statement on one compositional axis about the inclination of the whole series.

Perhaps the most important figure in the rainbow from a structural standpoint, however, is the one that is also the most topically problematic: the man walking in the arbor. He is important because he both holds the center ground of the upper horizontal band and marks the apex of the design's principal organizing triangle, inside which the shapes of the two sleepers—the lion and the man dreaming—form their own interior triangles, as previously described. The eye is naturally drawn to the controlling position occupied by the walking man, who thus seems to represent the culmination of the dreamer's own imaginative nature, the visionary fulfillment and release of the hampered animal and vegetative selves embodied under his aegis in the natural world below. Moreover, on the basis of figural transformation alone he can be taken to represent the risen counterpart of the prone and sleeping narrator. As the blue-robed narrator lies beneath the beech trees in the arbor of his dream, so the blue-robed man in the center of that dream stands erect beneath the arbor of Bunyan's Beulah. The two forms reflect and rely on each other, both compositionally and iconographically; here the message that the dreamer is striving to dream himself awake is made visual in a doubly compelling way.

Why, then, is this figure problematical? Because he has such an ambiguous referent in the actual story of the *Progress*. If, as I am claiming, he is meant to signify one of the dwellers in the vineyards of Bunyan's Beulah (the only dream location where there is an arbor with an archway once Christian, as here in the rainbow, has passed Apollyon), is he supposed to be Christian, the Gardener, or the "King" of that place (*PP*, 155)? A literal reading would demand that he be identified as the king (himself an avatar of Jehovah-Jesus), for only the king is described by Bunyan's narrator as walking there among the ancient trees. But Blake seems to have amalgamated all these personae into one figure capable of functioning as the summative projection of the dreamer's own identity. That this figure is synecdochic and interpretive, a distillation of all the characters rather than a depiction of any single dream entity, is further suggested by the fact that Blake offers no separate illustration of this episode in the ensuing series as he does of the other incidents pictured in the rainbow. Thus, it stands out as an occasion symbolizing, but not portraying, other symbolic occasions, and in particular it can be seen as a typological fulfillment of an earlier arbor episode, where Christian backtracks down Hill Difficulty to retrieve his abandoned identity scroll. *That* episode *is* lavishly illustrated by Blake in a separate drawing for the series, a drawing that prominently re-capitulates the rainbow motif of the opening design we are discussing here (see Plate 17). Clearly the motif of visionary self-recovery that the "Lost Traveller" episode in the arbor represents for Blake is the paradigmatic theme of the sequence as a whole; it is no wonder, then, that the initial design gives such structural importance to the figure in the rainbow who most strongly, if most subtly, alludes to that theme.[26]

The formal fitness and conceptual originality of this first drawing cannot be fully gauged until the whole series of twenty-eight designs has been studied. But its main innovation as an interpretive comment on Bunyan's *Progress* shows up the moment it is compared with the book's traditional frontispiece (Fig. 49). There, in a perennially reissued illustration that came to be known as "the sleeping portrait," the dreamer is represented in the clothes and with the features of John Bunyan himself.[27] Following the broad hints of the text, the designer of this standard frontispiece not only lumps together the personae of the author, narrator, and dreamer, but he renders the resultant personality as a worldly man (copied after Robert White's official likeness of Bunyan) who belongs in a separate category and is pictured as qualitatively different from the allegorical figures of his dream. Pictorial styles alone distinguish him unmis-takably from the creatures of his imagination (although other indicators, such as age and dress, also contribute to the disjunction). His portrait-bust, for example, is modeled and engraved in naturalistic detail according to a system of cross-hatching widely accepted as a technique of realism, while the dream characters, both here and in the subsequent prints of the series, are drawn in a

FIG. 49 Robert White, *The Sleeping Portrait* for *The Pilgrim's Progress*

comparatively primitive mode, their embodiment dependent largely on simple, linear definition. Also, the scale of the portrait figure, whose full form is too big for the picture frame, suggests that he derives from an order of reality alien to the visionary space and spiritual content of the dream.

Now if we turn again to Blake's opening design we see how emphatically and deliberately he has transformed the elements of the standard frontispiece in order to close the gap between the existential realms of dreamer and dream. The sleeping man in Blake's drawing is clearly not meant to represent the conventional likeness of Bunyan. He is not wearing puritan garb, he is not a portly middle-aged man older than the dream hero, and nothing about him suggests that he is either an author or a preacher. On the contrary, he is an idealized figure, dressed in a long flowing robe such as the idealized figures of his dream also wear. In form, in age, in dress he is of the same mold as the characters of his vision. This is the major change and the essential one. It alerts us to the fact that Blake (alone among his contemporaries) has taken the allegorical dream convention of the *Progress* not as a mere rhetorical cliché, but rather in a literal and modern psychological sense, as an authentic form of imaginal expression that both reflects and affects the psyche that generates it.[28] To put it another way, the implicit problematics of artistic unity that in this work both binds and separates the teller and the tale is viewed by Blake as part of the latent meaning of that tale. Blake knows that the phenomenology of mental life has its own aesthetic, its own imaginative or poetic justice whereby every aspect of a dream is an imaginal permutation of the dreamer; he knows that a dreaming man is an artist who can do neither more nor less than dream of himself while he dreams *up* himself, reaching for regeneration through psychic imagining which is at once self-dreaming and soul-making. Blake thus simply disallows Bunyan's authorial insistence that there is a separation between the name and nature of the dream narrator, on the one hand, and of the dream protagonists—especially Christian—on the other. Instead Blake reads that distancing device adopted by Bunyan as itself a fiction, behind which lies an antithetical fiction containing the allegory's visionary truth. The artistic meaning of Christian's story, in other words, depends entirely, for Blake, on its context as an archetypal vision projected by the partisan psyche of an individual seeking knowledge of his own being.

As we shall see, this reading enables Blake to interpret the many doublings, repetitions, and typological fulfillments of the primary text in a way that structures his own pictorial narrative into a revisionary myth about the hermeneutics of the imaginal and the quest for wholeness of self. Two more deliberate variations of the original frontispiece illustrate this procedure. First is the treatment of the figure of the lion. In the traditional portrait-frontispiece, the figure of the lion has an emblematic status separate from that of the other figures. It is a sort of visual pun, functioning as an incidental signifier of the word *Denn,* which appears in the text's opening sentence. That den, according to the author's marginal gloss on the text, is in its turn another incidental signifier, this time operating as a code word for the jail where Bunyan was incarcerated when he wrote the *Progress.*[29] The earliest illustrators, to ensure that the pictorialized lion in its den would serve the same arbitrary sign-function as the glossed image of the text, drew the creature and his lair on a scale noticeably different from the one used for the realistic portrait of Bunyan. It is a miniature lion and a miniature den that greet our eye below the bust of the author shown sleeping; the boundary line between the plausible, naturalistic environment and the metaphoric allusion is clear and abrupt, and what the viewer experiences most strongly is the dissociation of the two ontological realities. In Blake's drawing, however, the lion's world and the dreamer's world are continuous. Even if both figures are themselves asleep to that fact, *we* recognize their strategic interdependence, compositionally and conceptually, in the complex mapping of that opening scene. Later on, therefore, when the form of the lion returns, doubled, flanking Christian's pathway to House Beautiful, we are prepared to appreciate the recurrence as a significant transformation of the state of the dreamer's psyche (see Plate 18). The meaning of that transformation is a subject I leave for later discussion; here it is enough to point out Blake's careful seeding of pictorial images and forms that in the course of the series are themselves progressively integrated to tell a visual story *about* progressive integration of the personality on the inward, imaginal plane.

Blake's last noteworthy manipulation of the traditional frontispiece—his treatment of the representative dream content—presses the viewer even more certainly toward a psychological reading of the allegory. Thus, taking from the original "sleeping portrait" what appears to be a straight "film clip" of the early footage of Christian's journey (following him only as far as the wicket-gate),[30] Blake turns the upper portion of his picture into an interpretive overview of the whole dream: a panoramic vision, as we have seen, of the finished vision. In addition, he places this graphic prospectus of the complete narrative in a rainbow—a quintessentially metaphoric space according to scriptural tradition, and an iconographic sign in this instance that the dream is related to the dreamer as God's sign of promise in Genesis (the rainbow) relates to Noah and his descendents. Dream and rainbow, then, are emblems of the covenant between the human and the divine within the imagination of man; and so the dreamer, like Noah in "A Vision of the Last Judgment," can be understood to be an icon of that part of our nature that has the capacity to create images of our own transcendence.[31]

No such extension of meaning, no image of the comprehensive mapping of individual consciousness, is hinted at in the standard "sleeping portrait." On the contrary, both the vision and the present reality portrayed there is determinedly local. The figure of Christian is placed above the head of the author in a landscape that by normal pictorial conventions would readily be interpreted as continuous with the illusionist space of the main figure. Thus Christian actually appears to be trudging uphill *behind* Bunyan in a realistic environment; and despite his more sketchy delineation, the sense that Christian is a dream figure projected by the author's imagination is thereby visually blunted. Furthermore, the scene that Christian occupies is a scene limited to that of the first few pages of the text. In back of him is the City of Destruction;[32] ahead lies the wicket-gate, an initiatory threshold over which he soon will get to pass. The light emanating from the top of this gate, at the upper right of the engraving, is the light mentioned by Evangelist at a point only three pages into the narrative:

Then said *Evangelist,* pointing with his finger over a very wide Field, Do you see yonder *Wicket-gate?* The Man said, No. Then said the other, Do you see yonder shining light? He said, I think I do. Then said *Evangelist,* Keep that light in your eye, and go directly thereto, so shalt thou see the Gate; at which when thou knockest, it shall be told thee what thou shalt do. (*PP* 10)

The original "sleeping portrait" frontispiece thus lights the viewer's eye, like that of the still graceless Christian, up to and not further than the ritual starting line of the traveler's experience as a committed pilgrim. Apparently progress along the straight and narrow Way of Salvation does not begin for Bunyan's hero until after that juncture.[33] The city and gate pictured here are merely typological foreshadowings of the revelatory cities and gates to come, and Blake's handling of the dream scene in this first drawing utilizes that rhetorical fact.[34] Taking the iconography of the light over the wicket-gate from the original frontispiece engraving, he places it in his own design, position unchanged, yet proleptically transfigured into its fulfilled image: the light shining from the gate of the Celestial City where Christian at last will be welcomed home.

Blake's watercolor of the dreamer dreaming his dream is not, like the standard frontispiece, designed to be read on its own, divorced from the main sequence; rather, it is intended as an essential and corporate member of the full series that it initiates.[35] And because it has the function of an opening scene, it not only introduces a number of iconographic motifs that recur at significant points throughout the series, it also creates and teaches us a formal syntax governing the pictorial language of the compositions to come. Some of the elements of this graphic grammar involve a schematic color spectrum, symbolic directional attitudes, intimacy of scale, shallow depth perception, a meaningful use of frontality, and the dynamic interaction between vertical and horizontal movement. These factors, along with the many variations on figural themes, are the principal rhetorical devices we will chart and explicate in the course of describing the rest of the drawings below.

DRAWING 2

I dreamed, and behold *I saw a Man cloathed with Raggs, standing in a certain place, with his face from his own House, a Book in his hand, and a great burden upon his Back.* I looked, and saw him open the Book, and Read therein; and as he read, he wept and trembled: and not being able longer to contain, he brake out with a lamentable cry; saying, *what shall I do?* (*PP* 8)

This illustration (Plate 2, Fig. 22) shows Christian setting out from the City of Destruction under a storm cloud through which wrathful flames shine and shoot down. The guiding light of the previous design has now shifted to the left and become a goading fire. The lines in the text that describe this moment follow immediately the ones describing the first picture, and the composition renders that contiguity apparent by enlarging certain structural elements of its predecessor as if moving in with a zoom lens. The strong triangular configuration we observed in Plate 1, for example, is concentrated here into the shape of the main figure. Its triangularity is even emphasized by the pronounced contour and shading of Christian's upper arm, suggesting a right-angle perpendicular dropped from apex to base along an axis of symmetry running from the figure's right shoulder to his left heel. The ragged man and his shadow thus take the place of the dreaming man and lion in the opening design—another way Blake shows us Christian is to be considered a transformation of an aspect of the dreamer's psyche.

In equally important ways, though, this design contrasts with, rather than simply complements, Plate 1. First, the long side of the drawing's rectangular frame is now vertical. A certain swerving toward the personal is gained by this change alone, for the upright frame emulates the form of the upright human shape and acts somewhat like a full-length mirror for the viewer: as Christian makes a near-sighted scrutiny of the book that disturbs him, we look closely at the book-sized page on which he is portrayed and read his fretfulness with a matching perplexity of our own.[36] The viewer's perplexity has to do with focus and is occasioned in part by the scenic shift from external observation to internal confrontation. The schematic view of the dreamer's overall condition offered by the preceding design gives way here to a close-up of one of the emotional states his psyche is traveling through, and the transition is both sudden and drastic. Whereas the first illustration pictured the sleeping man in a wrapped serenity, suggesting a resolution of tempestuous mental weather through the natural symbolism of the rainbow, the tenor of this scene is of mounting turbulence. A storm is brewing, the man is bent double with wakeful pain and anguish, he wears ragged trousers and a torn shirt, and his limbs show extreme muscular exertion as if he were straining upward against the equal and opposite downward force of his burden. All these things tell us that the previous picture's peaceful dreamer is dreaming a dream of his own latent opposites. More details confirm it. The dome shape of the rainbow arch has become a double-curved, serpentine cloud form, and the colors that were integrated there are now dispersed into discrete objects: pants, shirt, burden, cloud, fire.

The fragmentation of the rainbow's color synthesis points up the fact that this picture not only contrasts with the previous picture but also is itself composed of self-contrastive forces. The dreamer's one garment is here differentiated into two, dividing the body at the waist into upper and lower portions. A similar clash of dualities is implied in the many countermovements of the composition as a whole, whereby downward vectors (such as the fire descending from heaven) are played against upward ones (such as Christian resisting his burden), creating a crisis of impinging pressures at the midpoint of maximal tension. The aesthetic midpoint of the entire picture exemplifies this fact, for there, at the juncture of opposing structural thrusts, Christian's burden is figured as itself an emblem of self-division, as if it were both growing from and striving with Christian's bodily form. It seems a human part of him, connected with ligaments at shoulder and waist: a humpbacked extension of his person exposing red streaks of raw flesh or blood-filled veins. At the same time, it displays a separate psychic autonomy, like a phobia or complex, in that it is grappling with the self-styled identity, that is, the ego portion of the personality. This psychological reading of the metaphor of the burden is strongly hinted at in the text—or at least a spiritual reading is, for later on, when the burden falls, Bunyan explicitly associates it with the guilt of Original Sin.[37] Nevertheless, Blake is alone among contemporary illustrators and commentators of the *Progress* in consciously stressing the burden's psychological nature, and he alone exploits the sense in which it is a metaphoric projection of both Christian and the dreamer-as-Christian.[38]

DRAWING 3

He looked this way, and that way, as if he would run; yet he stood still, because, as I perceived, he could not tell which way to go. I looked then, and saw a man named *Evangelist* coming to him, and asked, *Wherefore dost thou cry?* He answered, Sir, I perceive, by the Book in my hand, that I am Condemned to die, and after that to come to Judgment; and I find that I am not willing to do the first, nor able to do the second. . . .

Then said *Evangelist,* If this by thy condition, why standest thou still? He answered, Because I know not whither to go, Then he gave him a *Parchment-Roll,* and there was written within, *Fly from the wrath to come.*

The Man therefore Read it, and looking upon *Evangelist* very carefully; said, Whither must I fly? Then said *Evangelist,* pointing with his finger over a very wide Field, Do you see yonder *Wicket-gate?* The Man said, No. Then said the other, Do you see yonder shining light? He said, I think I do. Then said *Evangelist,* Keep that light in your eye, and go up directly thereto, so shalt thou see the Gate; at which when thou knockest, it shall be told thee what thou shalt do. (*PP* 9–10)

The scene depicts Christian's first encounter with a saving spiritual figure (Plate 3, Fig. 23). The man whom he faces is Evangelist, a personification of the New Testament. That he is here more than a mere representative of evangelical feeling, more than a stand-in for the ideal itinerant Puritan preacher of Bunyan's day, is suggested iconographically by his primitive biblical dress and compositionally by the fact that, in his head-on relation to Christian, he replaces the book (that is, the Bible) from the previous drawing. Typologically understood, he is that book numinously humanized, the inner life of the Christian Word itself come suddenly to life.[39] Blake emphasizes this sense of an attitudinal transformation by showing a continuous progression of like forms growing in size and building to a graphic climax over the first three designs. This progression, particularly with respect to the permutations of the triangular shape delimited by the central figures, can be schematically diagrammed as in Figure 50.

The flattened triangle of Plate 1 holds the dreamer and lion together in a relationship born of their mutual unawareness in a state of sleep; the larger isosceles triangle of Plate 2 shows an evolved form of the dreaming man struggling consciously toward an erect posture through his contact with the Word; finally, in the third plate of this minisequence, the triangle, which has become an elongated version of its immediate predecessor and a nearly congruent, upended complement of the triangle in Plate 1, features the dream protagonist standing upright and in contact with what might be considered an archetypal representative of his own, specifically human, spirit. The first drawing's tripartite mapping of man into his brute, vegetative, and visionary nature is thus echoed in the temporal sequence of drawings 1–3, wherein the projected Other of the central figure evolves from brute to book to "human form divine."

An added formal factor that makes Plate 3 appear as the culmination of a process is the increase in size of the figures. Nowhere in the series does Christian press closer to the foreground of the picture plane, nowhere does he fill so much of the space between plate top and plate bottom. In video-camera terms we might say the zoom lens has been extended to the fullest, and thus an ascendency of scale has reached its acme. This effect is enhanced by the horizontal presentation of the picture frame, which gives a strong, boxed-in feeling to the space, as if a lid had been put on the upward aspiration of figures too big for the enclosure (the apex of the imagined triangle they form is cut off by the top of the design). In the world of this illustration, even the near and far elements seem scrunched together, Alice in Wonderland fashion, by a spatial warping that has Christian standing with one toe still on the threshold of his house, although the text describes him as having left it far behind, while Evangelist's outstretched hand seems to be sowing the seeds of light over the distant hill.

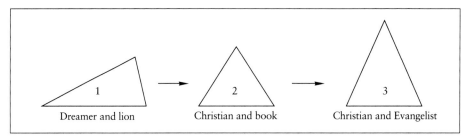

FIG. 50   Diagram of Plates 1–3

There is a curious inversion here in the association of these emblems of past and future. The architecture of the ruinous city Christian is leaving has suddenly become Gothicized, although in other surrounding drawings it is heavy and Romanesque.[40] This fact suggests again that Plate 3 is both a turning point and a prefiguration of things to come, since the Gothic style (Blake calls it "living form")[41] does not reappear until, in Plates 10 and 11, it is used to portray the wicket-gate. By the same token, the light hovering over the distant hill bears a much closer resemblance to its nearby, negative counterpart (the fire from Mount Sinai depicted in Plate 7) than it does to the far-off, benign influence it is supposed to represent. From these hints we may conclude that drawing no. 3 constitutes the closing of a gestalt having to do with beginnings and the opening of another concerned with future transformations of mistaken identities.[42]

DRAWING 4

> The Neighbors also came out to see him run, and as he
> ran, some mocked, others threatned; and some cried after
> him to return: Now among those that did so, there were
> two that were resolved to fetch him back by force. The
> name of the one was *Obstinate,* and the name of the other
> *Pliable.* Now by this time the Man was got a good
> distance from them; But however they were resolved to
> pursue him. (*PP* 10–11)

In this picture (Plate 4, Fig. 24) Christian is actively fleeing not only the City of Destruction but also the manifestation of his own divided being, the twin figures of Obstinate and Pliable. Blake portrays them as contraries by coloring the suit of one blue, the suit of the second pink—shades that are faded replicas of the colors of Christian's own two-toned clothing. That the opposite characters of Obstinate and Pliable represent the fallen moral traits responsible for leading Christian astray over and over again is demonstrated in several later episodes. As personality excesses, they signify the two extremes of an unintegrated will (overidentification of the ego with the will, both in pride and in despair, being Christian's besetting spiritual problem). The important fact conveyed here, though, is that each is a double of the other—two sides of one coin. It is this two-sidedness that Christian is turning from at full tilt. And under Blake's hand he turns so completely that he literally makes an about-face, heading for the first time in a leftward direction. This lurch toward the left has an obviously sinister connotation, which Blake plays up in his rendering of the landscape: the storm clouds crest the entire scene in a parody of the visionary rainbow arch, and the city, formerly downhill in relation to Christian, now has ascendency over him. In graphic terms, he appears to be moving both downward and backward, regressing instead of progressing.

At the same time, there is a singular advance in this picture vis-à-vis the spectator's relation to the main figure. For Christian is now presented in a nearly frontal pose, his anxious look seeming to appeal directly to our sympathies, his outspread arms seeming to request our embrace.

DRAWING 5

They drew near to a very *Miry Slough* that was in the midst of the Plain, and they being heedless, did both fall suddenly into the bogg. The name of the Slow was *Dispond*. Here therefore they wallowed for a time, being grievously bedaubed with the dirt; And *Christian*, because of the burden that was on his back, began to sink in the Mire.

Pli. *Then said* Pliable, *Ah, Neighbour* Christian, *where are you now?*

Chr. Truly, said *Christian*, I do not know.

Pli. At that *Pliable* began to be offended; and angerly, said to his Fellow, *Is this the happiness you have told me all this while of? . . . May I get out again with my life, you shall possess the brave Country alone for me.* And with that he gave a desperate struggle or two, and got out of the Mire, on that side of the Slow which was next to his own House. . . .

Wherefore *Christian* was left to tumble in the Slow of *Dispond* alone; but still he endeavoured to struggle to that side of the Slow, that was still further from his own House, and next to the Wicket-gate. (*PP* 14–15)

Although Christian's sinking in the Slough of Despond (Plate 5, Fig. 25) is one of the more memorable allegoric events of the *Progress,* it was curiously neglected by all serious illustrators of Bunyan's work before Blake.[43] Blake, though, saw its structural importance as the prototype of a set of depressive downswings in the dreamer's visionary cycle of self-revelation, and it provided him with a good opportunity for deepening the psychological turn of his pictorial narrative. The graphically regressive movement begun in the previous drawing is strengthened here as Christian, in profile, proceeds on all fours toward the ominous-looking lower left—a hellish nadir where a dark, forked storm cloud rises up like smoke emanating from a gutted fire. Insofar as these pictures can be said to diagram the dreamer's psyche, we can perhaps feel justified in calling on a traditional Jungian interpretation of the symbolism of the left to help explain Blake's weighting of it in this design. Usually such interpreters take the left in dreams to represent the threshold of repressed materials in the personal unconscious—the realm, particularly, of the dreamer's shadow or alter ego. If we read Blake's interpretation of Bunyan's slough passage in this light, we see that Christian's crawling-forward-while-heading-backward signifies a determined exploration of his own spectral unconscious at a point in the pictorial narrative where he understands that his difficulties stem from forces unrelated to the external behavior of others. That this is Blake's meaning is borne out by the fact that the smoky clouds of depression formerly hovering over the City of Destruction now have their source offstage in a location away from, and diagonally opposite, the city (which is now situated on the right of the picture plane), in the unknown psychic country toward which Christian doggedly strains.

One critic of Bunyan's story has compared this stage in the soul's journey to the first "dark night" of resistance experienced by patients in psychotherapy.[44] In Blake's rendition, the emphasis is more on the heroism of the struggle to wade through what Freud regarded as the cesspool aspect of psychic work.[45] For that task the figure of Christian appropriately emulates the posture and attitude of the lion in the first drawing. He has, however, developed into a more human and self-conscious version of that previously autonomous animality, related to the instinctual life, which was shown earlier in its sensual sleep of death. Similarly, the burden of guilt has now resumed its physically human aspect, this time resembling not a bodily growth but another self—a clinging, shadowy nature, perhaps a child, perhaps a ghost—being ferried across the muddy swamp by Christian.[46]

This plate represents a decisive psychological departure in that the dream-hero is now looking directly into the dark side of himself without the mediation of the word: neither book nor scroll nor human voice compels him at this point. Compositionally, too, there is a striking change that reinforces the effect

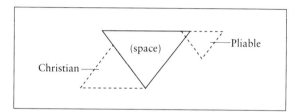

FIG. 51   Diagram of Plate 4

of a drastic shift in consciousness (Fig. 51). The controlling spatial structure no longer depends on one ground-based triangle that draws diverse elements into a focal unity. Instead, an upside-down triangular shape forms a large wedge of pictorial space at the center of the design, separating the two figures (one of whom, Pliable, repeats the inverse-pyramid form). In contrast to the layouts of previous drawings, the movement is centrifugal, suggesting that the division pictured is not merely a reflection of an unresolved inner conflict but rather an intentional pulling apart, a real drive toward differentiation. Two ways in which this meaning is enhanced are by the coloring of Pliable's clothes and by the shape of the storm cloud. Pliable, who wears a one-toned costume when paired antithetically with Obstinate in the preceeding design, is now shown in two-colored attire like Christian himself (though the color scheme is inverted). It is as if he is now subsuming the unconscious dualism that he formerly only half embodied and at the same time has become Christian's (obstinately) discarded double and counterpart. The difference between Christian's and Pliable's relation to the storm cloud reflects that same state of affairs: Christian heads toward the single source of the seemingly divided smoke screen, while Pliable's line of vision alerts him only to its "two-horn'd" appearance.

DRAWING 6

But I beheld in my Dream, that a Man came unto him, whose name was *Help,* and asked him, *What he did there?*

 Chr. Sir, said *Christian,* I was bid go this way, by a Man called *Evangelist,* who directed me also to yonder Gate, that I might escape the wrath to come: And as I was going thither, I fell in here.

 Help. *But why did you not look for the steps?*

 Chr. Fear followed me so hard, that I fled the next way, and fell in.

 Help. *Then,* said he, *Give me thy hand;* so he gave him his hand, and he drew him out. (*PP* 15)

The event illustrated in this design (Plate 6, Fig. 26) follows without a break the subject of Plate 5; thus the two incidents—a falling into and a lifting out of spiritual despair—are presented by Bunyan as directly related corollaries of a single experience. The implication is that Help's arrival on the dream scene is an immediate and natural result of Christian's determination to accept the reality of the unconscious (represented by the waters of despondency) despite its swamping power and yet to push on through the very midst of it with undeterred purpose. Blake's portrayal of the rescue of Christian by Help emphasizes the complementarity of these related attitudes—acceptance of and release from depression—by compositional inversion of the preceding plate. There, as we saw, the staged movement was centrifugal, whereas here it is centripetal. The focal void left in Plate 5 by the separating out of the various forces is now filled, moreover, as the figures of Christian and Help effect a central closure of the pictorial space in a redemptive embrace. Blake seems to be giving graphic expression here to a common psychological rule that goes beyond Bunyan's: the rule that active differentiation of the contents of the dark side of the self not only precedes spiritual assistance, but also literally creates a space for the healing powers of the psyche to move into as they well up from archetypal dimensions recognized as existing deep in the background of our mental landscape. This, at least, is the message of Plate 6 in its sequence.

The drawing shows Help, in a frontal pose, striding vigorously forward, his upper body bent far over into the picture plane as he leans down to pull Christian out of the bog. It is as if he had just now appeared at the top of the hill, a bright visitant from the mountainous backdrop, a magical runner along the pinkish-yellow road that streams behind him almost like an extension of his garment to connect him with the energy of the sun glowing on the distant horizon.[47] Below him, along the base of the plate, the water of the slough is pictured as a dark river from which Christian, submerged to his armpits, reaches strenuously upward.[48] This is the lowest visual level to which the figure of Christian descends in the entire series of designs. It is also the first time he is shown facing inward with his back completely to the audience. The call for spectator identification with a figure so positioned is very strong because the directional stance portrayed in the illusional space duplicates the actual, physical attitude of the viewer confronting the drawing in real space. Thus Blake has enticed us to feel ourselves Christian's double in this bodily way on the very occasion that he (Christian) reaches his literal nadir, with the result that we gain an added emotional investment in his recovery and his rise to wholeness.

This invitation to a more subjective involvement in the symbolic action of the present design is enhanced by the forward-reaching appeal of the numinous figure of Help (an appeal that builds on, and answers, the less focused play for an intimate response made by the arm-flailing posture of Christian in Plate 4). Our engagement with the meeting of Christian and Help is qualitatively different from the way we reacted to the portrayal of previous meetings, partly because an emphatic centering occurs here that resolves the upward and inward reaching of Christian with the downward and outward reaching of Help in a union of opposites that forms a womblike oval on the vertical axis of the drawing. This womb of interaction holds a strong charge, conveying a double sense of climax and continence, of excitement and satisfaction, with the moment of stasis held forever off by Christian's hands, which resist grasping Help's arm to complete the embrace.

Emotionally, then, this drawing makes special demands on the viewer even as it offers special rewards. In many ways it works as an icon not only of Christian's deliverance but also of our own imaginative release from a passive mode of viewing external reality. For just as Christian is lifted from the bog by Help, so we, as spectators, are yanked by Blake out of our sluggish and distanced way of relating to the passing scene. Certainly in terms of the sequence of pictorial events there is a radical break here in the continuity of onlooker objectivity. A break is made as well in the representational continuity, since the sudden change in both the landscape and weather of Plate 6 has no rational cause and no realistic explanation. In the drawings before and after this plate, the dream scenes are engulfed by turbulent clouds of either rain or smoke or fire, but Plate 6 is set serenely in the midst of that stormy world like a window opening onto another reality. What we glimpse through it is a vision of transcendence or ontological otherness that *itself* transcends the established order of the dream elements so far pictured. It also completely skews our sense of location and viewer orientation in that the background, formerly the locus of the City of Destruction and hence representative of a place to shun, is here suddenly a richly beckoning region, a dawning exemplar of the desired country toward which the entire dream is heading.

The iconic quality of this plate gives it a special structural function. Graphically it serves less to promote the movement of the narrative than to recapitulate the central imaginal theme and to refashion some of the visual motifs of the initial design. Thus the sun here appears as a variant of the light piercing the rainbow of Plate 1; the road curves backward like a grounded version of the rainbow arch; and the womblike oval formed by the joining arms of Christian and Help echoes, on the vertical plane, that protective, cocoon shape of the dreamer's garment in the opening illustration. Like several other such designs throughout the series, in other words, Plate 6 is constructed to remind us of the primary psychic context: the state of the dreamer dreaming. Even the coloring of the design works toward that end, for the fact that Christian, Help, the road, and the outer aura of the sun are all washed in the same shade—a warm, golden pink—gives them a consubstantiality that lets us recall their joint origin in the imagination of a single, main character bent on dreaming up his own agents and strategies of awakening.

DRAWINGS 7, 8, and 9

Now as Christian was walking solitary by himself, he espied one afar off, come crossing over the field to meet
him; and their hap was to meet just as they were crossing
the way of each other. The Gentleman's name was, Mr.
Worldly-Wiseman . . . [who] began thus to enter into some
talk with *Christian.* . . .

    Worl. *How camest thou by thy burden at first?*

    Chr. By reading this Book in my hand.

    Worl. *I thought so; and it is happened unto thee as to
other weak men, who meddling with things too high for them,
do suddenly fall into thy distractions . . . I could direct thee to
the obtaining of what thou desirest . . . in yonder Village, (the
Village is named* Morality) *there dwells a Gentleman, whose
name is* Legality, *a very judicious man . . . that has skill to
help men off with such burdens as thine are, from their shoulders.* . . .

    Chr. Sir, which is my way to this honest man's
house?

    Worl. *Do you see yonder high hill?*

    Chr. Yes, very well

    Worl. By that *Hill* you must go, and the first house
you come at is his. (*PP* 16–20)

So *Christian* turned out of his way to go to Mr. *Legality's*
house for help: but behold, when he was got now hard by
the *Hill,* it seemed so high, and also that side of it that
was next the way side, did hang so much over, that
Christian was afraid to venture further, lest the *Hill*
should fall on his head: wherefore there he stood still, and
wotted not what to do. Also his burden, *now,* seemed
heavier to him, than while he was in his way. There came
also flashes of fire out of the Hill, that made *Christian*
afraid that he should be burned: here therefore he swet,
and did quake for fear. (*PP* 20)

And now he began to be sorry that he had taken Mr.
Worldly-Wisemans counsel; and with that he saw *Evangelist*
coming to meet him; at the sight also of whom he began
to blush for shame. . . .

Then *Christian* fell down at his foot as dead, crying, Woe is me, for I am undone: at the sight of which *Evangelist* caught him by the right hand, saying, All manner of sin and blasphemies shall be forgiven unto men; be not faithless, but believing. (*PP* 20–22)

The next three drawings (Plates 7–9, Figs. 27–29) can most fruitfully be considered as a unit. They represent a six-page section of the text that tells a relatively contained drama of its own; and their grouping seems to reflect a historical precedent, set by Bunyan's first illustrator, to compare Evangelist and Worldly Wiseman, the characters Christian deals with in this portion of the dream.[49] The formal and conceptual principles behind Blake's grouping, however, do not coincide with the methods of the traditional pairings-off. Indeed, Blake makes his visionary commentary in this small sequence largely through a deliberate manipulation of the conventional graphic treatment of the subject. Illustrators up to Blake's day were content to point up the contrast between Christian's experience of Evangelist, on the one hand, and his run-in with Worldly Wiseman, on the other. Not so, Blake: he turns a simple juxtaposition of opposites into a complex tripling that has a dialectical relation to all that has gone before. In the process, the very question of Blake's structural numerology (if one may be permitted such a term to describe the metaphorical implications of his arrangement of pictorial elements in varying numerical units) presents itself. Before going into these issues, however, a brief description of the designs is in order.

Plate 7 shows Worldly Wiseman, disguised as a double of Evangelist, standing statuesquely on the left side of the plate. He faces forward in a three-quarter pose and with his left arm signals toward the "Hill" in the background, which is identified in the margin of the text as Mount Sinai. Christian, meanwhile, half stoops, half kneels before Worldly Wiseman, pointing out a passage in his Bible. The mountain looms up behind him and emits sparks of fire in a volcanic glow that is topped by a small cloud of black smoke. The rest of the sky is clear and colored a deep, intense blue. The operation of black magic is hinted at in this illustration; Worldly Wiseman's arm extends in a fiatlike gesture of supernatural power, as if he were creating the eruption of Mount Sinai rather than simply directing Christian to it.[50] The experience produced in the move from Plate 6 to Plate 7 is that this commanding figure has somehow usurped Help's position on the dream stage and has simultaneously altered the backdrop to suit his nefarious purpose, turning the bright sun of the previous drawing into the darkly dangerous volcano of this design.

The more orthodox conception of Worldly Wiseman is that he is a parodic counterpart not of Help but of Evangelist, an interpretation amply supported by the text. The exchange between him and Christian about the burden and the sight of "yonder high hill," for example, is clearly meant to be an ironic echo of the original meeting between Christian and Evangelist when Evangelist points the true way to the true light above "yonder Wicket-gate." Blake makes greater use of this resemblance than any other previous illustrator by having the light and the hilly location of "yonder Wicket-gate" in Plate 3 strongly prefigure the iconography of the fire from the mountain in Plate 7. In the original series of *Progress* designs, these contrasting episodes were the subjects of the opening two illustrations, but their very adjacency and their primacy encouraged the designer to point up more differences than likenesses so as to make the experiences represented into a clear pair of dialectical opposites (see Figs. B1 and B2).[51] Blake, borrowing from the invention of a later *Progress* illustrator (Figs. B37 and B38), abandons this tactic in favor of stressing the parity of Christian's psychological perception of the two events. His purpose is to give the viewer a more vivid experience of the inner dream process and to involve us dramatically in Christian's inability to discriminate the true from the false guide until rescued by Evangelist in Plate 9.[52] Then, retrospectively, we can compare the nearly identical figures and distinguish the rigidity of Worldly Wiseman (Plate 7) from the flowing vitality of Evangelist (Plates 9 and 3). Similarly, it is only after Evangelist lifts Christian up by the right hand—a commonplace icon of true faith[53]—that Christian, no less the dreamer and the viewer, can fully appreciate the significance of the fact that Worldly Wiseman had hidden *his* right hand behind his back.

Plate 8 shows Christian facing the viewer in a pose similar to the one he assumes in Plate 4, surrounded this time by flames of fire and bolts of lightning.[54] He is literally engulfed in the emblems of the wrath of God, the stormy moral weather of the Old Testament mentality that has dominated the landscape of most of the drawings in the series up to now. Fire and clouds of smoke circle him on all sides except for the small area occupied by his lower right leg and foot. The shape of this fiery circle is something like that of a womb holding Christian but permitting his escape through a birth canal that issues downward, to the ground where he has his true footing.[55]

These features of the design constitute a departure from the traditional iconography. In the standard illustrations involving this narrative moment, the emphasis had always been placed on the precipitous overhang of the mountain, which, according to Bunyan, made Christian "afraid to venture further lest the Hill should fall on his head" (Figs. B25 and B38). Blake, in contrast, has drawn a scene in which the mountain and indeed the whole sense of discernible, earthly location is being consumed in flames; thus the threatening overhang here is not the rock of the Mosaic Law but spontaneous fire and lightning erupting more or less on its own in a limbo of space and time. The scene is not so much a part of the ongoing action, then, as an interruption of narrative development, a mental stasis or parenthesis. Christian has evidently fallen into a psychological complex—a "state," in Blake's language—and is wrapped up in it as if he were in a decompression chamber designed to separate him from the flanking, mutually contradictory encounters of Plates 7 and 9.[56] This effect of static interposition between opposites is enhanced by the frontality of the image in Plate 8. As we noted of drawings 4 and 6, figures who face fully forward make an intimate appeal to the audience, like an actor who whispers an aside to explicate the latent meaning of some ambiguous or highly charged stage behavior. In this case, the appeal Christian makes is based on fear of the fiery experience he perceives to be in front of him in the drawing's illusional space—the same position we, as readers, occupy relative to him in real space. Thus we are drawn into his phobic complex more intensely here than at any other point in the series. In that regard, Plate 8 works as a development and heightening not only of the posturing but also of the response motif of Plate 4. Yet here Christian's pressing forward to the viewer takes place within a pocket of transpersonality comparable to the deeper layers of psychic landscape evoked in the frontally presented, womb-shaped configuration of Plate 6.

The design of Plate 6 with its theme of physical rescue is recapitulated in Blake's Plate 9, but this time the raising up of Christian is seen literally and psychologically from a different angle. Here the role formerly taken by Help is played by Evangelist, who, pictured in profile on the left side of the drawing, bends over toward Christian with both arms extended to the ground. Christian, also shown in profile, is prostrating himself at Evangelist's feet. He kneels facing the center from the right of the picture plane. Voluptuous rolls of flame swirl up from his back, and another spirals out like a giant seashell from his feet. In between, a thick finger of blue smoke rises and curves over the drawing in an arch that conforms to the arch of Evangelist's back. It is as if Christian had allowed the small opening in his phobia about God's wrath (the clear space breaking the circle of flames in the previous design) to expand and admit Evangelist. Simultaneously, of course, the cloud of fear begins to lift, and, as an integral part of that clearing-up, it is revealed that the source of the storm and stress is not Jehovah, not an external threat from the Mosaic Law on Mount Sinai, but Christian himself.

As I have tried to show, all the drawings in this unit of three extend, vary, or transform basic pictorial elements of Plate 6. In many ways this small series is best understood as a meditation on the meaning of that earlier, pivotal design in which Help, as an emblem of redemption, erupts spontaneously from the troubled unconscious. Plate 9 in particular gives us an opportunity to witness that process objectively, for its side-view presentation distances the spectator, discouraging partisan identification with the state of any one of the dream figures, and shows us what the psychic rescue pictured in Plate 6 looks like from the outside.[57] Drawings 7, 8, and 9 also work, though, to recapitulate and resolve motifs initiated in Plates 3, 4, and 5. In fact, the two triple-plate sequences have a quasi-mirror relation to each other, so that the third plate is tied to the ninth in a way that marks a completed movement in the visual plot—the closure of a large gestalt. Broadly speaking, the issues of that gestalt are projection and encounter, themes that Plate 9 brings together in a satisfying denouement just as it portrays the two characters into which the dream psyche originally split, blending in a continuous curve of compassionate interrelation. (Before, in Plate 3, when the same two figures first appeared, they held separate, upright postures in reversed positions on the dream stage, and Christian regarded Evangelist with that pulled-back gesture of fear and awe he later used to confront his overwhelming sense of divine wrath in Plate 8.)

Although I have been stressing that drawings 7, 8, and 9 make their statements by deliberately repeating and revising the pictorial themes of prior plates, it must be said that the sequence also radically cuts through the dream-vision's repetition compulsion. This occurs in two ways: first, by embedding firmly in the *visual* story line the fact that the recurrent landscape of gloom is a motif self-engendered by Christian—that is, it is a projection within the control of the ego-figure that can be (and is being) withdrawn; and second, by breaking one of the patterns of the plate arrangement—namely, the pattern of alternating vertical designs with horizontal ones. Up through the sixth design, that rhythm of alternation has been a part of the viewer's experience of the progression of the narrative. Thus, following Plate 6 we at least subliminally expect a flattening out of the scene, with its concomitant sense of movement along the horizontal axis; but fulfillment of that expectation is delayed until the appearance of design 9. This delay puts emphasis on the down-to-earthness of Plate 9, making its contents signify a consolidation on the literal plane, so to speak, of the doctrine of acceptance and forgiveness illustrated in a vision-ary/vertical mode in Plate 6. Henceforward there are twice as many vertically based compositions as horizontally based ones, with no conventional model of ordering them imposed from without. Rather, Blake begins from this point on to play with the rhetoric of frame shape as an element of meaning dictated purely by the spirit of the mythos itself.

All in all, this small unit of designs represents a major turning point in both the meaning and the method of the series as a whole. In addition to the stylistic devices mentioned above, the sequence introduces an aesthetic of narrative grouping by threes that has an important impact on the dynamic relation of later drawings, and promotes a practice (in defiance of the prior tradition of Bunyan illustration) whereby single dramatic events of the text are split pictorially into two or more moments, two or more compositions. We saw this already in the representation of the Slough of Despond, an episode to which Blake devotes two consecutive plates (5 and 6). In the present instance, however, the extension of a single, compact experience over three adjacent drawings is made more affecting, and more noticeable, by Blake's sticking to similar images and motifs.

As we shall see, this procedure is echoed frequently in the designs that ensue, with the result that narrative time undergoes a crucial slowing down to make visible the kinds of subtle, psychological, plot developments that happen only at very close range.

DRAWINGS 10 and 11

So in process of time *Christian* got up to the Gate. Now over the Gate there was Written, *Knock and it shall be opened unto you.* He knocked therefore, more *then* once or twice, *saying,*

> *May I now enter here? will he within*
> *Open to sorry me, though I have bin*
> *An undeserving Rebel? then shall I,*
> *Not fail to Sing his lasting praise on high. (PP 25)*

At last there came a grave Person to the Gate: named *Good-will,* who asked *Who was there? and whence he came? and what he would have?*

> *Chr.* Here is a poor burdened sinner, I came from the City of *Destruction,* but am going to Mount *Zion.* . . . I would therefore, Sir, since I am informed that by this Gate is the way thither, know if you are *willing* to let me in.
> *Good-Will.* I am *willing* with all my heart, said he; and with that he opened the Gate. *(PP 25)*

These two drawings (Plates 10–11, Figs. 30–31) carry forward Blake's strategy of giving double space to certain single incidents in the dream-story. Here the temporal and spatial realities embodied in each design are closer together than in any other pair of *Progress* illustrations. In fact, the scene of Plate 10 is literally only one step away from that of Plate 11, but the step is crucial—representing as it does the transition from a state of searching to a state of initiation—and Blake's desire to dwell on the numinous shifts of consciousness that beset souls at such junctures is characteristic of his interpretive approach to the entire text.

Taking the broad view, we can say that Plate 10 depicts Christian knocking at the wicket-gate from without, while 11 shows him being received—indeed, powerfully drawn in—over the threshold. Compositionally, too, Plate 10 is comparatively outer-directed, in the sense that its surface structure is busy and complex, full of dispersed forms and disparate details that represent conflicting world orders in the manner of Plate 1. This association to the initial design of the series is no accident, and Blake underscores it by painting a streak of rainbow colors, reminiscent of the dreamer's projected dream space, in a side arch over the right half of the gateway. Since the presence of the rainbow cannot be explained naturalistically, we know that its return is emblematic, a response to the lifting of projected turbulence in the previous drawing. That turbulence, for its part, seems to have been produced originally by the dream psyche as a screen or negative and unconscious transformation of the rainbow colors. Now it is as if Christian is about to step, with full knowledge of his act, into the place of his own visionary capacity, so that his quest and the dreamer's will henceforth be more consciously aligned.

The situation at the point of entry, however, is one of threatening *dis*alignment among the elements of the pilgrim's environment, with the realm of the quest (the gate), the desired landscape on the other side of the gate, and the place of menacing enmity to the left of the drawing all clashing with one another through formal means. To begin with, the wicket-gate expressly differentiates itself from its surroundings by its shape and continence. It is made up of a number of nesting Gothic archways plus a central panel carved with decorative replicas of those archways. Christian is a part of this self-sufficient ambiance, both because of his contact with the door and because of his figural stance, which adds to the heavy dose of triangular shapes constituting this portion of the design. A strong diagonal line on the picture plane, marking the top of the wall in which the gate is set, cuts the gate off sharply from the country above and beyond. There, in a world and climate of its own, is the "true" way of the pilgrim, looking pretty much as had been anticipated in the visionary landscape of Plate 6, with the sun showing and sparking its own rainbow rays on the horizon. Instead of expressing continence like the door arch, though, this glimpse of mountainous countryside is formed by lines radiating out like wings. Finally, on the left of the picture plane, the wall separating the seeker from the sought is itself truncated by an upright post, which incongruously supports a bow and arrow at its tip. The arrow points down, aiming at Christian and vying with the vectors of the right side of the design. This instrument of warfare is meant to illustrate the doubt and envy of those aspects of the psyche that are ready to attack the rest of the personality as it tenuously approaches the path of a healing individuation. Bunyan, through the voice of Good-will, explains the threat this way: "a little distance from this Gate, there is erected a strong Castle, of which *Belzebub* is the Captain: from thence both he, and them that are with him, Shoot Arrows at those that come up to this Gate; if happily they may die before they can enter in" (*PP* 25).

When we move from this moment to the moment illustrated in Plate 11, even though on the literal level of the story the two are only seconds apart, it is as if we were stepping out of time altogether. Gone are all the marks of the natural world and all the harsh dynamics of opposing forces. Instead of a Gothicized wicket-gate set in a blank and rigid garden wall, a virtually floating doorway, devoid of realistic setting, has now become a world of its own, alive with the sculpture of swaying human forms barely visible before. Instead of a closed door bearing biblical epigraphs, there is now a man, Good-will, who gives the appearance of being larger and more substantial than any character previously portrayed, a truly numinous figure ready to embrace Christian. And in place of a sun dominating an inaccessible landscape on a distant horizon, there is now a perfect halo shining in full view around the head of Good-will, a light brighter than the sun, which yet fills the doorway with sunshine.

But the connotation that this is a foretaste of eternity does not stop there. Structurally, the design stresses integration and concentricity, starting with the symmetry imposed by the architecture of the gateway, which centers and frames Good-will and initiates an intense interplay of circles and ovals. The oval of the door arch is matched by the oval inside it of Good-will's embrace; and within that embrace, the circle formed by Christian's head, burden, and chest is matched by the concentric circles of Good-will's face and halo. This wheeling within wheels and swirling within swirls heightens the sense that an infinite spiraling of spiritual libido is motivating the embrace and fulfilling the desire for union between Christian and Good-will.[58] One need only compare the formal elements of this design with those of Plates 6 and 9 to see how active the dynamic of the joining is here, though in other ways Plate 11 creates the most static and otherworldly of the three similar emblems. In fact, this drawing can fruitfully be considered a figural fulfillment of drawings 6 and 9, for the treatment of the archetypal embrace over the three pictures exhibits a progressive movement toward symbiotic ascension. We can observe how the helping figure in his various transformations through this series of designs straightens up and uses less and less strain to make contact, just as Christian in the same plates rises higher and higher on the picture plane, achieving greater parity with the stance and stature of his spiritual guide.

We must stop at this point to ask why Blake gave such iconographic weight to both the figure of Good-will and the action portrayed here. In Bunyan's narrative, after all, Good-will is no more than a gatekeeper, a rather minor spiritual official who is certainly lower in status than either Help or Evangelist. Why, then, does Blake dwell on his superior role? The answer, I believe, is that Good-will is associated, for Blake, with the Christian concept of forgiveness of sins—the cardinal doctrine, in his view, without which expansion of consciousness is not possible. Several facts from Bunyan's text and from its illustrations in popular editions assist this association. First, all of the standard editions contained pictures of the wicket-gate (see Figs. B3, B15, and B39),[59] and until well into the eighteenth century, below each was attached the following quatrain:

> He that will enter in must first without
> Stand knocking at the Gate, nor need he doubt
> That is a knocker but to enter in;
> For God can love him, and forgive his sin.

Here the principle of forgiveness is given recognition as the highest form of divine action—God's love—and it is definitely connected with the opening of the gate by Good-will. There are even grounds for reading the verse caption as a gloss to tell us that Good-will is God, or at least a typological representative of God. This was surely in Blake's mind when he drew the figure of Good-will, who has so many of the features and qualities that Blake elsewhere reserved for representations of the "human form divine," in its most developed aspect.[60]

Second, Bunyan's narrative introduces the term and concept of forgiveness on the occasion just preceding (which corresponds to Blake's Plate 9) when Christian is rescued by Evangelist from Mount Sinai. Evangelist speaks of it there as a promise of the New Testament modality that will replace the Mosaic moral code in the mature "believing" psyche: instead of accusation and punishment for sin, as Christian anticipates, there will be Grace and forgiveness: "Then *Christian* fell down . . . crying, Woe is me, for I am undone: at the sight of which *Evangelist* caught him by the right hand, saying, All manner of sin and blasphemies shall be forgiven to men; be not faithless, but believing" (*PP* 22). Because in Blake's narrative sequence this experience directly antedates Christian's arrival at the wicket-gate, we are prepared to find the promise and pattern of forgiveness carried forward there. And of course, the motto over the door taken from Christ's Sermon on the Mount, "Knock and it shall be opened" (Matthew 7:7–8), refers specifically to that aspect of immediate, suprapersonal response from the inner source of divine strength and wisdom that Christian forgiveness implies. Blake's inspired decision to let the representation of Christian's knocking be followed immediately by a representation of the instantaneous, welcoming result gives powerful expression in the very structure of the graphic narrative to the validity, and the striking efficiency, of an attitude of mutual trust and forgiveness.

In sum, this drawing in its sequential setting has the impact of aesthetic propaganda for a New Testament mentality, embodying the imagery of the motto Blake invented as a revisionary corollary to Christ's "Knock and it shall be opened," viz.:

Mutual Forgiveness of each Vice
Such are the Gates of Paradise.[61]

DRAWINGS 12 and 13

Now, said *Christian*, let me go hence: Nay stay (said the
Interpreter,) till I have shewed thee a little more, and after
that, thou shalt go on thy way. So he took him by the
hand again, and led him into a very dark Room, where
there sat a Man in an Iron Cage.

Now the Man, to look on, seemed very sad: he sat with
his eyes looking down to the ground, his hands folded together; and he sighed as if he would break his heart. . . .

Chr. Then said *Christian* to the Man, *What art thou?* The
Man answered, *I am what I was not once* . . . I am *now* a
Man of Despair, and am shut up in it, as in this Iron
Cage. I cannot get out; O *now* I cannot.

Chr. *But how camest thou in this condition?*

Man. I left off to watch, and be sober; I laid the reins
upon the neck of my lusts; I sinned against the light of the
Word, and the goodness of God: I have grieved the Spirit,
and he is gone; I tempted the Devil, and he is come to
me . . . I have so hardened my heart that I *cannot* repent.

(PP 34)

Chr. . . . Sir, is it not time for me to go on my way
now?

Int. Tarry till I shall shew thee one thing more, and then
thou shalt go on thy way.

So he took *Christian* by the hand again, and led him
into a Chamber, where there was one a rising out of Bed;
and as he put on his Rayment, he shook and trembled.
Then said *Christian*, Why doth this man thus tremble?
The *Interpreter* then bid him tell to *Christian* the reason of
his so doing: So he began, and said, This night as I was in
my sleep, I Dreamed, and behold the Heavens grew exceeding black; and also it thundred and lightned in most
fearful wise, that it put me into an Agony. So I looked up
in my Dream, and saw the Clouds rack at an unusual rate,
upon which I heard a great sound of a Trumpet, and saw
also a Man sit upon a Cloud, attended with the thousands
of Heaven; they were all in flaming fire, also the Heavens
was on a burning flame. I heard a voice saying, *Arise ye
Dead, and come to Judgement.* . . .

I . . . sought to hide my self, but I could not; for the
Man that sat upon the Cloud, still kept his eye upon me:
my sins also came into mind, and my Conscience did ac-
cuse me on every side. Upon this I awaked from my
sleep. (*PP* 35–37)

The previous plates were paired in a formal dialectic based on incremental
progression. Without changing the scene, movement occurred in the direction
of iconographic intensity as well as compositional focus. In other words, Blake
brought the eye of the viewer by a zoom-lens technique through Plate 10 into
Plate 11 and, literally and figuratively, made 11 magnify the inner significance
of the act begun in 10. Now, however, with drawings 12 and 13 (Plates 12–13,
Figs. 32–33), a different affective principle governs the grouping, for here
suddenly the two illustrations relate as symmetrically balanced opposites. Side
by side, *on* their sides, the formats of 12 and 13 match up in a way that takes full
advantage of the horizontal plane's ability to display contrast in terms of
right/left mirroring. Furthermore, as befits the analytical method of interpretation being taught to Christian in these episodes, the interplay between the
two pictures (like the composition of elements within each design) exemplifies
an urge for differentiation, not fusion. Nevertheless, the subjects shown as
antitheses also bear important similarities: both drawings portray Christian
deep in training at the House of the Interpreter; both show visions within
visions that reflect back on the dreamer's own visionary process; both offer a
comment on the pathology of spiritual despair; and both involve a guiding
figure new to the cast of dream characters—the Interpreter himself.

Considering that, of all the characters in the *Progress,* this figure is the one
after whom Blake was lovingly nicknamed by his admirers and with whom he
was most identified as a visionary artist, it is not surprising that he puts special
emphasis on the Interpreter's role in shaping the drama here at the literal center
of the design sequence. In fact, by a kind of graphic pun wholly in keeping
with the typical expressive ploys of dream rhetoric, Blake shows us that the
Interpreter is indeed a key figure—at least in Plate 12, where he literally "holds
the key" to this and the next room of the dream.[62]

On one level he can be said to hold the key simply because his lessons in
hermeneutics are supposed to help Christian (and us) unlock the meaning of
the immediate events in ways that illuminate other events of the plot. On
another level, he is himself a figure on the boundary of many realities; he is
therefore accessible to multiple truths, capable of opening us to the knowledge
of impulses that connect all facets of the dream world and the dream purpose.
Blake demonstrates the Interpreter's boundary nature in several ways. First,
the character iconographically combines, without assuming, roles established

by several other figures presented so far, so that he is neither friend nor foe nor rescuer to Christian yet builds on aspects related to all. He has the mien and stature of the Wise Old Man archetype (especially in Plate 13; Plate 12 is apparently uncompleted), but he does not—as others of this ilk in the series do—interact with Christian as if he were an opposing force either for evil or for good. Rather, he stands alongside the dream protagonist, doubling him like a silent partner representing an auxilliary function of the main personality. Second, the Interpreter's referential identity is confirmed by his blue gown, which allies him unmistakably with the dreaming self of Plate 1. Up to now, aside from the ambiguous figure in the rainbow vision of Plate 1, only the dreamer has worn a blue robe, as if to indicate that the characters of his vision were somehow not cut from the same conscious cloth as he, even though they represented parts of his imaginative reality.[63] The appearance here, therefore, of a character who seems to touch base with the core function of the dreaming psyche suggests that the narrative is on the verge of a major reorientation of its elements, spelling a leap in the progress toward awareness and integration of consciousness.

Plate 12 deals with the meaning of bodily garments in another way than simply through the Interpreter's blue-robed identity, though, for the issue of clothing (or rather its lack) is an important aspect of the emblem on the right side of the drawing. There a man sits naked in a cage, irons around his ankles and neck, spikes from the cage's grid constraining him at chest and throat. Nothing in Bunyan's text describing this tortured figure (the sixth of seven active visions presented to Christian for interpretation) hints that the man *is* in fact naked, but Blake depicts him that way to vivify the idea that the cage is his body's only real dress, the prison of despair in which the man, as he himself bewails, is totally "shut up." As we saw in Chapter 2 when discussing the naked dreamer on the last plate of the revised *Gates,* a man's outer dress is frequently for Blake a signal of his current state, his conscious condition, and not a measure of his permanent identity. But when people are caught in a dark or negative state, that very negativity robs them of the ability to distinguish their individual natures from the mental attitude they are wrapped (or, in this case, "shut up") in. Then each person becomes prey to his or her own satanic propensity, the Accuser within, whom the awakening dreamer of the *Gates* regarded as slightly retarded: "Truly My Satan thou art but a Dunce/And dost not know the Garment from the Man" (see Fig. 20). Plate 12 beautifully renders just such a cycle of self-entrapment, with Blake representing its dunce-like quality by means of the ridiculous, jerry-built iron cage. Thus we notice that the frame of the cage is lopsided, its corners angled so that it leans drunkenly to the right. Its grid work, moreover, is asymmetric, being made up of unequal bars, haphazardly joined. Finally, it has no solidity or depth: it casts a large angular shadow on the wall behind, but this only makes it look more than ever like a flat, cardboard stage prop.

At a certain point in Bunyan's description, when Christian suggests that the man might now cast aside his overblown structure of despair, the man suddenly deflects all the energy of his blame outward and starts accusing God instead of himself of being the architect of his cage:

> Chr. *But canst thou not now repent and turn?*
> Man. God hath denied me repentance; his Word gives me no encouragement to believe; yea, himself hath shut me up in this Iron Cage: nor can all the men in the World let me out. (*PP* 35)

The absurdity of this accusation and the neurotic childishness of its tactic are pointed up by the ungodlike, comical, and childish aesthetic of the cage in Blake's design and by the fact that the man, and no heavenly jailer, seems to be holding the shackles firm around his own feet.

The cage, in short, is an exteriorization of the state the man is in, and he has an investment in preserving it because he has confused it with his own identity: he "dost not know the Garment from the Man." Although he has tried to give his despair a concrete and autonomous existence, it still clings to him as an extension of himself—a fact that Blake expresses pictorially by showing that the iron collar on the man's neck is the missing link in the structure of the cage, from which the rest of the cage seems to emanate outward. There is, furthermore, a subliminal hint here that the erect, phallic spike aimed at the man's neck represents his own repressed sexuality, another visually punning way in which the cage figures as an extension of the man.

In the revised *Gates,* a work I have noted for its connection to the material in this segment of the Bunyan designs, Blake expressly exalted forgiveness over moral accusation as a method of self-knowledge. Now here, too, we see that the experience of being forgiven and accepted by Good-will in the previous illustration allows Christian to view, from an enlightened perspective inside the Interpreter's House, the crippling inadequacy of an accusatory mode that had formerly been his own. In many ways the emblem of the Man in the Iron Cage parodies the dream hero's earlier stances, especially his despair about the difficulty of losing his burden and escaping the wrath to come in Plate 2 and his imprisonment in the fiery state of fear in Plate 8. Similarly, the projective devices of the caged figure seem to exaggerate and mock the rhetorical strategies used by the dreamer in creating some of the past situations of the dream. That is, there is a certain kinship between, on the one hand, the melodramatic propensity of a dream that would produce a deadly bog and a violent volcano to express depression and fear (Plates 5, 7, and 8) and, on the other, the histrionic mentality of the man in the cage who aggravates his own dejection by envisioning it in terms of bars, bands, and spikes that nearly choke him. Both the dream psyche in those earlier scenes and the naked man's imagination in this plate utilize overblown images of disaster to confirm and dramatize the ego's sense that it is a witless victim of outside forces. Yet the differences in the content of the imagery allow the viewer as well as Christian to recognize the shackled man's state, by comparison, as a caricature and type of the obdurate sin of despair. For the Slough of Despond and the Fire from the Mountain are natural images that on the literal level refer to "acts of God"; they represent environmental conditions that are themselves subject to organic evolution and transformation—open systems, existing *in* the open, from which individuals can be rescued or through which they can pass. But the iron cage is a manmade object composed of inert material, a closed system constructed precisely to be impervious to change, whether from within or without. It is a structure of resistance, the kind that "Puts all Heaven in a Rage";[64] and when someone builds such a hard-hearted cell of confinement for him- or herself, that person by definition repels such redemptive figures as were met by Christian at the slough and the mountain.

Taken by itself, then, the pathetic image of the Man in the Iron Cage furnishes a dark and static moment in the ongoing train of visual motifs. In context, however, its effect is far from disheartening. Rather, it is energizing, because, as a work of visionary art composed by the Interpreter, it has been set out as a topos and an object of contemplation for our hero, who obligingly responds to its specific content with a good deal of vigor and psychological acumen. It is meaningful beyond its content, too, in that it is the first such interpretive emblem to be encountered in this pictorial series. (Here, again, Blake deliberately departs from Bunyan's text, where the carefully orchestrated sequence of seven tableaux in the House of the Interpreter begins with the viewing of a basically uninterpreted and uninterpretable religious icon-painting, as far removed from Christian's present state of mind as possible, and progresses only gradually toward the scenes reflective of Christian's actual condition, represented here by Plates 12 and 13.)[65] As the initiating emblem to call for a visionary hermeneutic on the part of the dream hero, it is representative of a new reflective consciousness in the dream. And so the plate itself acquires the status of an "image of wonder" and of "truth," signifying the creative function of the Interpreter who invented it and the objectifying imaginal capacity of the dreamer who invented the Interpreter.

The presence of the Interpreter is the steadying factor in the shift over to Plate 13. We even see his spiritual influence radiate in an aura arching over him like a doorway while he takes up the central position between Christian and the last emblem of instruction: the Man Who Dreamed of the Day of Judgment. As we saw in Chapter 2, this emblem treats a subject fraught with intense significance for Blake, since its theme, the Last Judgment, provides the apocalyptic pattern for almost all his prophetic poems and pictures, all his statements urging a radical, Christian aesthetic. No wonder, then, that he made so much of it here and gave the incident a place of honor as the resonantly penultimate drawing of the graphic journey's climactic midpoint: for in Blake's pictorial retelling of Bunyan's myth, the halfway mark of the serial narrative is the following design (Plate 14), where Christian loses his burden and gains a personal vision of his imaginal nature, the "human form divine."[66]

In the composition of Plate 13, the first thing we notice is that, compared to the previous plate, there has been a decided humanization of the environment and of the figure acting out the emblem. The iconographic elements of his situation integrate more plausibly and closely with the milieu of the whole; that is, whereas the presence of a cage inside a room, as in Plate 12, is incongruous and disconcerting, the presence of a bed inside a chamber is normal. Psychologically speaking, too, this man is more on a par with his interlocutors, being neither naked nor fettered like the iron man, but dressed in white "Rayment" (such as Christian himself will wear in future episodes)[67] and closed in only by the soft red folds of his bed curtains. He is presented as having already risen up out of *his* cage—the far more natural and quotidian cage of sleep; moreover, his emergent attitude causes the pronounced frontality of his posture as he sits on the edge of the bed to have a markedly more seductive effect on the sympathy of the viewer than did the equally frontal pose of the caged man. There is depth to this figure's personal reality, and we are drawn to it both visually and emotionally. An example: his bed curtains form vaulted recesses that entice us even as they seem to suggest the very shape and location of his prophetic visions. Similarly, our eye is pulled to follow the hem of his garment, which sweeps backward at floor level into the ruffles of his bedding as if still connected with the zone of sleep, the white pillowed world where imagination becomes (in this case, literally) Revelation.[68]

From Bunyan's text we know that the man in this emblem is meant to be a warning to Christian, just as the subject in the previous illustration was. But there is a big difference in the mentality of the two characters, a difference Blake picks up on and generously amplifies to his own interpretive purpose. For although Bunyan's version of this emblematic dreamer-within-the-dream shakes and trembles from his haunting fear that he is doomed, he is not so fixated or developed in his anxiety that he has lost all perspective on it. Unlike the Man in the Iron Cage, he talks about his fear and about his vision. He thus creates a certain amount of figural and dialogic distance between himself and his feeling state as figured in his dream. That is his saving grace, and indeed for Blake this figure from the *Progress* typifies the very possibility of a saving grace in everyone's psychic organization.[69] Thus, despite the man's dream-vision that he will be rejected by God at the Last Day, he has two invaluable attributes (themselves God-given) that help him to counteract the implosive effect of his negative intuition: he has the visionary power to create a clear embodiment of his fear and the capacity to reflect consciously on its imaged content. These two attributes suggest that the man in the emblem is functioning as a type both of the original visionary of this series—the dreamer dreaming the narrative— and his present avatar, the Interpreter interpreting it. It is as if there were here, in Plate 13, a sudden upwelling of the persona of Plate 1, the creative dreamer whose surge of self-reflective energy penetrates the literal story line in order to rehearse, contemplate, and revise the imaginal process of his own psychic unfolding. The episode is structured, as earlier noted, on the pattern of a dream within a dream: one of the oldest strategies used by the revisionary imagination to get generic forms to comment on themeselves.[70]

Actually, the reiteration of embedded contexts (deployed here in a mode that is itself typologically connected to the tactics and situation of Plate 1) follows a much more intricate model than that of simply a dream within a dream. Instead what we have is (1) a vision of a man (2) narrating (3) a recent eschatological dream within (4) a house of visions, which exist by virtue of (5) the embracing narration of (6) a recent eschatological dream told by its author (Fig. 52). Moreover, at every point the visions coalesce, each one recapitulating or anticipating the next in a mutual reflection of the overarching presentiment of deliverance and final judgment. That the narrations also coalesce can be verified by considering the way the man in the Interpreter's seventh chamber reports his dream. In the book, when this figure tells Christian about the initial moments of his dream, he could as easily be describing the landscape of the first few laps of *Christian's* dream-journey, at least as these are illustrated by Blake in Plates 2, 5, and 8. Here again is the passage in question: "This night as I was in my sleep, I Dreamed, and behold the Heavens grew exceeding black; also it thundered and lightened in most fearful wise, that it put me into an Agony. So I looked up in my Dream, and saw the Clouds rack at an unusual rate" (*PP* 36). If we agree that the imagery in this description is duplicated by Blake's version of the early *Progress* scenes, we may also agree that the diction and rhetoric here echo the speech-pattern of the main narrator in the opening sentences of Bunyan's text. We must therefore allow that Blake's insistence on the relation between these two dreamers heightens a feature already present in Bunyan's prose and hence is not an undue distortion of the original. Bunyan as well as Blake played up the relevance of this man's dream to all that went before and all that was to come; author as well as artist made it function as a premonition, in a static and negative mode, of the general denouement of the encompassing dream-journey; and both men let it react directly on Christian,

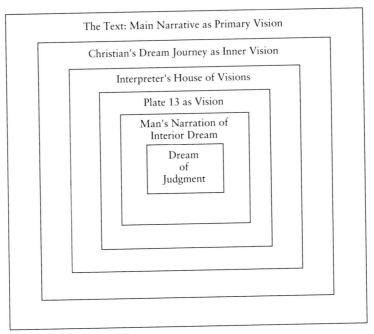

The Text: Main Narrative as Primary Vision

Christian's Dream Journey as Inner Vision

Interpreter's House of Visions

Plate 13 as Vision

Man's Narration of
Interior Dream

Dream
of
Judgment

FIG. 52   Diagram of the Dream-Within-the-Dream

who immediately goes off to experience his own, compensatingly optimistic, preview of deliverance. The differences between Blake's treatment of the episode and Bunyan's is that, by placing this design at the center of the graphic narrative (and so at the center of the viewer's experience), Blake gave it the structural prominence he felt its deeper psychological implications deserved. He made of its fearful symmetry—its ability to project beyond the limitations of its own intention the entire teleology of the main narrator's dream—an emblem and icon of the approaching midpoint in every pilgrim's map of imaginative change.

DRAWING 14

He ran . . . till he came at a place somewhat ascending;
and upon that place stood a *Cross,* and a little below in the
bottom, a Sepulcher. So I saw in my Dream, that just as
Christian came up with the *Cross,* his burden loosed from
off his Shoulders, and fell from off his back; and began to

tumble; and so continued to do, till it came to the mouth of the Sepulcher, where it fell in, and I saw it no more.

Then was *Christian* glad and lightsom, and said with a merry heart, *He hath given me rest, by his Sorrow; and life, by his death.* Then he stood still a while, to look and wonder; for it was very surprising to him, that the sight of the Cross should thus ease him of his burden. He looked therefore, and looked again, even till the springs that were in his head sent the waters down his cheeks. (*PP* 38)

The subject of this drawing (Plate 14, Fig. 34) is the experience of conversion. Blake states its principle of altered perception and response in a number of definitive ways, starting with its placement in the series as the initiator of the second half of the pilgrimage. These two swings of the dream-journey are symmetrically aligned in Blake's rendition and can be said to correspond to the Pauline doctrine of spiritual turning, which calls for a shedding of the old man and a putting on of the new. Plate 14 depicts the final shedding of the old in terms of the loosening of Christian's burden, while Plate 15 deals with the ritual donning in white raiment of the new. (The very idea of the relation between the Garment and the Man—or between the persona and the unique individuated identity—is thus another one of the attitudes undergoing conversion in this pivotal episode.)

It must be noted here that Blake's plotting of the *Progress* into two equal parts divided at the center by Christian's scene of spiritual conversion represents a major reapportionment of the original fictive structure. In Bunyan's text, the incident of the burden's release occurs only about one-fifth of the way through, leaving a great deal of narrative time for the amplification of what Blake likely regarded as secondary material fogging over the rest of the mythic content.[71] Indeed, with Bunyan the shape of the telling of the dream mushroomed intentionally, building as it went a momentum of repetition and commentary: for him, the temporal center of the narrative is the *discussion* of the narrative entered into by Christian and Faithful along the way (see Plate 21).

As to the iconographic treatment of narrative structure by other illustrators, most followed Bunyan more closely than did Blake. In the traditional sequence, a print of Christian at the cross appeared about one-third of the way through (illustration number 4 out of 14), and the design occupying the featured center position was devoted to Christian in full armor fighting Apollyon.[72] Artists who followed this pattern in effect slanted the story of *The Pilgrim's Progress* toward the militant myth of the Christian warrior doing battle against Satan's forces. Blake, however, made the pictorial tradition itself go through a significant transformation on this point. Thus, with drawing 14 he constructed a nonviolent, deeply Christ-centered interpretation of Bunyan's allegory, letting the cruciform apparition of Jesus (in its own right a symbol of counterforces joined at the center) serve as a spontaneous emblem of both the form of the work and the goal, not of warfare, but of the integration sought by the dreamer's psyche.

The drawing shows Christian standing at center stage with his back to us as he looks inward and upward at the figure of Jesus suspended above him in a wedge-shaped cloud. The vortexical contour of the cloud inverts, by upending, the shape of the curtain folds in the previous drawing. It is as though the articulation of the damnation-fantasy held by the man dreaming of the Last Judgment in the House of the Interpreter released this contrary image of deliverance through its own visionary opening in obedience to an inner law of psychological compensation in the mind of the original dreamer. There is a pronounced ambiguity here as to whether Christ's body is rising, descending, or fixed in place, as on the cross. One could say he is deliberately equipoised among all these interpretations, available to each according to need, in a flexibility of reference that is his hallmark.

By a motion answering Christian's gaze, mysterious streaks of dark light emanate outward and downward from the lower edge of the cloud. These rays are perhaps intended as a transfiguration of the crown of thorns worn by Jesus at his crucifixion. They also function as a redemptive version of the iron spikes pressing inward on the naked victim of despair in Plate 12—a creature who clearly figures as a reverse type of the transcendent image of Christ.

Flanking the apparition, a pair of thin sapling tree-trunks rises toward the heavens. Each tree is entwined with green-leafed vines whose stems are tinted a rusty red, like blood. Because this design makes it appeal on the grounds of its allusiveness to the death and resurrection of Christ, it is fair to regard the two trees as living reminders of the thieves killed and crucified on either side of Jesus at Golgotha. They may also be the dream's way of "converting" its own representations into the new significance, displacing the two emblems of Plates 12 and 13 (which function as counterexamples and also forerunners of Christian's ability to envision Christ) by superimposing Plate 14 on them in a manner comparable to the relation of Jesus and the thieves in scriptural mythology.

It is critical to understand the special way the images in this illustration do in fact embody symbolic significance; for they do so less by becoming symbols than by becoming images of the symbolizing process itself. Thus, it would be a mistake to believe that Blake intended them as occult allegorical references imposed on the visual narrative from an authorial distance. The motif just discussed, for example, is *not* Blake's way of saying "the trees Christian saw were like the thieves at the crucifixion." Rather, he is dramatizing Christian's experience of the shift in consciousness; hence, the statement the design makes in this particular might more accurately be worded: "the trees Christian saw were perceived *by him* to be like the thieves at Christ's side." This intention is borne out by examination of the drawing's relation to the text, which says simply that Christian "came up with the *Cross*" (*PP* 38). No mention is made of a vision or visitation or emblem of the "human form divine" (although Jesus is referred to by Christian as he cries out, alluding to scripture, "He hath given me rest, by his sorrow; and life, by his death"); and no illustrator other than Blake depicted Christ's presence here. Instead, most earlier pictorial treatments of the scene showed the pilgrim staring at the bare structure of a cross in awe at its magical charge, which had delivered him of his burden of Original Sin (see Figs. B40 and B52). Blake, however, takes the lines in the text describing Christian's attitude of wonder as a reference to the way a visionary imagination endows ephemeral objects with archetypal significance—and that, of course, is by observing them with the altered eye of "spiritual sensation" (E703/K794) and seeing eidetically the objects' inner image, with its store of overdetermined, polysemous meanings.[73] Here, then, we see that Christian sees not the apparent surface of the cross, but its personified, symbolic center. And this *act* of Christian vision *is* the vision: a resurrection of imaginative awareness conforming to the image of the risen Son of Man.

It is the identification Christian himself makes between his imaginative nature and Christ's resurrection that permits and denotes the falling away of the burden. Therefore, the burden in its death throes appropriately recalls the burial of Jesus, whereby a corruptible body was converted to an incorruptible. To enhance the hints Bunyan gives of this connection, Blake fashions the burden to look like an unborn human embryo crouched by the transcept of the sepulcher's angular doorway. It also has the appearance of crumpled clothing, a possible allusion to the linen cloth found folded up beside Christ's tomb after the resurrection.

In this pictorial image, the life cycle of the burden first invoked in Plate 2 comes to a close. Blake unifies the attributes of that life by revising in Plate 14 motifs associated with it in earlier designs. Thus, the ribbons of red streaming down like blood from the place of Christ's cross and merging at ground level with the huddled shape of the burden remind us of the bloody, humpbacked form that the burden took in Plate 2. Further, the episode in which the power of the burden nearly drowned Christian is recalled by a similarity between the structures of this composition and those of Plate 6. There, as we noted earlier, the body of Christian sank to its lowest point visually in the whole sequence, with the burden itself half submerged in the mire. Now again the burden takes that placement on the bottom line, but Christian, conversely, stands tall and by comparison is "raised a spiritual body."[74] Plate 14, in fact, is a formal and imaginal flowering of Plate 6, with the comparably inward-facing figure of Christian raised to the level to which Help tried to lift it and the frontal reach of

Help transformed to the widespread embracing vision of Christ. In short, the elements of the design of Plate 6 ascend on the picture plane of Plate 14 in unison with the visionary power gained here by Christian.

These transformations are Blake's work, but they are also meant to convey the creative work of the dreamer's psyche in the process of its own development. Blake gives us an opportunity to observe that progress from an aesthetic distance by alluding in Plate 14 to his external view of the dreamer in Plate 1. Juxtaposed, these two drawings, 1 and 14, comment on each other first and foremost on the basis of compositional stratification. Plate 1, as we saw, divided the dreamer's reality into three regions, the horizontal bands occupied by the lion, the man, and the visionary rainbow-dream. So, too, is Christian's world stratified in Plate 14, although the realm formerly dominated by the lion is now given over to the cast-off burden.[75] And just as the dreamer lay in a natural setting, so Christian stands amid natural trees and vines transformed by emblematic significance. Also, the rainbow swath holding the contents of the dreamer's dream is modulated here into the form of the cloud containing Christian's vision. The difference is that Plate 14 portrays an integration and interpenetration on the vertical axis of all the realms. With Christian, unlike the dreamer of Plate 1, meeting his divine vision here face to face, and with the stream of blood and vines flowing over the sacrificed burden, a link of differentiated elements is forged. At the same time, the role of Christian as mediator between his visionary and corruptible natures is seen to be an essential part of his conscious—not, as before, his unconscious—experience.

Plate 14, then, represents an accomplishment of imaginative cohesion aptly suited to the job of closing the first half of the dream-journey and introducing a new and necessary cycle of development for the dreamer. That continued development *is* necessary is suggested by the fact that the image of Christ that Christian envisions is noticeably incomplete—indeed, literally only half formed. Plates 15–28 work toward the resolution of this unfinished program to see whole the individuated reality of the dreaming psyche.

DRAWING 15

Now as he stood looking and weeping, behold three shining ones came to him, and saluted him, with *Peace be to thee:* so the first said unto him, *Thy sins be forgiven.* The second stript him of his Rags, and cloathed him with change of Raiment. The third also set a mark in his forehead, and gave him a Roll with a Seal upon it, which he bid him look on as he ran, and that he should give it in at the Coelestial Gate: so they went their way. (*PP* 38)

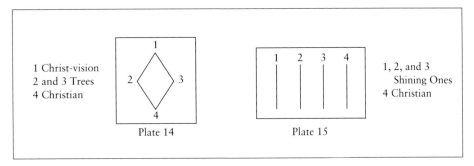

FIG. 53   Diagram of Plates 14 and 15

What immediately strikes the eye about this design (Plate 15, Fig. 35) is that it is crowded with full-sized figures spread out evenly across the horizontal plane. Here for the first time in the series we have more than three characters on view at once, and also for the first time more than two of them are shown as interrelating on the same level of consciousness (that is, person to person, rather than person to emblem), not to mention the same level of ground and in the same style of representation.[76] This fact is important because, although its efficient cause is the material of Bunyan's text, Blake uses the concept of a foursome as the basis for the aesthetic organization and symbolic revelation of much that follows. In fact, from a design standpoint, the second half of the *Progress* illustrations is dominated by a system of threes tending to fours, just as the first half was governed by groupings of twos leading to threes. This is true both in terms of the interrelation of key elements within particular drawings and in terms of many intracompositional units, or groupings of designs.

In the present case, the three-on-one arrangement of four figures standing in a line is an outcome of the incipient quaternity pictured in Plate 14. There, the image of Jesus flanked by the two vines formed a meaningful triadic gestalt that was pitted against the single figure of Christian in a combined fourfold config- uration best described as diamond-shaped (Fig. 53). In the structure of Plate 14, this diamond shape converged toward two other traditional emblems of spiritual wholeness, the cross and the circle, manifested in the cruciform pose of Christ's body and the mandala of light behind it. The relinquished burden and its grave remained outside the charged area of fourfoldedness like a fifth wheel, connected but nonfunctional. By contrast, in Plate 15 the theme of fourfoldedness becomes naturalized: we are *in* its world, having been brought over the threshold by force of the previous design. Therefore it is now appropriate to flatten the conversion experience out on the plane of normal interactions in rational space.

Here is no mix of modalities, no dialectical exchange between figures experienced as characters and figures experienced as visions, metaphors, symbols. Instead, the scene of drawing 15 depicts Christian meeting the "three shining ones," who of course can be interpreted allegorically but who in the dream's terms are the protagonist's existential equals. In a similar way, the rainbow coloration of Plate 14, a coloration reserved to identify the visionary realm according to a rhetorical principle established in the opening design, becomes diffused in pale washes throughout the entire atmosphere of Plate 15, tingeing the angels' wings, their coats, their halos, the sky. It is likely that Blake sought to differentiate the quality of drawings 14 and 15 thus because he saw them as representing emotionally distinct events—conversion and initiation—and he wanted to render that distinction through divergent visual stylistics. The deployment here of such a differentiating impulse is another example of Blake's revision of traditional practice through a characteristic double focus, for many influential illustrators lumped the two aspects of the event together in one design (see Figs. B40 and B52), while others simply excluded the second phase entirely. Remembering that Blake doubled the customary length of the complete graphic sequence, it is instructive of him to exhibit the semantic purpose of his expansion principle so dynamically at the pictorial narrative's exact midpoint.

The iconography of Plate 15 follows sedately and rather literally the content of Bunyan's text. The only major alteration is the gender of the angelic messengers. Bunyan refers to them in the conventional manner as men, but Blake renders them female. Usually it was Blake's habit (following the early masters of Christian art) to desexualize the figural appearance of angels: avoiding both virile and womanly body contours, he normally opted for a sort of prepubescent compromise. Here, though, the "Femin[in]e Portion" of existence (M 41) is deliberately constellated: an innovation in the imagery of the series so far. The effect is largely one of balance, a reprieve from the one-sided masculine world.[77] It also has the function of preparing us for the subtle sexual allusions of the following plates. From the point of view of the dream psyche, it would seem to have been introduced at this juncture in response to the vision of Christ, a traditionally androgynous figure capable of mediating all differences, whether of spirit or of form.

Looking at the drawing we see the three shining ones aligned close up in the foreground in the order described by Bunyan. Reading from left to right, the first carries a book, presumably the Gospels containing the passage about forgiveness, which this angel quotes for Christian by way of a formal blessing.[78] The middle angel, responsible for clothing Christian in a "change of Raiment," holds in either hand the top and bottom of the "Rags" she is said to have stripped him of. These remnants of Christian's former attire (associated with man's "Iniquity" in the scriptural reference alluded to in the margin by Bunyan)[79] are undergoing a noticeable metamorphosis at the angelic touch. No longer simply clothes, they look more like a sheath of leaves or an outpouring of liquid or a downward flow of torchfire. By this image, ambiguous and overdetermined as it is, Blake demonstrates the immediate effect of forgiveness on the structures of sin: they become what they always were—earthly perishables about to melt away.

The last "shining one" stands third in line and is closest to Christian, in three-quarter profile. She is shown holding a scroll in her left hand while with her right finger she places a mark on Christian's brow. This latter act is glossed in Bunyan's text with a reference to Ephesians 1:13, where the believer entering the faith is described as one "sealed with the Holy Spirit of promise." The same chapter and verse is cited to explain the other precious gift of this angel, that is, the "Roll," or guarantee, of heavenly inheritance and immortal identity that will become the psychological focus of Plate 17. As Christian receives the mark from the third angel he stands—also in three-quarter profile—dressed in his new garment. The coloration and style of this garment will change throughout the rest of the illustrations, but here it is presented as a white robe which matches that worn by the Man Who Dreamed of the Last Judgment in Plate 13. Again, the sense of this figural maneuver is to show how the understanding and value of reality—not just its look—have been transformed by the intervening conversion experience of Plate 14. On one side of that watershed we see a hell-fearing man who interprets his prophetic dream as a vision of personal doom and does not even relate to the fact that he is dressed in the costume of the elect, a dress betokening that his sins will in fact be forgiven him in eternity.[80] On this side of that same watershed, however, awareness of the white robe's significance is the very theme of the incident pictured, as it also was for Bunyan, who, in addition to having the first angel deliver the blessing of absolution just before the second angel "cloathes" Christian with the new robe, provides a set of biblical glosses for this passage that virtually equate the image of the garment with the idea of forgiveness.[81]

Plate 15 therefore can be compared to a musical chord sounding Blake's favorite Christian slogan, the forgiveness of sins, in four-part harmony. Even the embellishment of the vine-clad tree behind Christian is in tune with the keynote expression of divine forgiveness, for it carries over from Plate 14 the image associated with one of the reprobate sinners at Golgotha—the one, no doubt, who was redeemed along with Jesus on the cross. Thus, an unbroken connection is maintained between the archetypal scene of forgiveness in the previous drawing, on the one hand, and the ego-character's experience of its tangible effects, expressed here in the naturalistic mode of the dream's main story line, on the other.

The narrow way lay right up the Hill, (and the name of
the going up the side of the Hill, is called *Difficulty.*) *Christian* now . . . began to go up the Hill; saying,

> *This Hill, though high, I covet to ascend,*
> *The difficulty will not me offend:*
> *For I perceive the way to life lies here;*
> *Come, pluck up, Heart; lets neither faint nor fear:*
> *Better, tho difficult, th' right way to go,*
> *Then wrong, though easie, where the end is wo . . .*

I looked then after *Christian,* to see him go up the Hill,
where I perceived he fell from running to going, and from
going to clambering upon his hands and his knees, because of the steepness of the place . . . [and after sleeping
in the Arbour of Grace midway up the hill he] suddenly
started up, and sped him on his way, and went a pace till
he came to the top of the Hill. (*PP* 41–43)

Now when he was up to the top of the Hill . . . he felt in
his bosom for his Roll . . . and found it not. Then was
Christian in great distress, and knew not what to do, for
he wanted that which used to relieve him, and that which
should have been his Pass into the Coelestial City. . . .
Thus therefore he went back, carefully looking on this
side, and on that, all the way as he went, if happily he
might find his Roll. . . . He went thus till he . . . was
come to the *Arbour* again, where for a while he sat down
and wept, but at last . . . looking sorrowfully down under the Settle, there he espied his Roll; the which he with
trembling and haste catch'd up, and put into his bosom;
but who can tell how joyful this man was, when he had
gotten his Roll again! For this Roll was the assurance of
his life, and acceptance at the desired Haven. (*PP* 43–44)

Thus he went on his way . . . [and] he lift up his eyes,
and behold there was a very stately Palace before him, the
name whereof was *Beautiful,* and it stood just by the
High-way side.

So I saw in my Dream, that he made haste and went
forward, that if possible he might get Lodging there;
Now before he had gone far, he entered into a very narrow passage, which was about a furlong off of the Porters
Lodge, and looking very narrowly before him as he went,
he espied two Lions in the way. . . . Then he was

afraid . . . : But the *Porter* at the Lodge, whose name is *Watchful,* perceiving that *Christian* made a halt, as if he would go back, cried unto him saying, Is thy strength so small? fear not the Lions, for they are Chained; and are placed there for trial of faith where it is; and for discovery of those that have none: keep in the midst of the Path, and no hurt shall come unto thee.

Then I saw that he went on, trembling for fear of the Lions; but taking good heed to the directions of the *Porter;* he heard them roar, but they did him no harm. Then he clapt his hands, and went on. (*PP* 45–46)

The following three designs (Plates 16–18, Figs. 36–38) make up a triptych similar to the one treated earlier involving Plates 7, 8, and 9, which, particularly with regard to the sequential evolution of its three component parts, set the pattern for this unit. There, as here, the plates tell a well-ordered story about (1) a false step that is (2) realized and (3) corrected. There, as here, the last panel returns to the scene of the crime portrayed in the first. And there, as here, the middle design concentrates the energy of the series, placing the figure of Christian within an enclosed space of intense atmospheric charge where he both has a revelation and appeals to the viewer in a frontal pose of considerable strain and stretch. It is as if the dreamer were returning to the simple rhetorical formula of an old-time morality play in these passages, and the familiar rhythm of its three-act structure gives us a satisfying sense of clarity and finish. For here we see the progress of *The Pilgrim's Progress* consolidated in terms of character-building situations that are set apart from the flow of the literal journey through space; that is, these imagined acts take place in the undertow of the forward current, representing moments in the story when Christian's moral and imaginative backslidings force him to go back bodily over ground already covered in order to achieve a psychological *recovery.*

Blake's attempt to isolate the underlying motives of these narrative sections in a tripartite sequence comprehensible to the eye was influenced in each case by the counterexamples of the illustrative tradition. As we have seen, a confusion about the backtracking aspect of the action in these episodes had become a part of the history of the *Progress* designs and had fed Blake's revisionary impulse in the earlier three-plate series. In Plates 16, 17 and 18 we will observe the same process at work.

Plates 16 and 18, the outer panels of the triptych, can conveniently be looked at together. They are two of the more obvious derivative designs of the full series, although no less effective on that account. The first shows Christian reaching, by an enormous extension of his entire frame, the top of Hill Difficulty, where a set of buildings is pictured a ways off on the summit. Plate

18 gives us a closeup of the achieved summit, with the porter of Palace Beautiful standing in the distant gateway to urge Christian on through a rock chasm guarded by a pair of rigidly staring lions. Pictorially, these scenes match. Christian's push through a narrow passage in both drawings, the muscular reach and curve of his figure, the dark rocks at either side, the building at the top—all these things convince us that drawing 18 represents a revisitation of the territory of Plate 16. We note a discrepancy in the contour of the two buildings, but that can be explained as figuring forth the new perspective and perceptual faculty attained by Christian in the second of these three designs—a clarity of vision resulting, presumably, from Christian's recovery of the abandoned roll as depicted in Plate 17.

There is an alternative way of reading the iconography of Plate 16, though, that would equate the highpoint shown there with Hill Difficulty's *middle* plateau (*PP* 42). Then the building at the top of the design would represent not House Beautiful but the halfway shelter in the Arbor of Grace where Christian rests and forgets his identity papers. This was the subject of the two traditional illustrations (Figs. B19 and B41) that served as Blake's models for the formal conception of Plate 16. But even there, enough pictorial ambiguity remained that the publishers felt obliged to identify the scene with an inscription written on the picture itself, titling the building as the place where Christian "slept and dropt his Roll," making it clear that the structure was not to be confused with House Beautiful. No such identifying inscription accompanied the original engraving of this design, however (see Fig. B19), where the building in view probably *was* meant to represent House Beautiful (it has the look of a palatial edifice) and the event represented would then correspond to the one Blake's drawing first suggests: arrival at the Palace of Beauty.

Why, then, all the rigamarole about adding labels and manipulating the reference of picture to story in later reprints? The explanation entails a publishing misadventure. The original composition was one of the seven Flemish designs pirated for insertion in the fourteenth British edition of the *Progress*. It replaced an English engraving of Christian seated in the arbor, looking down at two of his former companions, Formalist and Hypocrisie, on their way to bad ends because they refused the difficult climb upward (see Fig. B5). Underneath the picture was attached one of those explanatory quatrains we spoke of earlier; and this one, instead of speaking for or about Christian, alluded rather to the doomed defectors, Formalist and Hypocrisie, as follows:

Shall they who wrong begin yet rightly end?
Shall they at all have Safety for their friend?
No, no in head-strong manner they set out,
And headlong will they fall at last no doubt.

When the Flemish engraving took over the slot of this English print, it inherited the old quatrain. Then, to make the old quatrain jibe with the new illustration, the editor had to ensure that the illustration could in fact reasonably refer to Christian's earlier meeting with Formalist and Hypocrisie. He therefore labeled it a picture of Christian climbing toward the arbor, when the "headstrong" pair who chose the opposite course would still be fresh in the mind of the commentator, reader and spectator alike.

Into this tradition of willful confusion stepped Blake. His intention seems to have been to preserve the most fruitful of these past manipulations of the image and show by the form of the sequence their necessary relation and inner meaning. For him, that inner meaning had its center in the center, the place occupied by illustration 17.

The subject treated is Christian's finding again, in the deep recesses of the arbor, the evidence of his divine identity. Thematically, this design functions as the positive contrary to Plate 8, its partner in the earlier series of three. There we saw Christian caught up in a state of fear, oblivious to the role of the self beyond states. Here, Christian himself *does* the catching up, retrieving his testament of selfhood from the zone of the state of grace (the arbor) so that it can serve him in the forward journey through all other states. Furthermore, Plate 8 portrayed its enclosure of fire and lightning as an assault of threatening, exterior forces. But in Plate 17, the protected environment of the arbor flourishes from within, its structure of palm trees, flowers, fruit, and carved benches pulsing with the sheer exuberance of color.[82] Its attracting force is so powerful that it seems to have drained the brightness out of the scenic panels on either side, like a fertile womb which draws nutriments from the mother's body to feed the embryo of the incarnating soul.

Another way of looking at the in-gathering vibrancy of this illustration is to see it as a metamorphosis in the dreamer's psyche of the centering power of Christ on the cross, portrayed in Plate 14. Three major design elements reinforce that reading. The first is the emphatic presence of the telltale rainbow in an arching configuration, developed from Plate 1, which inverts the shape of Christ's visionary cloud in Plate 14. The second is the general form of the arbor tent with its palm-tree pillars positioned like the three trees that evoked the three crosses at Christ's crucifixion in 14. And the third is the strong, prophetic gesture of Christian's arms connecting heaven and earth on the vertical axis, the way the design as a whole in 14 does, and the way the design of Plate 1 deliberately *avoids* doing.[83] By these flashback allusions to the two main examples of visionary power in the series, we get the sense that the ego figure of the dreamer's psyche has assimilated the message: through his experiential knowledge of his divine inheritance *he* mediates what is above and what is below. *His* imagination, stored in *his* "human form divine," can stretch so as to ground the transpersonal rainbow world and let it incarnate in the manifest forms of his personal reality. The phallic connotation of the "Roll," enhanced by its placement between Christian's legs, suggests that the dreamer's libido is being constellated in this design and that a release of pent-up energies is under way. It is instructive to remember that this episode was the one Blake chose as an emblem to help him recontextualize the *Gates of Paradise* into a graphic statement about self-recovery "For the Sexes." There, too, the image of erotic release proved central to the design, central to the revelation that there was such a thing as a permanent identity. But Plate 17 goes further than the lost traveler stranded under the hill of the *Gates:* along with the drawings on either side, it is concerned with the theme of conscious effort—effort that turns revelation into purposeful action and, in this case, helps Christian walk *through* a gateway (Plate 18) without the bodily assistance he required to pass the previous threshold (Plate 11).[84]

Of the many images of conscious effort in these drawings, the most unusual, perhaps, is that of the speckled garment that Christian wears in all three plates. On the literal level, these flecks of red simulate the embroidery that is described in the text as an attribute of Christian's new garment.[85] Embellishments of this sort in earlier illustrations became a part of the standard iconography (see Figs. B18 and B41). But Blake revises this tradition in two ways. First, he turns what was meant to be the noble mark of sumptuous decoration easily won into a symbol of spiritual exertion and martyrdom; for in his hands, these bits of embroidery resemble the scabs of tiny flesh wounds, or the trickle of blood from myriad scratches. Second, it is only in these three designs that the new cloak takes on the aspect of a robe of agony—as if it were suddenly but not permanently transformed from its pristine condition in Plate 15 by the strenuous drive and difficulty of this section of the journey.

The effort expended in any case proves a success, because it enables Christian to cut a pass (as Blake has rendered it) through the rocks that support the threatening lions in Plate 18. Notably, Christian manages the fearful transition by repeating the gesture adopted in Plate 17, the one that there reconciled the upper and the lower worlds. He is encouraged to take the middle way, moreover, by the porter, who waves a replica of the identity roll before his eyes for a sign and an inducement. This detail represents a departure by Blake from Bunyan's text, as well as from the iconography of all previous illustrators, and so is of some interest as a clue to the special implications he means to impart. Given that at this stage Christian's roll has begun to develop sexual connotations, as we saw in Plate 17, it would be plausible to anticipate an expansion of that libidinal theme here. And indeed, we see in this design another gratuitous allusion to the phallic force engendered by the experiences of climbing the hill, penetrating the passageway, and passing the lions—namely, the portrayal of a sword in Christian's right hand. As a literal item it is wholly anomolous: it comes from nowhere in the narrative and has no source even in the glosses of Bunyan's text. At most, on the mimetic level, it can be explained as an anachronism that anticipates the sword Christian will receive in the following scene (Plate 19), where he is shown leaving the palace armory. Yet if we read this sword as a figurative expression (which is the way "literal" images often do work in dreams and visions), it seems a perfectly justifiable metamorphosis and clear extension of the scroll handled by Christian in Plate 17. What was at hand there as text (the roll) has here instantaneously become weapon (the sword), and since both items in their contexts carry phallic connotations, we may justly infer that at the entrance to the domain of the beautiful (for so this way station is named), Christian's erotic identity is gaining power, albeit a rather defensive power. My sense, therefore, is that Plate 18 depicts an ac-knowledgment of the problem posed by physical desire and animal instinct in the life of an initiated pilgrim. Once the reality of the numinous connection between above and below has been experienced, it is not appropriate to maintain unexamined an ascetic attitude toward the instinctual capacities of the human makeup. Thus, the image of the lion signifying the dreamer's own brute nature in Plate 1 appears here, doubled and aroused, to challenge Chris-tian "in the way" of the dream. These two beasts, who are chained to the bedrock of earth, are nevertheless pictured on the level of Christian's head, indicating that they and the complex they represent have become a conscious issue to the ego of the dream.[86] It is precisely this issue that works itself out over the course of the following two designs.

DRAWING 19

> Now he bethought himself of setting forward, and [the
> Beautiful Damsels] were willing he should: but first, said
> they, let us go again into the Armory, so they did; and
> when he came there, they harnessed him from head to
> foot, with what was of proof, lest perhaps he should meet
> with assaults in the way. He being therefore thus ac-
> coutred, walketh out with his friends to the Gate, and
> there he asked the *Porter* if he saw any [other] Pilgrims
> pass by. (*PP* 55)

Blake emulated the earliest, traditional sequence of Bunyan designs by next illustrating the departure from Palace Beautiful (Plate 19, Fig. 39) and making it follow directly the subject of Christian's approach to the same locale. What goes *against* tradition in his treatment is the negative overtone he imputes to the palace. Admittedly, this drawing is in a very unfinished state, so the details are difficult to pick out. But the massive, square buildings and the heavy dome in the background echo ominously the architecture of the City of Destruction.[87] Also, the down-pressing spears in the palace's armory doorway, the lassitude of the guard sketched beside it, and the dejection of the figure seated within (posed in the stock iconographic attitude of Melancholia) all have an enervating effect on the atmosphere of the scene. Is Blake thus disparaging the lessons Christian learned from the Virgin Virtues of the palace? Portions of the passage in the *Progress* text that detail the exchanges between Christian and Prudence, and then Christian and Charity, constitute a flare-up of doctrinaire Puritan attitudes that may well have made Blake cringe. These passages take a hard-line approach to the pitfalls of "carnal cogitations" (*PP* 50) and of open, emotional transactions between husband and wife. Much of the sentiment expressed fundamentally contradicts the forgiveness principle, being full of the spirit of accusation produced by moral prudery. That this prudery is packaged in a seemingly pure but subtly seductive casing (the women of the house attend and detain Christian at suspicious length) only increases its incapacitating effect.[88] No wonder, therefore, that the Beautiful Damsels "harnessed" Christian "from head to foot" in religion's armor. And no wonder they felt obliged to give him the added potency of a phallic sword, in tacit substitution for his identity roll, as a protection against future attacks of repressed libido, which they themselves helped to create and thus had reason to fear.[89]

The above interpretation of the actions of the controlling virtues in Palace Beautiful clearly distorts the meaning *Bunyan* intended. Nevertheless, I believe it is a valid analysis of the material from a psychological standpoint, and—more important—I feel it tallies with *Blake's* revisionary view of the passage and of the underlying impetus of the dream. For in terms of the surrounding sequence of drawings, it appears that Blake regarded the interlude in House Beautiful as part of a regressive episode moving to culmination in the next design. This becomes clear if we look for a moment at the implications of the formal arrangement of Plates 14 through 20. What we see first is a seven-plate series laid out in three segments consisting of one double (14 and 15), one triple (16, 17, and 18), and another double (19 and 20). The scheme is perfectly symmetrical in both composition and conception, so that, with Plate 17 as the center, the designs on either side match up as opposites (Fig. 54; see also Figs. 34–40, which are arranged on the page according to this alignment). Thus 14 is brought into antithetical relation with 20, 15 contrasts with 19, and 16 counters 18. As far as Plate 19 specifically is concerned, it is made to function both as the direct contrary of 15 and as a prelude to the contrary of 14. That is, the

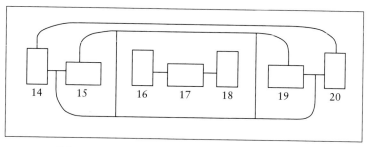

FIG. 54   Diagram of Plates 14–20

double-plate units, *qua* units, relate in bilateral symmetry just as do the individual designs.

This means that drawing 19 is heading toward an extreme concentration of spiritual "error," about to be embodied in the figure of Apollyon, the Antichrist—and, in its own right, by showing Christian paired with the porter instead of the damsels, it represents a breakdown of the realized quaternity achieved by Plate 15 in the visionary aftermath of Plate 14. A comparison of the narrative situations surrounding 15 and 19 tells this story in a nutshell. Just as the three "shining ones" invest Christian with his new raiment of forgiveness, the four virtues of House Beautiful issue him the uniform of ultimate resistance. And just as Christian goes upward once the angels leave, climbing Hill Difficulty in energetic imitation of Christ's passion, so he will go down slowly from House Beautiful, down to the satanic mills of the Valley of Humiliation, leaving behind in the armory the personifications of those so-called virtues who are the exemplars of Blake's old dictum about the lack of passion: "Those who restrain desire, do so because theirs is weak enough to be restrained" (*MHH* 5).

As mentioned earlier, an extra design of this incident exists outside the series (Fig. 55), and one scholar strongly suggests that it rightfully belongs here, within the series, between Plates 19 and 20.[90] Both because of the subject of that plate, which presents the damsels of House Beautiful in a positive light, to the degree that they are washed in the colors of the visionary rainbow motif, and because of its compositional discordance with the rhythm of the sequence from a design standpoint, I feel it is not a genuine part of the complete graphic narrative as Blake eventually shaped it. Instead I see the extra illustration as an alternate reading and a trial resolution of the repressive implications of Bunyan's passage. Such a resolution, however, would appear premature in the context of the present series, which seems to predict a rush toward the confrontation with Apollyon before amelioration occurs in Plate 21. I therefore argue that "Christian with the Shield of Faith, Taking Leave of his Compan-

FIG. 55 Blake, *Christian Takes Leave of His Companions* (formerly called *A Warrior with Angels*)

ions" was intentionally diverted by Blake from the current set of *Progress* drawings to stand or fall on its own merit.[91]

DRAWING 20

But now in this Valley of *Humiliation* poor *Christian* was hard put to it, for he had gone but a little way before he espied a foul *Fiend* coming over the field to meet him; his name is *Apollyon* . . . now the Monster was hidious to behold, he was cloathed with scales like a Fish (and they are his pride) he had Wings like a Dragon, feet like a Bear, and out of his belly came Fire and Smoak, and his mouth was as the mouth of a Lion. . . .

Then [after a long debate in which Apollyon attempts to seduce Christian into his service] *Apollyon* strodled quite over the whole breadth of the way, and said, I am

void of fear in this matter, prepare thy self to dye, for I
swear by my Infernal Den, that thou shalt go no further,
here will I spill thy soul: and with that he threw a flaming
Dart at his brest; but *Christian* had a Shield in his hand,
with which he caught it, and so prevented the danger of
that.

   . . . Then *Apollyon* espying his opportunity, began to
gather up close to *Christian,* and wrestling with him, gave
him a dreadful fall; and with that *Christian's* Sword flew
out of his hand. Then said *Apollion, I am sure of thee now;*
and with that, he had almost prest him to death; so that
Christian began to despair of his life. But as God would
have it, while *Apollyon* was fetching of his last blow,
thereby to make a full end of this good Man, *Christian*
nimbly reached out his hand for his Sword, and caught it,
saying, *Rejoyce not against me, O mine Enemy! when I fall, I
shall arise.* (PP 56, 59–60)

This drawing (Plate 20, Fig. 40) presents the most intense engagement of
conflicting powers in the entire *Progress* sequence. Before now we encountered
several designs showing close and numinous union between Christian and a
redemptive "other" (Plates 6, 11, and 14), but nowhere in this dream so far has
the opposite relation—a head-on clash between Christian and a mortally an-
tagonistic force—become manifest. Psychologically understood, this is therefore an extremely important moment, for constellating and confronting the
negativity of the individual psyche is the sine qua non for all durable self-
development, all awakening, all grounding of the personality in the real.

   In the composition, Apollyon looms up larger than life. We get the impression that he is a "Giant form" both because the character deliberately creates a
menacing appearance by spreading his arms, legs, and bat wings to the utmost
and because Blake makes this figure fill the entire picture plane. The tips of his
wings penetrate the frame at the upper corners, and his feet splay into the
lower corners, toes pressed to the very edge of the plate bottom. These
compositional measures are meant to make us feel the physical *emergency* of his
emergence in the dreamer's psyche. He really is "strodled quite over the whole
breadth of the way" in this rendering, preventing any further progress until he
is wholly attended to and dealt with.[92]

   Bunyan's description of Apollyon draws on three biblical sources: Revelation 9:11 and 13:2 and Job 41:15. Each scriptural place speaks of a different
metamorphosis of the satanic archetype, indicating that for Bunyan, as well as
for Blake, Apollyon is a composite exemplar of savage energy. Revelation 9
gives him his name and identity as the angel who is king of the bottomless pit;

Revelation 13 supplies the bear's feet and lion's mouth, derived from the body of the beast with seven heads; and Job 41 lends the image of the scales of pride from God's portrait of Leviathan.[93]

Blake faithfully illustrates each of these details, along with several others mentioned by Bunyan, but he outdoes himself in the rendering of two in particular: the crown signifying Apollyon's kingship, and the "Fire and Smoak" emitting from his "belly." The crown, and indeed the whole upper portion of the composition, takes on its full meaning only in relation to Plate 14, this plate's symmetric contrary in the group of seven discussed earlier. Plate 14's V-shaped cloud is duplicated by the contour and location of Apollyon's upper torso, and the diadem sprouting from Apollyon's head (formed by a system of head spikes, halo, and seven large, black coronal points) is an inversion of the rays that descend in spears of dark light from the edge of Christian's vision of Jesus. Notably, Plate 14's image of Christ inside the cloud is without crown of any kind, since in that drawing the sovereign energy comes rather from the visionary force field itself. In Plate 20, by contrast, the "foul Fiend" is unleashed as a real presence, not the symbol of a presence, so his power emanates directly from him and is "from the body" (*MHH* 4).

The emphasis on Apollyon's corporeal energy—especially compared to the restrained, indeed virtually amputated, embodiment of Jesus in the vision of Plate 14—reaches significant expression in the stream of fire ejaculating from the monster's genitals.[94] This is Blake's interpretation of the much less provocative image of the fire and smoke coming out of Apollyon's "belly" in Bunyan's account. For the loins, as the decreed seat of human desire, *are* what have bellied out in this eruption of libidinal instinct from the dreamer's unconscious. The fact that it is such a violent eruption is a measure of its former repression, and in this we begin to see the providential function of the hampering atmosphere of the previous plate. Indeed, taken in conjunction with the full sweep of drawings treating the activation of male sexual energy and erotic awareness, Plate 19 serves as the goad required by the dreamer to provoke orgasmic release. It is as if the issue anticipated by Christian in Plate 17 (an emblematic preview of orgasmic potency) had to be integrated into the rest of the dreaming personality by a passage through the dark nights of 19 and 20. These two plates, in fact, literally bring to a head (in this design's imagery of heads; see below) the tension between ecstacy and sexual incarnation—or between soul and body—that has been lurking in the wings of the dream all along.

The denouement of this conflict occurs through the subliminal symbolism of homoerotic oral sex—an important motif in Blake's iconology, as pointed out by W. J. T. Mitchell in his groundbreaking study of the *Milton* designs.[95] In the present case we observe the faint but deducible anticipation of such a union suggested at the start of the seven-part sequence when Christian stands, not so much face to face as head to loins, with his vision of Jesus. That Christ's lower body is not even imaged in this first stirring of the motif attests to how unconscious the drive for what Blake elsewhere calls "comingling" (a pun, perhaps, on "coming") still is in the dreamer. Plates 15–19, in fact, run through the alternate libidinal theme of heterosexual fulfillment as Christian meets the female angels, mounts and descends and again mounts a vaginal pathway, finds orgastic identity in the midst of it, pushes on through the now doubly dangerous instinctual gates into the interior of this palace of women, then leaves, "harnessed," through the gaping exit of that same "Female Space" (*M* 15). In Plate 20, therefore, when Apollyon begins to "gather up close to Christian" and attack him in a manner analogous to rape, the homosexual imagery returns, and the oral-genital climax is achieved just as Christian grasps the phallus-shaped hilt of his displaced sword.[96]

Hints of these erotic connotations are embedded in Bunyan's prose, as for example when Apollyon is said to wrestle Christian down to the ground and to cry "I am sure of thee now" as he "almost prest [Christian] to death." But it is Blake and not Bunyan (and not Bunyan's earlier illustrators) who develops the oral symbolism to represent a resolution of the dreamer's urge toward libidinal self-expression, an urge brought on by the dropping of the burden of guilt that occurred when Christian contemplated the image of the incarnate God. Call it self-love, call it a yearning for union with the archetype in divine brotherhood—in any event, the negative and combative aspects of this desire end with design 20, leading us over to the positive consequence of facing it through, as depicted in the following drawing.

DRAWING 21

> Now as *Christian* went on his way, he came to a little
> ascent, which was cast up on purpose, that Pilgrims
> might see before them: up there therefore *Christian* went,
> and looking forward, he saw *Faithful* before him, upon
> his Journey. Then said *Christian* aloud, Ho, ho, So-ho;
> stay and I will be your Companion.
> . . . Then I saw in my Dream, they went very lovingly
> on together; and had sweet discourse of all things that had
> happened to them in their Pilgrimage. (*PP* 66)

The subject of this illustration (Plate 21, Fig. 41) is the one that marks the halfway point of Bunyan's text. For Blake, however, in his interpretive rearrangement of the dream's narrative time, it establishes the three-quarter mark, dividing the whole second part of the journey itself into two.

The picture shows Christian still in his combat gear but without sword and shield, conversing along the way with his new companion, Faithful. The two figures are frontally posed, walking straight out at the viewer along a road that widens in our direction as it, too, seems to move from its illusional world into our real space. Although there have been many examples in the series so far of figures who have come with an emergent claim or purpose from the background of the psychic landscape to face the spectator head on, this is the first time that we experience ourselves being, like Apollyon from the opposite angle, "quite over the breadth of the whole way" in fellowship with the other travelers on the journey. No doubt Blake felt it fitting to involve us in this fashion at the very point that Christian finds a friend and an equal with whom to share his perception of the pilgrimage.

Above the pilgrims, two round bubbles contain representations of the events Christian and Faithful are narrating to each other. In Christian's case, the incident retold is the one just ended. It shows Apollyon in a much milder-looking form than in Plate 20, apparently stepping on Christian's groin (which seems to indicate Christian's awareness that the encounter had, among other things, a phallic connotation). Or perhaps Apollyon is emerging from Christian's genitals, in the manner of Satan issuing from the lost traveler in the epilogue engraving for the *Gates,* to indicate to us Christian's understanding that the fearfulness of the "foul Fiend" may have been his own projected creation. The figures in the other bubble, over Faithful's head, tell a different but not unrelated story. They illustrate Faithful's run-in with a character named Adam the First. Again, the incident represents a case of fleshly temptation, this time one in which Adam, by Faithful's account, did "take hold of my flesh, and give me such a deadly twitch back, that I thought he had pull'd part of me after himself" (*PP* 70). Blake's graphic digest of Faithful's narration of that event demonstrates the parity and the difference between it and Christian's experience. Both pilgrims have nude attackers in their stories, but Christian's marauder is more violent and direct; and the resultant responses of the victims vary, too, by posture and energy of gesture. The overall effect, however, is that these visitations of the past, reformed and suspended in narrations as though they were permanent emblems of trial, appear as time-lapse versions of each other: first the protagonist is pinched and twitched, then he is trampled on and "crusht" (*PP* 75). That, of course, is the purpose of the dream's present moment: to reassess its own passage through time and space and see the process as an unfolding of variant individual visions of unvarying archetypal states. By the same token, the act of recalling and refashioning these states in a transmittable form makes artists out of the characters in the dream. As they narrate their pasts, they imitate the art of the dream narrator (who in this case is Blake as well as the man shown sleeping in Plate 1), and momentarily they become visionary poets bent on turning their parallel realities to emblematic account.

Such moments are always vantage points of reorientation and breakthrough in Blake's work. For example, a very similar situation arises near the end of the Job illustrations when Job—like Christian and Faithful—becomes a storyteller to gain aesthetic mastery over the past of his mythic journey. The difference is that while Job takes on a much more obviously Blakean role than either Faithful or Christian (he is cast as a paradigm of the artist-interpreter at that stage), he is not simultaneously a figure in a dream.[97] Thus, he does not have to reflect the consciousness of the dreamer, who in the present series mediates between the visions of Blake, Bunyan, the characters and the audience.

How is the dreamer reflected in the drawing before us? Mainly by the visionary blue of Faithful's robe. As in the case of the Interpreter, Faithful's garment duplicates the one in which the sleeping man of Plate 1 is wrapped. Evidently, then, the shaping power of the dreamer's imagination has again assigned itself an independent role and worked its way into its own creation dressed in the dream's symbolic, imaginal blue; only this time the whole complex of self-reflexivity gets attached to the character of Faithful. The parallels between the Interpreter and Faithful are so strong that the event of Plate 21 amounts to a second coming. Even the specific contexts of these two epiphanies follow similar structures. Consider, for instance, the preludes to the appearance of each figure. Both times, a resolution of intense libidinal feeling is the key. Thus, the Interpreter enters the picture right after Christian melts into the loving arms of Good-will (Plate 11), and Faithful arrives on the scene as a direct reward of Christian's hot embrace with Apollyon, the paragon of *ill will* (Plate 20).

Despite the obvious contrasts in the quality of these close encounters—the positive numen versus the negative, the motherly versus the fatherly, a nourishing at the breast versus a fertilizing from the loins—there is a fulfillment of desired union in both cases. And from this union, like an heir apparent, springs the blue-robed presence of the dreamer in the dream. His major function seems to be to integrate the sudden discharge of affect. This is both a therapeutic service and an artistic one, requiring the use of those hermeneutic principles Blake saw as the redemptive core of the creative imagination. In short, these characters, the Interpreter and Faithful, are dynamic manifestations of the psyche's self-visionary instinct, and they function as archetypal guardians of the imaginal process that delivers us all from bondage to our own created states.

Alike as their roles may be, though, the two figures exist in different emotional relations to Christian, and the difference indicates Christian's development as an ego representative through the course of the dream. The

Interpreter is pictured as a being of slightly superior status, an instructor who demonstrates through visual aids, as it were, while Faithful is like a brother, a beloved companion, giving and receiving in equal measure through verbal interaction with Christian. Psychologically speaking, this change from subservience to friendship vis-à-vis the type of the visionary seems to be the result of Christian's having faced his oedipal aggression in the encounter with his darker self, the spectral Apollyon. Free now to experience other authorities as colleagues, he is able to risk more creative expression in his own right, telling his own tales, creating his own emblems.

Plate 21 ends the libidinal imagery of the previous drawings by transmuting it into a metaphor of balanced relatedness. That value of mutuality now appears to have been the dreamer's goal all along: not sex, but creative brotherhood; not internal stress, but emotion recollected in tranquility and transmuted into narrative art. Compositionally, also, the design expresses a return to stability, order, symmetry. Especially emphatic is the reestablishment of the quaternity as the formal basis of the drawing. In fact, groups of two converging toward groups of four in different combinations and permutations make up the layout of the design. Thus there is a foursome of the two pilgrims plus their two bubbles, another one consisting of the four small figures within the bubbles, yet another that takes into account the trees and the pilgrims (recalling the trees in Plate 14), and so on. Actually, the numerical foundation of the design is more complex than that, having, for example, a strong tendency to break down into paired units of threes. (One pair of matching trios is the threesome of Faithful plus his two characters in the bubble versus Christian and *his* two characters; another configuration of threes and twos is the triad of two trees, two travelers, and two bubbles.) Although the contrast and overlap of bondings by twos, threes, and fours will prove significant in the designs to come, the fourfold stability of Plate 21 is what hits us most as we first meet it in its proper sequence. That is in part because the composition does such a thorough job of resolving tensions and transforming quaternities set up in previous illustrations.

In a diagrammatic layout of Plates 14, 15, 20, and 21 (Fig. 56) we see that the diamond-shaped configuration of Plate 14 converts to the square form of 21. This squaring of the diamond involves a doubling of figures, a doubling of visions, with a concomitant inversion of the psychic intent of the images that the characters are picturing in their discourse (Christian at the cross sees an archetypal image of assent to the divine, but in Plate 21 the pilgrims see the warning examples of their own immediate past). Similarly, the alignment of forward-facing figures in Plate 15 is transferred to Plate 21 with the parallel effect of bringing the rhetorical form and content of the dream down from the sublime and back to the plane of the literal.[98] Finally, the powerful diagonal tensions of Plate 20 are both canceled and preserved by the squaring-off in the

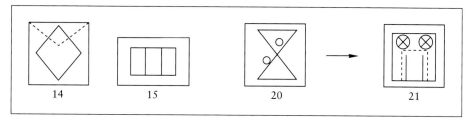

FIG. 56   Diagram of Plates 14, 15, 20, and 21

main design of Plate 21. Yet Apollyon's double-triangular thrusts are safely encapsulated, now, in the bubbles over the pilgrim's heads. Considered compositionally, then, the bubbles are a balanced rearrangement of the eccentric circles formed in Plate 20 by Apollyon's halo and Christian's shield. The next seven designs (Plates 22–28) constitute an asymmetrical, freely linear interplay of all these forms, dealing with the symbolic implications of the distinction between splitting and doubling hinted at here in Plate 21.

DRAWINGS 22 and 23

Then I saw in my Dream, that when they were got out of the Wilderness, they presently saw a Town before them, and the name of the Town is *Vanity;* and at the Town there is a *Fair* kept called *Vanity-Fair* . . . because all that is there sold, or that cometh thither, is *Vanity* . . . And moreover, at this Fair there is at all times to be seen Juglings, Cheats, Games, Plays, Fools, Apes, Knaves, and Rogues, and that of all sorts. . . .

Now these Pilgrims, as I said, must needs go thorow this *Fair:* Well, so they did; but behold, even as they entred into the *Fair,* all the people in the *Fair* were moved, and the Town it self as it were in a Hubbub about them; and that for several reasons: For . . . First The Pilgrims were cloathed with such kind of Raiment, as was diverse from the Raiment of any that traded in that *fair.* . . .

 . . . Then were these two poor men brought before their Examiners . . . and there charged as being guilty of the late Hubbub that had been in the *fair.* So they beat them pitifully, and hanged Irons upon them, and led them in Chaines up and down the *fair,* for an example and terror to others. (*PP* 88–89, 91–92)

They therefore brought [Faithful] out, to do with him
according to their Law; and [tortured him] . . . and last of
all they burned him to Ashes at the Stake. Thus came
Faithful to his end. Now, I saw that there stood behind the
multitude, a Chariot and a couple of Horses, waiting for
Faithful, who (so soon as his adversaries had dispatched
him) was taken up into it, and straightway was carried up
through the Clouds, with sound of Trumpet, the nearest
way to the Coelestial Gate. But . . . *Christian* for that
time escaped [the town], and went his way.

   . . . Now I saw in my Dream, that *Christian* went not
forth alone, for there was one whose name was *Hopeful,*
(being made so by the beholding of *Christian* and *Faithful*
in their words and behaviour, in their sufferings at the
fair) who joyned himself unto him, and entring into a
brotherly covenant, told him that he would be his Companion. Thus one died to make Testimony to the Truth,
and another rises out of his Ashes to be a Companion
with *Christian. (PP* 97–98)

The following two designs (Plates 22–23, Figs. 42–43) take the pilgrims
through the trials and tribulations of Vanity Fair. In the two most popular
illustrated editions of the *Progress,* a sequence of three designs was devoted to
this episode, lending an inordinately heavy proportion of graphic narrative
time (over one-fifth of the total fourteen designs) to an incident that Blake
regarded as only subliminally instructive of the dreamer's progress. Even in
Bunyan's time it was one of those sections recognized principally for its social
satire, not its imaginal content. Blake therefore reversed his normal way of
manipulating the graphic tradition here, and instead of increasing the number
of drawings in order to include all conventional variants in a reformed and
recentered unit, he cut back. This tactic was conservative for two reasons: first,
Blake was upholding thereby the precedent of the earliest English illustrated
edition, which also covered the incidents of Vanity Fair in two designs (see
Figs. B10 and B11); and second, even with the cutting back, Blake managed to
keep most of the iconographic motifs used by his predecessors.[99]

    When we look at Blake's condensed version of the incident, we see that he
has played down the linearity of its plot by picturing its component parts as a
pair of contraries, seen from an energetic standpoint. These contraries are
opposed not just thematically; they are also disjunctive in style and feeling.
Accordingly, the structure of Plate 22 is presented as a virtual parody of the
order and symmetry evoked in Plate 21, and Plate 23 radically upsets that
parodic order by an apotheosis of the diagonal emphasis already prefigured in

the composition of Plate 20. In this way Blake makes the interlude in Vanity Fair function for the dreamer as a critique of the unfinished business hidden within the image of a temporary resolution of tensions achieved by him in Plate 21.

The first drawing of the pair exemplifies that critical procedure. Here we see Christian and Faithful literally raised on a pedestal and pushed into the background by the taunting populace of Vanity Fair. There, instead of walking and conversing freely in "Visionary forms dramatic" (J 98), as they did in Plate 21, the pilgrims are chained at the ankles, immobilized, and separated from each other by a bare and ill-proportioned cross. Below in the foreground, two figures costumed as jesters fill the positions vacated by Christian and Faithful in their transference from Plate 21: by contrast, however, these jesters face inward, one directly, the other obliquely in a contorted dance pose—and both pick up on the gestures used by the little figures envisioned within the bubbles of Plate 21. Are we perhaps seeing the pilgrims from the point of view of the mentality closed up in those bubbles? In any case, it seems fair to say that Blake wants to present the citizens of the town of Vanity as the shadow aspects of the dreamer's personality, the underside of the faithful Christian persona cultivated through the creation of Faithful and Christian in consort in the previous design.

The rest of the citizenry carry a similar meaning. Two coy women holding masks in a seductive manner stand on either side of the jesters; faintly sketched in behind the women are, to the left, the figure of a man with a bishop's hat and, to the right, a man with a three-pronged royal crown. These figures all represent vainglorious and tyrannical elements of the social order, each of which Blake regarded as a perverse, institutionalized form of psychic repression: that is, "female will," kingship, religion, and the multiform dancers of philosophic and scientific doubt.[100]

The jesters symbolize a model of scientific doubt both by their function as mockers of the religious quest and by their costumes, which segment the human form in mathematically divisive ways. The fellow on the left has things separated into black and white distinctions so neatly that his body seems to contradict itself in a parodic image of the fourfold ideal: instead of being in harmony with himself, he seems split into four centrifugal parts like one who has been drawn and quartered. His stance can also be viewed as a trivialized, turned-around version of Apollyon's posture in Plate 20—another clue to the tortured and torturing heritage of his psychological state. The design of the costume of the twisting dancer to the right, on the other hand, is a geometrically regularized rendition of Apollyon's scales of pride, as well as a sort of spoof of the blood-flecked embroidery on Christian's cloak in Plates 16–18. The fact that the pattern of this dancer's suit consists of atomized particles in the shape of diamonds with circles in them is suggestive, too, of imagery used by Blake in the kind of complaint he frequently voiced against Newtonian and Democritian ideas of universal order—namely, the complaint that those systems treat discrete items as lifeless counters in a game of quantification, regarding individuals, too, as static singularities dissociated from their expansive contexts or translucent possibilities.[101] In short, diamonds and circles are geometric forms that often connote for Blake a single-visioned view of reality such as he believed was fostered by "demonstrative science" ("Anno Reynolds," E659/K475). But whether or not that private association applies, Blake's criticism of the closed order portrayed here, with its heavy domed architecture and its reliance on "Grecian Form," comes across to the spectator as negative and deflating simply in contrast to its neighbor plates.[102]

In Plate 23, for example, the death of Faithful causes a complete disruption of the symmetric principle governing the picture of Vanity Fair in Plate 22. To the left, now, the monument of that old order, the church dome, is hemmed in by bars of flame that shoot up in spires around the faintly discernible skeleton of Faithful being burned at the stake. To the lower right, the human remnants of the same repressive society fall down in a heap as they veer away from the ascension of Faithful's spirit. The major part of the right side of the drawing is thus given over to the strong diagonal movement that constitutes the rendering of Faithful's abrupt translation to the Celestial City. Here the flames lose their rigidity, curving around the departing form of Faithful's ghost and horses, creating a current of widening air to promote the upward flow. The same widening is repeated by the arm spreads of Christian and his new companion, Hopeful, who are watching from below in the places where the harlequins danced in the previous illustration. Those former figures spread their arms also, but Blake has given an angularity to the gestures of Christian and Hopeful that seems to be a deliberate reparation of the too-contained, formal-balletic motions of the dancers in Plate 22.

The death and resurrection of Faithful represent a revival, then, of the dynamic energies last fully manifested in the scene of Christian's fight with Apollyon (Plate 20). Now, however, that vitality not only has returned, it has undergone a sudden and impressive transmutation predictive of the final goal of the dream. Here again we have to admire Blake's ability to turn the standard iconography of the illustrative tradition to psychological account. For while all the early engravings of this subject showed Faithful's spirit riding sedately off in the heavenly chariot poised in the clouds above, Blake centers his design on the rising motion of man and horse reminiscent of the naive pictorial urgencies in the earlier parts of the dream (such as the dark clouds in Plates 2 and 5 or the fire in Plate 8). Gone altogether from Blake's depiction is the chariot; rather, it is Faithful's full-length form—a spirit without benefit of extraneous vehicle—

that serves as the penetrating force to reopen the way in the mind to the vision of Bunyan's "Desired Countrey" (*PP* title page). Faithful's departure is thus an important preview of coming attractions for Christian and Hopeful. But in the natural unfolding of the psychic life of the dreamer, its very force and violence suggests that its achievement as an apotheosis of the values of faithfulness is premature—a meaning that, indeed, Blake draws out in the following two drawings.

DRAWINGS 24 and 25

Now there was not far from the place where they lay, a *Castle* called *Doubting-Castle,* the owner whereof was *Giant Despair,* and it was in his grounds they now were sleeping; wherefore he getting up in the morning early, and walking up and down in his Fields, caught *Christian* and *Hopeful* asleep in his grounds. Then with a *grim* and *surly* voice he bid them awake, and asked them whence they were? and what they did in his grounds? They told him, they were Pilgrims, and that they had lost their way. Then said the *Giant,* You have this night trespassed on me, by trampling in, and lying on my grounds, and therefore you must go along with me. . . . They also had but little to say, for they knew themselves in a fault. The *Giant* therefore drove them before him, and put them into his Castle, into a very dark Dungeon, nasty and stinking to the spirit of these two men. (*PP* 113–14)

Now a little before it was day, good *Christian,* as one half amazed, brake out in this passionate speech, *What a fool, quoth he, am I, thus to lie in a stinking Dungeon, when I may as well walk at liberty?* I have a *Key* in my bosom, called *Promise,* that will, (I am perswaded) open any Lock in *Doubting-Castle.* Then said *Hopeful,* That's good news; good Brother pluck it out of thy bosom, and try: Then *Christian* pulled it out of his bosom, and began to try at the Dungeon door, whose bolt (as he turned the Key) gave back, and the door flew open with ease, and *Chris-tian* and *Hopeful* both came out. Then he went to the out-ward door, that leads into the *Castle yard,* and with his Key opened the door also. After he went to the *Iron* Gate, for that must be opened too, but that Lock went *damnable* hard, yet the Key did open it; then they thrust open the Gate to make their escape with speed; but that Gate, as it opened, made such a creaking, that it waked *Giant Despair,* who hastily rising to pursue his Prisoners, felt his Limbs to fail, for his fits took him again, so that he could by no means go after them. Then they went on. (*PP* 118)

In Bunyan's story the pilgrims go through many vicissitudes between the time they escape the magistrates of the town of Vanity and the time they are captured by Giant Despair. Their fall into the deep depression signified by the dungeon of Doubting Castle thus comes as part of a long cycle of changing moods that flow naturally from changing circumstances. The immediate cause is a lapse of moral vigilance on Christian's part which sends the travelers off course and makes them lose their way. The resultant despair is giant, or double-sized, because Christian feels double guilt—both for being out of the "way" and for making the error of judgment that led him there.

In Blake's illustration of the text, no such intervening narrative separates the capture shown here in Plate 24 (Fig. 44) from the prior event envisioned in Plate 23: Faithful's final escape from the world by death. Considered psychologically as a sequel to Plate 23, then, Plate 24 represents the personality's instinctive response to permanent loss: the locked-in feeling of terrible deprivation and grief caused by the death of a beloved. When Faithful died, something precious was lost to the dreamer's psyche as far as the believing ego was concerned, and repercussions signaling loss of faith were inevitable. That is one meaning of Plate 24 cultivated by Blake. The other more expansive and assimilative implications can best be appreciated by a look at the work of earlier *Progress* illustrators.

In most of the standard series, even though some juxtaposition of subjects occurred, an accompanying quatrain supplied a commentary to fill the hiatus in the plot, and this served to weaken the viewer's experience of a direct emotional link between the present episode and Faithful's death.[103] Nevertheless, Blake in his rendition seems to have picked up on the one hint of development that the old design sequence contained: the faint, formal resemblance between the figures of Faithful tied to the stake on the one hand and Giant Despair on the other (see, for example, Figs. B11 and B12). Then, in typical revisionary fashion, Blake turned that hint of likeness around to his own multilevel interpretive purpose. Thus here, Giant Despair is not seen as a figure reminiscent of Faithful; rather, he is drawn in pointed *contrast* to Faithful's resurrected, living form. For instance, Faithful in Plate 23 is dressed in the raiment of heavenly ascension, but the giant is naked; Faithful mounts upward on a left-right diagonal axis, whereas Giant Despair leans downward along the opposite diagonal created by his own threatening gesture; and Faithful rises through the fiery colors of the rainbow aflame, while Giant Despair dominates a world of black.

But Giant Despair does not function only as an antithesis to Faithful. He also reflects figures among the drawings with whom he *shares* decided attributes and attitudes. In fact, he is a kind of culmination of all the nude men pictured, as well as all the strong gesturers as far back as Worldly Wiseman in Plate 7 and even Evangelist in Plate 3. From Plate 20 onward, however, as the dream environment localizes around this last scene of imprisonment, the pace of the dream psyche's self-reflexive cross-references increases to show a hint of the giant's nature in each design. At least a bit of this tyrannical character's salient quality—despair—permeates the lamentation poses of the pilgrims watching Faithful's demise; and more of that derisive energy is prefigured in the postures of the jesters of design 22. Most clearly of all, though, the body stance that Giant Despair takes in Plate 24 can be seen as an amalgamated blowup of the stances of the two marauders, Apollyon and Adam the First, who appear in the pilgrims' conversation bubbles in design 21: learning well from the imaginations of Christian and Faithful, Giant Despair copies the outstretched right arm of Adam the First, while he keeps his left arm raised in the position of Apollyon. It is almost as if the new tyrant, forced into service so abruptly by Faithful's martyrdom, had not yet developed an individual form of his own; and so he had to turn inward to the "exemplars of Memory and Intellect" (*J* 98), there to take lessons in deportment from those ranting and raving types fashioned earlier by his victims.

The result of condensing all these allusions from the past of the dream and casting them into the form of Giant Despair is that the dreamer, in typical dream-work style, creates thereby a fresh allusion, this time to a figure outside the dream: the central attacker in Raimondi's famous engraving of Raphael's *Massacre of the Innocents* (Fig. 57).[104] That Giant Despair is meant to be an inward-facing analogue of Raphael's chief slaughterer cannot be proved, of course, but there is an aptness to the association that greatly enriches the meaning of the dream event. For if we consider the slaughter of the infants of Bethlehem (Matthew 11:16) as a mythic occurrence, we will understand it as the last-minute, desperate attempt of recalcitrant forces (represented by Herod and his men) to halt the earthly development of the archetypal Divine Child. On the level of the personal psychological journey, this interpretation of the myth corresponds to the fierce and often deadly devaluation of the self encountered in the unconscious of depressed persons. Yet the myth of the massacred children can also be interpreted as an emblem of the painful sacrifice of infantile attitudes demanded by a conscious urge toward psychic integration such as is signified by the birth of Christ. Something like this latter meaning was recognized in the tradition of the church, where the murdered infants were regarded as the first Christian martyrs and equated symbolically with the redeemed who were sealed with the blood of the lamb in the Apocalypse at the Last Judgment.[105]

FIG. 57 Marcantonio Raimondi, *The Massacre of the Innocents*

Blake applies both these views of the myth to the dream situation, and he coalesces them by dwelling on the regressive imagery common to each. He makes Christian and Hopeful appear diminutive, vulnerable, and naked like the children at the massacre of Bethlehem; yet at the same time he indicates that this "innocent" condition is composed of infantile, neurotic adaptations left over from an earlier portion of the dreamer's progress. Thus Hopeful, the naked pilgrim who occupies the center of the design, assumes the standard pose of melancholy last seen in one of the figures in the armory of House Beautiful (Plate 19). As for the image of Christian, it is a truly hybrid embodiment of all the old emblems of neurotic dejection, for here Christian combines the physical attitudes of the Man in the Iron Cage (Plate 12), the Man Who Dreamed of the Last Judgment (Plate 13), and the cast-off burden of guilt sent tumbling into the sepulcher at the sight of Christ on the cross (Plate 14).[106] It is interesting to note that Christian's postural forerunners, called up here just before he and Hopeful set themselves free in a sudden act of consciousness, are themselves emblems in a progression of consecutive plates (12–14) that led to the dream's midpoint image of deliverance by conscious vision.

The key to the double meaning symbolized by this emblematic moment of the dream lies—as before in Plate 12—in the very metaphor of the keys themselves. Here they dangle from the hand of Giant Despair as if to remind

FIG. 58   Blake, *Alas!*

both us and the pilgrims of their earlier function as attributes of the interpreter's art. In this picture even Giant Despair himself seems caught between a
cruel desire to taunt the miserable pilgrims with his power to detain them in
darkness and a compassionate wish to wake them up and show them the
way—the keys to liberty. For from a certain perspective the giant looks to be
clanging the keys over the heads of the victims, trying to arouse the infant
forms, amazed at the dejection that his actions have inspired. It is as though he
were in the same state of bewilderment about his role as is the boy in the
seventh emblem of the revised *Gates* (Fig. 58), another composition that
alludes deliberately to the iconography of Raphael's *Massacre* print; and he
could be saying here, in paraphrase of that infanticidal boy: "What are these?
Alas! the [Christian] martyr/Is [he] also the Divine Image?"

In the next design (Plate 25, Fig. 45), the superiority of divine imagining
over tyrannical force is expressed by another artistic allusion, this time to a
famous example of Greek sculpture personifying bodily strength. For Giant
Despair stands here, debilitated by a seizure of weakness, in the pose of the
Farnese Hercules, a popular antique marble showing Hercules as the archetypal strong man (Fig. 59).[107] Christian and Hopeful, meanwhile, dressed once
more in the clothing of pilgrimage, are positioned face to face in the foreground, running off to the left in a kind of side-stepping motion like partners
in a dance. In short, the paragon of strength becomes fainthearted and immobilized while the cowering, belittled pilgrims grow vigorous and joyful.

The meaning here is obvious and also somewhat comic, depending on a
species of dream irony that tends to be more broad than dry. The scenario in
fact verges on the slapstick when Christian, doing a double take at the giant's

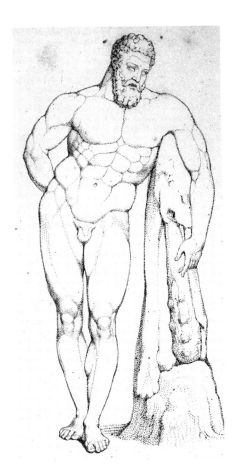

FIG. 59   Blake, *The Hercules Farnese*

boast about holding the keys, suddenly remembers to remember his own key of Promise and is thus instantly liberated both from the dungeon and from his morbid perception of the dungeon. As a result, he and his sidekick, Hopeful, witness the truth of Doubting Castle from the outside, where it appears as a jumble of crooked stone slabs and bricks arranged in a flat pattern without regard to the laws of rational space, like a child's drawing. Blake is using the same device here as in Plate 12 (the dream's other objective view of paralyzing self-doubt) to illustrate the psyche's awareness that the structure of despair is flimsy and aesthetically flawed.

An identical flaw is now also seen in the castle's giant guardian. His shrunken manhood (represented by diminished genitals), his muscle-bound lassitude, his stupefied expression—these things show that *his* weakness, too, is structural, making him an artistic travesty of the antique ideal of self-sufficient strength embodied in the Farnese Hercules. Or is Blake suggesting here that the classical aesthetic itself, and not just this version of it, is inherently inadequate to the expanding energies of a redemptive world view? We know from other sources in the Blakean canon that he often held the "Greek [and] Roman Models" responsible for a deadening of imaginative perception.[108] And increasingly, around the time of his work on the Bunyan illustrations, he lambasted the classical paradigms as exemplars of a "Mathematic Form" antithetical to the "Living Form" of Christian art.[109] Moreover, he became more and more explicit in this period about his conviction that spiritual development not only resembled the dynamic structures of visionary Christian art but was also, in its own right, an aesthetic process.[110] But to assume that Blake was simply exploiting Bunyan's myth as a convenient platform from which to voice again his own separable views on the theory of art would be to miss the point. Rather, I believe it is meant as an important step in this particular dreamer's own progress that he can envision the ego personality's penultimate triumph before awakening—its release from the structures of despair and doubt—as an act of aesthetic judgment. In the commentary where Blake first mentions Bunyan's fable as a visionary work, he also outlines the way such a focus on artistic formulations furthers psychic awakening:

> The Last Judgment is an Overwhelming of Bad Art & Science. . . . Some People flatter themselves that there will be No Last Judgment & that Bad Art will be adopted & mixed with Good Art That Error or Experiment will make a Part of Truth & they Boast that it is its Foundation these People flatter themselves I will not Flatter them Error is Created Truth is Eternal Error or Creation will be Burned up & then & not till then Truth or Eternity will appear. (VLJ, E565/K617)

At the top of Plate 25, in the sky behind the kindergarten architecture of Doubting Castle, the dawn of the dream's "Truth or Eternity" glows in rainbow colors expectantly on the horizon.

DRAWINGS 26 and 27

> Now there was on the tops of these Mountains, Shepherds feeding their flocks, and they stood by the high-way side. The Pilgrims therefore went to them, and leaning upon their staves, (as is common with weary Pilgrims, when they stand to talk with any by the way,) they asked, *Whose delectable Mountains are these? and whose be the sheep that feed upon them?*
> *Shep.* These Mountains are *Immanuels Land,* and they are within sight of his City, and the sheep also are his, and he laid down his life for them. (PP 119)

Now I further saw, that betwixt them and the Gate was a River, but there was no Bridge to go over; the River was very deep; at the sight therefore of this River, the Pilgrims were much stounded. . . . The Pilgrims then, especially *Christian,* began to dispond in his mind, and looked this way and that, but no way could be found by them, by which they might escape the River. Then they asked the men [who led them from Beulah] if the Waters were all of a depth. They Said . . . *You shall find it deeper or shallower, as you believe in the King of the place.*

They then addressed themselves to the Water; and entring, *Christian* began to sink, and crying out to his good friend *Hopeful;* he said . . . Ah my friend, the sorrows of death have compassed me about, I shall not see the Land that flows with Milk and Honey. . . . *Hopeful* therefore here had much adoe to keep his Brothers head above water, yea sometimes he would be quite gone down, and then ere a while he would rise up again half dead. *Hopeful* also would endeavour to comfort him, saying, Brother, I see the Gate, and men standing by it to receive us.

(PP 156–57)

With the twenty-sixth and twenty-seventh drawings (Plates 26–27, Figs. 46–47), the pictorial scene returns to a horizontally based format, ending a six-plate run of designs that stress the vertical. Again as with Plates 15 and 19, these wide-based compositions tend to translate the inward aspirations of ascension onto the external plane of the journey. Plate 26, particularly, recapitulates the theme and motifs of Plate 15 in this regard. There the three shining ones faced Christian with emblems of initiation; here the shepherds, occupying the same relative placement in the composition of the drawing, show Christian and his companion the signs of the journey's end. There the angels' heads were ringed with halos; here the shepherds all wear hats whose wide brims give an excellent earthly imitation of heavenly auras. There the full palate of the familiar rainbow was diffused through all the angelic wings; here the gown of each mountain shepherd is a different color of the same visionary rainbow. Even the dreamer's blue robe is represented in the dress of the shepherd to the far left; and this is an innovation, because in his two other appearances (in the forms of the Interpreter and Faithful) the dreamer-identified figure stood alone next to Christian, not as one among equals in a larger group.

The fact that the shepherds are differentiated from one another, while in their combination as a foursome they contrast with the twosome of Christian and Hopeful, raises a set of key issues. First, it reintroduces the subject of the numerology of the dream sequence. As we remarked earlier, the second half of the pictorial journey is dominated by the joining and dissolution of dualities into quaternities, and quaternities into dualities. The glaring exception to this principle occurs in the organization of the two designs just discussed: the Doubting Castle sequence. There the triadic symbolism of the first half of the dream reasserts itself, its appearance adumbrated by Plate 23 but fully personified and brought to a fitting denouement only in the conflict between the pilgrims and Giant Despair. Now again in the final plates, the tension between, on the one hand, the quaternity of wholeness and, on the other, the differentiation of individuated existence represented by threefoldness becomes a thematic concern and a formal vehicle of meaning which works itself out to a resolution in the last design, as we shall see.

It is Bunyan's imagination first, of course, and Blake's only second, that conceives of the four shepherds of the Delectable Mountains as a typological fulfillment of the three shining ones who appeared at the cross. But it is Blake alone who brings the *issue* of the groupings of like forms into play as an effective design motif. Moreover, he goes a step further in suggesting a second set of questions worrying the mythic plot of the dream, namely: what is happening here to Christian's individuated character, how does his identity relate to the identity of other characters, and how do all these figures dovetail with the self-actualizing process of the dreamer? At the start of the dream-journey, there seemed to be no conflict between Christian's progress and that of the personality dreaming him up. Christian fulfilled his double function as individual hero and ego representative by being the one who gained the necessary consciousness to proceed. After the interjection of the Interpreter, however, a disruption of the dreamer's focus altered the quality of the narrative's psychic investment in Christian. These were the scenes (Plates 12 and 13) in which the two emblematic characters took center stage to reflect elements of the *dreamer's* situation and personality, elements that could also be seen as unconscious aspects of *Christian's* personality—with Christian and the dreamer-as-Interpreter standing by, witnessing and assimilating these caricatures of themselves. Later still, when Christian found a companion (Plate 21), the dream energy withdrew even more of its investment in the ego identity of Christian, spreading the hero work equally between Christian and Faithful. Then when Faithful passed on and Hopeful immediately replaced him, "joyn[ing] himself" to Christian and "entring into a brotherly covenant" with him (*PP* 98), Christian's own boundaries as an ego figure became diffuse. This feature is found in Bunyan's text to some degree, but it is a major part of the design strategy in Blake's drawings. Increasingly, he paints the pair of pilgrims as identical twins, purging their differences as they move through Plates 23–28, thus showing that they have become more and more available to the dreamer's psyche as assimilable aspects of the central self: their loss of individual distinctness is the dreamer's individual gain. In Plate 26, the sense of an approaching equalization and recombination of once-autonomous forces is conveyed visually, first by the comparable stature of all the figures pictured, and then by the likeness, with variations, among the staves and the crooks—instruments that represent the personal extensions and projective devices of both the shepherds and the pilgrims.

Plate 27 (which is the least finished drawing of the lot and therefore possibly the most tentative in significant form and content) sets up the final round in the dreamer's individuation process. The dialectic established between the pilgrims and the shepherds in Plate 26 is intensified and simplified here in the relation between men and angels. Though spaced farther apart than were the sets of figures in Plate 26, the human and the divine seem to yearn for union across the water—a situation quite different from the static, planar array of collective pilgrims and shepherds in the previous design. There Christian and Hopeful witnessed the shepherds as a completed fourfold unit from a standpoint *outside* the quaternity, a fact that lessened the push toward closure. Now, in Plate 27, the pilgrims are crossing the river in order to be *inside* a relation of four that will lift the dreamer's whole empathic imagination up to the place of maximal psychic energy and freedom which Christian tradition calls heaven.

It must be said that the sketch of that crossing over is not only unfinished; it is also almost totally dependent on the iconography of previous illustrators of the *Progress*. From the standard treatment of the subject found originally in the seventeenth-century Flemish edition (Fig. B23), Blake borrows the poses of Christian and Hopeful, showing Hopeful with one arm stretched out along a strong diagonal, the other cupped under Christian's chin in an approved life-saving hold. Blake wants to preserve the diagonal emphasis here, for reasons discussed below, and thus he seems to have superimposed the Flemish model over his other source, John Sturt's engraving (Fig. B51), from which he took the relative placement of the figures on the dream stage. This repositioning of the angelic host on the far side of the river, on the heavenly shore (instead of on the earthly side as in the Flemish design), was called for by Blake's own compositional symbolism in which, as we have seen, the suprapersonal powers of psyche and spirit are consistently pictured emerging from the depth of the drawing's illusional space.[111]

Perhaps one reason for the incomplete state and derivative conception of Plate 27 is the difficult role it had to play in the aesthetic gestalt of the series taken as a whole: Blake may well have wanted to wait until all the other designs were done before he took this one further. As a prelude to the finale, after all, it should serve a full-blown recapitulative function, without slowing the narrative action—which is what Blake seems to have been trying to work out formally by stressing the diagonal structure of the design. A panoramic glance back over the whole sequence of drawings shows that the compositional format here, as well as the iconography, does indeed mirror and transform elements of many earlier pictures. Take, for example, the nearby precedent of Plate 24 and the far away models of drawings 5 and 1. (I single out those three because I believe Blake wanted especially to engage them, and the episodes they represent, as prefigurations of the dream's penultimate moment.) In the case of Plate 24, the thematic connection with drawing 27 is obvious—both show Christian weakened in his faith—but their comparative relation also shows moral and emotional progression. By loosely matching the layout of this fearful crossing of the river of death with the earlier pictorial pattern of imprisonment in Doubting Castle, Blake indicates not just the similarity of the two psychic states but, even more pointedly, the critical differences. One scene (24) is dark, the other (27) light; one peril is stony, the other is fluid and flowing; in the first situation the two figures in trouble resist interrelation, in the second the more conscious friend helps his brother out. Finally, of course, one scene shows the diagonal gradient of energy following a downflow controlled by a demonic presence, while the other makes a parallel diagonal seem to move upward by virtue of the visionary pull of the angelic appearances.

Bunyan, for his part, took a somewhat dimmer view of this scene. He used it much more admonitorily, dwelling with a good deal of Puritan fervor on Christian's final failing of character. In fact, according to the text, the dream hero's doubting tendency becomes stronger in this last trial of the spirit than ever before. As Stanley Fish has observed, Bunyan seems to have had a stake in keeping the pilgrims from making too much progress, in the modern sense of the word.[112] Indeed, in a sense Christian as described by Bunyan never gets anywhere in his own development as he moves through the states of the dream.[113] Ever bedeviled by his penchant for despair, ever doubting his election to Divine Grace, ever fearing the wrath to come, and ever mistrustful of the power of mutual forgiveness, each cure of the soul brings a new wounding; but the dialectic does not raise Christian's consciousness enough to permit him to break the pattern.

Blake avoided this impotent view of man's imaginative nature by showing at every step that the fable derives from the wider perspective of the dreamer's creative consciousness. That wider perspective exists also in Bunyan, of course, but submerged, subversive, unrealized. By liberating the dream context from the restraints that Bunyan imposed on it for doctrinal reasons, Blake liberated as well the meaning of Christian's last reactive behavior.[114] From the standpoint of the dreamer's psyche, Christian's sinking in Plate 27 takes on an expansive rather than a regressive connotation, as the drawing makes clear by

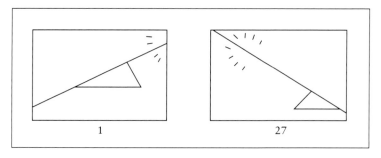

FIG. 60 Diagram of Plates 1 and 27

compositionally reflecting (Fig. 60), and thematically reflecting *on,* the initial design of the series. Hence we understand that the original mapping of reality is being balanced out in this second-to-last design. In the first plate, the figure of an unconscious (that is, sleeping) man filled the diagonal of the picture plane, his head veering all unawares toward the light of his own dream. By contrast, in Plate 27 the swimmers represent the enhanced conscious identity of the dreamer striving along an opposite diagonal (like Jesus countering the easterly motion set against the "current of Creation" in *Jerusalem*)[115] to close the gap between themselves and the light of eternity, here personified by angels. The two men in the water represent the dreamer's unawakened mentality because they unite in a configuration that echoes the shape of the folded arms and head of the man in Plate 1. Yet they show him to himself in an awakened version: Hopeful's head is raised higher than that of the first plate's dreamer; Christian looks up where that figure looked down; and Hopeful's arm breaks through the triangular enclosure of sleep maintained by the dreamer in that initial design. This last fact suggests that Hopeful is an evolved aspect of the dreamer's psyche, capable of carrying the former ego quotient (Christian) to higher and more expansive consciousness. In this way Plate 27 signifies a real evolution, a real push by the creative dreamer toward the integration of his own personality.

Finally, Plate 27 modulates the dream's earlier scene of sinking, where Christian struggles through the Slough of Despond (Plate 5). In the text, the episode of the slough is constructed as a clear and obvious preview of the events at the River of Life and Death.[116] For Blake, however, the two events are revealed to be contrasts rather than analogues: whereas in Plate 5 the psyche as a whole is divided against itself, pulling in opposite directions, its component parts heading toward the periphery while the whole is wedged and weighted downward, in Plate 27 the evolved conscious personality struggles to meet as a peer with its separated aspects. The once-harassed ego has made a "Friend & Companion" of its own good angel, Hopeful (shown embracing Christian in a pose that has assimilated the affective power of Christian's former embrace with Good-will in Plate 11), and the whole psychic structure is now aligned with its entelechal purpose so that all forces within it move centripetally toward that goal.

DRAWING 28

> Now upon the bank of the River, on the other side, they saw the two shining men again, who there waited for them. Wherefore being come up out of the River, they saluted them, saying, *We are ministring Spirits, sent forth to minister for those that shall be Heirs of Salvation.* Thus they went along towards the Gate, now you must note that the City stood upon a mighty hill, but the Pilgrims went up that hill *with ease,* because they had these two men to lead them up by the Arms; also they had left their *Mortal* Garments behind them in the River: for though they went in with them, they came out without them. They therefore went up here with much agility and speed, though the foundation upon which the City was framed was higher then the Clouds. They therefore went up through the Regions of the Air, sweetly talking as they went, being comforted, because they safely got over the River, and had such glorious Companions to attend them. . . .
> . . . Then the Heavenly Host gave a great shout, saying, *Blessed are they that are called to the Marriage Supper of the Lamb.*
> There came out also at this time to meet them, several of the Kings Trumpeters. . . . [They were] continually sounding as they went, with melodious noise, in notes on high; so that the very sight was to them that could behold it, as if Heaven it self was come down to meet them. . . . And now were these two men, as 'twere, in Heaven, before they came at it; being swallowed up with the sight of Angels, and with hearing of their melodious notes. (*PP* 158–59, 160–61)

In the previous three plates we saw again how deftly Blake shifts the focus of Bunyan's story away from Christian's spiritual development and onto the individuation process of the dreamer and his images. Just as in his revision of the *Gates,* where he recontextualized the whole emblem sequence by stressing its relation to the image of the lost traveler who had created its mental forms,

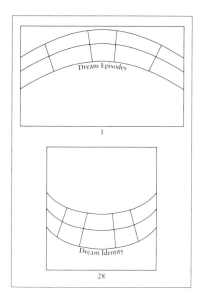

FIG. 61   Diagram of Plates 1 and 28

Dream Episodes

1

Dream Identity

28

this series, too, follows and at the same time questions a profoundly Hegelian pattern in which consciousness finds itself "coming to itself," its "goal of knowledge . . . set for it with the same necessity as the sequence of its progression."[117] Indeed, nowhere among the full complement of *Progress* illustrations is this pattern made more vivid than in design 28 (Plate 28, Fig. 48), especially when considered in its dynamic relation to the first design showing the dreamer dreaming the dream.

The most striking aspect of the final drawing is its blend of rainbow colors running in bands through the bodies of all four ascending figures. These men, the pilgrims and their two "glorious Companions," are at once apparently *in* the rainbow and *of* it. As they mount in unison, the colored segments of their garments together form a U-shaped arc that balances and seems to complete the circle begun by the broad dome of the dreamer's visionary rainbow in Plate 1 (Fig. 61). It is less significant that a segmented circular closure is reached in this last drawing, though, than that fulfillment here is displayed as an awakening *within,* not a waking *from,* the visionary element of the dream. In the first drawing, which shows the dreamer's psychic condition from the outside, as it were, the dream's apotheosis was pictured to the far right of the visionary band as an explosive sunrise that shatters the rainbow structure. But now, experienced and portrayed from within, the directional forces move from the periphery toward the center where Christian and Hopeful face each other, thus reconstituting rather than destroying the reality of the rainbow world. Furthermore, that rainbow world is no longer represented as an alienated system of imaginal otherness existing apart from the figure of the dreamer. Instead,

Plate 28 stresses the integration of the dreamer and the dream. The dreamer's new fourfold identity, then, represented by the quaternity of figures who rise to an "Above" that is "Within" (*J* 71), is seen to *be* the constitutive medium of the dream. Here the medium, the content, and the creator of the dream seem mutually engaged in a kind of objective self-knowledge, a recognition that the whole process (to use the Hegelian formulation) "may be regarded as the way of the soul, which travels through the sequence of its forms, like stations marked out for it by its own nature, in order that it may purify itself into pure spirit in reaching through the complete experience of itself, the knowledge of what it is in itself."[118] Of course, Blake's inclusive image here in the final plate of the series has more elements of indeterminacy than any strict Hegelian vision would want to entertain. In principle, though, the "progression" or "supplementation" of the graphic narrative up to this point is pictured now at the last as "return[ing] to itself . . . in a new and immeasurably greater—or smaller—form."[119]

Other differences between Plates 1 and 28 confirm the quasi-Hegelian route of the dream psyche represented here. Thus in Plate 1, the picture is horizontally based, giving scope to the lateral direction of the figures within it and emphasizing the division into three autonomous segments along the horizontal axis. The state depicted is one of expectant evolution. Even the triadic organization of the space, following the archetypal significance often accorded ternary groupings in the psyche, "seems to symbolize adequately and completely a developmental process in time."[120] In Plate 28, by contrast, the compositional numerology expands to a tetradic structure on the vertical axis, but incorporates the threefold within it, thereby canceling and preserving—or differing and deferring—its earlier entelechally loaded forms.[121] We see this the moment we attempt to schematize the drawing (Fig. 62). At first view, the ascending figures stand out as a fourfold unit. But because of the gothic arch formed by the inner wings of the angels, enclosing Christian and Hopeful in its "doorway," the space can also be seen to be divided into three main vertical partitions. Since the upper region of the plate, in its turn, has a tripartite structure (consisting of a stylized palace gate flanked by two groups of the "Heavenly Host"), the lower triad gains visual validity as its natural parallel. More permutations and combinations of the three-in-four scheme exist in this design, but the main point of such a fusion is that it emblematizes the unending interpenetration in the imaginal world of the dynamic with the static, of process with structure, time with eternity, dialectic with synthesis, the way of individuation with its "goal or completed state."[122]

That expansive imaginative attitude which accepts the mutual identification of the *goal* with the *way* is again reflected in the work of Blake's contemporary, Hegel, who writes of the spirit's being-at-home-with-itself-in-its-otherness as

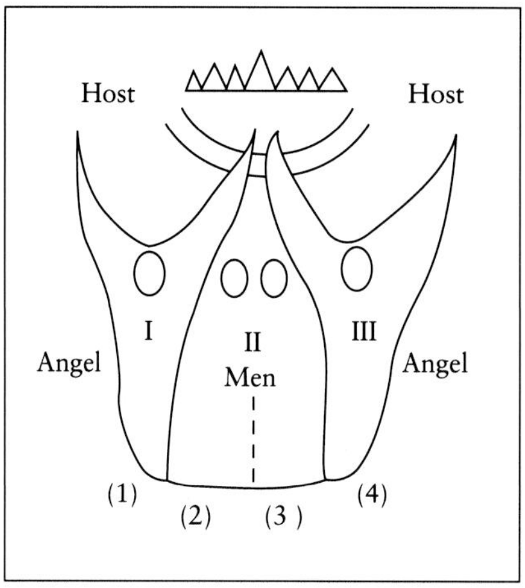

FIG. 62 Diagram of Plate 28

the highest goal: "Everything that happens—the life of God and everything that is done in the course of time, are nothing other than the striving to the end that the spirit may recognize itself, make itself objective to itself, find itself, become for itself, and unite with itself. It is a division, alienation, but only so that it can find itself, so that it can return to itself."[123] Blake's Plate 28 expresses this return of the self to the self by having all the figures in the design (with the exception of the trumpeters) focus on the center of the pictorial space. We may compare the centeredness here with the desire for convergence pictured in the preceding drawing and in Plate 14, for those designs have a natural rhetorical relation to the final vision.

Simply by placement, drawing 27 is obviously meant to represent the immediate precondition of the last depicted shape of the dreamer's psyche, and, as we noted earlier, it bespeaks an expected union by creating a gradient along which runs an implied centripetal attraction of men to angels and angels to men. Plate 14, conversely, does not so much anticipate Plate 28 as stand in an analogous relation to it, both thematically and in terms of some of its compositional features on the vertical plane. For there Christian meets his projected image of Christ in a dynamic interaction of visionary ascent and descent, a motion that parallels the way the two pilgrims in Plate 28 move to meet the male and female heavenly host who float down toward them between the angels' wingtips.[124] But Christian in Plate 14, without a fraternal companion, seems to reflect an ego still in a state of relative alienation, lacking a sense of its rightful place in a self-referential psychic system. As we have seen, Blake suggests this partial alienation between the envisioner and the quality envisioned in the fourteenth plate by showing only half of Christ's form, from the

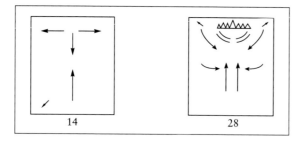

FIG. 63 Diagram of
Plates 14 and 28

waist up, thus signifying an imaginal entity incompletely conceived by Christian. But there are no partial bodies in Plate 28. Also, the Christ figure of Plate 14, though in manifold ways a powerful force for integration, still images an emotional situation in which the self suffers "crossed" and contrary functions, enduring them rather than enjoying them. That sufferance counters the equally valid containment principle of the design, showing Christ's agonistic influence shooting outward along the horizontal axis of his cruciform pose, the result being a dialectic of directional tensions (Fig. 63).

Here it is plain that the spiritual advance of the situation pictured in this last drawing, compared with its typological precursor at the midpoint of the dream, is expressed in terms of an agreement among the directional forces of the composition. In short, Blake's concluding design, though it depicts a rising, is structured in the manner of an *infolding* and so pulls the eye of the viewer—like the mind of the dreamer—into its center. Such a center within, according to the testimony of Blake's late prophetic thought, is a trope for the constellation of the objective inner life where both the personal and the transpersonal aspects of the psyche merge in a state of mutually gratifying congress, producing "new Expanses" (*J* 98), new creative vision.

In its culminative reach for an open-ended yet harmonic closure, the twenty-eighth illustration of Blake's *Pilgrim's Progress* differs from the last view of the dream offered by Bunyan. In fact, Bunyan's finale, by contrast, is deliberately discordant and disruptive. Above all, it insists on leaving us with a jarring reassertion of the book's original premise that there is an absolute, ontological distinction between the narrator and the main protagonists of the dream—the very opposite of Blake's premise. In Bunyan's hands, as the book draws to a close, this ontological distinction is first emphasized by the penultimate scene, where the narrator tells of watching Christian and Hopeful disappear through the gates of Paradise, leaving him—the author, narrator, and dreamer—excluded and indeed bereft on the outside of his own proleptically imagined

"Desired Countrey" (*PP* titlepage, facing xxxvi): "And after that," he reports, gazing at his departing hero, "they shut up the Gates: which when I had seen, I wished myself among them" (*PP* 162).

The wish for inclusion, however, is not fulfilled, and in this respect Bunyan's narrator/dreamer remains stuck in the outcast state and position that Christian occupied at the very start of the imaginative journey. It is as if the fictive dreamer's reading of his own dream-vision is finally so weak that it does not permit him to learn as much as either his characters or we, his privileged listeners, have gradually learned. At the end of the dream, then, we find ourselves stymied by what might be regarded as an unreliable allegorical narrator—one who has eschewed interpretive development, proving himself an inadequate reader of events, and who has remained for the most part a mere voyeur of the unfolding story. According to some theorists of the genre, such a normally passive reader is in fact allegory's prime target. In this reading, the goal of the form, *qua* form, is to subvert the indolence of its audience (or, as Blake put it, to "rouz[e] the faculties to act"),[125] using rhetorical strategies that force the reader to "out-hero" the hero by going through more interpretive transformations than are required of the main protagonist. In this way the erstwhile passive (or innocent or ignorant) reader becomes "the central character" of the text, even though not named in the story; in the end, it is the reading process itself that is plotted as the principal generator of action and reflection in most allegorical narratives.[126]

Bunyan's narrator-cum-reader, however, strongly resists that role. On all but two occasions he basically refuses to be a character, refuses to act or reflect or otherwise participate in the quasi-apocalyptic form of the work. At the last, it is this very refusal that seems to invoke and become reified in the personified figure of Ignorance; for just when the dreamer, unable to follow Christian and Hopeful into heaven, turns his head "to look back" (*PP* 162)—that is, literally to reflect—Ignorance appears. In other words, the dreamer's unredeemed ignorance of how to act and how to reflect with respect to his own mental imagery comes to the surface in the denouement, where it is allegorized as an ignorant allegorical character—the last to be seen—receiving final judgment.

Thus the text of *The Pilgrim's Progress* ends not with the protagonist's triumphal entry into the Celestial City, but with the cautionary tale of Ignorance's defeat. While the creative dreamer of *Blake's* graphic series imagines an apotheosis of the imagination as the fitting signal of an awakening in and from the dream, Bunyan's narrator dreams up an anticlimactic fall. His is an envoi that is a literal tailspin, in which Ignorance, thwarted and abused by angelic messengers for trying to walk uncredentialed into heaven, is trussed and then dumped through a celestial side door that chutes him down to eternal perdition. This vision of a final fall—or perhaps more compellingly, this fear of finally falling (the very thing that set the action of the allegory going in the opening pages of the book)—is what catapults Bunyan's dreamer at long last out of his sleep: "Then I saw that there was a way to Hell, even from the Gates of Heaven, as well as from the City of *Destruction*. So I awoke, and behold it was a Dream" (*PP* 163).

The inconclusiveness of such a conclusion, which seems to exert an entropic force drawing us back to the blurred perspectives of square one, can be explained and defended on the grounds of its generic traditionalism: allegories—like *The Faerie Queene*, for example, or like Chaucer's *House of Fame*—tend naturally to teleological ellipses.[127] It is their way of affirming the structural importance of the reader's role. For the ideal audience of what Blake called a "sublime allegory" is an interpreter who does more than uncover a link between the hermeneutic and the *protagonal* quest; the allegorical reader's task is also to enact that quest by taking on (and, as it were, transfiguring) the imaginative burdens of the *author*, as well. Thus, the unresolved finishes of many allegorical dream-visions are like prophetic legacies: they invite the reader not only to dream the author's dream and its interpretation onward, but also to pursue the fulfillment of the dream in personal belief and action.[128]

It is possible that the plotting of the denouement of *The Pilgrim's Progress* had this rhetorical intent. But Bunyan's deliberate turning away from his hero's transcendental homecoming in the narration of the dream may have had another, less heuristically motivated, cause as well. For Bunyan was in part constrained here by his Calvinistic beliefs and by a desire within that context to remain rhetorically true to both the literal and metaphoric terms of his allegorical equation. That is, from the start he had set up a fixed, one-to-one semiotic relationship between tenor and vehicle regarding the Celestial City, whereby the metaphoric image of the city (the vehicle) served to signify the domain of the elect in a literal afterlife (the tenor). It would therefore have seemed illogical, sinfully prideful, and even perhaps blasphemous for him to represent his dream narrator—a time-bound, corporeal, realistic character, not an emblematic figure like Christian—as one who could cross over while yet in this life, this language, to the realm of the eternally redeemed to share their privileged viewpoint.

In sum, Bunyan could engineer and promote a double-visioned reading of his own text, in which an internal sense complemented an external and in which "the slippery tensions between literalness and metaphor" were brought dynamically into focus;[129] but at crucial junctures he seemed doctrinally blocked from taking the further step that would have allowed him freely to evoke the polysemous imaginal world that gave his allegory life. On those occasions, the implied aesthetic of "the Bunyan of the Conventicles" would war with that of "the Bunyan of Parnassus," causing him to abandon the stance from which many contradictory and paradoxical meanings are seen to lie comfortably folded within a single word or image. So if the heavenly city, through the weight of scriptural tradition, stood in the end for that wholly other eschatological condition, the afterlife, it could not at the same time in Bunyan's book also stand for a merely mortal state or cognitive process belonging to the mind of the reader or dreamer.

Blake's view, as we know, is just the reverse. For him, all images identify and indeed *are* mental states; they refer to things and ideas as perceived in the imagination, and they also reflect the rhetorical process by which perception claims them. Thus, the signifier is on an ontological par with the signified in Blake's work. But while any Blakean image can therefore shed light on both the structure and function of its psychic content (opening the "immortal Eyes/of Man inwards into the Worlds of Thought"; *J* 5), his eschatological imagery in particular bespeaks a state of self-awareness *about* states and "the liberty both of body & mind" (*J* 77) to choose among them, as in the familiar dictum quoted earlier: "Whenever any Individual Rejects Error & Embraces Truth, a Last Judgment passes upon that Individual."

It is with the depiction of this free and inclusive embrace of imaginative reality that Blake chose to end his pictorial narrative of *The Pilgrim's Progress*. And the fact that he, ironically, followed the earliest conventional graphic treatment of the text, picking the scene of the pilgrims' transumptive ascension as the subject for his otherwise quite *un*conventional denouement in Plate 28, should not blind us to the extreme originality of either his overall intent or his final achievement.[130]

We have discussed that intent and achievement at many stages of this study; but because Blake's vision both of the *Progress* and of the visionary hermeneutics required to read it stand out in sharp relief when compared judiciously with Hegel's view of consciousness awakening to itself, I would like to conclude by quoting M. H. Abrams's succinct digest of the plot of Hegel's *Phenomenology*. To make that digest function as at least a partial gloss on the entire set of Blake's drawings analyzed in this chapter, we need only imagine an identity existing between Hegel's term *spirit,* on the one hand, and Blake's extended image of the dreamer dreaming the dream of the *Progress* on the other:

> For example, the spirit, the protagonist of the story, maintains no one phenomenal identity, but passes through bewildering metamorphoses in the form of outer objects and phenomenal events, or "shapes of consciousness" . . . as well as multiple human personae, of particular "spirits"—"a slow procession and sequence of *Geister,* a gallery of pictures, each of which is endowed with the entire abundance of the *Geist.*" . . . This protagonist, the spirit, is also his own antago-

nist, who appears in a correlative multitude of altering disguises, so that the one actor plays all the roles in the drama; as Hegel says of one stage of the evolution, "the I is We, and the We is I." . . . It eventuates, in fact, that the one spirit is all there is in the story. It constitutes not only all the agents, but also the shifting setting in the phenomenal world of nature and society which it sets up as object against itself as conscious subject or subjects, and since the spirit's being involves all of its own ceaseless development, it constitutes the totality of the plot as well. In a sustained dramatic irony, however, the spirit carries on this astonishing performance all unknowingly. We are privileged to watch this process, as Hegel puts it, in which "consciousness doesn't know what is happening to it," as though "it goes on, so to speak, behind its back" . . . —until, that is, the process discovers itself to consciousness in its own latest manifestation, the thinking of the philosopher Hegel [substitute: "the vision of the artist Blake"], in an on-going revelation with which our own consciousness is privileged to participate as we read. For the reader, no less than the author and the subject matter . . . , is one of the *Geister* in which the spirit continues to manifest itself.[131]

To the extent that this epitome of the *Phenomenology* does bear a telling relation to Blake's goal and procedure in illustrating Bunyan's allegory, it reminds us that the *Progress* watercolors share the strategy and hermeneutical vision of most of his other interpretive and artistic acts. For here in the form of images screened through the imagination of the dreamer, Blake "rouzes the faculties to act" in a Last Judgment of creative recognition that forges a fearful symmetry between the wonder of the object and the ever-unfolding imaginal truths of the self.

Influential Changes in the Established
Iconography of Bunyan Illustrations

Below are indicated the plagiarisms, borrowings, and amalgamations of design motifs that were established and played off against one another in the earliest important illustrated editions of *The Pilgrim's Progress, Part I,* published between 1682 and 1728. Also cataloged is the influence of this iconographic manipulation on the later pictorial narratives offered first by Thomas Stothard, Blake's friend and rival, and then by Blake himself. Unless otherwise noted, all the designs collated here are reproduced in Appendix B, with the exception of Blake's drawings, which are grouped both as Plates 1–28 (in color) and as Figs. 21–48 (pp. 130–33).

1. THE "5TH" EDITION, 1682 (FIGS. B1–B14)

There were two so-called "fifth" impressions of *The Pilgrim's Progress.* One appeared in 1680 carrying only two illustrations: the traditional frontispiece engraved by Robert White (Fig. 49) and a woodcut of the burning of Faithful in martyrdom at Vanity Fair (Fig. B11). In several copies of this edition, however, thirteen extra "copper cuts" were advertised, on the recto of page A, as a supplement available to interested purchasers at additional cost. The second "5th" edition was published in 1682—after the sixth and seventh impressions had been issued—and, besides the frontispiece portrait of Bunyan, it contained for the first time the full complement of fourteen designs listed below:

1. Christian Meets Evangelist
2. Christian Directed by Worldly Wiseman
3. Christian at the Wicket Gate
4. Christian Loses his Burden at the Cross
5. Christian in the Arbour
6. Christian Passes the Lions
7. Christian Goes Forth Armed
8. Christian Fights Apollyon
9. The Valley of the Shadow of Death
10. On Trial at Vanity Fair
11. The Burning of Faithful
12. Giant Despair Before Doubting Castle
13. The Shepherds of the Delectable Mountains
14. The Pilgrims Riding the Clouds

2. THE FLEMISH EDITION, 1685 (FIGS. B15–B23)

In 1685, the Dutch publisher Joannes Boekholt brought out a Flemish-French edition of *The Pilgrim's Progress* entitled *Voyage d'un chrétien vers l'éternité*. Three years earlier, he had issued an illustrated edition in Dutch, but none of the designs for that volume had an impact on future English illustrators, with the possible exception of an engraving of the Man Dreaming of the Last Judgment (Fig. A1). The Flemish edition contained nine new copper plates engraved by Jan Luiken, an artist of some renown. One of these plates served as a frontispiece, but was not a portrait of the author, as in the case of the English editions; instead it was intended as an integral part of the pictorial dream-narrative. The sequence of pictured events progressed as follows:

1. (Frontispiece) Christian at the Wicket Gate
2. Christian at Mount Sinai
3. The Man Sweeping the Interpreter's Parlor
4. Christian Meets Simple, Sloth, and Presumptuous
5. Christian Climbs Hill Difficulty
6. Christian Fights Apollyon
7. The Valley of the Shadow of Death
8. Vanity Fair
9. Christian and Hopeful in the River

3. THE 14TH EDITION, 1695 (IDENTICAL TO FIGS. B24–B36 FROM A LATER PRINTING)

This edition, while retaining White's portrait of Bunyan as frontispiece, pirated seven of Luiken's designs from the 1685 Flemish edition and intermingled them with seven of the engravings printed in the "5th" edition of 1682. The resultant mixture, which remained the standard iconographic model for over thirty years, was ordered in the following manner:

1. Christian Meets Evangelist = *English 5th, #1*
2. Christian at Mount Sinai = *Flemish, #2*
3. Christian at the Wicket Gate = *Flemish, frontis*
4. Christian Loses His Burden at the Cross = *English 5th, #4*
5. Christian Climbs Hill Difficulty = *Flemish, #5*
6. Christian Passes the Lions = *English 5th, #6*
7. Christian Fights Apollyon = *Flemish, #6*
8. The Valley of the Shadow of Death = *Flemish, #7* (not included in Appendix B)
9. Vanity Fair = *Flemish, #9*
10. On Trial at Vanity Fair = *English 5th, #10*
11. The Burning of Faithful = *English 5th, #11*
12. Giant Despair Before Doubting Castle = *English 5th, #12*
13. The Shepherds of the Delectable Mountains = *English 5th, #13*
14. Christian and Hopeful in the River = *Flemish, #9*
    (also known as "Pilgrims Riding the Clouds" because the plate contained the same poetic epigraph as *English 5th, #14*)

Dream of the Man Dreaming of the Last Judgment (from *Eens Christens reyse node euwigheyt*, 1682)

4. THE "QUEEN CAROLINE" EDITION, 1728 (IDENTICAL TO FIGS. B37–B50 FROM TWO LATER PRINTINGS)

In commemoration of Queen Caroline's coronation in 1728, J. Clarke published the 22d edition of the *Progress* "adorned with twenty-two copper plates engraven by J. Sturt." These were all new designs supplied by Sturt to illustrate both Parts I and II of Bunyan's text. Fourteen of the twenty-two plates referred to Christian's dream, and their iconographic relation to the example of the previous editions can be charted as follows:

1. Christian Meets Evangelist; cf. *English 5th & 14th, #1*
2. Christian at Mount Sinai (also known as "Christian Loses His Way and Meets Evangelist a Second Time"); cf. *English 5th & 14th, #2* and *Flemish, #2*
3. Christian at the Wicket Gate; cf. *English 5th, #3* and *Flemish, frontis*
4. Christian Loses His Burden at the Cross; cf. *English 5th & 14th, #4*
5. Christian Climbs Hill Difficulty; cf. *Flemish, #5*

6. Christian Passes the Lions; cf. *English 5th & 14th, #6*
7. Christian Fights Apollyon; cf. *English 5th & 14th, #8; Flemish, #6;* and *English 5th, #9*
8. The Valley of the Shadow of Death; cf. *Flemish, #7*
9. Vanity Fair; cf. *Flemish, #9,* but mostly sui generis
10. On Trial at Vanity Fair; cf. *English 5th & 14th, #10* and *Flemish, #9*
11. The Cruel Death of Faithful; cf. *English 5th & 14th, #11*
12. Christian and Hopeful Escape Doubting Castle; cf. *English 5th & 14th, #12,* but mostly sui generis
13. The Shepherds of the Delectable Mountains; cf. *English 5th & 14th, #13*
14. The Pilgrims Pass the River; cf. *English 14th, #14* and *Flemish, #9*

5. DESIGNS BY THOMAS STOTHARD, 1788 (FIGS. B51–B58)

These designs were engraved and issued separately from the text in 1788 and later incorporated into the 1792 edition of *The Pilgrim's Progress,* along with engravings by other artists. Many were also included in subsequent editions of the text through the first decade of the nineteenth century. Their debts to the influence of the English 5th edition, the Flemish edition, and John Sturt's designs for the Queen Caroline edition are listed below.

1. The Alarm: Christian Breaks His Mind to His Wife and Family; sui generis
2. The Consolation: His Burden Lost, Christian Meets Three Shining Ones; cf. *English 5th, #4*
3. Entering House Beautiful; sui generis
4. Victory: Christian Fights Apollyon; cf. *English 5th, #8 & #9; Flemish, #6;* and *Sturt, #7*
5. Faithful and Christian Meet Evangelist Before Vanity Fair; sui generis
6. Christian and Hopeful Escape Doubting Castle; cf. *Sturt, #12*
7. The Shepherds of the Delectable Mountains; cf. *English 5th, #13* and *Sturt, #13*
8. The Pilgrims Cross the River to Heaven's Gate; cf. *English 5th, #14; Flemish, #9;* and *Sturt, #14*

6. BLAKE'S TWENTY-EIGHT WATERCOLOR DRAWINGS OF *THE PILGRIM'S PROGRESS,* CA. 1824 (FIGS. 21–48; PLATES 1–28)

Collated below are Blake's twenty-eight subjects and the iconographic influences on them of the designs previously listed. Instead of including the 14th edition of the *Progress* as a separate reference, I cite the English 5th and the Flemish editions (though in most cases these engravings would have been familiar to Blake from their reappearances in the 14th edition). Blake's compositional allusion to the unique 5th edition's ninth illustration in his Plate 8, and his evident knowledge of the equally unique third Flemish design (Figs. 1 and 2), indicate he had seen and studied well the engravings of these publications.

1. The Dreamer Dreams a Dream
2. Christian Reading in His Book
3. Christian Meets Evangelist; cf. *English 5th*, *#1* and *Sturt*, *#1*
4. Christian Pursued by Obstinate and Pliable
5. Christian in the Slough of Despond
6. Christian Drawn out of the Slough by Help
7. Christian Directed by Worldly Wiseman; cf. *English 5th*, *#2* and *Sturt*, *#2*
8. Christian Fears the Fire from the Mountain; cf. *English 5th*, *#2 & #9* and *Flemish*, *#2*
9. Christian Falls at the Feet of Evangelist
10. Christian Knocks at the Wicket Gate; cf. *English 5th*, *#3; Flemish, frontis;* and *Sturt*, *#3*
11. The Gate Is Opened by Goodwill; cf. *Sturt*, *#3*
12. The Man in the Iron Cage
13. The Man Who Dreamed of the Day of Judgment; cf. Boekholt's 1682 Dutch edition (Fig. A1)
14. Christian at the Cross; cf. *English 5th*, *#4* and *Sturt*, *#4*
15. Christian Met by the Three Shining Ones; cf. *Sturt*, *#9* and *Stothard*, *#2 & #3*
16. Christian Climbs Hill Difficulty; cf. *Flemish*, *#5* and *Sturt*, *#5*
17. Christian at the Arbour; cf. *English 5th*, *#5*
18. Christian Passes the Lions; cf. *English 5th*, *#6* and *Sturt*, *#5*
19. Christian Goes Forth Armed; cf. *English 5th*, *#7*
20. Christian Fights Apollyon; cf. *English 5th*, *#8; Flemish, #6; Sturt, #7;* and *Stothard*, *#4*
21. Christian and Faithful Conversing
22. Vanity Fair; cf. *Sturt*, *#9*
23. Faithful's Martyrdom; cf. *English 5th*, *#11* and *Sturt*, *#11*
24. Christian and Hopeful in Doubting Castle; cf. Flaxman's drawing (Fig. 13)
25. Christian and Hopeful Escape Giant Despair; cf. *Sturt*, *#12* and *Stothard*, *#6*
26. The Shepherds of the Delectable Mountains; cf. *English 5th*, *#13; Sturt, #13;* and *Stothard*, *#7*
27. Christian and Hopeful in the River; cf. *Flemish*, *#9* and *Sturt*, *#14*
28. At the Gates of Heaven; cf. *English 5th*, *#14*

Five Popular Sets of Bunyan Illustrations
Before Blake's: 1685–1788

Engravings from *The Pilgrim's Progress* (5th ed., 1682)

FIG. B1 *Christian Meets Evangelist*

FIG. B2 *Christian Directed by Worldly Wiseman*

FIG. B3 *Christian at the Wicket Gate*

FIG. B4 *Christian Loses His Burden at the Cross*

FIG. B5 *Christian in the Arbour*

FIG. B6 *Christian Passes the Lions*

FIG. B7 *Christian Goes Forth Armed*

FIG. B8 *Christian Fights Apollyon*

FIG. B9 *The Valley of the Shadow of Death*

FIG. B10 *On Trial at Vanity Fair*

FIG. B11 *The Burning of Faithful*

FIG. B12 *Giant Despair Before Doubting Castle*

FIG. B13 *The Shepherds of the Delectable Mountains*

FIG. B14 *The Pilgrims Riding the Clouds*

Engravings by Jan Luiken from *Voyage d'un chrētien vers l'éternité* (1685)

FIG. B15 *Christian at the Wicket Gate*

FIG. B16 *Christian at Mount Sinai*

FIG. B17 *The Man Sweeping the Interpreter's Parlor*

FIG. B18 *Christian Meets Simple, Sloth, and Presumptuous*

FIG. B19 *Christian Climbs Hill Difficulty*

FIG. B20 *Christian Fights Apollyon*

FIG. B21 *The Valley of the Shadow of Death*

FIG. B22 *Vanity Fair*

FIG. B23 *Christian and Hopeful in the River*

Woodcuts from *The Pilgrim's Progress* (17th ed., 1710)

FIG. B24 *Christian Meets Evangelist*

FIG. B25 *Christian at Mount Sinai*

FIG. B26 *Christian at the Wicket Gate*

FIG. B27 *Christian Loses His Burden at the Cross*

FIG. B28 *Christian Climbs Hill Difficulty*

FIG. B29 *Christian Passes the Lions*

FIG. B30 *Christian Fights Apollyon*

FIG. B31 *Vanity Fair*

FIG. B32 *On Trial at Vanity Fair*

FIG. B33 *The Burning of Faithful*

FIG. B34 *Giant Despair Before Doubting Castle*

FIG. B35 *The Shepherds of the Delectable Mountains*

FIG. B36 *Christian and Hopeful in the River*

Engravings by John Sturt from *The Pilgrim's Progress* (23d ed., 1741; 29th ed., 1757)

FIG. B37 *Christian Meets Evangelist*

FIG. B38 *Christian at Mount Sinai*

FIG. B39 *Christian at the Wicket Gate*

FIG. B40 *Christian Loses His Burden at the Cross*

FIG. B41 *Christian Climbs Hill Difficulty*

FIG. B42 *Christian Passes the Lions*

FIG. B43 *Christian Fights Apollyon*

FIG. B44 *The Valley of the Shadow of Death*

FIG. B45 *Vanity Fair*

Engravings by John Sturt from *The Pilgrim's Progress* (23d ed., 1741; 29th ed., 1757) *continued*

FIG. B46 *On Trial at Vanity Fair*

FIG. B47 *The Cruel Death of Faithful*

FIG. B48 *Christian and Hopeful Escape Doubting Castle*

FIG. B49 *The Shepherds of the Delectable Mountains*

FIG. B50 *The Pilgrims Pass the River*

Engravings by Thomas Stothard (1788)

The Alarm: Christian Breaks His Mind to His Wife and Family

The Consolation: His Burden Lost, Christian Meets Three Shining Ones

Entering House Beautiful

Victory: Christian Fights Apollyon

Engravings by Thomas Stothard (1788) *continued*

FIG. B55 *Faithful and Christian Meet Evangelist Before Vanity Fair*

FIG. B56 *Christian and Hopeful Escape Doubting Castle*

FIG. B57 *The Shepherds of the Delectable Mountains*

FIG. B58 *The Pilgrims Cross the River to Heaven's Gate*

NOTES

PREFACE AND ACKNOWLEDGMENTS

1. Cf. "The Mental Traveller," line 62, E485/K426.

2. *All* may well have been Blake's favorite word: it appears 1,595 times in the various verse and prose texts mined by David V. Erdman for *A Concordance to the Writings of William Blake,* 2 vols. (Ithaca: Cornell University Press, 1967), making it the most frequently used item in Blake's vocabulary; see app. A, 2:2181.

3. M. Esther Harding, *Journey into Self* (London: Longman's Green, 1956).

4. I borrow the term *writerly* from the English translation of Roland Barthes's famous discussion of the distinction between readerly (*lisible*) and writerly (*scriptible*) narratives, wherein the writerly texts are spoken of as those that actively involve the reader in the production of meaning, emphasizing reader response over reader "consumption"; see *S/Z: An Essay,* trans. Richard Miller (New York: Farrar, Straus & Giroux, 1974), 4 and passim. These narratives "are *scriptible* or 'writable,'" John Sturrock explains, "because the reader as it were re-writes them as he reads, being induced to mimic in his own mind the process by which the Text came to be written in the first place" (*Structuralism and Since: From Lévi-Strauss to Derrida,* ed. Sturrock [Oxford: Oxford University Press, 1979], 71).

5. Many recent commentators seem to agree in a general way that the elements of surrealism and/or magical realism in Bunyan's *Progress* owe as much to his imitation of actual dream and fantasy structures as they do to the formal determinants of allegory and literary dream-visions. See, for instance, remarks on this score by Vincent Newey, Roger Sharrock, James Turner, and David Mills in *"The Pilgrim's Progress": Critical and Historical Views,* ed. Vincent Newey (Liverpool: Liverpool University Press, 1980), 24, 25, 29, 66, 94, 155. None of these critics, however, has proposed, as I do, that specific problematic instances of narrative anachrony or other rhetorical displacements should be regarded as deliberate representations on Bunyan's part of the dreamer/narrator's unconscious oneiric strategies.

One example of a place in the *Progress* that critics consistently deem thorny but that can readily be shown to follow common dream logic is the episode of the "key of Promise" (*PP* 118). There Christian, locked up for days by Giant Despair in the dungeon of Doubting Castle, suddenly recalls that he has all the while been holding the means of his own release in the form of a key placed "in his bosom" long since. This instrument of deliverance, however, is one that the narrative never previously mentioned and so could not itself re-call or, strictly speaking, allow to be re-called. In mystery stories and other popular fictional constructs, such last-minute appearances of significant objects or unforeshadowed clues are critically dismissed as the result of poor plotting. But in the discourse of dreams and fantasied remembrances, similar paralipses, metalepses, and so forth carry the kind of significance associated with extremely well plotted fictions, for in the former such narrative discontinuities can be seen as having symptomatic value and psychical effectiveness, often operating as defense mechanisms that serve the individual fantasizer's inner economy of desire. It was Freud who first gave such processes theoretical dignity and a name, *Nachträglichkeit* ("deferred action" in the standard English translation). Since then, in Lacan's belated (mis)reading of Freud, that very notion of pseudorecollection and pathogenic revisionism has been simultaneously enacted and transformed, giving rise in turn to renewed discussion by literary theorists of its complex narrative function. See Sigmund Freud, *The Standard Edition of the Complete Psychological Works of Sigmund Freud,* 24 vols., ed. James Strachey et al. (London: Hogarth Press, 1953–74), 17:45n. and passim; Jacques Lacan, "The Function and Field of Speech and Language in Psychoanalysis" in *Ecrits: A Selection,* trans. Alan Sheridan (New York: Norton, 1977), 48 and pt. 1 passim; Peter Brooks, "Fictions of the Wolf Man: Freud and Narrative Understanding" in *Reading for the Plot: Design and Invention in Narrative* (New York: Knopf, 1984), 275–81; Malcolm Bowie, *Freud, Proust, and Lacan: Theory as Fiction* (Cambridge: Cambridge University Press, 1987), 160ff.; Ned Lukacher, *Primal Scenes: Literature, Philosophy, Psychoanalysis* (Ithaca: Cornell University Press, 1986), 35ff. (Not addressed here are writings by narratologists, from Gerard Genette to Mieke Bal, who also speak of expressive manipulations of narrative order, causality, duration, and so on, but not from a psychological perspective.)

6. Prolific signification is of course a salient concept for Blake, one that he both methodizes and thematizes even as he simultaneously destabilizes it, as in his play on the symbiosis of the prolific and the devourer in *The Marriage of Heaven and Hell,* plates 16–17. That his images are too overdetermined to be treated as fixed symbols and that the resultant semantic excess is manipulated by Blake to cause the reader/viewer to function as a visionary hermeneut is part of my thesis throughout this book and will be amply demonstrated in the chapters to follow. But it is relevant to stress here that Blake's insistence on making us face the play of the mind's own polysemous concretism is the very thing that irritated Yeats when he complained that Blake was a "too literal realist of imagination" (William Butler Yeats, "Blake's Illustrations to Dante," in *Essays and Introductions* [New York: Collier Books, 1968], 119). See also Hazard Adams, "Blake and the Philosophy of the Literary Symbol" (rev. version), in *Essential Articles for the Study of William Blake, 1970–1984,* ed. Nelson Hilton (Hamden, Ct.: Archon Books, 1986), 1–14.

7. See James Hillman, *Archetypal Psychology: A Brief Account* (Dallas: Spring Publications, 1985), 6–10.

8. Ibid., 3.

9. See Janet E. Warner, *Blake and the Language of Art* (Kingston and Montreal: McGill-Queen's University Press, 1984), chap. 4.

10. For a discussion of these concepts and their application, see Stephen Behrendt, *The Moment of Explosion: Blake and the Illustration of Milton* (Lincoln: University of Nebraska Press, 1983), 1–8; and Joseph Anthony Wittreich, Jr., "William Blake and *Paradise Regained*," in *Calm of Mind: Tercentenary Essays on "Paradise Regained" and "Samson Agonistes,"* ed. Wittreich (Cleveland: Press of Case Western Reserve University, 1971), 25–26; and Wittreich, *Angel of Apocalypse: Blake's Idea of Milton* (Madison: University of Wisconsin Press, 1975), chap. 2.

INTRODUCTION

1. For a definition and explication of the term *imaginal,* see Preface.

2. See Paul Ricoeur, *Freud and Philosophy: An Essay on Interpretation,* trans. Denis Savage (New Haven: Yale University Press, 1970), 28–36.

3. See Freud, *Standard Edition* 5:499, 13:95.

4. See David Couzens Hoy, *The Critical Circle: Literature, History, and Philosophical Hermeneutics* (Berkeley and Los Angeles: University of California Press, 1978), 2.

5. Consider, for example, the following from Blake's *A Descriptive Catalogue:* "This Drawing [*The Penance of Jane Shore*] was done above Thirty Years ago, and proves to the Author, and he thinks will prove to any discerning eye, that the productions of our youth and of our maturer age are equal in all essential points" (E550/K585–86). For a penetrating discussion of Blake's recalcitrant attitude toward development in art, identity, and visionary power, see Morris Eaves, *William Blake's Theory of Art* (Princeton: Princeton University Press, 1982), 107–23.

6. Cf. Hans-Georg Gadamer, *Truth and Method,* 2d rev. ed., trans. Joel Weinsheimer and Donald G. Marshall (New York: Crossroad, 1990), 447.

7. Using the figure of the Möbius strip to express how the subject and object of imaginal knowing not only interinvolve each other but also become identical during acts of visionary hermeneutics is, I recently discovered, no more than an "original derivation" on my part. Lacan, for one, has claimed the image as a topological trope for some of the more paradoxical aspects of subjectivity that he explores; see, for example, "Sexuality in the Defiles of the Signifier" and "Of the Subject Who Is Supposed to Know, of the First Dyad, and of the Good," in *The Four Fundamental Concepts of Psycho-Analysis,* ed. Jacques-Alain Miller, trans. Alan Sheridan (New York: Norton, 1978), 156 and 235. And in *The Continuing City: William Blake's "Jerusalem"* (Oxford: Clarendon Press, 1983), 33, Morton D. Paley suggests that criticism of Blake's work should ideally be inscribed on a Möbius strip to simulate the fourfold visionary perspective that Blake's composite art attempts first to represent and then to recreate in his audience.

8. Martin Butlin was the first correctly to identify this extra design as one representing a scene from the *Progress;* see "An Extra Illustration to *Pilgrim's Progress,*" *Blake Newsletter,* no. 19 (Winter 1971–72): 213–14. Along with James T. Wills, Butlin notes

that the drawing bears signs of belonging to the existing series (rather than being intended as an independent work); see Wills's article "An Additional Drawing for Blake's Bunyan Series," *Blake Newsletter* 23 (Winter 1972–73); 63–67; and Butlin's catalog entry no. 829 in *The Paintings and Drawings of William Blake*, 2 vols. (New Haven: Yale University Press, 1981), "Text": 603. My reasons for believing that this design is a rejected alternate for one of the drawings of the series and not an intended addition to the twenty-eight-plate sequence are discussed in Chapter 3.

9. To compare plates from Blake's Bunyan series with designs by previous illustrators of *The Pilgrim's Progress*, see Appendix A and Figs. B1–B58.

10. For the information we do have on the genesis and execution of these watercolor drawings, see Geoffrey Keynes, *Blake Studies: Essays on His Life and Work*, 2d ed. (Oxford: Clarendon Press, 1971), 167–85, and my discussion below.

11. It was William Michael Rossetti, Blake's first cataloger, who initially proposed that these drawings were not colored by Blake; see his "Annotated Catalogue of Blake's Pictures and Drawings," in Alexander Gilchrist's *Life of William Blake, Pictor Ignotus*, 2 vols. (London: Macmillan, 1863), 2:201–64, "Works in Colour," entry no. 211. Rather, he suggested, the "injuries" he saw in the tinting and finishing of the designs could be attributed to "the handiwork of Mrs. Blake," who was known to have assisted her husband on several other projects. Thus began the convenient scapegoating of Catherine Blake, who is held responsible for any number of touches in Blake's pictorial work that a particular critic regards as infelicitous. My own assessment is that Blake himself was entirely capable of executing what some see as objectionable work without the help of his wife or anyone else. In the case of the *Progress* watercolors, however, I reserve judgment. Martin Butlin (*Paintings and Drawings*, "Text": 599–605) finds many signs of work done by another hand (he does not specify Catherine Blake); and while I agree that there is a good deal of reworking, "overpainting," and retracing of outlines, I am not so ready as Butlin is to state categorically that such "finishings" are not done by Blake.

12. In this accounting I have included variants, multiple sets, and preliminary sketches; see Butlin, *Paintings and Drawings*, for numberings and descriptions of all these works.

13. The *catalogue raisonné* referred to here is Butlin's *Paintings and Drawings of William Blake;* for his black-and-white reproductions of the *Progress* designs, see "Plates": pl. 1093–1120.

14. See *"The Pilgrim's Progress" by John Bunyan, 1628–1688, Illustrated with 29 Watercolor Paintings by William Blake*, ed. G. B. Harrison, intro. Geoffrey Keynes (New York: Limited Editions Club, 1941).

15. James T. Wills completed a dissertation on these watercolor drawings entitled "William Blake's Designs for Bunyan's *Pilgrim's Progress*" (Ph.D. diss., University of Toronto, 1975), but because of the Canadian custom of refusing public access to doctoral dissertations for a set period, this work did not become available to me until after my own study was finished.

16. See Jerome J. McGann, *The Romantic Ideology: A Critical Investigation* (Chicago: Chicago University Press, 1983); and Clifford Siskin, *The Historicity of Romantic Dis-*

course (Oxford: Oxford University Press, 1988). All references to the writings of McGann and Siskin in the ensuing discussion are to these two books.

17. Cf. Dan Miller's interesting overview of these issues as they relate to Blake criticism in his introduction to *Critical Paths: Blake and the Argument of Method,* ed. Dan Miller, Mark Bracher, and Donald Ault (Durham, N.C.: Duke University Press, 1987), 1–18, esp. 9. More sustained arguments for a sophisticated intrinsic-valorizing approach to the reading of Blake's narratives are provided by Mark Bracher in *Being Form'd: Thinking Through Blake's "Milton"* (Barrytown, N.Y.: Station Hill Press, 1985); and especially by Donald Ault in "Re-Visioning *The Four Zoas,*" in *Unnam'd Forms: Blake and Textuality,* ed. Nelson Hilton and Thomas A. Vogler (Berkeley and Los Angeles: University of California Press, 1987), 105–40. See also Ault's book-length elaboration of this essay, *Narrative Unbound: Revisioning Blake's "Four Zoas"* (Barrytown, N.Y.: Station Hill Press, 1985).

18. Freud, *Standard Edition* 16:404.

19. Jonathan Culler, "The Mirror Stage," in *High Romantic Argument: Essays for M. H. Abrams,* ed. Lawrence Lipking (Ithaca: Cornell University Press, 1981), 149–63.

20. Martin Heidegger, *Being and Time,* trans. John Macquarrie and Edward Robinson (New York: Harper & Row, 1962), 195.

21. Some places in Blake's writings where he distinguishes between negativity and contrariety are "Annotations to Lavatar" (E601/K88); *Milton* 5 (E98/K484), 34 (E134/K524), and 40 (E142/K533); and *Jerusalem* 17 (E162/K639).

22. Siskin (*Historicity,* 53) explains the dynamic interrelation of (a) sympathetic identification, (b) "the collapsing of distinctions of kind into distinctions of degree," and (c) the elitism of a "politics of creativity" as follows: "Eliminating kinds makes sympathetic identification possible; positing degrees makes it desireable. Poets can speak to men, for example, because they are of the same kind. The men *want* to listen because the poet is more sensitive." The problem for me here, as in his larger argument, is that Siskin seems to assume that sympathetic identification is generated by, rather than attempts to effect, the penetration of generic boundaries. My understanding is that sympathetic identification—an early form of *Einfühlung* or the aesthetic notion of empathy—is anything but dependent on the elimination of differences of kind. To the contrary: it is precisely differences of kind that evoke the need for, and the problems attendant on, identifying. In fact, I would argue that the plea for a willing identification with otherness, like that for a willing suspension of disbelief, can and does occur only given a full appreciation of radical alterity.

Moreover, I find an arbitrariness operating in what Siskin is willing to call either "kind" or "degree." Sometimes the distinction between kind and degree seems itself a matter of degree rather than of kind. This, of course, is the same complaint that Siskin assiduously levels against the Romantics, but in fact the problem seems inherent in the very process of classification. Blake wittily suggests as much when he remarks: "As Newton numbered the stars, and as Linneus numbered the plants, so Chaucer numbered the classes of men" (*DC,* E533/K567). Here three distinctly different kinds of catalogers of "kinds" are being classed and compared in an ordering that emphasizes differences in the degree of their focus on the human dimension of experience. As

Gavin Edwards notes in an essay on related issues, "A similar permutation of similarity and difference is made beautifully explicit in 'The bird a nest, the spider a web, man friendship'" ("Repeating the Same Dull Round," in *Unnam'd Forms,* 42).

It is Blake, then, who most relentlessly abjures such artificial differences of kind, lumping even painting and poetry together as cognate productions of imaginal activity. At the same time, it is also Blake who, in "A Vision of the Last Judgment," is most adamant about preserving other generic distinctions, such as the one between "allegory" and "vision" that he claimed was collapsable only on pain of forfeiting eternal life (VLJ, E554/K605; I explore this example at length in Chapter 1).

23. See, for example, Heinz Kohut and Ernest S. Wolf, "The Disorders of the Self and Their Treatment: An Outline," *International Journal of Psychoanalysis* 59 (1978): 413–25; Arnold Goldberg, ed., *Advances in Self Psychology* (New York: International University Press, 1980); and Joseph Lichtenberg, Melvin Bornstein, and Donald Silver, eds., *Empathy,* 2 vols. (Hillsdale, N.J.: Analytic Press, 1984).

24. See my discussion below and in Chapter 1 on the passage from "A Vision of the Last Judgment" in which Blake tells the spectator how to read his painting of the Last Judgment (VLJ, E560/K611).

25. Blake's claim that "Mental things are alone Real" does not imply, as some readers have assumed, that he denied the actuality of material existence. Rather, his aphoristic comment is spoken from the point of view of the experiencing consciousness, which is the only thing capable of measuring what is or is not real. The observation he is making, therefore, is simply that everything, even "objective" reality, must be processed by an interpreting psyche in order to be experienced as real. As the neo-Jungian psychologist James Hillman puts it: "In terms of logical priority, all realities (physical, social, religious) are inferred from psychic images or fantasy presentations to a psyche" (*Revisioning Psychology* [New York: Harper & Row, 1975], 173).

26. For Hillman's (misquoted) references to Blake as one of archetypal psychology's forerunners, see *Archetypal Psychology,* 26; and *Revisioning Psychology,* ix, 16. It is Jung who figured psychic images as "transformers," taking the metaphor from electrical mechanics; see Carl Gustav Jung, *The Collected Works of C. G. Jung,* 20 vols., Bollingen Series, 2d ed., trans. R. F. C. Hull (Princeton: Princeton University Press, 1960–1978), vol. 5, par. 344.

For representative examples of previous, more orthodox Jungian readings of Blake, see W. P. Wittcut, *Blake: A Psychological Study* (London: Hollis & Carter, 1946; reprinted Port Washington, N.Y.: Kennikat Press, 1966); Margaret Rudd, *Organiz'd Innocence: The Story of Blake's Prophetic Books* (London: Routledge & Paul, 1956); George Wingfield Digby, *Symbol and Image in William Blake* (Oxford: Clarendon Press, 1957); June Singer, *The Unholy Bible: A Psychological Interpretation of William Blake* (New York: Putnam, 1970); Joseph Natoli, "A Study of Blake's Contraries with Reference to Jung's Theory of Individuation" (Ph.D. diss., State University of New York at Albany, 1973); Christine Gallant, *Blake and the Assimilation of Chaos* (Princeton: Princeton University Press, 1978); Edward F. Edinger, *Encounter with the Self: A Jungian Commentary on William Blake's "Illustrations of the Book of Job"* (Toronto: Inner City Books, 1986); and Barbara Frieling, "Blake at the Rim of the World: A Jungian

Consideration of *Jerusalem,*" *Journal of Evolutionary Psychology* 8 (1987): 211–18. These and other Jungian studies are interestingly set off (and in some cases countered) by such competing psychoanalytic readings of Blake as Morris Dickstein's "The Price of Experience: Blake's Reading of Freud," *The Literary Freud: Mechanisms of Defense and the Poetic Will,* ed. Joseph Smith (New Haven: Yale University Press, 1980), 67–111; Diana Hume George's *Blake and Freud* (Ithaca: Cornell University Press, 1980); Margaret Storch's "The 'Spectrous Fiend' Cast Out: Blake's Crisis at Felpham," *Modern Language Quarterly* 44 (1983): 115–35; Storch's *Sons and Adversaries: Women in William Blake and D. H. Lawrence* (Knoxville: University of Tennessee Press, 1990); Brenda Webster's *Blake's Prophetic Psychology* (Athens: Georgia University Press, 1983); Jerry Caris Godard's *Mental Forms Creating: William Blake Anticipates Freud, Jung, and Rank* (Lanham, Md.: University Press of America, 1985); and Mark Bracher's "Rouzing the Faculties: Lacanian Psychoanalysis in the Marriage of Heaven and Hell in the Reader," in *Critical Paths,* 159–203.

27. This conception of the psyche as the larger body and the individual as the smaller is echoed by James Hillman: "Man can never be large enough to possess his psychic organs; he can but reflect their activities" (*Revisioning,* 173). Compare this to Blake's own Devilish principle in *The Marriage of Heaven and Hell,* pl. 4: "Man has no Body distinct from his Soul for that calld Body is a portion of Soul discernd by the five Senses. the chief inlets of Soul in this age."

28. For a fuller understanding of Blake's position on the place of subjectivity in psychic life, see my discussion of Blake's doctrine of states and individuals in Chapter 2.

29. Morris Eaves provides an important discussion of the crucial idea of metaphoric identity and its relation to the concepts of self identity and "identical form" in Blake, in *William Blake's Theory of Art.*

30. Hillman makes reference to this idea in *Archetypal Psychology,* 6, 12; *Revisioning Psychology,* 121, 126, and passim; and *Healing Fiction* (Barrytown, N.Y.: Station Hill Press, 1983), 36.

31. Jung, *Collected Works,* vol. 11, par. 889.

32. Hillman discusses the idea of psychological faith in *Healing Fiction,* 54. For Coleridge's famous adage about poetic faith and the willing suspension of disbelief that constitutes it, see *Biographia Literaria,* ed. James Engell and W. Jackson Bates, 2:6, in *The Collected Works of Samuel Taylor Coleridge,* 7 vols., ed. Kathleen Coburn (Princeton: Princeton University Press, 1983).

33. Hazard Adams, "Synecdoche and Method," in *Critical Paths,* 41–71. References to Adams in the ensuing discussion are to this essay.

34. See Eaves, *Blake's Theory of Art,* 189, for a discussion of Blake's use of the figure of the Old Testament prophet as type of the poetic genius operating alike in poet, work, and audience.

35. Cf. William Wordsworth, "Essay Supplementary to the Preface," in *The Prose Works of William Wordsworth,* 3 vols., ed. W. J. B. Owen and Jane Worthington Smyser (Oxford: Clarendon Press, 1974), 3:80. The pertinent line reads: "Every author as far as he is great and at the same time *original,* has had the task of *creating* the taste by which he is to be enjoyed."

36. For example: "Predestination after this Life is more Abominable than Calvins & Swedenborg is Such a Spiritual Predestinarian" ("Annotations to Swedenborg's *The Wisdom of Angels Concerning Divine Providence*," E610/K133).

CHAPTER ONE

1. For accounts of the Shoreham Ancients and Blake's relationship to them, see, among others, Gilchrist, *Life of Blake,* chap. 31; Mona Wilson, *The Life of William Blake,* ed. Geoffrey Keynes (London: Oxford University Press, 1971), 342–55; David Cecil, *Visionary and Dreamer: Two Poetic Painters—Samuel Palmer and Edward Burne-Jones* (Princeton: Princeton University Press, 1969), 34–60; Robert Rosenblum, "The International Style of 1800: A Study in Linear Abstraction" (Ph.D. diss., New York University, 1956), 220–23; G. E. Bentley, Jr., *Blake Records* (Oxford: Clarendon Press, 1969), pt. 5; Joseph Viscomi, *Prints by William Blake and His Followers* (Ithaca: Herbert F. Johnson Museum of Art, Cornell University, 1983); G. E. Bentley, Jr., et al., *Essays on the Blake Followers* (San Marino, Calif.: Huntington Library and Art Gallery, 1983); Raymond Lister, *Samuel Palmer and "The Ancients"* (Cambridge: Cambridge University Press for the Fitzwilliam Museum, 1984); and Morton D. Paley, "The Art of 'The Ancients,'" *Huntington Library Quarterly* 52 (1989): 97–124. Included in the group were the artists Samuel Palmer, George Richmond, Edward Calvert, Francis Oliver Finch, and Frederick Tatham. Blake exerted a significant stylistic influence on the best of these painters, but the fact that art historians usually refer to them as his "disciples" (following the example of Gilchrist's *Life,* which drew heavily on reminiscences exacted from the men themselves) indicates also the heavy freight of religious transference the young Ancients made to Blake.

2. For a more extended discussion of Blake's associations to the term *ancient,* see Paley, "Art of 'The Ancients.'"

3. Rosenblum, "International Style," 155. The author documents here a deliberate and characteristic trend toward "retrogressive evolution" in the style and theory of a wide range of artists of the period. A more succinct, and also a more suggestive, treatment of the same theme is given in his later study, *Transformations in Late Eighteenth Century Art* (Princeton: Princeton University Press, 1970), 146–191.

4. George Richmond, quoted in Alexander Gilchrist, *Life of William Blake,* rev. ed., ed. Ruthven Todd (London: J. M. Dent, 1942), 299.

5. Francis Oliver Finch, quoted in ibid., 300.

6. Samuel Palmer, quoted in A. H. Palmer, *The Life and Letters of Samuel Palmer* (London, 1892), 9–10.

7. For a preliminary discussion of what I mean by this term, see my introduction. Here I would simply stress that Blake's visionary hermeneutics is a reader-response tactic. As such, it inheres in both audience and text, being at once a performative property of Blake's structural poetics and a method of reading forced on us by that same poetics. In both cases it involves the art of seeing in multiple perspective a controlling event, moment, or identity such that its inner or "identical form" (E693/

K439; and see Eaves, *Blake's Theory of Art,* 35–44) comes to be recognized as consistent with all perspectives. In this way, visionary hermeneutics creates and requires what Hazard Adams calls the trope of radical and progressive synecdoche ("Synecdoche and Method," 42–48). It incorporates the means of interpreting a vision within the aesthetic structure of that vision, a method of operation that became an integral part of Blake's program for renovating the imagination through art. Swedenborg's externally coded reading of the Bible is a good example of nonvisionary hermeneutics, which, according to Blake's metaphor in the *Marriage of Heaven and Hell,* was about as useful in activating the imaginal and transcending the traps of "the corporeal understanding" ("Letters," E730/K825) as Christ's linen clothes left folded at the tomb on the day of resurrection (*MHH* 3). Visionary hermeneutics, by contrast, strives to reveal the power of the "risen" imagination by requiring its use simply to perceive that that is its subject.

8. Northrop Frye, "The Road of Excess," in *The Stubborn Structure: Essays on Criticism and Society* (Ithaca: Cornell University Press, 1970), 160–61 (reprinted from *Myth and Symbol: Critical Approaches and Applications,* ed. Bernice Slote [Lincoln: University of Nebraska Press, 1963]). I cannot agree with Frye's assertion that Blake saw poetry solipsistically as being always and only about poetry, unless Frye's definition of "poetry" includes the play of all the imaginal "Mental Things" that are "alone Real." Furthermore, Frye does not distinguish Blake's discussion of poetry from his treatment of painting when quoting here from the letters. In fact, the context from which Frye takes his second reference (to Blake's claim that implicit allusion "rouzes the faculties to act") is a strong defense by Blake of his deliberately heuristic method— *not* of writing, but of "Moral Painting." See "To Revd Dr Trusler, August 23, 1799" (E702/K793); here Blake denies that he "want[s] somebody to Elucidate [his] Ideas," and affirms instead that his visual forms are "fittest for Instruction" because they are fashioned precisely to invite interpretation and to provide for it.

9. The concept of the *mundus imaginalis* is explained in the Preface.

10. The notion that visionary art simply "illustrates" imaginal reality (doing for the imagination what naturalistic art does for nature) is stated by Blake in this same commentary, viz.: "the Writings of the Prophets illustrate these conceptions of the Visionary Fancy by their various sublime & Divine Images as seen in the Worlds of Vision" (VLJ, E555/K605). A similar idea is articulated again in Blake's "Public Address" written during the same period: "Men think they can Copy Nature as Correctly as I copy Imagination this they will find Impossible. & all the Copies or Pretended Copiers of Nature, from Rembrat [*sic*] to Reynolds Proves that Nature becomes . . . to its Victim nothing but Blots & Blurs. Why are Copiers of Nature Incorrect while Copiers of Imagination are Correct this is manifest to all" (E574–75f/K595).

11. In Genesis, Noah's rainbow is the sign God gave of the covenant between him and Noah that there would never again be a dissolution of the world by a universal flood. Traditionally it is a promise both of earthly fulfillment and of immortality. It can be seen "below," from an earthly perspective, by man, and "above," from a heavenly perspective, by God, and stands conventionally for the hope of the permanent joining

of those two perspectives. It has a double valence in another way, too: its beauty is caused by the reflection of the flood waters held in suspension within it, and as such it becomes a fitting emblem not only for the power of bestowal but also for the power of withholding that is repeatedly attributed to God in the Hebrew Bible. In the history of Christian art, rainbows often appear as the principal material of the judgment seat in representations of the Last Judgment, following the description of Revelation 4:2–3. Considered typologically, therefore, a rainbow is a prefiguration of the completed Apocalypse.

According to S. Foster Damon in *A Blake Dictionary: The Ideas and Symbols of William Blake* (Providence, R.I.: Brown University Press, 1965; reprinted Boulder, Colo.: Shambhala, 1979), the rainbow represents for Blake a "prevision of eternity" (340) and a token of the spiritual body: "The rainbow, as a form of water sublimated and transfigured, is the perfect symbol of the spiritual body" (301). Tying its meaning to the argument for aesthetic empathy given in the passage about the spectator, we can say that the rainbow denotes the whole science of imaginal representation and transformation: for in the Bible (Genesis 9:9–17), God mentions the setting of the bow in the cloud three times within the space of four short verses and repeatedly stresses how it will be an imaginal remembrance as much to him as to man of their mutual, immortal bond. To enter Noah's rainbow, then, would be to exist imaginatively in a state symbolic of the art of symbol making, at the dividing line between earthly and eternal revelation. These are all significant associations to bear in mind when, in Chapter 3, we come to examine the rainbow motif that figures so prominently in Blake's Bunyan drawings.

12. "All Things are comprehended in their Eternal Forms in the Divine body of the Saviour the True Vine of Eternity the Human Imagination" (VLJ, E555/K605–6).

13. Since Noah is the middle figure (between Shem and Japhet) of the three who represent poetry, painting, and music, we can safely assign him the allegoric function of representing the middle-named art. Poetry belongs to Shem, painting belongs to Noah, and music belongs to Japhet. There is an indication in the positioning here that Blake at this time and in this particular context considered painting to be the central image literally and figuratively of all imaginal activity.

14. *Active imagination* is a term used in Jungian and archetypal psychology to describe a self-therapeutic method of participating fully in one's own spontaneous imagery without the undue interference of egoconsciousness. The other expressions mentioned here are currently used more or less interchangeably by a large range of practitioners in the helping professions, from gestalt therapists to new-age spiritual healers.

15. It should be stressed that this apocalyptic lesson in right reading has nothing to do with the dogmatic beliefs of sectarian Christian theology. On the contrary, it is a deliverance from parochial interpretations of the psychic events represented in visionary art. The Last Judgment, Blake tells us (referring at once to his own picture and to the underlying paradigm), is above all "an Overwhelming of Bad Art & Science" (E565/K617), and its heuristic teaching to embrace truth is stated to be synonymous with its hermeneutic teaching to "Embrac[e] True Art" (E562/K613). Furthermore, the truth that an individual is supposed to embrace is not an absolute or fixed idea: that

would not be "True Art." Rather, it involves a widening of the imagination to include more fluid notions of potential imaginative truths. One might fairly say that Blake's vision is less a vision of Truth, with a capital *T*, than a vision of Images of truth, with a capital *I*.

16. Exploration of this issue by modern scholarship has begun; see, for example, W. J. T. Mitchell, "Blake's Visions of the Last Judgment: Some Problems of Interpretation," in *Blake's Visions of the Last Judgment,* (a *Blake Newsletter* pamphlet for the MLA Blake seminar, December 1975), 3 pp.; and Irene H. Chayes, "Blake's Ways with Art Sources: Michelangelo's *The Last Judgment,*" *Colby Library Quarterly* 20 (1984): 60–89. Nevertheless, more art-critical and art-historical work remains to be done in this area.

17. On Blake as a linear abstractionist, see Rosenblum, *Transformations,* passim; and "International Style," 70–135. Morris Eaves adds an important perspective on the significance of Blake's love of line in *Blake's Theory of Art,* 18–44. Blake's native predilection for the vivid and definite, reiterated by him in many different ways, may well have been related to the eidetic constitution of his visualizing faculty (about which see note 19 below). Finally, the expressive term *bounding outline*—suggesting both a limit (to bind) and a leaping of that limit (to bound)—is from the following passage of Blake's "Descriptive Catalogue," which I quote at length as a summary of much of the material alluded to above:

> The great and golden rule of art, as well as of life, is this: That *the more distinct, sharp, and wirey* the *bounding line, the more perfect the work of art.* . . . The want of this determinate and bounding form evidences the want of idea in the artist's mind. . . . How do we distinguish the oak from the beech, the horse from the ox, but by *the bounding outline?* How do we distinguish one face or countenance from another, but by *the bounding line and its infinite flexions and movements?* What is it that builds a house and plants a garden, but the *definite and determinate?* What is it that distinguishes honesty from knavery, but the hard and wiry line of rectitude and certainty in the actions and intentions. *Leave out this l[i]ne and you leave out life itself;* all is chaos again, and the line of the almighty must be drawn out upon it before man or beast can exist. (*DC,* E550/K585; italics added)

18. Blake's peculiar stance toward imaginal truth as that which is at once *definite* and *infinite,* historical and eternal, original and derived, makes his position toward what we today often disparage as "totalism" and "essentialism" a matter of some complexity. Although he so often works with structures of identity when it comes to inventing synchronic systems of metaphor and the like, I find his reliance on polysemy, diachronic unfolding, and the "logic of difference," as Stephen Carr puts it, to be the most compelling components of his approach to such ideas as "universal truth." Speaking of Blake's printing practice in the illuminated books, Carr notes that "Blake's pages insistently signal that they are not transparent mediums for some canonical 'vision.' . . . They point to an ongoing, open-ended production of meanings rather than a representation of an original meaning" ("Illuminated Printing: Toward a Logic of Difference," in *Unnam'd Forms,* 190). Nelson Hilton's important book *Literal Imagination: Blake's Vision of Words* (Berkeley and Los Angeles: University of California Press, 1983) pursues even further the idea of Blake's deliberately "irreducible polysemy"; and Steven Shaviro's article " 'Striving With Systems': Blake and the Politics of Differ-

ence," *Boundary 2* 10 (1982): 229–50 [reprinted in *Essential Articles,* 271–300]—gives an exemplary reading of Blake's "Tyger" from this perspective. Finally, the revised version of Hazard Adams's by now classic article "Blake and the Philosophy of Literary Symbolism" tells a similar cautionary tale.

19. Yeats, "Blake's Illustrations to Dante," 119. It has often been suggested that Blake's adherence to this "literal realism" of imagination is the outgrowth of a functional "abnormality," that is, his special gift for eidetic fantasy, memory, and even ESP. The classic work on eideticism is E. R. Jaensch's *Eidetic Imagery and Typological Methods of Investigation,* trans. Oscar Oeser (London: Kegan Paul, 1930). Joseph Burke discusses the subject in relation to Blake in "The Eidetic and the Borrowed Image: An Interpretation of Blake's Theory and Practice of Art" (1964), in *The Visionary Hand: Essays for the Study of William Blake's Art and Aesthetics,* ed. Robert N. Essick (Los Angeles: Hennessey & Ingalls, 1973), 253–302; as does Morton D. Paley, *Energy and the Imagination: A Study of the Development of Blake's Thought* (Oxford: Clarendon Press, 1970), 201–6; and (briefly) Anne K. Mellor, *Blake's Human Form Divine* (Berkeley and Los Angeles: University of California Press, 1974), 237. People with eidetic mentation create and/or remember extremely vivid images that are not like dreams or hallucinations but "seem to approach the completeness of scenes directly perceived in the physical environment; like that outer visual world, they seem to have the character of something objectively given, which can be explored by active perception the way one scrutinizes a painted or real landscape" (Rudolf Arnheim, *Visual Thinking* [Berkeley and Los Angeles: University of California Press, 1971], 104, working from Wilder Penfield and L. Roberts, *Speech and Brain Mechanisms* [Princeton: Princeton University Press, 1959]). Clearly Blake's belief in the reality of the psyche's sensory and self-regulating powers, his insistence that imagination has a body ("Annotations to Berkeley's *Siris,*" E663/K773; *Laocoön; J* 74, etc.), and his sense that the "outward creation" is epiphenomenal may well have been affected (if not actually formed) by habitual eidetic thinking. Whether eidetic individuals are born or made, whether their abilities are physiologically or psychologically determined, are still open questions as far as modern scientific investigation goes. But obviously Blake thought the power of "spiritual sensation" was latent in everyone and teachable through involvement in the acts of art.

20. On Blake and the Jungian notion of psychic images as transformers of consciousness, see Introduction, n. 26.

21. Consider the condition of Albion, shrunken, sick, asleep in Ulro, suffering a "soul's disease" in the opening plate of chapter 1 of *Jerusalem,* where he is described as "the perturbed Man" who "away turns down the valleys dark," denying the reality of the Divine Vision of imagination which he calls a "Phantom of the over heated brain" (*J* 4).

22. Blake's concept of eternal forms differs from Platonic and Neoplatonic notions of ideal reality in that for him the so-called absolute was not an abstract, rational, foundational formula of which the particular manifestation was a deformity (see "Annotations to *The Works of Sir Joshua Reynolds*" E637/K459). In his view, every ephemeral thing had a spiritually perfect identity that was its own central or "imaginative Form" ("Annotations to Berkeley's *Siris,*" E663/K774). This identity, despite its

dynamism, never in itself changed, although in the material world of space and time it went through many states that looked like change. These states in their turn each had a valid ontological status and could be thought of as *a priori* psychic archetypes with concrete, humanized characteristics: "The Giants who formed this world into its sensible existence" (*MHH* 16). For another discussion of the way Blake's concept of eternal forms differs from the Platonic, see Adams, "Synecdoche and Method," 45–46. On the relationship between changeless states and changing individual manifestations of those states, see my treatment of the doctrine of states and individuals in Chapter 2. For a full and rigorous account of Blake's position on these matters within the tradition of scientific and philosophical thought, see Donald Ault, *Visionary Physics: Blake's Response to Newton* (Chicago: University of Chicago Press, 1974), 57–95.

23. The *Marriage* remains the basic source in Blake's canon for statements about and demonstrations of his revisionist, aesthetic intentions. See especially the full text of plate 14, from which I quoted above.

24. On the systemic organization of coherence and change, see Ault, *Visionary Physics,* chaps. 1 and 2.

25. Blake's father, James Blake, Sr., is spoken of by Gilchrist and others as a devout man, but the sect in which he worshipped was never clearly recorded. Although his family received Anglican christening in the parish church of St. James, he is believed to have practiced outside it. In *Blake Records,* Bentley presents strong evidence to suggest that, at least for a while, the Blakes were members of the local Baptist church. It is also generally conceded that both father and son were drawn to Swedenborgianism even before it burgeoned as a full-fledged nonconformist sect, and many of Blake's closest friends and associates (such as Flaxman, Butts, Varley, and Tatham) seem to have followed the same route. See Bentley, *Blake Records,* 8; and Gilchrist, *Life of Blake,* 47 and passim.

26. *PP* 29. Bunyan is drawing on the words of Saint Paul from Galatians 4:19, 1 Corinthians 4:15, and 1 Thessalonians 2:7, as he clearly glosses in the margins. This passage is a curious one in many respects, as I show further in Chapter 2. The figure being described is labeled by the Interpreter as "the only Man, whom the Lord of the Place whither thou art going, hath Authorized, to be thy Guide in all difficult places thou mayest meet with in the way." But whether this man signifies the ideal seventeenth-century minister, the Apostle Paul, Evangelist (whom Christian has already met and should therefore recognize), the Gospels personified, the Holy Spirit, or Christ ("authorized" by God the Father as author and actor of the Gospel's self-interpretations) is not stated and has never been agreed upon by critics. For divergent opinions, see Wharey in *PP* 316; Harding, *Journey into Self,* 100–109; Henri Talon, *John Bunyan: The Man and His Works,* trans. Barbara Wall (Cambridge, Mass.: Harvard University Press, 1951), 145; U. Milo Kaufmann, *"The Pilgrim's Progress" and Traditions in Puritan Meditation* (New Haven: Yale University Press, 1966), 67; Brian Nellist, *"The Pilgrim's Progress* and Allegory," in Newey, *"Pilgrim's Progress,"* 141; and Dayton Haskin, "The Burden of Interpretation in *The Pilgrim's Progress," Studies in Philology* 79 (1982): 256–78.

What strikes a reader attuned to the art of repetition, revision, and interior duplication practiced by Bunyan in this work, however, is that the portrait of this "Man," introduced to Christian by the Interpreter as the first of seven lessons in hermeneutics, is in one sense the portrait of the Interpreter's own archetypal self or idealized image, and the fact that it could also be a symbol of Saint Paul or the Word or the Holy Ghost is a function of that idealization. The ambiguity of identity appears deliberate and seems to serve the purpose of raising questions in the mind of the reader about the issues of guidance and identity and how to interpret the Interpreter—even though these are the very issues that are supposedly being resolved for Christian by the Interpreter's briefing.

27. Thomas Case, *Mount Pisgah: or, a Prospect of Heaven* (London, 1670), 67, quoted in Kaufmann, *"Pilgrim's Progress,"* 26. I am indebted to Professor Kaufmann's book for my understanding of the ways and means of Puritan hermeneutics as they affect the structure of *The Pilgrim's Progress*.

28. The greater the Calvinistic influence, the more rigorously the search for salvation was replaced by the search for *certainty* of salvation. This was so because the choice between election and damnation, judged to be a foregone conclusion determined by God, was not a matter subject to human process at all. Yet transformation of the personality was still believed to be desirable and effective, since, as Wolfgang Iser remarks, "It is in fact the ultimate uncertainty of salvation that leads to closer and closer inspection of the self, for it is only through his own transformations that the believer can detect the signs he is looking for. As the idea of salvation is intangible, he can only observe its reflections and refractions in the spectrum of human conduct" (*The Implied Reader: Patterns of Communication in Prose Fiction from Bunyan to Beckett* [Baltimore: Johns Hopkins University Press, 1974], 7).

29. See William Haller, *The Rise of Puritanism* (New York: Harper & Row, 1957), 82 (from which I am here paraphrasing).

30. See Richard Greenham, *The Workes* (London, 1599–1600), 40, quoted in Kaufmann, *"Pilgrim's Progress,"* 42–43, 127.

31. Kaufmann, *"Pilgrim's Progress,"* 55.

32. William Whitaker, *Disputation on Holy Scriptures Against the Papists, Especially Bellarmine and Stapleton,* trans. Rev. William Fitzgerald (London: Cambridge University Press, 1849), 404, quoted in Kaufmann, *"Pilgrim's Progress,"* 30.

33. Kaufmann, *"Pilgrim's Progress,"* 109; and John Owen, "An Exposition of the Epistle to the Hebrews," in *The Works,* ed. Rev. William H. Goold and Rev. Charles W. Quick, 17 vols. (Philadelphia: Leighton Publications, 1850), 13:315.

34. John Owen, "Meditations and Discourses on the Glory of Christ," in *Works* 1:275, quoted in Kaufmann, *"Pilgrim's Progress,"* 42.

35. Kaufmann, *"Pilgrim's Progress,"* 42.

36. That Blake makes a point of distinguishing the translucent from the transparent may be due in part to his interest in refining some of Swedenborg's concepts, of which translucency was one. But for Swedenborg, the term is equivalent to, not differentiated from, "transparent," as in the passage Paley (*Continuing City,* 77n.2) quotes from *Apocalypse Revealed,* 3 vols. (Manchester: C. Wheeler, 1791), 2:547–48 (no. 981):

By precious Stones, when speaking of the Word, is signified Divine Truth in the literal sense of the Word transparent or translucent in it's [sic] spiritual sense. . . . The reason why it is translucent, is because Divine Truth in the literal sense is in spiritual Light, wherefore when spiritual light flows into natural light with a Man, who is reading the Word, he is illuminated, and sees truths there, for the object of spiritual Light are Truths.

37. Other recent critics of Bunyan's work have remarked on the same dynamic ambivalence, as for example Vincent Newey in " 'With the Eyes of my Understanding': Bunyan, Experience, and Acts of Interpretation," in *John Bunyan Conventicle and Parnassus: Tercentenary Essays,* ed. N. H. Keeble (Oxford: Clarendon Press, 1988), 213: "Bunyan subordinates the claims of truth (man's plots) to those of Truth (God's plots). . . . Yet in the final analysis *The Pilgrim's Progress* is paradoxical, and subverts Truth . . . for the absolutes it upholds are inscribed in an overall structure of indeterminacy that on various levels calls them in question."

38. See *PP* 4, line 34 of the verse Apology.

39. Ibid., line 26. The full couplet that contains this phrase is set off from the preceding and following arguments in a paragraph of its own and reads: "My dark and cloudy words they do but hold/The Truth as Cabinets inclose the Gold." This nothing-but attitude toward metaphor is contradicted later in the "Apology" when Bunyan's latent visionary bias surfaces as follows:

> . . . but yet let Truth be free
> To make her Salleys upon Thee, and Me,
> Which way it pleases God. For who knows how,
> Better then he that taught us first to Plow,
> To guide our Mind and Pens for his Design?
> And he makes base things usher in Divine.
>   3. I find that holy Writ in many places,
> Hath semblance with this method, where the cases
> Doth call for one thing to set forth another:
> Use it I may then, and yet nothing smother
> Truths golden Beams; Nay, by this method may
> Make it cast forth its rayes as light as day.

(PP 6.7–18)

40. I am borrowing my phraseology here from the seventeenth-century alchemist Thomas Vaughan, twin of the poet Henry Vaughan, for in one of his alchemical myths he states the case exactly: "In the summer translate thyself to the fields, where all are green with the breath of God and fresh with the powers of heaven. Learn to refer all naturals to their spirituals by way of secret analogy; for this is the way the magicians went and found out miracles" (*The Works of Thomas Vaughan, Mystic and Alchemist,* ed. Arthur Edward Waite [New Hyde Park, N.Y.: University Books, 1968], (115–16). For the idea that present pleasures are prophecies, see Kaufmann, *"Pilgrim's Progress,"* 136.

The phrase "Spiritual Sensation," which Dan Miller calls "almost oxymoronic" ("Blake and the Deconstructive Interlude," in *Critical Paths,* 157), comes from Blake's famous letter to Dr. Trusler where it is given as a term defining and describing

"Imagination" (E703/K794). This letter can be regarded as an early position paper by Blake on the imaginal and its role in the production and hermeneutical understanding of visionary art.

41. Richard Sibbes, *A Glance of Heaven* (London, 1638), quoted in Kaufmann, *"Pilgrim's Progress,"* 134.

42. Blake mentions Beulah 170 times in his poetry from *The Four Zoas* through *Milton* and *Jerusalem*. It appears first as a place and a "state" in the *FZ*, Nights I, IV, VII, VIIb, VIII, and IX. Since there seems to be a pattern here of alluding to the term only in those sections of the manuscript that Bentley conjectures were written or revised after Blake was under Hayley's influence (see G. E. Bentley, Jr., *William Blake, "Vala or The Four Zoas": A Facsimile of the Manuscript. A Transcript and a Study of Its Growth and Significance* [Oxford: Clarendon Press, 1963], 157–66)—and since Hayley seems to have been the one interested in pushing the parallel between Blake and Bunyan's pilgrim (see my discussion below, Chapter 2, in the section entitled "The Personal Reference")—it is likely that Blake's use of a Bunyanesque Beulah to represent one of his mythological categories was indebted to a renewed evaluation of the Bunyan passage brought on by Hayley's needling. The only *dated* mention of Beulah is in the verses sent to Thomas Butts from Felpham, November 22, 1802—at just the time that Blake was contending most heavily with Hayley's attitude toward Bunyanesque "enthusiasm" (again, see Chapter 2, "The Personal Reference," for further elaboration). A summary of the uses and meanings of Beulah in Blake's mythic "system" is offered by Damon in *A Blake Dictionary*, c.v. "Beulah."

43. On the imaginary and symbolic, see Lacan, "The Function and Field of Speech and Language in Psychoanalysis," in *Ecrits*. On my phrase *inflexibly literalistic* it should be noted that I am making a distinction between the terms *literal* and *literalistic*—a differentiation applicable to and indeed implied by both Bunyan's and Blake's imaginal rhetoric. To be literal is to be focused on the imbricated play of signifiers that make up the "speech" of imaginative expression, an approach lovingly endorsed by Blake, as Nelson Hilton demonstrates with much flair in his *Literal Imagination*. To be literalistic, however, is to reverse the process, turning the play of signification into a "solid without fluctuation" (*Urizen* 4): it is to be fixated on a single meaning derived from the identification of signifier and signified. According to Blake's poetics, the very act of equating the "letter" thus with a fundamentalist determinacy is what makes it a killer in the style prophesied by Saint Paul (2 Corinthians 3:6).

44. See my discussion of the Beulah allusion that appears in Blake's first drawing of the *Progress* series (below, Chapter 3) where the dreamer's vision of himself, arisen in Beulah, is pictured as being at the center of the rainbow representing his dream.

45. In Bunyan's text, too, there are several places where characters are featured in a state of sleep within the narrator/dreamer's state of sleep. Blake alludes to two of them, but he portrays the characters themselves after the fact, at a point in the narrative when they have awakened. The first of these two *mise-en-abîme* sleepers is the Man Who Dreamed of the Last Judgment in the House of the Interpreter (Plate 13); the second is Christian himself, shown making up for his unconsidered sleep in the Arbor of Grace—the sleep that made him drop his identity roll (Plate 17).

46. Blake equates the dreamer specifically with the Interpreter and with Faithful, so that their presence on the scene functions as a sort of authorial interruption (see my discussions of Plates 12 and 13 and Plate 21 in Chapter 3). Bunyan, for his part, also allows the dreamer/narrator to intervene directly in the action of the dream on two occasions, including the Beulah incident. The other occasion is after Christian's rescue by Help from the Slough of Despond, when the narrator steps up to Help and engages him in a discussion about the phenomenology of despondency in the Christian psyche, though Christian himself has at that point gone on his way (*PP* 15–16).

47. See Kaufmann, *"Pilgrim's Progress,"* 159–60, for a discussion of the Puritan practice of infernal meditation and its use as a corollary of heavenly meditation. Kaufmann notes also that Bunyan's tendency was to lace the infernal with the heavenly, as in his treatment of the Valley of the Shadow of Death, an incident that "clearly owes something to common formal meditation on hell, but, ironically, it owes even more to meditation on heaven" (160). The same mixture of meditational modes can be seen operating in the dreamer-within-the dream's report of his dream of the Last Judgment.

48. This image of the man in the clouds recalls Blake's annotation to Swedenborg's *Wisdom of Angels Concerning Divine Love and Divine Wisdom:* "Think of a white cloud. as being holy you cannot love it but think of a holy man within the cloud love springs up in your thoughts. for to think of holiness distinct from man is impossible to the affections. Thought alone can make monsters, but the affections cannot" (E603/K90).

49. "I hope that all our three years trouble Ends in Good Luck at last & shall be forgot by my affections & only rememberd by my Understanding to be a Memento in time to come & to speak to future generations by a Sublime Allegory which is now perfectly completed into a Grand Poem" (E730/K824–25).

50. "Whenever any Individual Rejects Error and Embraces Truth a Last Judgment passes upon that Individual" (E562/K613).

CHAPTER TWO

1. See Martin K. Nurmi, "Negative Sources in Blake," in *William Blake: Essays for S. Foster Damon,* ed. Alvin Rosenfeld (Providence, R.I.: Brown University Press, 1969), 303–18. Many changes have been rung on the theme of influence in Blake's work since Nurmi's formulation, most notably by Harold Bloom in *The Anxiety of Influence* (New York: Oxford University Press, 1973), *A Map of Misreading* (New York: Oxford University Press, 1975), and *Poetry and Repression* (New Haven: Yale University Press, 1976); by Ault in *Visionary Physics;* and, more recently, by Chayes in "Blake's Ways with Art Sources"; William Dennis Horn in "Blake's Revisionism: Gnostic Interpretation and Critical Methodology," in *Critical Paths,* 72–98; and Edward Larrissy in *William Blake* (Oxford: Blackwell, 1985), who (36–37) puts it this way:

> Blake has to "graft" different discourses onto each other, to borrow a term from Derrida. But when ideas from different traditions are spliced together, naturally "their sense and their function change," as Derrida says ["Economimesis," *Diacritics* 11 (1981): 3]. . . .

We have already seen that "The Chimney Sweeper" is the product of grafts: children's hymns, liberal educational theories and occult emblems. Furthermore . . . it is highly self-conscious in its grafting: it exposes the graft. . . . There are historical reasons why Blake's grafting was so self-conscious. And . . . his work is marked by deep anxieties about whether the discourses and conventions he uses are tainted parasites, grafted onto some original tree of meaning, or whether it is impossible to articulate any idea in the "Fallen World" . . . without it being tainted.

2. The date of composition of this engraving is conjectural. Its designation by Geoffrey Keynes as a work of the 1790s (a designation I continue to support) has in the last decade been contested. Originally thought by William Michael Rossetti, Archibald Russell, and Laurence Binyon to be a product of the 1820s, it was given the earlier date by Keynes when in the 1950s he discovered a prior state of the work on paper associated with Blake's prints of ca. 1794. See Rossetti, "Annotated Catalogue," 258; Russell, *The Engravings of William Blake: A Critical Study Together with a Catalogue Raisonné* (London: Grant Richards, 1912), 32, 101–2; Binyon, *The Engraved Designs of William Blake* (London: Benn, 1926), 139; Keynes, *William Blake's Engravings* (London: Faber & Faber, 1950), 21; and Keynes, *Engravings by William Blake: The Separate Plates and a Catalogue Raisonné* (Dublin: Emery Walker, 1956), 30–33.

David Bindman, however, in *The Complete Graphic Works of William Blake* (New York: Putnam, 1978), 485, challenged Keynes's dating, and Robert N. Essick concurred with Bindman's opinion both in *William Blake, Printmaker* (Princeton: Princeton University Press, 1980), 160–61, and (more tentatively) in *The Separate Plates of William Blake* (Princeton: Princeton University Press, 1983), 108–9. Bindman and Essick suggest "ca. 1824" as a likely date, for plausible, but to my mind not compelling, technical reasons. Like their predecessors, neither links his dating arguments to issues of interpretation, as the plate itself seems to require. A fuller explanation of my position in favor of the early dating of the plate is given in my article "Critical Appraisal and the Dating Game: The Case of Blake's *Man Sweeping the Interpreter's Parlor," Blake: An Illustrated Quarterly* (forthcoming).

3. See E694/K440. As with the date of the engraving, there is a controversy over the date of the "woodcut" entry in the *Notebook*. Keynes believes it was made in the year 1807 (K907–8), but David V. Erdman and Donald K. Moore, eds., *The Notebook of William Blake: A Photographic and Typographic Facsimile*, rev. ed. (New York: Readex Books, 1977), N4, transcript and note, suggest a date of 1794.

4. On the relationship between technical medium and message in Blake's work, see (among many sources) W. J. T. Mitchell, "Style and Iconography in the Illustrations of Blake's *Milton," Blake Studies* 6 (1975): esp. 48–57; and Essick, *William Blake, Printmaker,* who (xxi–xxii) sums it up in the following statement: "Blake's high level of consciousness, as both aesthetic theorist and a practicing artist, of the interactions between concepts and the media in which they are expressed led him to exploit the fullest possibilities for making such interactions an essential part of his art."

5. "Woodcut," it should be noted, is a general term that signifies white-line block printing, such as can be produced by hand or in a letter press. It does not necessarily mean that the block is actually made of wood, or that the block has been "cut" with a

graver. Metal woodcuts may achieve their effects by the use of "mordants" as well as carving tools. A mordant is an acid bath in which the acid eats the unprotected surfaces of the metal by its corrosive "bite."

In a woodcut, unlike plates that are intaglio-engraved or etched, the portion of the block that takes the ink and prints is the raised area, a feature that it has in common with all other relief-printing methods. It is distinct from the "relief etching" process that Blake invented for his illuminated books, however, in that the image raised on the surface of the woodcut plate represents the background or "negative space" of the image printed, and results from being left alone and carved around, whereas the raised portions of Blake's relief etchings held the lineaments of the printed designs and were "worked" on the plate with special varnishes and "stopping-out" fluids. For a general description of these and variant woodcutting methods, see Arthur Hind, *An Introduction to a History of Woodcut,* 2 vols. (New York: Dover, 1963), 1: chap. 1 ("Process and Materials"); and Essick, *William Blake, Printmaker,* 106–9.

6. Consider, for example, these lines from the verse "Conclusion" to Part 1 (*PP* 164):

> Take heed also, that thou be not extream,
> In playing with the *out-side* of my Dream:
> Nor let my figure, or similitude,
> Put thee into a laughter or a feud;
> Leave this for *Boys* and *Fools;* but as for thee,
> Do thou the substance of my matter see.
> Put by the Curtains, look within my Vail;
> Turn up my Metaphors and do not fail:
> There, if thou seekest them, such things to find,
> As will be helpful to an honest mind.

7. Although it is often assumed that Blake went through a period in which he repudiated nature, it is not true that he ever discounted the images of nature as carriers—or metaphors—of "truth." He railed against the tendency to become snared by a literalistic interpretation of their bodily referents, though—a snare that obviously tempted him or else he would not have had to defend against it, as in his statement countering Wordsworth's belief that nature's influence strengthens the imagination: "Natural Objects always did & now do Weaken deaden & obliterate Imagination in Me" (E665/K783). Note that Blake's complaint here is specifically about the "object-ness" of the object, and not about the image of the object. The image of the object ("it is impossible to think without images of somewhat on earth"; E600/K88) is what remains for Blake when the positivistic view of the object, as part of the Demiurgic "Creation," is finally identified with "Error" and instantaneously gets "Burned up" (see VLJ, E565/K617). This attitude toward the substantiality of matter is really quite consistent with Blake's earlier position in the *Marriage,* though superficially the VLJ view seems to contradict the *Marriage*'s exuberant defense of "sensual enjoyment." In fact, the very imagery of a purging conflagration that will cleanse the "doors of perception" is shared by the two works. (cf. *MHH*14 in relation to E565/K617).

8. See Stanley E. Fish, *Self-consuming Artifacts: The Experience of Seventeenth-Century Literature* (Berkeley and Los Angeles: University of California Press, 1972), 240, where

Fish comments on the aesthetics that result from such a Puritan world view: "There is in the *Pilgrim's Progress* an inverse relationship between visibility and reliability."

9. On the problematic identity of this figure, see Chapter 1, note 26.

10. Roger Sharrock discusses the resemblances between the description of this figure and various emblem-book frontispieces in "Bunyan and the English Emblem Writers," *Review of English Studies* 21 (1945): 107.

11. A different view, expressive of a further irony in Bunyan's strategy, is provided by U. Milo Kaufmann (*"Pilgrim's Progress,"* 68), who sees the significance of the portrait quite oppositely: "As Evangel, or good news, he is a necessary counterpoise to the staticity of the Word as it is allegorized by Interpreter's House, and there is good reason for his likeness to be shown at the beginning of Christian's tour."

12. The reproduction here of this print (Fig. 1) is of the second state of the engraving executed, many conjecture, some twenty-five or thirty years after the first state we are considering (see note 2, above). There are some observable differences between the two states, mainly in the amount of "white" carved behind the Damsel, but the salient iconographic details are not significantly altered. See Keynes, *Engravings: The Separate Plates;* or Essick, *The Separate Plates,* for reproductions of both states.

13. The term *comparison,* like the term *example,* has a specialized meaning in the vocabulary of Puritan hermeneutics. See Kaufmann's discussion and application of the terms to the rhetorical structure of the *Progress, "Pilgrim's Progress."*

14. The figure of butterfly wings used as a symbol either of fairy natures or of the human soul is widespread in the iconography of Western art. Blake employs it often: see, for example, the design of "Infant Joy" in the *Songs of Innocence* or the illustration Blake made for Thomas Gray's poem "Spring," reproduced in Irene Tayler, *Blake's Illustrations to the Poems of Gray* (Princeton: Princeton University Press, 1971), pl. 6.

On one copy of the "Interpreter's Parlor" print there is an inscription that names all the creatures "Devils." It reads: "The parable of the relapsed Sinner & her seven Devils." Russell, in *The Engravings,* 101, claims this inscription to be in Blake's hand, a belief that is echoed by Laurence Binyon (*The Engraved Designs,* 139) and S. Foster Damon (*A Blake Dictionary,* 62). Yet it is emphatically denied by Keynes, *The Separate Plates,* 31, as well as by Bindman and Essick. Thomas Wright, *The Life of William Blake,* 2 vols. (Olney: Thomas Wright, 1929), 2:92, suggests that the inscriber (whether Blake or another) is conflating the event of the Interpreter's Parlor with two passages from Scripture: Luke 8:2 and Luke 11:24–26. Luke 8 cites the incident of "certain women, which had been healed of evil spirits," among whom was Mary Magdalene, "out of whom went seven devils"; and Luke 11 speaks of the reincorporation of "seven other spirits more wicked" who made the "last state of that man . . . worse than the first." The context of the whole of Luke 11 is richly associative to many elements of *The Pilgrim's Progress;* the connection with this print is thus instructive, at the very least. Nevertheless, identifying all seven figures as devils without differentiating among them seems to overlook distinctions that Blake deliberately included in the engraving, thereby blunting his meaning.

15. For a complete survey of the six different versions in several media (pencil, watercolor, engraving), see David Bindman, ed., *Colour Versions of William Blake's*

Book of Job Designs from the Circle of John Linnell (London: William Blake Trust, 1987); and Bindman, ed., *William Blake's "Illustrations of the Book of Job": The Engravings and Related Materials with Essays* (London: William Blake Trust, 1987). Also helpful is the earlier study of the several versions edited by Laurence Binyon and Geoffrey Keynes, *Illustrations to the Book of Job by William Blake* (New York: Pierpont Morgan Library, 1935).

16. See Lawrence Lipking's article "Quick Poetic Eyes: Another Look at Literary Pictorialism," in *Articulate Images: The Sister Arts from Hogarth to Tennyson,* ed. Richard Wendorf (Minneapolis: University of Minnesota Press, 1983), 6, for the suggestion that visual representations of the literal level of poetic language should be called "pictural."

17. Although not currently in contention, the later dating of the tempera remains conjectural. Anthony Blunt, in *The Art of William Blake* (New York: Columbia University Press, 1959), 31, seems to have decided that it postdated the copper-cuts on the basis of what he considers its aesthetic advance over plate 6 of the etched Job series. He finds that the "new formal theme of the design as a whole" contributes to "a sharpness and brilliance . . . entirely lacking in the engraved version." Butlin, in *Paintings and Drawings,* "Text": no. 806, follows Blunt and affirms the 1826 date of the tempera for the same reason: "The general effect is more monumental and, although the borders of the engraving add further subtleties of meaning, the painting *seems to* represent the final stage of the composition" (italics mine). Butlin's greater caution at least leaves room for the possibility that what he sees as "development" may in fact be a falling off of "subtlety" and therefore not so clearly an artistic improvement. My point here is that correct dating cannot be established on the grounds of personal preference alone. What is overlooked in such an aesthetic judgment is the differing aims of print and tempera and the likelihood that each is as developed as the other within its appropriate context. The formal composition of the print has a symbolic value exactly suited to Job's state of consciousness at the point in the series where it appears. Satan's power to afflict evil depends, at that juncture, on Job's perceiving him as akin to an atmospheric storm over which he has no control, a naturalized act of God and not a monster bat apparition. The rhetorical purpose of the plate is to reveal Job's dissociated condition by letting us glimpse reality from his limited point of view. This way of seeing has peculiar impact because it is part of a staged sequence of such views dramatizing a gradual development of consciousness over the full complement of twenty-one plates that chart Job's progress. In the tempera painting, however, where the identical scene is removed from the context of temporal process, Satan's symbolic nature and its relation to the landscape has to be conveyed in one showing. The engraving's heuristic lesson about satanic inversion is therefore sacrificed in favor of a starker and more immediate vision of Satan's spectral participation in Job's redemptive ordeal. Were this composition to be imported into the series, it would lose much of its force and diminish the affective stylistics of the graphic narrative. This principle has a bearing on our readings of both Blake's *Progress* series and the "Interpreter's Parlor" print.

18. See above, note 10. What Keynes calls the "spurious" inscription, the one that identifies the Damsel as a "relapsed sinner," and the Law, in consort with his imps, as

the product and/or cause of her bedevilment, supports this negative evaluation of her act (unless we suppose the language of the inscription uses Blake's own ironic vocabulary in the *Marriage*). Even if we accept the assertion by Keynes and others that the inscription "has no authority," because it is not in Blake's hand, it may have some value as a spontaneous response to the print by one of Blake's contemporaries. It appears on an impression of the engraving owned first by Cumberland and then by Linnell.

19. See Roger Sharrock's notes to lines 33–34 of page 29 of the *Progress* in *PP* 316 ("Commentary: The First Part") for evidence of Bunyan's debt to Wierix; and cf. Rosemary Freeman, *English Emblem Books* (London: Chatto & Windus, 1948; reprinted New York: Octagon Books, 1966), 178–79 for more on the belated quality of Bunyan's emblematics. For a discussion of the Wierix engraving, see my "Critical Appraisal and the Dating Game"; and Mario Praz, *Studies in Seventeenth-Century Imagery*, 2d ed. (Rome: Edizioni di Storia e Litteratura, 1964), 152–55. Wierix's print is cited as a source for Bunyan's text in Roger Sharrock, "Bunyan and the English Emblem Writers," 109. The place of the Wierix design in its own sequence of twenty engravings depicting the dedicated heart's progress toward mystical enlightenment may be seen in a unique copy of Henry Hawkins's *The Devout Hart*, reissued in facsimile by John Horden, ed., *The Devout Hart, 1634* (London: Scolar Press, 1975) and in Marie Mauquoy-Hendrickx, ed., *Les étampes des Wierixs conservées au cabinet de la Bibliothèque Royale Albert Premier: catalogue raisonné* (Brussels: Bibliothèque Royale Albert 1er, 1978), 56–58.

20. Bunyan's demotion of the personifications in his verbal emblem from the sublime status of the figure in his pictorial "source" is duplicated by the weakening of power observable in a comparison between Wierix's design and that of Luiken mentioned earlier (Figs. 5 and 2 respectively). Luiken's engraving of this *Progress* episode appeared in the Flemish edition of 1685 but was totally ignored by later Bunyan illustrators (until Blake's print), even though six of his other eight designs were fully recognized, copied, and incorporated into the tradition (see Appendix A).

21. For mention of some of the publications other than *The Devout Hart* in which Wierix's illustrations were reproduced "down to the end of the nineteenth century," see Praz, *Studies in Seventeenth-Century Imagery*, 154.

22. On Blake's changing usage of the word *allegory*, see his own definitions in his letter to Thomas Butts, July 6, 1803 (E730/K825), and in VLJ, as well as discussions by Joseph Anthony Wittreich, Jr., "Sublime Allegory: Blake's Epic Manifesto and the Milton Tradition," *Blake Studies* 4 (Spring 1972): 15–44; Robert Gleckner, *Blake and Spenser* (Baltimore: Johns Hopkins University Press, 1985), app. B; and Miller, "Blake and the Deconstructive Interlude," 155–159.

23. On the relationship between *MHH* 14 and the "Interpreter's Parlor" print, see my "Critical Appraisal and the Dating Game."

24. When Blake uses this term in the *Marriage*, he is probably punning, at one level, on Swedenborg's persistent phrase throughout his writings: "internal sense." Swedenborg's concept of internal versus external matched Bunyan's, being based on a dichotomous world view. For Blake, this dualistic attitude denied the possibility of an integration of inner and outer reality; he thus polemically insists on an infernal/internal sense that by definition contains all the energies of the otherwise repressed portion of existence.

25. See Fish, *Self-consuming Artifacts,* 238, where this passage is cited in exactly these terms.

26. David V. Erdman, *Blake: Prophet Against Empire. A Poet's Interpretation of the History of His Own Times,* 3d ed. (Princeton: Princeton University Press, 1977), 203–4. A fuller treatment of the relationship between Blake and Gillray is given in Erdman, "William Blake's Debt to James Gillray," *Art Quarterly* 12 (1949): 165–70. For the reproduction of another Gillray cartoon based on the imagery of Christian's journey in the *Progress,* see Morton D. Paley and Michael Phillips, eds., *William Blake: Essays in Honour of Sir Geoffrey Keynes* (Oxford: Clarendon Press, 1973), 264 (the plate illustrates Paley's article "William Blake, The Prince of the Hebrews and The Woman Clothed with the Sun," 260–93). Gillray used Bunyan a third time in an 1808 print satirizing Napolean's hardships and entitled "The Valley of the Shadow of Death"; see *The Works of James Gillray, from the Original Plates* (London: Henry G. Bohn, 1851), no. 349, or the more readily available Draper Hill, ed., *Satirical Etchings of James Gillray* (New York: Dover, 1976), no. 93.

27. Erdman, *Blake: Prophet Against Empire,* 204.

28. The sport of parodying Bunyan had become quite popular by Gillray's and Blake's day. See Chapter 3 below (the first section, entitled "The Tradition of Bunyan Illustration"); and John Brown, *John Bunyan: His Life, Times, and Work,* rev. ed., ed. Frank Mott Harrison (London: Hulbert, 1928), 439–89. Particularly common was the use of Christian/Bunyan as a type of fanatical Jacobin (if the writer was a Tory), or at least as an exemplar of dissenting liberal politics. Gillray's exploitation of the figure was quite conventional in this respect.

29. In Gillray's caricature, the outcry of Charles Fox (inscribed in the cartoon bubble over his head) starts off with the plea "Help! Help!" Bunyan's text, however, has no such exclamation coming from Christian at this point in the story; thus, Blake's use of the caricature's initial words betokens once again his debt to Gillray.

30. In a very literal way, the *Gates* can be read as a series of variations on the theme of projection, since almost every design makes its compositional impact through a play on the visual dynamics of extended hands, limbs, torsos, or extrasomatic protrusions. Furthermore, reaching gestures and thrusting attitudes are a leitmotif throughout, causing the projecting stance of a figure in one emblem to echo or complement the stance of other figures in nearby designs.

31. A further difference between the two phrases relates to a difference between the targets of Blake's satire. As mentioned above, the *Natural Religion* tracts aimed to deflate the importance of the quantitative model of the universe revered by the followers of Newton and Locke. "More! More!" in Blake's view aptly represented the futile cry of such empirical testers of objective reality. But the same testing attitude, transposed to the plane of a lust for individual salvation, required a shift from a quantitative to an experiential verbal mode. "I want! I want!" emphasizes the active searching ever necessary, and ever doomed of fruition, in a predestinarian setting that by its own rules could guarantee no evidences. The *Gates,* like the *Marriage,* was directed at an enthusiast audience, not a deistic one, and its polemic consisted largely in showing up the restrictive moral and metaphysical paradigm perpetuated by predestinarian religious systems, Swedenborgian and Calvinist alike.

32. None of the literature on the *Gates* known to me mentions this feature of the design, no doubt because it is ambiguous and difficult, perhaps impossible, to identify with certainty. After examining it carefully, however, I have come to the conclusion that some floater is intended: one part protrudes from the figure's head, the other part from about the region of his waist. See Mellor's *Blake's Human Form Divine*, 79, where this emblem no. 10 of the series is reproduced with slight enlargement.

33. Erdman (*Blake: Prophet Against Empire*, 221–22) reproduces the print in question and describes with elegant conciseness the many threads of allusion to the contemporary historical situation on which Gillray deftly draws in this parody. Yet he does not mention the popularity of the Miltonic source as a subject for painting and as a *locus classicus* of aesthetic controversy—a context that adds a great deal of punch to the irreverent wit of the burlesque. For the Sin and Death passage in *Paradise Lost* was frequently cited as a problematic crux in critical discussions of the day on the nature and use of allegorical personages in fiction. This, incidentally, it had in common with Bunyan's fable and with key passages from Shakespeare, which were also travestied by Gillray and subsequently rehabilitated as serious archetypal sources by Blake.

The range of opinion over the artistic viability of the *Paradise Lost* scene went from admiring it as a trope of the Miltonic sublime to regarding it as an unsightly intrusion on the decorum of the epic structure of Milton's Grand Poem. See Joseph Addison's *Spectator Papers* no. 273, January 12, 1712, in James Thorpe, ed., *Milton Criticism: Selections from Four Centuries* (New York: Collier Books, 1969), 30; Samuel Johnson, *Lives of The English Poets*, quoted in *Milton Criticism*, 83; Samuel T. Coleridge, *Miscellaneous Criticism*, quoted in Joseph Anthony Wittreich, Jr., ed., *The Romantics on Milton: Formal Essays and Critical Asides* (Cleveland: Press of Case Western Reserve University, 1970), 247, for a representative sampling of negative evaluations of the passage through the period. The phrase *unskillful allegory* is Johnson's disparaging epithet for the scene, which he characterized as "one of the greatest faults of the poem." For more on eighteenth-century criticisms of Milton's figures of Sin and Death, see Steven Knapp, *Personification and the Sublime: Milton and Coleridge* (Cambridge, Mass.: Harvard University Press, 1985), chap. 2. Gillray himself plays satirically on an opposite reaction—the uncritical popularity of this episode among artists of his time—when he inscribes the following original legend at the bottom of the print: "The above performance containing Portraits of the Devil and his relatives drawn from the life is recommended to Messrs. Boydell, Fuseli and the rest of the Proprietors of the 385 editions of Milton now publishing." See Marcia Pointon, *Milton and English Art* (Toronto: University of Toronto Press, 1970), 117 and passim, for a fuller tracing of the conscious line of descent from Hogarth to Barry to Fuseli to Gillray and Blake with regard to the iconographic treatment of this subject.

34. Erdman, *Blake: Prophet Against Empire*, 211. Erdman is applying the concept a bit differently, seeking to disentangle the historical narrative of Enitharmon's dream from its surrounding "mythological envelope" in Europe.

35. Ibid., 204.

36. Ibid., 209.

37. The prototypical illustrations of this episode from the *Progress* did not show the inside of the prison (see my discussion of the standard subjects in Chapter 3). However,

FIG. 64 John Flaxman,
Untitled

the drawing by Flaxman, signed and dated June 1792, which does depict the interior scene (see Fig. 13), has an unmistakable resemblance to Blake's design for plate 13 of *Europe* (see Fig. 12). In Blake's version, while the presentation of the prisoner is completely altered, the jailor escaping up the dungeon stairs, filling the door frame with his large form seen from the back, retains Flaxman's iconography. The only evident differences between the two treatments come from those small, telling details that were normally changed when one artist borrowed, or "quoted," from another.

Yet Blake's debt to Flaxman here (if indeed it can be called a debt) is puzzling, for Flaxman was in Rome between 1787 and 1794 (see *Dictionary of National Biography* [*DNB*], vol. 7). To assign a direct influence, we must suppose either that Flaxman circulated his illustrations of the *Progress* episodes by mail (perhaps in response to the reissue of Stothard's designs, which were published in book form in the *Progress* edition of 1792) or that Blake saw and reacted to them with astonishing rapidity after Flaxman's return in late 1794. The drawings may well have circulated among friends at home in 1792, because Flaxman was known to have shipped many designs back from Italy (though usually not the originals). Also, Blake's figure for "The Traveller Hasteth in the Evening" (design no. 14 of the *Gates;* see Fig. 14) shows a striking family likeness to Flaxman's (undated) drawing of Christian attempting to rouse Simple, Sloth, and Presumption (Fig. 64). Blake's first sketch of this subject appears in the *Notebook* on a page covered with studies of a devouring monster reminiscent of Flaxman's famous (1793) design for Dante's Lucifer; see Erdman and Moore, *Notebook of Blake*, N15; and Rosenblum, *Transformations,* fig. 202.

A third hypothesis—still assuming that conscious borrowing was involved—is that the dates on Flaxman's drawing were affixed *post facto,* with inaccurate hindsight. Perhaps, in that case, it is Blake rather than Flaxman who supplies the influence, which would jibe with his own gnomic quip addressed to Nancy Flaxman: "How can I help thy Husbands copying Me/Should that make difference twixt me & Thee" (E507/ K539). For reference to an example of such copying by Flaxman, see Butlin, *Paintings and Drawings,* "Text": no. 152, where Butlin writes of some now untraced Blake drawings that "perhaps formed the basis for the three outline drawings done by 'J. Flaxman from memory of the drawings of Blake June 1792' while he was in Italy where he had been for five years." The only bibliographic information I know of on Flaxman's Bunyan drawings is in Robert Wark's *Drawings by John Flaxman in the Huntington Collection* (San Marino, Calif.: Huntington Library and Art Gallery, 1970), 35–36.

Wark has located over thirty drawings illustrating the *Progress,* but in this catalog he does not identify them individually.

38. For representative treatments of the way prophetic structures strain toward the genre of apocalypse in Blake's work, see Kenneth Stein, "Blake's Apocalyptic Poetry: A Study of the Genre of Blake's Prophetic Books" (Ph.D. diss., Brandeis University, 1969); Leslie Tannenbaum, *Biblical Tradition in Blake's Early Prophecies: The Great Code of Art* (Princeton: Princeton University Press, 1982), chap. 2; and Joseph Anthony Wittreich, Jr., *Visionary Poetics: Milton's Tradition and his Legacy* (San Marino, Calif.: Huntington Library and Art Gallery, 1979), pref. and chap. 1 ("Revelation's 'New' Form: The Recovery of Prophecy by Spenser and Milton").

39. Erdman and Moore, *Notebook of Blake,* 9, 16. See also my discussion of Stothard's designs below, Chapter 3. In fact, the similarities between Blake's pilgrim and Stothard's are much less strong than the likenesses that exist among Blake's and some of the pilgrim figures of early Bunyan illustrators. Consider, for example, the traveler hasting toward the gate in the frontispiece of the first edition of the *Progress* (Fig. 49). Except for the burden and the book, Blake's emblem "quotes" the stance and arrangement of this figure almost "verbatim." Indeed, as far as the pictorial narrative of the *Gates* is concerned, the absence of burden and book—appurtenances no longer necessary when at death's door—emphasizes Blake's "corrected" (dis)placement of the figure at the conclusion, rather than the beginning, of his scheme. On the basis of iconographic resemblance, my own candidate for a contemporary influence, if one need be assumed, is the Flaxman drawing discussed in note 37 (Fig. 64), questions of availability notwithstanding. Blake made an earlier use of this same figure in his first emblem series, *All Religions are One,* pl. 7. There the "traveler" even occupies the same position on the page, and is about the same size, as the pilgrim in the cuts of the *Progress* frontispiece. See David Erdman, ed., *The Illuminated Blake: All of Blake's Illuminated Works with a Plate by Plate Commentary* (New York: Doubleday, 1974), 25. For another possible intertext or source of this much overdetermined image, see Joseph S. Salemi, "Emblematic Tradition in Blake's *The Gates of Paradise,*" *Blake: An Illustrated Quarterly* 15 (Winter 1981–82): 117–18.

40. *MHH* 3. In the critical literature on the *Gates* with which I am familiar, only Erdman and Keynes regard the emblems as a demonstration of "progression by contraries": see Erdman, *Blake: Prophet Against Empire,* 203–4; and the commentary of Geoffrey Keynes in Blake, *The Gates of Paradise,* 3 vols., ed. Geoffrey Keynes (London: Trianon Press Facsimile, 1968). No one, to my knowledge, has dealt with this theme in terms of the compositional structures of consecutive emblems, again with the exception of incidental comments by Erdman, this time in *Illuminated Blake,* 268–79, and *Notebook of Blake,* 40–44. Other important treatments of the *Gates* are Digby, *Symbol and Image,* 5–53; Gail Kemtz, "A Reading of Blake's *The Gates of Paradise,*" *Blake Studies* 3 (Spring 1971): 171–85; Mellor, *Blake's Human Form Divine,* 67–85, 227–35; Frank M. Parisi, "Emblems of Melancholy: *For Children: The Gates of Paradise,*" in *Interpreting Blake: Essays,* ed. Michael Phillips (Cambridge: Cambridge University Press, 1978), 70–110; and Salemi, "Emblematic Tradition."

41. See the sixteenth emblem with its biblical inscription (adapted from Job 17:14),

"I have said to the Worm: Thou art my mother & my sister," and note the elaboration of this theme of the negative mother in the 1818 version, *For the Sexes: The Gates of Paradise*. The closing couplets of "The Keys of the Gates" in particular express the corrupting influence of a material view of life by highlighting the conventional association of matter with the Latin, *mater:*

> The Door of Death I open found
> And the Worm Weaving in the Ground
> Thou'rt my Mother from the Womb
> Wife, Sister, Daughter to the Tomb
> Weaving to Dreams the Sexual strife
> And weeping over the Web of Life.

The fact that Blake has eliminated from his biblical source all mention of the corruptible father (Job 17:14 actually reads, "I have said to corruption, Thou art my father: to the worm, Thou art my mother and my sister") is a further indication that he deliberately cast mortality in matriarchal guise. See also the grasping, repressive role of the mother in the opening couplets of the "Keys."

From the point of view of the visual experience of the plates, this negative dreamer-mother clearly exists outside the "parenthesis" formed by the traveler emblems, 14 and 15. The circle created from the joining of those two emblems is a womb and tomb of its own that excludes "her" as a corruptible force; that in so doing it gives birth to her final formulation is part of the Blakean "redemptive" process that sought to give "a body to Falsehood that it may be cast off for ever" (*J* 12).

42. In the earliest copy of the *Gates* (copy A of the Lessing J. Rosenwald Collection, Library of Congress, Washington, D.C.), the inscription on this plate appears in a first state and reads: "Fear or Hope are—vision." Although the subsequent alteration of the connective *or* to *&* brings Blake's motto in closer alignment with Bunyan's comment on "hope and fear" (see text below), the Blakean motto remains an inversion of Bunyan's diction ("Fear & Hope" replacing the *Progress's* "*hope* and *fear*"), perhaps deliberately.

43. In Bunyan's text, too, a reminder of heaven immediately precedes the acknowledgment that hope and fear are visionary actants. In the *Progress,* however, that reminder is more fearful than hopeful. The episode in question is the last lesson in the Interpreter's House, in which the Man awakened from his dream of the Last Judgment imagines not deliverance but only his own eternal damnation. It is Christian's readiness to understand both the nature of the dream and the limitations of its dreamer that marks him as a graduate of the Interpreter's school of visionary hope and fear.

44. "What is Above is Within, for every-thing in Eternity is translucent" (*J* 71).

45. The compositional relationship of these two designs is neither an identity nor an opposition but involves symmetric permutations that have obvious semantic overtones. Figure 17 provides a diagrammatic representation of the similarities and differences.

46. Northrop Frye notes this connection between the epilogue's tailpiece and the *Progress* in his essay "Keys to the Gates," in *Stubborn Structure,* 194.

47. Freeman, *English Emblem Books*, 206.

48. Ibid., 206, 209. Bunyan's book changed its title three times, through three editions. The earliest title was simply *A Book for Boys and Girls; or, Countrey Rhymes for Children,* and in this form had no pictures. See Frank M. Harrison, *A Bibliography of the Works of John Bunyan* (London: Bibliographic Society Transactions, 1932); and E. S. Buchanan, ed., *John Bunyan's "A Book for Boys and Girls": Country Rhymes for Children* (New York: American Tract Society, 1928).

49. "For Children" refers, of course, to the full title of the 1793 version of Blake's emblem series: *For Children: The Gates of Paradise.* The Bunyan title quoted appeared on the cover of the revised, second (and posthumous) edition of his book of emblems, the first edition with cuts.

Despite the fact that several recent critical analyses have treated the relationship between the genre of children's literature and the genre of Blake's *Songs,* the whole question of Blake's indebtedness to the design element of children's books (including page layouts, script fonts, and colophons, as well as illustrations) remains ripe for further study. Some relevant discussions of the issue are provided by, among others, Gary J. Taylor, "The Structure of *The Marriage:* A Revolutionary Primer," *Studies in Romanticism* 13 (Spring 1974): 141–45; Zachary Leader, *Reading Blake's "Songs"* (London: Routledge & Kegan Paul, 1981), chap. 1; Heather Glen, *Vision and Disenchantment: Blake's "Songs" and Wordsworth's "Lyrical Ballads"* (Cambridge: Cambridge University Press, 1983), chap. 1; Samuel F. Pickering, *John Locke and Children's Books in the Eighteenth Century* (Knoxville: University of Tennessee Press, 1981); Warren W. Wooden, *Children's Literature of the Early Renaissance,* ed. Jeanie Watson (Lexington: University Press of Kentucky, 1986); and such standard comprehensive works as Percy Muir, *English Children's Books, 1600–1900* (London: B. T. Batsford, 1954); Mary Thwaite, *From Primer to Pleasure in Reading* (Boston: Horn Books, 1972); F. J. Harvey Darton, *Children's Books in England,* 3d ed., rev. Brian Alderson (Cambridge: Cambridge University Press, 1982); and Gerald Gottlieb, ed., *Early Children's Books and Their Illustrations* (New York: Pierpont Morgan Library, 1975).

50. The return to ancient models for inspiration—seeking ideal forms in the products of a previous age—is of course not an exclusively neoclassical impulse. But the late-eighteenth-century tendency to purify the Rococo of its illusionist extravagances, to eschew contemporary and naturalistic settings in art and fiction, and to resuscitate the "Gothic" all grew out of that taste for antiquity which neoclassicism had created. The legacy was the method of reversion—what Robert Rosenblum (*Transformations,* 154) calls a "retrogressive evolution" toward increasingly archaic standards of willful simplicity in form and outline.

51. See Blake, *The Gates,* Intro.: 7; and Erdman and Moore, *Notebook of Blake,* N14(4) and pp. 15–16. Both scholarly treatments agree that the "Good" and the "Evil" announce a compendium of antithetical emblems. Erdman further notes (and makes mileage out of the fact) that the title is placed on the page in such a way that it "is partly hidden by the marriage picture beneath it"; the resultant "suggestion of a marriage of contrary ideas, a marriage of 'Good & Evil,' affords guidance to a peruser of the emblems."

52. This left/right alteration is a specific dynamic of the two *Natural Religion* tractates, but the relation of plate to plate in *All Religions Are One* follows a different rule, being more concerned with the movements from plate top to plate bottom. These tractates still await full critical treatment from an art-compositional point of view. Helpful and highly suggestive statements for the student embarking on such a study are to be found, once again, in Erdman's *Illuminated Blake,* 24–32. For a checklist of the kinds of pictorial elements that affect sequential impact in Blake's emblematic texts, see Myra Glazer-Schotz and Gerda Norvig, "Blake's Book of Changes: On Viewing Three Copies of the *Songs of Innocence and of Experience,*" *Blake Studies* 9 (1980): 100–121. For a more theoretical discussion of pertinent issues related to the same question, see Carr, "Illuminated Printing."

53. Five of the songs in the separately issued *Songs of Innocence* covered two plates each, and the combination poems "The Little Girl Lost" and "The Little Girl Found" covered one and one-half plates each, or three plates jointly.

54. A convenient list of the variant arrangements, with comments supplied by Donald Ross, appears in Erdman, *Illuminated Blake,* 69–70.

55. See the tables charting Blake's altering conceptions of that order in Erdman and Moore, *Notebook of Blake,* 7–12.

56. The *Notebook* also supplied motifs for illustrations to other of Blake's works in the illuminated canon; see Erdman and Moore, *Notebook of Blake,* 48–50, for a handy listing. Regarding the motivation for these extractions: there is much evidence that Blake's interest in setting up a system of symbols expressive of his doctrine of contraries pulled him in two directions—toward a one-volume edition of poems and designs based on a dialectic of progression, and toward a set of matching volumes "shewing the two contrary states of the Human soul" (subtitle of the combined *Songs*). It is possible that he first contemplated dividing the *Notebook* emblems themselves up into two matching *Gates* volumes, since there exists a drawing of an alternate title page: "For Children/The/Gates/of/Hell." Keynes offers this explanation, and at the same time speculates that the sketch may represent Blake's "first version of the title-page for the revised series" (*Gates,* 3–4). Erdman and Moore suggest another possibility: that the "Gates of Hell" page may have been a sketch not of a title page for a second volume of emblems, but for a transition title for the 1793 edition of the *Gates,* hit upon between the *Notebook*'s "Ideas of Good and Evil" and the finally selected "Gates of Paradise." Readers of Bunyan will recall a similar equivocation in the last lines of the *Progress,* Part I: "Then I saw that there was a way to Hell, even from the Gates of Heaven, as well as from the City of *Destruction.* So I awoke, and behold it was a Dream" (*PP* 163).

57. The emblem entitled "The Traveller Hasteth in the Evening" (Fig. 14) initiates the whole series in the *Notebook,* where it receives extended narrative treatment in the subsequent pages, following more or less the typical story that Bunyan also relies on— the very progression carefully inverted in the later *Gates* sequence, as we have seen. For more on Blake's access to Bunyan's example, see in Chapter 3, my discussion of the Queen Caroline edition of Bunyan's works, which contained both the *Progress* and the *Divine Emblems,* with influential cuts.

58. Blake's manipulation of the emblem-book structure (as distinct from his bor-

rowings and alterations of the form and content of individual emblems) is a subject still in need of analytic scrutiny. For my purposes here, I need only stress that most products of the convention retained the character of a "gallery" or compendium, structured by nonnarrative ordering principles, except in the case of some religious emblem collections. Especially process-conscious were the Jesuit emblem books, seconding as devotional manuals. They normally had a spiritual-betterment theme and sometimes showed personified agents or objects (like Divine Love, the Soul, the Heart) undergoing transformations throughout the designs. Still, the adventures depicted were not usually presented in a graphically significant sequence. For example, in Wierix's series of cardiomorphic emblems mentioned earlier, and in the work of Quarles and of Christopher Harvey (who used Wierix's plates), the narrative line was emphasized, but the verbal text was relied on to explain the associative causality connecting plate to plate, episode to episode. Among these popular emblem authors, only Quarles in his *Hieroglyphikes of the Life of Man* (London: M. Flesher for John Marriot, 1638), used engravings that on their own told a significant story of progress. Even here, the order of the plates clocked changes in the iconography of a symbolic figure but did not utilize the compositional rhetoric of serial illustration to tell a tale of psychological experience the way Blake's emblems did.

One other important exception to the rule of the picaresque modality of emblem literature ought to be mentioned: the case of alchemical texts such as the *Atalanta Fugiens,* the *Mutus Liber,* and other extremely popular collections of symbolic figures designed to demonstrate stages of transformation in the quest for wholeness.

59. There are differences as well as similarities between this later design for the *Progress* and the emblem on page N41 of the *Notebook*. But the possibility that the imagery common to both held Bunyanesque connotations for Blake, even in the earlier form, is suggested by the placement of the emblem in what might be termed a Bunyan "run." The preceding *Notebook* page, namely, carries the Gillray-Bunyan emblem of the ladder reaching for the moon, while a figure based on the motif of the spider in the Interpreter's House (*PP* Part II) occupies the following page, N42.

60. Kaufmann, *"Pilgrim's Progress,"* 90.

61. Tayler, *Blake's Illustrations,* 49. Here Tayler cites Blake's dependence on Gray's poem "Ode on the Spring" as a mainly negative source. Other critics recall Shakespeare's "flies to wanton boys," notably John E. Grant in "Interpreting Blake's 'The Fly,'" in *Blake: A Collection of Essays,* ed. Northrop Frye (Englewood Cliffs, N.J.: Prentice-Hall, 1966), 37.

62. Proverbs 30:28 reads: "The spider taketh hold with her hands and is in Kings' palaces." For a citation of the places where Bunyan uses the analogy, see *PP,* Commentary, 342. See also Freeman, *English Emblem Books,* 217, where a portion of the dialogue between the Sinner and the Spider in an emblem poem from *A Book for Boys and Girls* is quoted and discussed.

63. Kaufmann, *"Pilgrim's Progress,"* 190. The spider is mentioned in one of the meditation manuals quoted here, not just as a particular instance in the general category of instances on which a person might piously reflect, but as an emblem of the very act of occasional meditation itself:

There is nothing more easie than this ejaculatory meditation to you that are spiritual; deliberate and solemn meditation is very hard and difficult; but this way of meditation is very easie; and the reason is this, because there is no Creature of God but is a teacher of some good thing; thou canst not behold a Spider but thou maist make some good use of it; the Scripture doth make many rare uses of a Spider; a wicked man may be lookt upon in a Spider, as in a glass. (Edmund Calamy, *Art of Divine Meditation* [London, 1680], 14, quoted in Kaufmann, *"Pilgrim's Progress,"* 190)

64. Kaufmann, *"Pilgrim's Progress,"* 190.

65. When Blake illustrated Gray's poem on the comparison of men to flies (see note 61, above), he placed a spider-militant among the insects from whom the speaker moralist drew his meaning; this may indicate Blake's awareness of the complementarity between the two devices, fly and spider, as traditional self-reflexive emblems of emblematic contemplation. But see Tayler, *Blake's Illustrations,* 52–53, for another explanation of the spider image. For what seems to me to be a visual allusion to Bunyan's use of the spider motif, see the emblem of page N41 of the *Notebook.*

66. The episode in Part II detailing Christiana's pilgrimage simply did not stir Blake's visual imagination, with the possible exception of the *Notebook* emblem mentioned above. In fact, Christiana's plight fell behind Christian's story in its appeal to most artists who took up the challenge of illustrating Bunyan—with the notable exception of Stothard (see Chapter 3, the section entitled "The Tradition of Bunyan Illustration," for a discussion of Stothard's designs).

67. Mary Lynn Johnson, "Emblem and Symbol in Blake," *Huntington Library Quarterly* 37 (February 1974): 155. Other traditional comments on Blake and the verbal emblem (for example, by Freeman, *English Emblem Books,* 27–32; Northrop Frye, "Poetry and Design in William Blake," *Journal of Aesthetics and Art Criticism* 10 [1951]: 25–42; and Jean Hagstrum, "Blake and the Sister Arts Tradition," in *Blake's Visionary Forms Dramatic,* ed. David V. Erdman and John E. Grant [Princeton: Princeton University Press, 1970], 82–91) have become somewhat dated and might well be interestingly revisioned in the light of such recent work as Nelson Hilton's *Literal Imagination* and Hazard Adams's "Synechdoche and Method."

68. Angus Fletcher, *Allegory: the Theory of a Symbolic Mode* (Ithaca: Cornell University Press, 1970), 322. Fletcher does not place Bunyan in the same borderland region as he places Blake, but in an adjacent one that he names "accommodation and syncretism" (331), because he is here talking about the novelistic, rather than the emblematic, aspect of Bunyan's form.

69. See William F. Halloran, *"The French Revolution:* Revelation's New Form," in *Blake's Visionary Forms Dramatic,* 30–56, esp. 38: "Just as the Hades of Revelation holds men and women who have defied God, this hell holds men and women who have defied the King. . . . [Thus the] shaking of the seven dens . . . ironically echoes the breaking of the seven seals in Revelation."

70. See Erdman and Moore, *Notebook of Blake,* 85 and N85.

71. Halloran, *"French Revolution,"* 38.

72. Most likely the *locus classicus* informing this whole progression from Dragon to Book—and indeed the central idea of a Hellish Printing house as the guardian of

knowledge and liberty of imagination—is the following passage from Milton's *Areopagitica:*

> I deny not, but that it is of greatest concernment in the Church and Commonwealth, to have a vigilant eye how Bookes demeane themselves, as well as men; and thereafter to confine, imprision, and do sharpest justice on them as malefactors: For *Books are not absolutely dead things, but doe contain a potencie of life in them to be as active as that soule was whose progeny they are:* they do preserve as in a violl the purest efficacy and extraction of that living intellect that bred them. I know they are *as lively, and as vigorously productive, as those fabulous Dragons teeth;* and being sown up and down, may chance to spring up armed men. And yet on the other hand unlesse warinesse be us'd, as good almost kill a man as kill a good Book: who kills a Man kills a reasonable creature, God's Image; but hee who destroyes a good Booke, kills reason itself, kills the Image of God, as it were in the eye. Many a man lives a burden to the Earth; but *a good Booke is the pretious life blood of a master spirit, imbalm'd and treasur'd up on purpose to a life beyond life.* . . . We should be wary therefore what persecution we raise against the living labours of publick men, how we spill that season'd life of man preserv'd and stor'd up in Books. (In *The Prose of John Milton*, ed. J. Max Patrick [New York: Doubleday, 1967], 271–72; italics added)

73. "Allegory addressd to the Intellectual powers while it is altogether hidden from the Corporeal Understanding is My Definition of the Most Sublime Poetry"; see Blake's letter to Thomas Butts, July 6, 1803 (E730/K825).

74. There is surprisingly little agreement in the critical literature as to the connotations of this image. Indeed, the entire Printing house allegory has never received a consistent reading acceptable to the general audience, and most critics tend to avoid direct confrontation with this material. Some of those who have sought to identify the "rubbish" offer the following readings: Martin. K. Nurmi (*Blake's "Marriage of Heaven and Hell": A Critical Study* [Kent, Ohio: Kent State University Press, 1957], 46) calls the rubbish "sexual codes" that block the doors of perception; S. Foster Damon (*William Blake, His Philosophy and Symbols* [Gloucester, Mass.: Peter Smith, 1958], 324) implies it is a virginal hymen; June Singer (*Unholy Bible*, 133) names it "the debris of materialism"; David V. Erdman, Tom Dargan and Marlene Deverell–Van Meter ("Reading the Illuminations of Blake's *Marriage of Heaven and Hell*," in *William Blake: Essays in Honour of Keynes*, 191) hint that it is curls of copper plate being lifted by the artist's burin; and Thomas R. Frosch (*The Awakening of Albion: The Renovation of the Body in the Poetry of William Blake* [Ithaca: Cornell University Press, 1974], 175) refers to it as "habitual and institutionalized restrictions." That most of these interpretations work within the context of their authors' individual approaches simply testifies to the resonance and resilience of the image.

75. See Milton's *Areopagitica* as quoted above, note 72.

76. For detailed treatments of this aspect of the *Marriage*, see Erdman, Dargan, and Van Meter, "Reading the Illuminations"; and Morris Eaves, "A Reading of Blake's *Marriage of Heaven and Hell*, Plates 17–20: On and Under the Estate of the West," *Blake Studies* 4 (Spring 1972): 81–117.

As to Swedenborg, the nature of Blake's polemical disagreement with him in the *Marriage* has been frequently studied; see Erdman, *Blake: Prophet Against Empire*, 127–

28, 160–62; Nurmi, *Blake's "Marriage,"* 25–30; Damon, *A Blake Dictionary,* 392–94; Paley, *Energy and the Imagination* 11–18; John Howard, "An Audience for *The Marriage of Heaven and Hell," Blake Studies* 3 (Fall 1970): 19–51; and the essays in Harvey F. Bellin, ed., *Blake and Swedenborg: Opposition Is True Friendship: The Sources of William Blake's Art in the Writings of Emanuel Swedenborg* (New York: Swedenborg Foundation, 1985). Paley and Howard both describe the extent to which Blake's criticism of Swedenborgian hermeneutics is really directed against the corrupt, institutional use to which Swedenborg's writings were put by the puritanical elders of the New Church in 1790. Blake may have linked Swedenborg's methodology to Bunyan's display of Calvinist doctrine because he wanted to expose the way in which their common, predestinarian mentality encouraged a too rigid treatment of the Bible as a code of fixed symbolism rather than as a "Code of Art" (*Laocoön,* E274/K777). Blake's epithet for Swedenborg as a "Spiritual Predestinarian" is discussed below.

77. As John Howard ("An Audience," 33) observes concerning the ideological clampdown promoted by the founders of the Swedenborgian New Church, "Blake had reason to see in the New Church a growing priestcraft destroying a once liberal religious movement. The machine of that priestcraft was the restrictive morality of the old church," as well as a deepening political conservatism.

78. An earlier letter, also to Butts, dated November 22, 1802, contains a passage in which the imagery of Christian's travail flashes through Blake's description of his own depression: "Tho I have been very unhappy I am so no longer I am again Emerged into the light of Day I still & shall to Eternity Embrace Christianity and Adore him who is the Express image of God but I have traveld thro Perils & Darkness not unlike a Champion I have Conquerd and shall still Go on Conquering" (E720/K815–16). Emerging into the light of day, though a common enough figure for the revival of spiritual health, seems here to have the specific reference of Christian's experience in the Valley of the Shadow of Death, where daylight dawns halfway through his ordeal, after he, too, had "traveld thro Perils & Darkness not unlike a Champion." The metaphor of repeated warfare—to have conquered and to go on conquering—is also appropriate to the stance of Christian in his two valleys. My sense is that Blake's identification of himself with Christian, on the one hand, and of Hayley with one of the foul fiends at hell's mouth, on the other, is already operating, even though at this point Blake gives Butts no clue that the "Perils" encountered related to either his personal or his cosmic quarrel with Hayley.

Note that I quote Blake's letters from Erdman's *Complete Poetry and Prose* rather than from the standard source, Geoffrey Keynes's *The Letters of William Blake* (London: Rupert Hart-Davis, 1956), in order to retain, as Erdman does, most of the holographic integrity of Blake's original punctuation, orthography, and so on.

79. The applicability of Psalm 139 to Blake's predicament is clearly echoed in other parts of this letter. We may suppose a very thorough reading of the psalms at this point in Blake's career, as he was just then learning Hebrew (see his letter to James Blake, January 30, 1803; E727/K821). Also, the psalter imagery may easily have recalled subliminal memories of Bunyan, since Bunyan built much of the landscape of the *Progress* out of this store, including the elaboration of the figure of the Valley of the

Shadow of Death (see Psalms 23:4, 69:14, and 44:19—all of which are cited by Bunyan as marginal glosses on, respectively, pages 64, 62, and 61 of the *Progress*). Furthermore, when Blake mentions "the sore travel" of his stay at Felpham, we may be entitled to think again of Bunyan, who also made pertinent use of the interchangeable meaning of the words *travel* and *travail;* see "The Author's Apology," *PP* 6.33.

80. The complete story of Cowper's effect on Blake via the mediation of Hayley, who was a "corporeal Friend" to both, has a number of unexplored twists worth investigating. Cowper died in the spring of 1800, just before Hayley took Blake under his wing for the express purpose of having Blake assist him in the project of fashioning Cowper's *Life*. The sense of substitution, with Blake filling Cowper's place in Hayley's psychological ecosystem, may have been only partly conscious on Hayley's side. But it did clearly feed his need to have in his debt at least one seemingly half-mad enthusiast at a time. Actually, Blake himself seems to have recognized the syndrome only late in his three-year stay at Felpham (see his January 30, 1803, letter to James Blake with regard to Romney, another of Hayley's unstable artist-protégés (E725/K819); and consider also the nature of the role that Hayley plays in *Milton*).

Hayley had attempted to hoist Cowper out of his debilitating melancholy by extravagant means (see David Cecil, *The Stricken Deer; or The Life of Cowper* (London: Constable, 1943), 288ff. But he had finally to give way to the course of Cowper's severe depressive psychosis—a disease that, in this case, was often expressed in terms of the tenets and fantasy structures of methodical Calvinism. Cowper's poetry, especially such hymns as "The Valley of the Shadow of Death," gave Hayley a real basis for conflating the popular poet's evangelical anxiety with Bunyan's imagery, and when Blake showed signs of a melancholic frame of mind during the period of intense work on Cowper's *Life,* the neat alignment of Blake's with Cowper's and Bunyan's "symptoms" was probably too inviting for Hayley to resist. I quote Cowper's hymn on the Shadow of Death in full to demonstrate its reliance on Bunyan's topos:

> My soul is sad, and much dismay'd
>   See, Lord, what legions of my foes,
> With fierce Apollyon at their head,
>   My heavenly pilgrimage oppose!
>
> See, from the ever-burning lake
>   How like a smoky cloud they rise!
> With horrid blasts my soul they shake,
>   With storms of blasphemies and lies.
>
> Their fiery arrows reach the mark,
>   My throbbing heart with anguish tear;
> Each lights upon a kindred spark,
>   And finds abundant fuel there.
>
> I hate the thought that wrongs the Lord;
>   Oh! I would drive it from my breast,
> With thy own sharp two-edged sword,
>   Far as the east is from the west.

> Come, then, and chase the cruel host
> Heal the deep wounds I have receiv'd!
> Nor let the powers of darkness boast,
> That I am foil'd and Thou art griev'd!

For further relevant material on Hayley and Cowper, see Wright, *Life of Blake* 1:97–131; Cecil, *Stricken Deer;* H. J. Norman, *Cowper and Blake* (Olney, Eng.: Thomas Wright, 1913); Morchard Bishop, *Blake's Hayley: The Life, Works, and Friendships of William Hayley* (London: Gollanez, 1951); Morton D. Paley, "Cowper as Blake's Spectre," *Eighteenth-Century Studies* 1 (1968): 236–52; and James King, *William Cowper: A Biography* (Durham, N.C.: Duke University Press, 1986). Blake himself comments on Hayley's attitude toward Cowper's illness in the *Notebook* (see Erdman and Moore, *Notebook of Blake,* N50); he also refers to the psychology of Cowper's Methodistical insanity and its relation to his visionary work in his "Annotations to Spurzheim's *Observations on Insanity"* (E663/K772).

81. Hayley's two-volume *Life of Cowper,* published in London by J. Johnson, came out originally on December 29, 1802; a second edition appeared, with an extra volume and more engravings, in 1804. It is first mentioned in Blake's correspondence in a letter to Butts, September 11, 1801 (E716/K809). Hayley was simultaneously working on an edition of Milton's Latin poems translated by Cowper, for which Blake was to have contributed designs—a fact that no doubt drew Cowper into the vortex of associations operating on Blake's *Milton,* where a transvaluation of the Calvinist system of election, it will be remembered, is thoroughly developed. In addition, Cowper had become a silent partner with Hayley in the matter of Blake's Greek lessons, as it was Cowper's translation of the *Iliad* that served as Blake's Homeric trot.

82. Lady Hesketh sponsored Hayley's *Life* of her cousin, despite her often valid misgivings about Hayley's good sense (or rather, the lack thereof) as she had observed it over the many years of their acquaintance. Her control of the material was absolute, because she held—and withheld—most of the pertinent letters.

83. Bentley, *Blake Records,* 112. The "two dear Angels" that Hayley refers to here are likely Cowper himself, as "the Bard," and Flaxman as "the Sculptor." Flaxman's role in the publication was, on the surface, slight (see Hayley, *Life of Cowper* [2d ed.], 2:421 and 3: opp. p. 1), yet his regard for both Blake and Cowper, as well as for Hayley, was genuine and influential in the careers of all three. Flaxman played another "angelic" role when he let it be announced that he would execute a national monument in the late poet's honor, pending adequate profits from Hayley's efforts—a good guarantee, Hayley hoped, of the book's success.

84. Consider the following lines from the poem in the *Notebook* written ca. 1807 and addressed to Hayley. In Erdman and Moore's restored version it is entitled, "Epitaph for William Cowper" (N50):

> He calls you to his help be you not movd
> Untill by being Sick his wants are provd.
> You see him spend his Soul in Prophecy

Do you believe it a Confounded lie
Till some Bookseller & the Public Fame
Proves there is truth in his extravagant claim.

Part of the satiric wit of this verse is its title and form, the Epitaph, since Hayley had himself composed over one hundred epitaphs and was sometimes referred to, playfully, as "Epitaph Hayley" (Wright, *Life of Blake* 1:114).

85. See Wright, *Life of Blake* 1:122–23; and see note 92, below.

86. See Brown, *John Bunyan* (rev. ed. by Harrison), 462–63, for a review of Bunyan criticism in Blake's day.

87. I stress *unconscious* contempt because one of the hallmarks of Hayley's personality was his tendency to hide, even from himself, his negative feelings. There is no record of his having looked upon himself as ill disposed either toward Bunyan or Cowper or toward Blake—though he frequently was. Blake's habit of reinforcing Hayley's prejudices—pretending to be the wild enthusiast Hayley thought he was—goes back to the beginning of their relationship as patron and protégé. See, for example, Blake's letter to Hayley of November 26, 1800, where he calls himself "your affectionate, Enthusiastic, hope-fostered visionary," despite the obviously tempered value that Hayley placed on these terms.

88. John Bunyan, *Grace Abounding to the Chief of Sinners,* ed. Roger Sharrock (Oxford: Clarendon Press, 1962). Subsequent references to this text are abbreviated as *GA*.

89. Hayley, *Life of Cowper* 2:288.

90. Cecil, *Stricken Deer,* 289.

91. See ibid., 288. The exact place of this report in Hayley's *Memoirs* is not given by Cecil, and I was not able to locate it owing to unavailability of the text. Blake would have heard about the episode from Johnny Johnson, Cowper's cousin, who had a hand in it and was particularly fond of Blake. See Wright, *Life of Blake* 1:120–23; and, for more on the Blake-Johnson connection, G. E. Bentley, Jr., "William Blake and 'Johnny of Norfolk,'" *Studies in Philology* 53 (1956): 60–74.

92. See the letter quoted by Wright, *Life of Blake* 1:122–23, to Lady Hesketh, sent July 15, 1802, where Hayley likens Blake to Cowper with respect to the "tenderness of his heart," that is, a frenzied sensibility that prevented Blake, Hayley thought, from being able to take Lady Hesketh's adverse criticism—criticism which might "reduce him to the capacity of an ideot." Blake reminds Hayley of Cowper, he says, "by little touches of nervous infirmity when his mind is darkened with any unpleasant apprehension" and "by being a most fervent admirer of the Bible," and again by a "too apprehensive spirit" common to all such evangelistic imaginations.

93. See Wright, *Life of Blake* 1:122–23. It is interesting to note that Apollyon's shifting tactics to subdue Christian in the *Progress* read like a catalog of Hayley's misdemeanors vis-à-vis Blake. They include the following, as expressly glossed in the margins by Bunyan: "Apollyons *flattery;* Apollyon *undervalues Christs service;* Apollyon *pretends to be merciful;* Apollyon *pleads the grievous ends of Christians, to diswade* Christian *from persisting in his way;* Apollyon *pleads* Christian's *infirmities against him*" (*PP* 57–58). This last gloss uses the very words in which Hayley expresses his distorted view of Blake to Lady Hesketh in the letter quoted in the preceding note.

94. On Flaxman's drawings, see above, note 37. Blake's illustrations of Milton's poems began (with a series of designs for "Comus") in 1801; see Butlin, *Paintings and Drawings,* "Text": 373–74. Also to be considered as part of Blake's Milton identification at this time, of course, are the designs for *Milton,* begun by Blake during the Felpham period.

95. When we recall the importance of the plow symbolism as it is linked to the role of Hayley-playing-Satan in the "Bard's Song" of *Milton,* we catch a further ironic resonance in the language of Blake's claim here that he wished "two so unequal labourers might not be yoked to the same Plow."

96. For details of Blake's trial for sedition, see Wilson, *Life of Blake,* 171–78; and Bentley, *Blake Records,* 140–47.

97. Although Blake equated his plight with Christian's in letters to Butts written before the trial, he never wrote to Hayley in this vein until the affair was over. See above and E739–40/K833–34 for the first such letter, dated January 14, 1804—three days after the trial.

98. Blake's reference to Cowper's "Glorified Band" of just spirits may simply be another roundabout compliment to Hayley's use of the phrase in the effusive peroration of the *Life.* Or it may refer to a comment made by Cowper himself. If so, I have been unable to locate such a remark in Cowper's works, though it may lurk there unbeknownst to me. Cecil (*Stricken Deer,* 105), for example, quotes (without giving his source) one use of the Hebrews 12 rhetoric in a passage where Cowper mourns the supposedly reprobate condition of his cousin Lady Hesketh: "How lovely must be the saints of just men made perfect," said Cowper, according to Cecil, "since creatures so lovely in our eyes may yet have the wrath of God abiding in them."

99. Revelation features the sound of trumpets, and Hebrews 12 mentions harps, but bells were not a scriptural appurtenance. This is one of Bunyan's contemporary touches—and also a personal one, for his love of church bells (which he considered a vain and sinful enjoyment) is well known through the example he made of it in his spiritual autobiography (*GA,* par. 33). Here, however, in the paradise of the *Progress,* the art of bells is apparently divinely "redeemed."

100. Blake's developing interest in the dream, both as a symbol of imaginative reality and as a literary genre, is too broad a subject for inclusion here. Suffice it to say that a tendency to portray dreams as delusive, rather than as prospective or visionary, dominates the poet's employment of this topos from 1789 up to about the time of his abrasive contact with Hayley at Felpham. Until then, even in those cases where the dream is acknowledged as an "image of truth," its value is usually depreciated because of its unstable, evanescent, self-obliterating quality, which is the factor emphasized. See, for example, *Tiriel* 2:9, *Thel* 1:10, *America* 6:12, *Europe* 9, and *Urizen* 13: chap. V, v. 3. Only once between the printing of *Songs of Innocence* (which contained such dream scenes as that in "The Chimney Sweeper") and the Felpham period did the verbalization of the concept of dreaming have a clearly creative and visionary sense. That once was in the epigraph to Blake's illustrations to the poems of Gray (ca. 1798):

> Around the Springs of Gray my wild root weaves
> Traveller repose & Dream among my leaves.

Note the connection here with the traveler motif that Blake had already, in 1793, associated with Bunyan through the imagery of the *Gates*. Then, during the writing of *The Four Zoas*—in part a recasting of the structure of Young's waking "night thoughts" into a formal dream genre—the visionary aspect of dreams became more functionally important through the agency, mainly, of the dominion of Beulah. Beulah itself, of course, is in Blake's mythography a state of dreams and visions that probably derived much of its character and status as a gateway to Eden from Bunyan's portrayal of the "Country of Beulah" in the *Progress* (PP 154–56). See also the positive connotation of the dream motif in "The Land of Dreams" (E486–87/K427), a poem from the Pickering manuscript believed to have been composed between 1800 and 1804, and the crucial function of visions-in-sleep in *Milton*. The history of the value of the dream as an image in Blake's writings thus shares many points with the history of his use of the term *allegory*—and both, as we have seen, were specifically associated by Blake with Bunyan.

101. The epigram is titled "On H——— the Pick thank" and reads: "I write the Rascal Thanks till he & I/With Thanks & Compliments are quite drawn dry" (Erdman and Moore, *Notebook of Blake,* N41; E506/K549). There is a problem with the date of this entry. Keynes suggests that the lines were written between 1808 and 1811; but these years do not jibe with the dates of Blake's extant correspondence with Hayley, which comes to a close in 1805. Mona Wilson's solution is to speculate that there were further and more sycophantic exchanges, now missing, between the two men, and that the Pickthank soubriquet applies to Hayley only in Blake's changed view of him anent the character of those later, lost letters (Wilson, *Life of Blake,* 220). In any case, the Bunyanesque allusion applies to the roles both men more or less habitually played with respect to each other. An interesting coincidence, perhaps meaningful, perhaps not, is that this little satiric couplet shows up on a page of the *Notebook* already occupied by a Bunyan-related design in a series of three emblems that I term a Bunyan "run" (see note 59, above).

102. On Bunyan, see William York Tindall, *John Bunyan, Mechanick Preacher* (New York: Columbia University Press, 1934), 22–24. As for the *Commedia,* an interesting comparison may be drawn between Dante's celebrated letter to Can Grande introducing the *Paradiso* and Blake's two letters to Butts (April 25 and July 6, 1803) announcing the composition of his "immense number of verses" (E728/K823). Dante states that the aim of *his* Grand Poem, also a "Sublime Allegory," is "to remove those living in this life from a state of misery and to bring them to a state of happiness," while Blake hopes his work will "be a Memento in time to come & speak to future generations"; see Paget Toynbee, ed., *Dantis Alagherii Epistolae: The Letters of Dante* (Oxford: Clarendon Press, 1920), 197–202, esp. par. 15.

103. Tindall, *John Bunyan,* 23.

104. Erdman points out both this and other related (visual) puns in *The Illuminated Blake,* 217, 233, and in "The Steps (of Dance and Stone) That Order Blake's *Milton,*" *Blake Studies* 6 (Fall 1973): 73–87.

105. "Milton's journey to the fallen world, or part of it, repeats the journey of Moses through the Wilderness to the boundaries of the Promised Land," says Northrop Frye

in *Fearful Symmetry: A Study of William Blake* (Princeton: Princeton University Press, 1947), 337. For a discussion of the widespread use of Exodus as an established figure for the experience of conversion, see Charles Singleton, "In Exitu Israel de Aegypto," in *Dante: A Collection of Essays,* ed. John Freccero (Englewood Cliffs, N.J.: Prentice-Hall, 1965), 102–21. Note also Bunyan's repeated reliance on these traditional associations in his preface to *GA* 2.

106. Cf. *MHH* 9 and *America* 8. Although this refrain appears within Blake's work in political contexts that refer to libidinal liberty, it belongs as well to Blake's deeper quarrel with Milton's Puritan ethic, the errors of which the poem *Milton* was expected to correct. The phrase itself was probably conceived as a direct counterstatement to the following passage from "Comus":

> . . . when lust
> By unchaste looks, loose gestures, and foul talk,
> But most by lewd and lavish act of sin,
> Lets in defilement to the inward parts,
> The soul grows clotted by contagion,
> Imbodies, and imbrutes, till she quite loose
> The divine property of her first being.
>
> (*A Mask,* lines 463–69)

Here Milton, through the voice of the elder brother who is speaking "sweet philosophy" while his sister is being abducted by Comus, images a soul of sweet delight that not only *can* be defiled but *will* be, the moment it gives in to lust.

107. See Eckhard H. Hess, "The Role of Pupil Size in Communication," *Scientific American,* November 1975, 110–19; and Hess, "Attitude and Pupil Size," *Scientific American,* April 1965, 46–54.

108. See C. G. Jung, *Collected Works,* vol. 8: *The Structure and Dynamics of The Psyche,* par. 159.

109. "No man can Embrace True Art till he has Explord & Cast out False Art. . . . Thus My Picture is a History of Art & Science the Foundation of Society Which is Humanity itself. What are all the Gifts of the Spirit but Mental Gifts whenever any Individual Rejects Error & Embraces Truth a Last Judgment passes upon that Individual" (VLJ, E562/K613).

110. See the inscriptions on the *Laocoön* engraving, E274/K777.

111. For more on the relationship between the identity of line and the identity of personality, see Eaves, *Blake's Theory of Art.*

112. This idea, and the term embodying it, are both derived from the classic critical essay by Edward J. Rose, "Blake's Metaphorical States," *Blake Studies* 4 (Fall 1971): 9–31. Much of my earliest thinking about Blake's doctrine of states was influenced by this article, which seeks to relate "states" to both Blake's theory of art and his gospel of forgiveness.

113. "The Oak dies as well as the Lettuce but Its Eternal Image & Individuality never dies. but renews by its seed. just so the Imaginative Image returns by the seed of Contemplative Thought" (VLJ, E555/K605; deletions omitted).

114. See Rose, "Blake's Metaphorical States," 16: "The imagery of states and classes permits Blake to continue a running commentary on the nature of the symbolizing process while at the same time employing that process."

115. Bunyan's use of "Remember Lot's wife" is a scriptural reference, but not one alluding directly to the Old Testament. Rather, it is a New Testament quote citing an Old Testament example—a reference to a reference—and it is spoken by Jesus to his disciples (Luke 17:32) as a typological reminder of the results of looking back toward one's earthly attachment when the Apocalypse (described as an inner event in Luke 17:20) arrives. There is a certain paradoxicality (perhaps even irony) in Jesus' cautionary use of this figure, however, since the typological reference and the admonition to "remember" are themselves forms of "looking back"—the very action Jesus is warning against.

116. The phrase derives from Jung, whose explorations into the way meanings manifest in the psychic life of individuals led him to postulate a principle of universal operation that he called "synchronicity," or meaningful coincidence. See "Synchronicity: An Acausal Connecting Principle," in *Collected Works,* vol. 8, and in C. G. Jung and W. Pauli, *The Interpretation of Nature and the Psyche* (New York: Pantheon Books, 1955). This principle is seen by Jung to complement the law of cause and effect and to apply to a special class of events that are unexplained by the mechanisms of causality. Such events are characterized by their "self-subsistent meaning[s]" (*Interpretation,* 119) and are seen by Jung to occur according to a formal factor of "psychophysical parallelism" (124), which is to say by metaphoric or symbolic contingencies. The whole concept of "acausal orderedness" (138) has interesting affinities with some postmodern methods and modalities of Blake's art and poetics; and echoes of its fundamental assumptions are to be heard in many of Blake's statements about Eternal or Imaginative reality, for example: "The Philosophy of Causes & Consequences misled Lavatar as it has all his contemporaries. Each thing is its own cause & its own effect" ("Annotations to Lavatar," E601/K88)—a radically poetic idea that is elaborated in the text of "A Vision" discussed above.

117. Kaufmann (*"Pilgrim's Progress,"* 72) points out in his treatment of the way Puritan hermeneutics relates to the *Progress* that, "without question, the approach to biblical circumstance as example invited allegorical interpretation."

118. Kaufmann (ibid., 72n.6) notes the double bind of the Puritan position in re the figural truth of the Bible as follows: "Curiously, in insisting upon doctrine as the fullest realization of the literal meaning, the Puritan cultivated a situation in which heavy didacticism would obscure the historicity of the materials." From Blake's point of view, the doctrinal-allegoric sense would appeal to the "Corporeal Understanding," sapping the energy of the vision by rational reductivism, and the historical-literal approach would foster a concretistic fixation on the material aspects of the figure. For a Jungian approach to the reductive and concretistic "fallacies" as they affect individual encounters with the imagery of dreams and fantasy, see Edward F. Edinger, *Ego and Archetype: Individuation and the Religious Function of the Psyche* (New York: Putnam, 1972), 110–17.

119. I attempt no listing even of the greater masterpieces in this genre, but refer the

reader instead to Blake's own commentaries, verbal and visual, on such standard Christian journey-poems as *The Divine Comedy, The Canterbury Tales, Paradise Lost,* and *Paradise Regained,* as well as our subject here, *The Pilgrim's Progress.* See also James Blanton Wharey, *A Study of the Sources of Bunyan's Allegories, with Special References to Deguilleville's "Pilgrimage of Man"* (Baltimore: J. H. Furst, 1904), which acquaints us with popular models of the *pèlerinage de l'âme* theme available in Bunyan's day.

120. "The Christian system of symbols . . . is based largely on analogy of personality. God, though in his essence beyond human comprehension, is to be dealt with as a person, rather than as an abstraction or an absolute. The personal quality of God is conveyed through virtually every revealing accomodation of the Biblical symbols . . . and is ultimately manifested in the historical person of the incarnate Son in a way which is unique, final, adequate and indispensable" (Roland Mushat Frye, *God, Man, and Satan: Patterns of Christian Thought and Life in "Paradise Lost," "Pilgrim's Progress," and the Great Theologians* [Princeton: Princeton University Press, 1960], 13).

121. A succinct treatment of this theme from the perspective of Jungian depth psychology is offered by Edinger, *Ego and Archetype,* chap. 5 ("Christ as Paradigm of the Individuating Ego"). His premise is stated in the opening paragraphs, of which I quote the first: "The image of Christ and the rich network of symbolism which has gathered around Him, provide many parallels to the individuation process. In fact when the Christian myth is examined carefully in the light of analytical psychology, the conclusion is inescapable that the underlying meaning of Christianity is the quest for individuation" (131).

Jung also has written repeatedly and from various angles about the psychological implications of Christ as a symbol of the Self; see especially, *Collected Works,* vol. 9, pt. 2: *Aion: Researches into the Phenomenology of the Self,* pars. 68–126. For one of Blake's earliest formulations of this idea in the illuminated canon, see the final plate of *There Is No Natural Religion,* ser. B, in Erdman, *Illuminated Blake,* 32.

122. The suggestion that the way of the cross (the way of the pilgrim) is also the way of individuation can be found in Matthew 16:24–26, where Jesus in effect asks his followers to forgo their ties to the collective norm in favor of fulfilling their individual life patterns, taking up their "crosses," and finding their own soul.

123. The concept of a multitude of only-begotten sons derives from the religious prose of Thomas Traherne; see Louis L. Martz, *The Paradise Within: Studies in Vaughan, Traherne, and Milton* (New Haven: Yale University Press, 1964), 35–105, for a good exposition of this paradoxical image.

124. The conformity of these two commentaries to a single methodology is no accident, of course, since "A Vision" was meant to be incorporated into a revised edition of the *Descriptive Catalogue.* See its heading in the *Notebook:* "For the Year 1810 Addition to Blakes Catalogue of Pictures," Erdman and Moore, *Notebook of Blake,* N70.

125. See Karl Kiralis, "William Blake as an Intellectual and Spiritual Guide to Chaucer's *Canterbury Pilgrims," Blake Studies* 1 (Spring 1969): 139–90. This article set a precedent for modern scholarship interested in Blake's "genius as a literary critic" (ibid., 139).

126. For instance, the oft-quoted letter to Butts of November 22, 1802, (E722/K818), which contains Blake's poetic revelation of the fourfold structure of vision:

> Now I a fourfold vision see
> And a fourfold vision is given to me
> Tis fourfold in my supreme delight
> And three fold in soft Beulahs night
> And twofold Always. May God us Keep
> From Single vision & Newtons sleep

Other places in Blake where Newton is invoked in satanic guise are too numerous to mention here; see Ault, *Visionary Physics,* for a full account.

127. Here and in what follows I disagree with Rose, who lumps "classes" and "states" together in Blake's usage ("Blake's Metaphorical States," 9). Actually, the term *classes* has both a circumscribed life span and a rather specialized application in the history of Blake's vocabulary, as is clearly shown in Erdman, *A Concordance.* After its early function in the *Marriage* as a word to describe those two "portions of existence" that are also "two classes of men," the Prolific and the Devourer, the term does not reappear until Blake's "Annotations to Reynolds," ca. 1802–8 (the dating is Erdman's, E801). Then it flourishes for a short period in *Milton,* the *Descriptive Catalogue,* the "Public Address," and "A Vision of the Last Judgment." And in all these cases it carries the kind of significance it picked up as a response to Reynolds's use of the word in the academician's statements about categories of form, of character, and of the representation of character in art. Thus, it always held for Blake a certain psycho-aesthetic connotation, and to understand the ramifications of the term in his work it is instructive to examine it as a reaction to the general views on mimetic classification expressed in the "Third Discourse" of Sir Joshua's *Discourses on Art* (New York: Collier Books, 1961), 43–52. For further commentary on this point see Hazard Adams, "Revisiting Reynolds' *Discourses* and Blake's Annotations," in *Blake in His Time,* ed. Robert N. Essick and Donald Pearce (Bloomington: Indiana University Press, 1978), 132–35.

At one place in his Chaucer commentary Blake even paraphrases Reynolds on the subject. When Blake writes that "Chaucer makes every one of his characters perfect in his kind, everyone is an Antique Statue; the image of a class, and not an imperfect individual" (E536/K570–71), we hear the loud echo of Reynolds's comment (*Discourses,* 47) on the three ideal statues of classical beauty—the Hercules, the Gladiator, and the Apollo: "These figures are each perfect in their kind, though of different characters and proportions but still none of them is the representation of an individual, but of a class." The same source feeds into Blake's discussion of the "three general classes of men" represented in his (lost) picture "The Ancient Britons" (E542–45/K577–81).

Only in *Milton* does the term *class* seem at first to merge its meaning with the idea of states, the "Class of Satan" (*M* 11) standing for an aggregate of individuals in the state of Satan. But it must be remembered that the whole treatment of classes in this epic depends largely on a deliberate, "Miltonic" parody of the Calvinists' spiritual class system, a system that, from Blake's point of view, was guilty most of all of confusing temporal states with fixed classifications of being, thus tyrannically frustrating the energy of the individual will to change and impeding the inner call to develop through the pilgrimage of states. After *Milton,* the concept of class disappears from Blake's poetic canon, and the word, too (except for an incidental usage in *J* 72), is abandoned.

128. See Erdman, *A Concordance,* and the preceding note.

129. Witness the heading of the prose introduction to chapter 3 of *Jerusalem:* "To the Deists," a title flanked by the marginal caveats: "Rahab is an Eternal State" and "The Spiritual States of the Soul are all Eternal Distinguish between the Man & his present State."

130. *J* 25.11–12; *J* 32/36.37–38; *J* 35.113–16; *J* 49.65–75; *J* 52, heading; and *J* 73.2.

131. All of the plates were worked on to some degree to bring them to a second state, either by altering aspects of the design or by adding inscriptions, or both. A good presentation of these changes, conveniently arranged for comparison, appears in Erdman, *Illuminated Blake,* 268–79.

132. Hilton, *Literal Imagination,* 166; and Hilton, "Some Sexual Connotations," *Blake: An Illustrated Quarterly* 16 (1982–83): 169. For an earlier observation and articulation of the same point, see my "Images of Wonder, Images of Truth: Blake's Illustrations to *The Pilgrim's Progress*" (Ph.D. diss., Brandeis University, 1979).

133. In some copies of *For the Sexes: The Gates of Paradise,* the demonic form pictured in the epilogue appears white-winged. The engraved plate went through four versions, and in the first and second states (I have not seen an example of the third) no lines darken Satan's figure. (For a reproduction of the design in its second state, showing the devil in this less imposing aspect, see Mellor, *Blake's Human Form Divine,* 234.) Besides strengthening the aesthetic effect of the plate as a whole, the blackening of the dream figure draws attention to the phallic quality of the devil's foot, the sole of which (occupying the position of the dreamer's semierect penis) is the only portion of the devil's body that remains the same white color as the dreamer's body; thus it is seen to belong in substance more to the dreamer than to the form of the wet dream. Other changes in the final state of this image further reinforce both the latent connection and the manifest split between the lost traveler and his projected psychic content; see ensuing discussion.

134. In this observation I am partly anticipated by Jean H. Hagstrum, *William Blake, Poet and Painter: An Introduction to the Illuminated Verse* (Chicago: University of Chicago Press, 1964), who notes (7) that Satan "is connected to the sleeper's head by a black line" but neglects to mention the main service of that line as part of the contour of the sleeper's neck. Hagstrum also overlooks the other, phallic connection that Satan has with the pilgrim. Finally, it is a matter of visual record that the outline of the sleeper's neck is in fact *not* a black line connecting sleeper and devil in the first states of the engraved plates. See, for example, the reproduction in Mellor, *Blake's Human Form Divine,* 234.

135. Nelson Hilton, in "Under the Hill," *Blake: An Illustrated Quarterly* 22 (Summer 1988): 16–17, points out that this epithet for Satan may also be an allusion to the deliverance of the Mosaic law at Mount Sinai, which took place "under" (at the foot of) a "hill" (Sinai) to the gathered company of "lost travelers" in the wilderness. Further-

more, says Hilton, "the Hill" can be thought of as a transliteration of one of Satan's other names, "Hillel," and thus the epithet can be seen to recapitulate the critique of the Law of Sinai announced in the prologue to the revised *Gates*.

136. Erdman calls the lines at the tip of the walking stick a spider web (*Illuminated Blake*, 279), and as far as I know he is the first to so note and identify this detail. Whether the lines are accurately identified is another matter. It is surely a very strange configuration for a spider to make, and the presence of what appears to me to be a tiny moth or butterfly with folded wings at its underside casts further doubt on the nature of this web or thread. See below for additional speculations.

137. Blake's purpose in substituting a walking stick for the Puritan image of the roll of election is probably manifold, but it is typical of the emendments he liked to make on Bunyan's behalf to widen the scope of the allegory. In the first place, the roll or scroll is a credential conferred by an external authority, whereas the staff is a functional item chosen by the owner to help him on his way. In the dynamic of the plate we are considering, however, there is a further purpose that has to do with the phallic quality of the staff; for the picture hints at a trade-off relation between the unenergized staff with its tip tied to the material earth, on the one hand, and the sexually aroused "devil's foot" on the other. While one "sleeps," the other rises and produces all the demonic conflicts that in the "Keys of the Gates" are in fact called "sexual strife." These conflicts would refer to what Erdman (*Blake: Prophet Against Empire*, 203) has seen as a "progression by contraries" evidenced in the serial relation of the preceding emblems, but also to all the antinomies embodied in the epilogue plate itself including night vs. day, accusation vs. forgiveness, picture vs. poem, and lost selfhood vs. the expanded consciousness of a poetic speaker connected to a transpersonal reality.

138. Apart from its placements in *Jerusalem*, which are virtually undatable (owing to the long period of time it took Blake to complete that poem), the phrase "Mutual Forgiveness" and its cognates appear only in works executed ca. 1818 and after. See the supplementary prose prologue to *The Everlasting Gospel* (E875/K757), *The Ghost of Abel* 2:24 (E272/K781), "Notes on the Illustrations to Dante" (E690/K785), "Annotations to Thornton" (E669/K788), and the headings for the illustrated manuscript of *Genesis* (E688/K940), as well as *For The Sexes: The Gates of Paradise*. In *Jerusalem*, mention of it is located on plates 7, 38/43, 49, 54, and 92. As for the dream-within-a-dream, this motif can be observed working in a diffuse way as far back as *The Four Zoas*, and it is suggested as a metaphoric possibility in *Milton* 15 (see below, note 142).

139. See Erdman, *Illuminated Blake*, 279. Except for Hilton (see above, note 132), most commentators have simply assumed that the figure is getting ready to flee or disperse. An example is Mellor's description: "he scurries away in fear and confusion at the first glimpse of the sun rising behind the mountains" (*Blake's Human Form Divine*, 233).

140. On illusional space, see Rosenblum, *Transformations*, chap. 4.

141. See *Jerusalem* 71: "What is Above is Within, for every-thing in Eternity is translucent." Blake follows Paracelsus here in transmuting to a psychological dimension the dictum of the famous hermetic doctrine: "What is below is like what is above and what is above is like what is below, to perpetuate the miracles of One Thing"; see

Jolande Jacobi, ed., *Paracelsus: Selected Writings,* 2d ed. (Princeton: Princeton University Press, 1958), 120; and Stanislas Klossowiski De Rola, *Alchemy: The Secret Art* (New York: Avon Books, 1974), 15. In its simplified form, the motto read even more like Blake's, viz.: "What is above is below, what is below is above: know this and be happy." In the plate under discussion, Blake incorporates the truths both of his revisionist slogan and of the hermetic original by according certain similarities to, on the one hand, the pilgrim figure below and, on the other, the representation of the inner voice, seen as text, above. The poem and the dreamer reflect a common concern with garmentless man; each exists in a predominantly white area of the design; and both face outward to the picture plane—in all these respects they oppose the figure of the devil who comes between them.

142. Cf., for example, the situation in *Milton* 15: "As when a man dreams, he reflects not that his body sleeps, / Else he would wake; so seem'd he entering his Shadow: but / With him the Spirits of the Seven Angels of the Presence / Entering; they gave him still perceptions of his Sleeping Body."

143. To this degree my reading differs from Hilton's ("Some Sexual Connotations," 169), for Hilton interprets the ejaculation as an emblem of the traveler's copulating or sleeping "with" the satanic figure, while my sense is that the night-winged form is the manifestation of the traveler's spent, and hence no longer desired, desire.

144. M. H. Abrams, *Natural Supernaturalism: Tradition and Revolution in Romantic Literature* (New York: Norton, 1971), 230.

CHAPTER THREE

1. Although evidence for Blake's familiarity with the convention is solely circumstantial, it is extremely strong. Design after design borrows motifs, plays on standard compositional structures, or transforms the accepted iconography in deliberate ways. Discussion of many such debts to the tradition is supplied in the course of the analysis of the drawings below. See Figs. B1–B50 for reproductions of some of the most popular illustrations of early editions of the *Progress.*

2. A good chronology and descriptive bibliography of all the impressions of the *Progress* published during Bunyan's lifetime can be found in Wharey and Sharrock's introduction to *The Pilgrim's Progress,* xxvi–lxxiii. Other sources are Brown, *John Bunyan,* chap. 19; Frank Mott Harrison, "Some Illustrators of *The Pilgrim's Progress* (Part One): John Bunyan," *Library,* 4th ser., 3 (December 1936): 241–63; and Keynes, *Blake Studies,* 167–85. A list of subjects illustrated in three of the standard editions up through Blake's day appears in my Appendix A ("Influential Changes in the Established Iconography of Bunyan Illustration").

3. The illustrations "ordinarily printed" in editions prior to that of the embellished "Fifth Impression" were the frontispiece portrait (Fig. 49) and a woodcut of Faithful's martyrdom, re-engraved later on copper (Fig. B11).

4. See Brown, *John Bunyan,* 441.

5. The number of pages varied from edition to edition, mostly because of variation

in type sizes. When the book's format switched with the printing of the twenty-second edition from small duodecimo to quarto, the illustrations also changed. See below, note 9.

6. For a general overview of visual representations accorded Milton's epic, see Marcia Pointon, *Milton and English Art* (Toronto: University of Toronto Press, 1970). Blake's two sets of watercolor drawings illustrating *Paradise Lost* are discussed by Pointon and by the following: C. H. Collins Baker, "Some Illustrations of Milton's *Paradise Lost* (1688–1850)," *Library,* 5th ser., 3 (1948): 1–21, 101–19; Kester Svendson, "Some Illustrators of Milton: The Expulsion from Paradise," in *Milton Studies in Honour of Harris Francis Fletcher,* ed. G. Blakemore Evans et al. (Urbana: University of Illinois Press, 1961); Edward J. Rose, "Blake's Illustrations for *Paradise Lost, L'Allegro,* and *Il Penseroso:* A Thematic Reading," *Hartford Studies in Literature* 2 (1970): 40–67; Wittreich, *Angel of Apocalypse,* chap. 2; Pamela Dunbar, chapter 3 of *William Blake's Illustrations to the Poetry of Milton* (Oxford: Clarendon Press, 1980); Behrendt, *Moment of Explosion,* chaps. 3–5; and Bette Charlene Werner, *Blake's Vision of the Poetry of Milton* (Lewisburg, Pa.: Bucknell University Press, 1986), chap. 3. A comparison of the traditions of illustrating Bunyan, on the one hand, and Milton, on the other, adds an extra nuance to Blake's comment to Hayley, discussed above in Chapter 2, that his working with Flaxman for Hayley would be like "putting John Milton with John Bunyan" (E758/K941).

7. See Dorothy Van Ghent, *The English Novel: Form and Function* (New York: Harper & Row, 1953), 21–32, for a commonsense discussion of Bunyan's double appeal on this score. Other pertinent comments on Bunyan's concrete abstractionist method appear in Fletcher, *Allegory;* Maureen Quilligan, *The Language of Allegory: Defining the Genre* (Ithaca: Cornell University Press, 1979); essays by Philip Edwards, David Mills, Brian Nellist, Vincent Newey, Roger Sharrock, and James Turner in Newey's *"Pilgrim's Progress";* and Valentine Cunningham, "Glossing and Glozing: Bunyan and Allegory" in *John Bunyan Conventicle and Parnassus,* 217–40.

8. For a listing of the designs from each set, and for other comparisons among major illustrated editions, see Appendix A.

9. This was the twenty-second edition, published in quarto format, of both parts of Bunyan's allegory. Besides the traditional number of illustrations allotted Christian's journey (Part I of the *Progress*), eight prints were included depicting episodes from Part II. All twenty-two prints were then reproduced again in the so-called Queen Caroline edition of Bunyan's complete works in 1736–37, a handsome folio volume where the serial interest of the prints was heightened by their appearing four to a page.

10. See, for example, the influence of Sturt's ninth design (Fig. B45), depicting Vanity Fair, on Blake's rendition of the same scene with respect particularly to the representation of the harlequin figure as a type of worldly fool. Another striking motif is the embroidered coat received by Christian from the shining ones and rendered thrice by Sturt in three adjacent designs. Unlike his predecessors, Sturt gives lavish attention to the embroidery, which he depicts with delicate strokes of the burin. This is an effect that Blake adopts and adapts, to make Christian appear garbed in a robe flecked with tiny stains of blood in his parallel sequence of three drawings (Plates 16–

18). The borrowings from Sturt are made without parodic intent. Indeed, a case could be made for considering Sturt's inventions as having a major positive influence on Blake, one going far beyond the business of imitating iconographic details. Specifically, Sturt's experimentation with narrative groupings is echoed in Blake's series: both artists exploit in a similar manner the concept of doubling (sometimes tripling) design motifs, and both organize thematic material in overlapping sets and subsets of consecutive plates. See the discussion below for an analysis of Blake's interpretive use of these expressive devices.

11. The term *gallery* refers to the then-popular habit among artists and publishers of promoting subsidized exhibitions of paintings on a single theme, often literary. Lavishly engraved reproductions of these paintings were simultaneously offered in book form to subscribers, who footed the bill in advance for the entire project. Famous examples in the annals of eighteenth-century art history are Boydell's "Shakespeare Gallery" and Fuseli's abortive "Milton Gallery."

12. Note that the practice of issuing *Progress* designs separately from the text dates back to the first set of copper-cuts offered as an auxiliary purchase with the 1680 version of the fifth impression. But Stothard was not reviving an old tradition so much as following a current fad based on the great success of Hogarth's independent "picture stories."

13. In 1728, when Sturt agreed to illustrate Part II of the *Progress* along with Part I, he, too, executed eight prints for it, though he meanwhile kept the conventional fourteen plates for Part I. The plan of Stothard's series could be seen as an attempt to right the balance of Sturt's lopsided pairing of parts. Yet whereas Stothard had the chance to do this by augmenting the number of plates devoted to Christiana's progress from 8 to 14 (to make twenty-eight prints, the same number as in Blake's set), he chose instead to limit the visuals illustrating Part I with the results described above.

14. See Abrams, *Natural Supernaturalism*.

15. For documentation of these versions and others, see Brown, *John Bunyan,* 481–86; and James K. Forrest and Richard L. Greaves, eds., *John Bunyan: A Reference Guide* (Boston: G. K. Hall, 1982).

16. See Figs. 13 and 64 and my discussion of same above, Chapter 2.

17. "These are rather small designs, having quite a sufficient measure of Blake's spirit in them, but much injured by the handiwork of Mrs. Blake, the colour being untidy-looking and heavy for the most part, and crude where strength is intended. Two of the designs, at any rate, may be considered untouched by Mrs. Blake" (Gilchrist, *Life of Blake* 2:235).

In 1941, Geoffrey Keynes, the next to describe and publish a critique of the Bunyan watercolors, showed a somewhat kinder face to the primitivistic element in the design series as a whole, but saw no semantic value in particular distortions in individual drawings. Thus, on the one hand he could write that "in no instance . . . were the refined productions of a Stothard or a pre-Raphaelitic artist suited to the plain style of Bunyan's writing. The rough and homely wood-cuts of a chap-book are more in tune with the tinker-preacher's spontaneous art than the polished products of the sophisticated book-illustrator." On the other hand, he remarked about Plate 6 ("Help Draws

Christian out of the Slough of Despond") that "the figures, particularly that of Christian, are naively drawn, much violence being done to anatomical accuracy, but the color is fully finished with a strong effect" (*Blake Studies,* 169). For the perpetuation of this view into the 1960s, couched in very similar (perhaps borrowed) terms, see the statement of Robert M. Coates below. As pointed out earlier, even Butlin's 1981 *catalogue raisonné* assumes that the drawings were largely finished by "a later hand" and so many of the effects that Butlin personally undervalues or devalues are on that account dismissed as spurious "later accretions" (*Paintings and Drawings,* "Text": 599, 605).

18. Robert M. Coates, "The Art Galleries: William Blake and the Frick," *New Yorker,* June 9, 1960, 69.

19. The term *pseudosimplicity* is Rosenblum's (*Transformations,* 190). See also Rosenblum's dissertation, "International Style," 102–14. W. J. T. Mitchell has written importantly on the uses of crude, figural forms in Blake's art in "Style and Iconography in the Illustrations of Blake's *Milton,*" as well as in *Blake's Composite Art: A Study of the Illuminated Poetry* (Princeton: Princeton University Press, 1978). Janet Warner's essay "Blake's Use of Gesture" in *Blake's Visionary Forms Dramatic,* 174–95, together with her expanded treatment of this topic in her book *Blake and the Language of Art,* gives a good defense of the repetitive, seemingly melodramatic posturing that has often been taken for stereotypic crudity in Blake's art. Finally, Bo Lindberg, in *William Blake's Illustrations to the Book of Job* (Åbo: Åbo Akademi, 1973) chap. 3, ably describes and explains the formulas of distortion as well as other, previously undiscussed compositional strategies used by Blake.

20. There is, of course, a crucial difference between Blake's idea of the relation between signifier and signified and Bunyan's. For Blake, the removal of an "apparent surface" reveals not something hidden but only the overdetermination of the original appearance in which other surfaces with other meanings "apparently" reside, in the sense that meaning itself *is* the play of signifiers, the play of surfaces. See Hilton's *Literal Imagination* for further discussion of Blake's focus on the polysemy of texts and images in the "Litteral expression."

21. For greater elucidation of Blake's psycho-aesthetic notions of identity and "identical form," see Eaves, *Blake's Theory of Art;* and Adams, "Synecdoche and Method." See also Blake's own comment in his "Annotations to Reynolds": "Identities or Things are Neither Cause nor Effect They are Eternal" (E656/K470).

22. The role of the dreamer/narrator as a presence in the text of his own dream is an interesting narratological issue. He is there principally to remind us of what the energy of the reported dream narrative simultaneously tries to make us forget: that what we are reading is a "secondary revision" (that is, "original derivation") of a lived dream-experience, not the dream itself. But his first-person interjections, which appear on almost every other page (mostly by way of the formulaic phrase "then I saw in my dream that . . ."), work also to underscore his scopic agency as purveyor of the scene and to indicate that his understanding is outside the point of view held by Christian. Several times he sees things that Christian has turned his back on; and, as mentioned earlier, on two occasions he actually functions as a dream figure interacting with

another dream figure. But on both these occasions—the episode involving Help's rescue of Christian from the Slough of Despond (PP 15) and the episode in Beulah land when Christian and Hopeful drink the wine of garrulous sleep (PP 156)—the interchange results only in the narrator's receiving exegetical instruction on a perplexing aspect of the event.

23. The identification of trees and flowers in Blake's art is sometimes extremely conjectural, and in this case I am adding to that tradition. But while my knowledge of arboreal horticulture is practically nil, my eyes tell me that these trees resemble in leaf and trunk the silver beeches in the back yard of my family home.

24. A similar motif governs the first design in the Gates (Fig. 18), where the cocooned, chrysalitic infant rests on a leaf, merging with it at the stem. The Gates, as we have seen, had several associations in Blake's mind with the Progress, and this theme of an unfolding from vegetative existence is one of them.

25. Blake used this device of intentional obscurity, leaving certain figural designs somewhat vague for heuristic purposes, on several other occasions as well—this despite the fact that in general he derided artists who preferred chiaroscura over clear and determinate outlines, calling the practice "blotting and blurring" (DC, E528/K562, E546/K581). The clearest cognate example of Blake's intentional obscurity is in the design of the "Introduction" poem to Songs of Innocence, where the figures in the medallions on the side of the plate are in most copies left indistinct, as if to suggest that their reality needs "bringing out" by the artistic activity both of the reader and of the Piper piping the songs in the volume to come; see Glazer-Schotz and Norvig, "Blake's Book of Changes," 113–16.

26. See the epilogue to For the Sexes: The Gates of Paradise, and my discussion of it in Chapter 2.

27. A good source for observing historical developments in the use of the frontispiece engraving is Wharey's introduction to the Progress, xxxvi–cxvi, including several reproductions of interesting variants of the plate. The convention of representing Bunyan's portrait along with designs of the text remained dominant down through Blake's day. Even Stothard's loose-leaf set of sixteen prints, issued separately from the book, contained an initial plate with Bunyan's portrait in the center. Stothard did not represent Bunyan as the dreaming narrator, however, since his genre was more in the "gallery" tradition, being an anthology of "conversation pieces" related to the theme of the Progress rather than a continuous pictorial narrative.

28. Cf. the antidream treatment given the subjects of Stothard's designs as I have described them above and in the preceding note. For an oft-quoted assessment by one of Blake's contemporaries, see the comments of Coleridge in T. M. Raysor, ed., Coleridge's Miscellaneous Criticism (London: Constable, 1936), 31; there Coleridge claims that Bunyan's "piety was baffled by his genius, and the Bunyan of Parnassus had the better of Bunyan of the conventicle, and with the same illusion as we read any tale known to be fiction, as a novel, we go on with his characters as real persons, who had been nicknamed by their neighbours." Elsewhere Coleridge cites Bunyan's "faulty allegory" as a blot on the work, referring especially to the passages in which several dimensions of reality intermingle: apparently he prefers either a straight allegorical or a

straight realistic genre over the necessarily mixed mode of the dream. See Samuel T. Coleridge, *Notes on English Divines,* 2 vols., ed. Rev. Derwent Coleridge (London, 1853), 1:339–40.

29. In the text of most early editions, the word *Denn* is printed with an asterisk, and in the margin its "comparison" is named "The Gaol." Right away, therefore, the reader is let in on the fictional pretense that will govern the rest of the book: the things represented in it will be at once signs and symbols. As a sign, the den refers to Bedford Jail, and the sleeping narrator of the opening sentence refers to Bunyan made inactive there. As symbols, however, the wilderness and the den exist as traditional images of psychic trial and contemplation—mythologems appearing often in Scripture and other spiritual or symbolic literary modes. This symbolic element is underplayed by the visual rhetoric of the "sleeping portrait," but it is vigorously reinstated by Blake, who may even have had the many pictorial renditions of Saint Jerome and his lion in the wilderness in mind when inventing the initial design for his *Progress* illustrations. (Blake is known to have kept near his work table a copy of the famous Dürer print of Jerome at *his* work table with lion underfoot in a position not unlike that of the lion of Plate 1.)

30. One copy of the first edition of the *Progress* (the Palmer-Nash copy; see Fig. 49) identifies the city pictured on the plate by the inscription *Vanity,* thus implying that the engraved vision encompasses a later segment of the dream-narrative. However, the inscription is obviously a careless error; for the pilgrim marching up the hill retains both burden and book, appurtenances lost by Christian in the text long before he reaches Vanity Fair. In later copies the city is renamed *Destruction.*

31. See my discussion in Chapter 1 of the meanings that Blake attributed to Noah and the rainbow.

32. See note 30, above.

33. The wicket-gate is identified by Good-will himself as "the strait gate" of Scripture, *PP* 22.

34. The text of the *Progress,* too, is structured on the principle of typological figuration and fulfillment. Almost all its major motifs are doubled in a system demonstrating "before" and "after" visions, indicating the difference between this life and the one to come or, metaphorically, the "earthly" and the "heavenly" perspectives. Some motifs, though, occur more often, exhibiting a triadic or tetradic pattern. The city and the gate treated by Blake in Plate 1 are examples of triadic motifs. Thus, the City of Destruction surfaces a second time in the dream as Vanity Fair, and then is transfigured to become the Celestial City, while the image of the wicket-gate is echoed by the gate of House Beautiful, countered by the iron gate of Doubting Castle, and later "redeemed" by the image of the heavenly gate at dream's end.

35. A clue to Blake's intention is found also in the number of plates executed. Since the standard number of illustrations was fourteen, not including the frontispiece, and since Blake's designs numbered twenty-eight *with* the first plate, it seems fair to infer that he regarded the first design as part of the sequence proper, a sequence that exactly doubled the standard number of plates devoted to the text itself. For a counterview suggesting Blake's full complement of intended *Progress* designs was twenty-nine, not

twenty-eight, see Wills, "An Additional Drawing"; and Butlin, "An Extra Illustration"; see also Introduction, note 8.

36. The book that Christian looks into is evidently the Bible; this we understand from the fact that his outcry, "What shall I do to be saved?" derives from the Pauline texts of conversion in Acts 9:6 and 16:30. Because it is an overdetermined dream image, however, it has other possible connotations as well, including that the volume is *The Pilgrim's Progress* itself. Christian looking for guidance in the Good Book is analogous to the reader looking for guidance in the book that records his dream. Blake gives credence to this multivalent meaning by showing us the book in the duodecimo format common both to scriptural texts and to chapbook editions of the *Progress*.

37. The identification comes as a gloss to the experience of release, when Christian's burden was spontaneously "loosed from off his Shoulders, and fell from off his back" (*PP* 38). At the words "Then was *Christian* glad," an asterisk in the text marks the marginal comment: "When God releases us of our guilt and burden, we are as those that leap for joy." Of course, the Christian meaning of guilt does not coincide with our modern, psychological notion, which refers only to the subjective sense of guilt. Instead, Christian guilt is essentially a legal term defining both sin and the responsibility for sin. It is synonymous with criminality, and its contrary is the state of grace.

38. From the first set of illustrations to the *Progress* down through those invented by Blake's contemporaries (and including a range of later illustrators), the figure of Christian starting out was shown with an ordinary backpack strapped to his shoulders (see Figs. B1, B15, B24, and B37 for representative examples). The effect in these cases never reached beyond a naturalistic and literal rendering of the image. Blake's innovation is the attempt to portray simultaneously both sides of the metaphor equating the burden with guilt. In his version, we see not only that the burden is experienced by Christian as an external weight, but also that it is created from within as a reflection of his mental suffering. Blake learned this double-valenced technique through a lifetime of illustrating spiritual and psychic metaphors, but he brought it to perfection in his *Illustrations of the Book of Job,* still in the process of being engraved when he began these drawings for the *Progress*.

39. A common interpretation of the function of Evangelist among Bunyan critics is that he represents the perfect role model of Protestant pastors or else that his character is based on the personality of the real-life preacher who was Bunyan's mentor. See Tindall, *John Bunyan,* 19f.; Sharrock's commentary to *PP,* 316; and Henri Talon, *John Bunyan,* 142. Blake, of course, preferred an archetypal interpretation. Another clue that he plants to tell us Evangelist is indeed a living transformation of Scripture is the notable *absence* of the book in this illustration. Bunyan's text states that Christian still has the book in hand at this juncture (*PP* 9.31); but Blake pictures only the book's human replacement: Evangelist with the testamentary scroll. Blake's own private symbolism (whereby scrolls frequently represent the vital energy of the Word released from its dogmatic bondage in the dead format of books) corresponds perfectly in this case to Bunyan's latent meaning; and Blake's elimination of the book from the scene is simply a way of heightening the sense of a shift of value appropriate to the methods of dream-journeying. It is significant that Blake defied iconographic tradition in this

regard, for all previous illustrators of this passage, which was a standard subject, retained the image of the book in fidelity to Bunyan's text. See, for examples, Figs. B1 and B37.

40. Rather than a static building *within* the city, this Gothic arch is most likely intended to represent a city gate and thus is in itself an image of liminality. Furthermore, although the fact of the temporary proleptic shift away from squat, Romanesque stolidity toward the more mobile and uplifting qualities of the Gothic is significant, it is the strategy of the shift that both enacts and points toward the lability of imagination required of the pilgrim protagonist and the pilgrim reader in his/her unfolding negotiations with the world of dream imagery. Thus, while Blake may indeed have used "Gothic architectural motifs" as unvarying images of "the Good" (Hagstrum, *Blake, Poet and Painter,* 28), I believe it is inappropriate to impose that fixed coding on the interpretation of this design. The viewer (and dreamer) have no context for such a signification at this point: instead this first appearance of the Gothic shape of imagination is indeterminate and rather provides the context for future interpretations of it.

41. "Rome and Greece swept Art into their maw & destroyd it. . . . Mathematic Form is Eternal in the Reasoning Memory. Living Form is Eternal Existence./Grecian is Mathematic Form/Gothic is Living Form" ("On Virgil," E270/K778).

42. Blake's decision to give so much structural prominence in the arrangement of his series to this drawing may have been influenced by the fact that its subject provided the initial illustration of the standard sequence (see figs. B1 and B37). For nearly a century of English publishing, it was this event that opened the pictorial narrative, and the quatrain printed as an epigraph below the picture in most editions suggests its emblematic import for the meaning of the dream as a whole:

> *Christian* no sooner leaves the World but meets
> *Evangelist,* who lovingly him greets
> With tidings of another: and doth show
> Him how to mount to that from this below.

43. As noted in Chapter 2, the graphic satirist James Gillray used the episode of the Slough of Despond as a parodic context for his caricature of Charles Fox subtitled "The Patriot's Progress." Otherwise I know of no illustrators who gave space to this subject.

44. See Harding, *Journey into Self,* 59.

45. See C. G. Jung, *Memories, Dreams, Reflections,* ed. Aniela Jaffe (New York: Pantheon Books, 1961), 150–52.

46. An interesting analogy can be drawn between the image of Christian sinking under his burden during the crossing of the slough and the image of Saint Christopher bowing under the weight of the world and the world's Lord while carrying the Christ child across another river. In both cases, the experience for the individual is one of an "obligation attached to the process of individuation which is felt to be a burden rather than an immediate blessing" (M.-L. von Franz, writing about the psychological significance of the Saint Christopher story in "The Process of Individuation," in *Man and his Symbols,* ed. Carl G. Jung and M.-L. von Franz [New York: Doubleday, 1964],

219). As Jean Hagstrum has pointed out ("Christ's Body," in *William Blake: Essays in Honour of Geoffrey Keynes,* 146–48), Blake alludes elsewhere to the iconography of the Saint Christopher myth, too, namely in his frontispiece illustration to the *Songs of Experience.*

47. Blake considered the visual representation of the garment to be an extension of the human form in art; "Annotations to Reynolds," E650/K462: "Drapery is formed alone by the Shape of the Naked." Also, it was a favorite device of his to show an inexplicable overflow of the garment exuding from the ungarmented body, as in his famous color print of Newton and in the design for his print "Ancient of Days." When it occurs, this overflow seems to suggest that the naked personality is creating or affecting his environment to the point of excessive contamination, or excessive joy. See also Morton D. Paley, "The Figure of The Garment in *The Four Zoas, Milton,* and *Jerusalem,*" in *Blake's Sublime Allegory: Essays on "The Four Zoas," "Milton," "Jerusalem,"* ed. Stuart Curran and Joseph Anthony Wittreich, Jr. (Madison: University of Wisconsin Press, 1973), 119–39.

48. The prototype of this deep-sinking figure is the political caricature by Gillray cited in Chapter 2 and in note 43 above (Fig. 7). As the discussion in Chapter 2 explains, the cartoon served Blake originally as a parodic model for emblem 10 of *For Children: The Gates of Paradise* (Fig. 6). Blake departed from Gillray in that case by drawing the arm of his drowning figure extended to the full. Here he departs from Bunyan in the same way. Bunyan's text speaks only of Christian's being extracted from the slough by a hand pull, but Blake, attempting a more energetic expression, insists on a complete arm stretch for both Christian and Help. In each revision of his original, Blake's point would seem to be that sinking into despondency is reversible by extended effort. Nevertheless this drawing has been criticized by Geoffrey Keynes (*Blake Studies,* 169) for containing "figures, particularly that of Christian, which are naively drawn, much violence being done to anatomical accuracy." Keynes leaves no room here for Blake's expressionist purpose. But it should also be noted that part of Keynes's negative assessment is due to a misapprehension of Christian's figural contour. His back is *meant* to be humped here by the presence of the burden; it is not anatomical inaccuracy that has distorted it.

49. The original series of engravings in the "fifth" edition of the *Progress* devoted the first two of its fourteen copper-cuts to Evangelist and Worldly Wiseman, respectively (see Figs. B1 and B2). These cuts did not illustrate contiguous events of the story, however. The one picturing Evangelist corresponded to Christian's first encounter—the prototype of all his other meetings with guides, rendered by Blake as Plate 3—and the one evoking Worldly Wiseman illustrated a much later episode corresponding to Blake's Plate 7. Nevertheless, the two engravings were designed as a pair, the second reflecting the composition of the first as if they were back-to-back opposites, with the figure of Christian holding the pivotal position. The rhymed quatrains attached to these illustrations in the early editions reinforce the idea that the two events represented a juxtaposition of moral contraries that would lead the pilgrim in exactly opposite directions: right and wrong. Thus, the first picture was captioned as quoted in note 42, and the second picture held the following legend:

> When Christians unto carnal men give ear
> Out of their way they go, and pay for't dear,
> For master *Worldly Wiseman* can but show
> A saint the way to Bondage and to woe.

Later, when half the designs of this original set of engravings were mixed in with seven designs from the Flemish series, the explanatory and moralizing quatrains were retained, even when they no longer suited the new picture. In the present case, the imported picture showed Christian fearing the fire from the mountain, an event that occurs *after* Worldly Wiseman directs him to "Bondage and to woe" (this is the incident Blake represents in Plate 8). The next standard illustrator, perceiving the problem, revised the graphic examples so that the designs more nearly matched each other and suited the rhymed captions, with exceptions as noted in the text below and in note 52.

50. This gesture is like, but not identical to, the iconographic pose in Christian art that signifies divine creative power. Blake uses it almost exactly as here in his two versions of God creating Eve made for his *Paradise Lost* designs. See Butlin, *Paintings and Drawings,* "Plates": pls. 639 and 652.

51. Although Evangelist and Worldly Wiseman take comparable poses in these drawings and gesticulate with their hands in similar ways, as if they were doubling each other, they are easily distinguished by their very different garments. There is also no attempt to make the fiery mountain in the second design resemble the light that Evangelist alerts Christian to in the first, except that the two light sources occupy roughly similar locations in the two compositions.

52. The illustrator whom Blake is following here is John Sturt. His engravings restored with a vengeance the compositional principle of pairing adjacent designs. In this case, as Figs. B37 and B38 show, not only does the image of Christian in the first illustration mirror his image in the second, but also Evangelist and Worldly Wiseman are presented as virtually identical. When the two designs are placed side by side (as they were in the folio editions), Evangelist and Worldly Wiseman stand back to back in the pivotal position originally occupied by the figure of Christian in the earliest *Progress* illustrations of these subjects—and this substitution seems to have contributed to their being represented as mutually identified. In fact, one can tell them apart in Sturt's work only by means of either the accompanying quatrains, when they are used, or the halo over Evangelist's head. That these signs were overlooked by many viewers and that readers sometimes confused the figures, or interpreted them as the same character, can be inferred from the fact that in the edition from which my Fig. B38 was reproduced, the illustration featuring Worldly Wiseman was retitled "Christian Loses His Way and Meets Evangelist [*sic*] a Second Time." The editor who renamed this design, effectively transposing an earlier event (Worldly Wiseman pointing the way to Mount Sinai) to a later one (Evangelist saving Christian from Sinai's fire), had his reasons. Principally, it seems, he was responding to the fact that the robed character in Fig. B38 is standing directly below the overhanging mountain rather than remarking on it from "yonder" distance, as in the text. The second detail encouraging an interpretation consonant with the new caption is that this figure, despite his lack of halo, has a more saintly and evangelical expression than his twin *with* halo. Finally, we note that the newly captioned design clearly influenced Blake, not only in his decision to exploit further the

physiological resemblance between Evangelist and Worldly Wiseman, but also in his strategy of giving separate graphic attention to the subject of Christian's second meeting with Evangelist, in his Plate 9.

53. "A cliché of seventeenth-century Puritanism was the identification of hand with faith and . . . this identification is one of the constants of the allegory in *The Pilgrim's Progress*" (Kaufmann, *"Pilgrim's Progress,"* 62).

54. The ordering of the plates here, with 8 as the middle design flanked by 7 and 9, follows the placements adopted by Butlin, *Paintings and Drawings,* "Text": 600–601. Butlin reverses the sequence 8 and 9 held in Keynes's presentation of the designs (see the Limited Editions Club publication of the *Progress*) on the authority of numberings inscribed on the drawings (even though some of those numberings, as he duly notes, are incorrect and not in Blake's hand). My reasons for endorsing Butlin's arrangement are based less on the inscriptions than on the thematic and compositional analyses given in the text below.

55. It is well known that throughout his career as an artist Blake frequently exercised his penchant for drawing the lower legs and feet of his figures in such a way as to hide, replace, or evoke association to the male sexual organ. (Nelson Hilton discusses some appearances of this motif—including the example from the revised *Gates* analyzed in Chapter 2, above—in *Literal Imagination,* 166–67). Less recognized, however, is the fact that he also sometimes used legs and feet (as here) to suggest a vaginal birth passage; see, for instance, the Arlington Court Picture, reproduced in color in Butlin, *Paintings and Drawings,* "Plates": pl. 969; and in Milton Klonsky, *William Blake: The Seer and His Visions* (New York: Harmony Books, 1977), 105. There the figure of Odysseus is kneeling with his left, lower leg and foot embedded in the blood-red folds of his robe. The folds at just that place are made to look like folds of human tissue and have a strong vaginal connotation. In this way the image recapitulates the picture's overall theme of rebirth, and echoes a similar image formed by the riverbank carrying the three fates.

56. Note the resemblance of this plate's compositional structure to the design of Fig. B9, the first *Progress* illustrator's representation of Christian's much later encounter with hell fiends in the Valley of the Shadow of Death. Interestingly enough, Blake gave no separate treatment to the subject of that hellish valley, although the incident had special personal meaning for him and he quoted the passage from Bunyan's text several times in his Felpham letters, as we have seen.

57. Compare this objectifying technique with *Bunyan's* earlier-noted habit of forcing us periodically to step back from the action of the text as the narrator reminds us that the events under review occurred and were witnessed by him in his dream. The specific effects of these authorial intrusions (nearly one hundred of them are peppered throughout the text) are not consistent with any scheme I have been able to work out. Generally, though, they function in a different way from Blake's distancing procedures, for they seem to set the narrator/dreamer up as a competitor of Christian, thereby diminishing Christian's power to act for the dreamer in the dream. This attitude, of course, contrasts sharply with Blake's view that Christian and the dreamer are one.

58. It is appropriate to call this configuration an infinite spiraling, I believe, since the

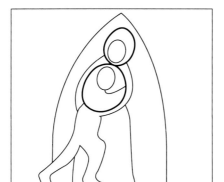

FIG. 65 Diagram of Plate 11

schematic mapping of the interrelation of the circles produces a tipped figure eight, which resembles the sign ∞, the mathematical symbol for infinity (Fig. 65).

59. Comparing the iconography of the three main treatments of this subject, we can see that Blake borrowed motifs from each and spread them over his two plates. For Plate 10, he took from the first English cut (Fig. B3) the idea of the arched door in a high wall with an endpost. And from the Flemish design later amalgamated into the second English series (Fig. B15) he borrowed the door knocker and the stance of Christian approaching the gate. From Sturt's engraving (Fig. B39) he developed both the motif of the sun shining over the gate (see Plate 10) and the concept of the robed figure standing in the doorway (Plate 11).

60. See, for example, plate 99 of *Jerusalem*.

61. This is the message announced in the opening verses of the prologue poem inscribed on the title page of *For The Sexes: The Gates of Paradise*.

62. This phrase is from a line in the poem "To Clio, Muse of History," by Howard Nemerov in his collection *The Next Room of the Dream* (Chicago: University of Chicago Press, 1962), 3–4. I have used the quote in both the title and epigraph for this chapter because of its relevance to the incident pictured in Blake's Plate 13, which exposes the *mise-en-abîme* relation that Blake saw operating between interpretation and imagination and which therefore emblematizes key aspects of his own visionary hermeneutics.

63. One earlier character, a member of the duo of Obstinate and Pliable, wears blue in Plate 4. But the costume there is not otherwise similar to that of the dreamer, and in any case neither Obstinate nor Pliable functions as an individual personality in that plate. In the next plate, when Pliable is pictured as a separate figure, he no longer wears the same clothing.

64. "Auguries of Innocence," line 6 (E490/K431).

65. See my earlier discussion (Chapter 2) of the first two tableaux encountered by Christian at the House of the Interpreter in Bunyan's text. There both the room with the picture of the man who was to be Christian's guide and the picture itself, which we encounter in close-up, exhibit some of the same claustrophobic and static qualities that are shown in their pathological aspects by the example of the Man in the Iron Cage.

66. "The Divine Image," *Songs of Innocence,* line 15 (E13/K117).

67. See, for example, Plate 15. On the shifting characteristics of Christian's heavenly garment, see the text below.

68. See note 47 above. It should be mentioned that while none of the standard illustrators chose to depict this subject, one maverick example (Fig. A1) exists in a copy of the Dutch edition of 1682, cut in half-size plate and unlisted in the bibliographic information on illustrated Bunyan editions. See Appendix A.

69. A curious train of allusion and overdetermination surrounds this image, providing a typical example of the way Blake often used borrowed motifs from the storehouse of traditional iconographic themes in art. The paradigmatic source in this case is Michelangelo's figure of Aminadab, on the Sistine ceiling (Fig. 66). Aminadab is one of the ancestors of Christ added by Michelangelo, at the end of his chapel-painting task, to the border of the main fresco. These ancestors signify the prefiguration of the human ideal existing before, and anticipating the advent of, Jesus. An Italian critic says of the haunting quality of these figures: "Present is the latent conviction that the final event will not occur in their times but always in a succeeding epoch," and he accords them a separate, dreamlike reality (Valero Mariani, *Michelangelo the Painter* [New York: Abrams, 1964], p. 79). In this respect the connection between the design and Blake's Man Who Dreamed of the Day of Judgment seems fitting enough. But add to that the fact that Blake once made a copy of Michelangelo's figure from an engraving (entitling it "The Traveller in Repose," thus calling up associations with the *Gates* tailpiece and with the *Progress*) and that the copy was duplicated by Blake's friend Fuseli for an engraving Fuseli did of Shakespeare's Pericles dreaming of the goddess Diana, and the connections strengthen. In Fuseli's treatment, tented curtains over Pericles' bed recall strongly the shape of the curtains over the bed in Blake's Plate 13. An additional association ties all three uses of the motif together, for Pericles, in the scene from Shakespeare's play represented by Fuseli, is being addressed by an interpreting dream figure who tells Pericles to go to her temple at Ephesus (the town where Christ first appeared to his disciples after the resurrection) and there experience a revelation, which Blake would surely class as a Last Judgment such as Bunyan's dreamer defends against from fear. See Figs. 66–69. See Hagstrum, *Blake, Poet and Painter,* 39–40, for an earlier citing of some of these interrelations.

70. For a helpful overview of the history and use of *mise-en-abîme* as a literary device, see Lucien Dallenbach's *The Mirror in the Text,* trans. Jeremy Whitely and Emma Hughes (Chicago: University of Chicago Press, 1989).

71. Bunyan devoted many long passages of his text to homiletic discussions delivered by the characters, and other portions to satiric treatments of typical human foibles. Blake (in common with most of the early illustrators) avoided these subjects. The only satirical figure he raised to archetypal status was Worldly Wiseman. Otherwise all figures and episodes represented by him refer to what he felt were "eternal" mental states and not topical allusions.

72. In the original English series, the "central" design could be considered either the seventh, as the last of the first septad, or the eighth, as the first of the last septad. Since the seventh design is of Christian leaving House Beautiful fully armed (Fig. B7), and

FIG. 66
Michelangelo,
Aminadab

the eighth design deals with Apollyon, the focus on the theme of Christian warfare remains at the center of the series no matter which definition of midpoint is applied.

73. Later on in Bunyan's text, in one of those passages of retelling of which Bunyan was so fond, Christian reveals his sight of the cross to have been visionary after all: "I saw one, as I thought in my mind, hang bleeding upon the Tree; and the very sight of him made my burden fall off my back" (*PP* 49). Blake's design can be seen as a proleptic interpretation of this later passage, and a reversal of Bunyan's habit of

FIG. 67 Adam Ghisi,
Aminadab (after
Michelangelo)

FIG. 68 Blake, *The Reposing
Traveller*

FIG. 69 Henry Fuseli,
Pericles

delaying the report of visionary experience so that it occurs only as a narrative analepsis.

74. Cf. Blake's use of this scriptural phrase in his design for the poem "To Tirzah," *Songs of Experience,* where it is engraved on the side of the plate in a rising position matching the rising of the awakening figure.

75. The placement of the cast-off burden in Plate 14 balances the location of the lion in Plate 1, and the two images are related by meaning as well. In fact, the burden's fall into the sepulcher seems to activate the rebirth of the lion image after the intervention of Plates 15 and 16 and after the transmutation of the roll, in Plate 17, into an aspect of man's libido. For in Plate 18, the lion form arises, doubled, to threaten the pathway of Christian, and in Plate 20 Apollyon himself is said to have the mouth of a lion (see discussion below).

76. In Plate 4, three figures appear (Christian, Pliable, and Obstinate), but Obstinate and Pliable are background figures, distanced in space and lifted to a higher latitude on the picture plane. They have the significance, furthermore, of a single character, although with a double aspect. In Plates 12 and 13, the group of three characters is presented as a unit on one horizontal plane, but the emblem figures exist as semisymbolic manifestations and are not on a reality par with Christian and the Interpreter. As described above, Plate 13 then begins the process of bringing the figurative character into the same realm as the protagonist.

77. In Part I of the *Progress,* references to women are generally avoided, though in the case of the damsels of Palace Beautiful Bunyan gives women special prominence. There he is representing "the virtues," who are traditionally figured as female (see Blake's extra illustration of this scene, Fig. 55, and my discussion of same below). The female figures in Plate 15 may have been influenced by Blake's own coterminous work

on the Dante designs, in which the role of woman of course has an extremely important place. But see also the final drawing of the *Progress* series (Plate 28), where Blake again introduces the image of woman for the sake of completeness. Pertinent to this point may be the revised evaluation of the status of the female in the second state of emblem 7 of *For the Sexes: The Gates of Paradise* (1818, the version dominated by Bunyan associations), where he asks the question ignored by Christian: "What are these? Alas! the Female Martyr, Is She also the Divine Image?" For more discussion of gender issues in Blake's work, see George, *Blake and Freud,* chap. 6; Susan Fox, "The Female Metaphor in William Blake's Poetry," *Critical Inquiry* 3 (Spring 1977): 507–519 (reprinted in *Essential Articles for the Study of William Blake, 1970–1984,* ed. Nelson Hilton [Hamden, Conn.: Archon Books, 1986], 75–90); Alicia Ostriker, "Desire Gratified and Ungratified: William Blake and Sexuality," *Blake: An Illustrated Quarterly* 16 (1982–83): 156–65 (reprinted in Hilton, *Essential Articles,* 211–36); Irene Tayler, "The Woman Scaly," *MMLA Bulletin* 6 (Spring 1973): 74–87 (reprinted in *Blake's Poetry and Designs,* ed. Mary Lynn Johnson and John E. Grant [New York: Norton, 1981], 538–53); Anne Mellor, "Blake's Portrayal of Women," *Blake: An Illustrated Quarterly* 16 (1982–83): 148–55; Anne Mellor, "Blake's *Songs of Innocence and of Experience:* A Feminist Perspective," *Nineteenth-Century Studies* 2 (1988): 1–17; Harold O. Brogan, "Blake on Women: Oothoon to Jerusalem," *CEA Critic* 48 (1986): 125–36; Brenda Webster, "Blake, Women, and Sexuality," in *Critical Paths,* 204–24; Elizabeth Langland's "Blake's Feminist Revision of Literary Tradition in 'The Sick Rose'" in *Critical Paths,* 225–43; David Aer's "William Blake and the Dialectic of Sex," *ELH* 44 (1977): 500–514; Margaret Storch's "Blake and Women: 'Nature's Cruel Holiness,'" *American Imago* 38 (Summer 1981): 221–46, and her *Sons and Adversaries;* and Camille Paglia's *Sexual Personae: Art and Decadence from Nefertiti to Emily Dickinson* (New Haven: Yale University Press, 1990), chap. 10: "Sex Bound and Unbound: Blake."

78. See Bunyan's gloss in the margin of the text telling us that this shining one is quoting Mark 2:5, which reads: "When Jesus saw their faith, he said unto the sick of the palsy, Son, thy sins be forgiven thee" (*PP* 38).

79. The reference cited, Zechariah 3:4, is a response to the situation of Joshua the high priest, seen standing before the Lord in filthy garments in Zechariah's vision; it reads as follows: "And he answered and spake unto those that stood before him, saying, Take away the filthy garments from him. And unto him he said, Behold, I have caused thine iniquity to pass from thee, and I will clothe thee with change of raiment."

80. The error of the dreaming man in the House of the Interpreter is the obverse of the error of Satan in the last plate of the revised version of the *Gates* discussed earlier. Satan overidentifies the garment with the man, but the paranoid dreamer of doom underidentifies it, ignoring the seeds of psychic power contained in such images and outward appearances.

81. In the margin, Bunyan conflates three biblical sources: Mark 2:5, on forgiveness; Zechariah 3:4, on change of raiment; and Ephesians 1:13, on the significance of belief as an inheritance and seal of promise.

82. There is another prefigurative contrary to this design: Plate 13, where the position of the dreamer inside a tented space seems to be a tight and repressed version

FIG. 70 Blake, *Isaiah Foretelling
the Destruction of
Jerusalem*

of the open, erotic implications of Plate 17. The posture of Christian in 17 could well be
seen as phase two of an aerobic stretching exercise, the first phase of which is demonstrated by the dreamer of Plate 13.

83. A cognate design, done in three versions by Blake, is an emblem of another
mediator between heaven and earth: the prophet Isaiah. The first two versions of the
composition are sketches, one on either side of the same piece of paper, both titled
"Isaiah Foretelling the Crucifixion"; see Raymond Lister, "Two Blake Drawings and a
Letter from Samuel Palmer," *Blake Newsletter* 22 (Fall 1972): 53–54. The third version is
called "Isaiah Foretelling the Destruction of Jerusalem" (an interesting shift of perspective) and was prepared for a woodblock engraving never completed (Fig. 70). Thomas
Wright (*Life of Blake* 2: pl. 68, opp. p. 93) claims that Samuel Palmer, who owned the
sketched version, called the figure "Evangelist," and Lister cites Palmer's letter to an
unknown addressee stating that the fainter of his two sketches (the one most like Plate
17) "is a design perhaps for the Pilgrim's Progress—the first inventive line—from
which he was always most careful not to depart" (Lister, "Two Blake Drawings," 54).

Lister denies this attribution by Palmer, since the sketches are believed to have been done in 1821 and the *Progress* drawings in 1824. But that discrepancy may rather indicate that Blake was thinking of the *Progress* series as early as 1821, just after he revised the *Gates* according to the Bunyanesque model of the very same episode to which the Isaiah design so strongly relates. For more on the three versions of this design, see Butlin, *Paintings and Drawings,* "Text": nos. 772 and 773 and "Plates": pls. 1015–17.

84. Christian is encouraged across the threshold in this design too, but by gesture only, and from a distance: see the figure of the Porter egging him on from the palace gateway at the top of the plate. (In Bunyan's text, the encouragement is vocal, not gestural, but the fact of a nontactile, distant spur to action remains the same in both cases; see *PP* 45–46.)

85. See *PP* 49: "Yea, and while I stood looking up, (for then I could not forbear looking) three shining ones came to me: one of them testified that my sins were forgiven me: another stript me of my rags, and gave me this Broidred Coat which you see." This passage occurs in the episode within House Beautiful where Christian laboriously retells his (and the reader's) past experience. It is the first time we hear of the embroidery of the coat, however. Bunyan's narrative functioned often in this way, reshaping past reality with each retelling of the action. Such destabilizing use of narrative analepsis is an authentic dream device that Blake picks up on, as we have seen, changing the appearance of Christian's "coat" as often as Bunyan gives him license to do so.

86. Compare this feature of Plate 18 with the relations of head, libidinal instinct, and the lion's mouth assimilated by the figure of Apollyon in Plate 20.

87. Note that in the previous drawing, Plate 18, the architecture of the same building anticipates what will become the seven-point-tiara design of Heaven's Gate pictured in Plate 28 (except that the palace roof in 18 has six rather than seven points). The implication of presenting the contrasting architectural motifs in Plates 18 and 19 is that Palace Beautiful has a changing aspect: heavenly at the entry, repressive and martial at the rear. Thus the six roof peaks of 18 seem to have been transformed into the six spears cresting the exit of the armory in Plate 19.

88. Cf. *MHH* 7: "Prudence is a rich ugly old maid courted by Incapacity." The Blake who illustrated the *Progress* in 1824 must not be expected to have an outlook identical with that of the Blake who wrote the *Marriage* in 1793. But on the subject of sexual repression, his attitude seems to have remained consistent enough to make the cross-referencing apt.

89. Throughout the sequence of designs from Plate 15 to Plate 20, in all but one drawing (Plate 16) Christian appears with something in his hand. As described above, there does not seem to be a rational scheme dictating the appearance (Plate 15), disappearance, and reappearance (Plates 17–20) of the walking stick–scroll–sword, and one wonders whether Blake intended this loose dream-rhetoric to signify subtle turns of thought or whether the shift from stick to roll to sword was meant to meet only the literal situations evoked by the text.

90. See Wills, "An Additional Drawing"; and Butlin, "An Extra Illustration." A

color reproduction of this design appears in Butlin's *Paintings and Drawings,* "Plates": 976.

91. Wills argues for the design's inclusion on the basis of its exemplifying, in sequence, what he refers to (without definition) as "Blake's method of illustrating *Pilgrim's Progress*" ("An Additional Drawing," 67). By this he may mean Blake's frequent habit of devoting two plates to cover a single incident in Bunyan's text. But as my analysis has tried to show, there is an apparently overriding symmetric schema governing the seven-plate series involving drawings 14–20—an important schema, which an extra illustration would interrupt and, indeed, destroy. Even if we posit that this extra illustration was intended to replace Plate 19 (and thus match up with Plate 15, a fairly close analogue of it in some respects), serious objections remain. These principally concern the positive presentation of the Virgin Virtues as angels with full halos awash in rainbow colors—a departure from the text that requires some justification, though Wills supplies none. It is possible that Blake intended the viewer to interpret the halos ironically, but the treatment he has given the figures (especially their coloring, which associates them with the redemptive rainbow motif) mitigates against such a reading. Another problem with supposing this design an integral part of the series is its premature presentation of so strong a frontal composition, taking much of the thunder from the extreme frontality of Plate 20. Finally, Wills's contention that "the maiden to Christian's immediate right may be holding a bottle in her left hand" (66), as in Bunyan's text, seems to me unsupportable, unless bottles came in the shape of books in Bunyan's or Blake's day.

92. Note how much more forbidding Blake's Apollyon is than the usual figure in the standard illustrations (see Figs. B8, B20, B43, and B54). Some of the terror and awe-full-ness that Blake concentrated in Plate 20 is spread over two drawings in those earlier illustrated series, where the Valley of the Shadow of Death was represented as the nadir of dreadfulness on Christian's journey. For his own reasons, Blake eschewed representing this confrontation with the void and instead drew all its power into the intensity of Christian's face-off with Apollyon. See note 56 above and Chapter 2 for more on Blake's graphic "silence" regarding the topos of the Valley of the Shadow of Death.

93. The motif of the lion reaches a conclusion here in the representation of the mouth of the creature with bolts of lightning shooting from its source. This characteristic of Apollyon shows yet again how he has absorbed the dream's earlier representations of the instinctual life as bestial. In the text, as a character speaking with the wiles of Satan, he alludes directly to the theme of the threatening lions when he taunts Christian with a review of his (Christian's) past weaknesses: *"Thou didst sinfully sleep, and loose thy choice thing* [sic]: *thou wast also almost perswaded to go back, at the sight of the Lions"* (PP 58).

94. Blake may have received the pictorial suggestion for the monster's genital potency from Sturt's design (Fig. B43), where Apollyon's quiver of arrows has a clear, phallic connotation. The smoke, however, in Sturt's version as in several other standard versions, comes out of Apollyon's chest rather than out of his loins. The earliest illustration of this subject (Fig. B8) has placed the smoke even further from the genitals, representing it as emitting from the foul fiend's mouth.

95. W. J. T. Mitchell, "Style and Iconography," 67: "There are even more drastic homoerotic implications in the direct conjunctions of head and loins in Blake's union with Los . . . and in Milton's baptism of Urizen . . . , implications which are certainly latent in the central concept of loving brotherhood. Blake makes it clear that the magnetism which draws the prophets together over gulfs of time and space is not any abstract sense of duty, but love for each other." In a note to this passage, Mitchell cites John Grant as having suggested to him that Plate 20 of the *Progress* designs is an "important analogy" to plate 47 of the *Milton* illustration, which for its part shows the character, Blake, positioned head to loins with the figure of Los.

96. The sword here occupies the same position, in mirror imagery, as did the burden in Plate 14, and there is concomitantly a suggested trade-off of power over instinct in the two situations. Note, too, that the misplacing of the sword in midcareer during this episode of the narrative follows the pattern of the misplacing of the roll, earlier, in the incident of the arbor.

97. It is fair to call Job a paradigm of the Blakean artist-interpreter in this design, for Blake himself gives us justification through associations to an early version of the composition (the watercolor first made for Butts) in which the three daughters whom Job addresses are designated as representing the three arts of music, poetry, and painting. Job, therefore, is teaching the (personified) arts themselves the *use* of art, demonstrating its purpose in forwarding the growth of human consciousness. For more on similar interpretations of this plate see Diane Filby Gillespie, "A Key to Blake's *Job*: Design XX," *Colby Library Quarterly* 19 (June 1983): 59–68; and Lindberg, *Blake's Illustrations to Job*, 342–43.

98. An additional transformative relation between Plates 15 and 21 is the conversion of the angelic halos into the narrative bubbles of the latter design.

99. See Figs. B31–32 and B45–46, and note 10 above.

100. Blake's addition here to the cast of characters represented by Bunyan's previous illustrators is the presence of the women, the "Female Will." Note that this is not the first place in which Blake has interjected the female figure into the iconographic tradition of *Progress* illustration.

101. See the *Notebook* poem (E477/K418):

> Mock on Mock on Voltaire Rousseau
> Mock on Mock on! tis all in vain!
> You throw the sand against the wind
> And the wind blows it back again
>
> And every sand becomes a Gem
> Reflected in the beams divine
> Blown back they blind the mocking Eye
> But still in Israels paths they shine
>
> The Atoms of Democritus
> And Newtons Particles of light
> Are sands upon the Red sea shore
> Where Israels tents do shine so bright

Perhaps Blake is himself mocking the dot-and-lozenge pattern of this harlequin suit as an ironic repudiation of the technical process of engraving that he abandoned (as a vanity equal to the vanities of Vanity Fair) in favor of his more classical and expressive style, recently employed so successfully on the Job illustrations. (The dot-and-lozenge method of engraving, in brief, consisted in constructing pictorial patterns out of a mechanical system of diamonds and dots.) See Morris Eaves, "Blake and the Artistic Machine: An Essay on Decorum and Technology," *PMLA* 92 (1977): 903–27 (reprinted in Hilton, *Essential Articles,* 175–210); and Robert N. Essick, "Blake and the Traditions of Reproductive Engraving" *Blake Studies* 5 (Fall 1972): 59–104; as well as the more recent salient passages of Essick's *William Blake, Printmaker.*

102. See "On Virgil": "Rome & Greece swept Art into their maw & destroyd it a Warlike State never can produce Art. It will Rob & Plunder & accumulate into one place, & Translate & Copy & Buy & Sell & Criticise, but not Make. Mathematic Form is Eternal in the Reasoning Memory. Living Form is Eternal Existence. Grecian is Mathematic Form/Gothic is Living Form" (E270/K778).

103. The earliest rendition of this subject (used in both the first and the second series of standard *Progress* illustrations) showed a frontally positioned, menacing Giant Despair standing guard outside his castle (see Fig. B12). No attempt was made to portray Christian's and Hopeful's experience inside the dungeon. The picture represented the oppressive character of the retribution taken against the pilgrims for their having given in to a need for ease. This was expressed in the accompanying quatrain:

> The Pilgrims now to gratify the Flesh
> Will seek its ease, but oh! how they afresh
> Do thereby plunge themselves new grieves into
> Who seek to please the flesh, themselves undo.

It would be possible to argue that this quatrain contains within it a scenario of the stages of grief, from denial to depression, and it may be that Blake was influenced to do two designs by his perception that some such latent meaning had been left undeveloped by the original illustrators. In the case of the next designer, John Sturt (see Fig. B48), the focus of the episode in Doubting Castle was shifted to the pilgrims' escape from the gate (Blake's Plate 24). But Sturt seems really to have been more interested in drawing a parallel between this event and its obvious contrary, the arrival of Christian at the Wicket-gate (see Fig. B39 in relation to Fig. B48). Finally, as we saw in Chapter 2, John Flaxman, the artist Blake ironically referred to as a Milton to his Bunyan, made a drawing of this subject that had an important impact on Plate 24 as well as on plate 13 of *Europe* (see Figs. 12 and 13).

104. This figure served Blake in at least two other significant instances: the *Job* design called "Satan Smiting Job with Sore Boils" (Fig. 3) and emblem 7 of the *Gates* (Fig. 58). The *Gates* emblem follows the iconography of Raphael's "Massacre" not only in the gesture of the infanticidal boy swatting at the female babes, but also in the placement of the dead babe on the ground—a figure that duplicates one of the murdered innocents in Raphael's design.

105. See Gertrud Schiller, *Iconography of Christian Art,* 2 vols., trans. Janet Seligman (Greenwich, Ct.: New York Graphic Society, 1971), 1:114–16.

106. The burden in Plate 14 held an additional connotation appropriate here: its fetal shape. That aspect suggests that it, too, was undergoing a transmutation into its

opposite—from assumed sin to martyred innocence—and that its "massacre" was the beginning of its rebirth as a new capacity to bear witness to the evolving of an infant divinity within the human form.

107. This identification was first noted by Stephen A. Larabee, *English Bards and Grecian Marbles* (New York: Columbia University Press, 1943), 100. Blake remarks on the Hercules as the ideal of the Strong Man in the *Descriptive Catalogue* (E544/K579), and he responds to Sir Joshua Reynolds's discussion of the ideal in his "Annotations to Reynolds" (E648/K459–460), where he advances the notion of "central from." Reynolds's own comments appear in the "Third Discourse," in *Discourses on Art,* 43–52. The Farnese Hercules was one of the full-sized casts set up in the studios of the Royal Academy as models for art students to copy, and a miniature replica of it was among the small casts purchased for the young Blake by his father. For more on Blake's relationship to the paradigms of Greek sculpture, see Morton D. Paley, "Wonderful Originals—Blake and Ancient Sculpture," in *Blake in His Time,* 170–97.

108. Cf. the "Preface" to *Milton,* E95/K480: "We do not want either Greek or Roman Models if we are but just & true to our own Imaginations, those Worlds of Eternity in which we shall live for ever."

109. See "On Virgil," quoted above, note 92.

110. Consider the many statements and aphorisms to this effect festooned around the engraving of the classical statue of Laocoön and his sons, renamed Satan and Adam, on Blake's plate *Laocoön* (E273–75/K775–77). Note especially: "A Poet a Painter a Musician an Architect: the Man/Or Woman who is not one of these is not a Christian/You must leave Fathers & Mothers & Houses & Lands if they stand in the way of ART/Prayer is the Study of Art/Praise is the Practise of Art/Fasting &c. all relate to Art."

111. These last-ditch-standing shining ones are in fact movable creatures, according to Bunyan's narrative, for when first met they are simply "two men" in clothing that happens to shine "like Gold," and they inhabit the near side of the river where all mortals live (*PP* 156–57). But as soon as Christian and Hopeful actually make it across the barrier of material life, these men suddenly appear there too, like ghostly epiphanies, to greet the pilgrims and to reveal their true natures as "ministring Spirits, sent forth to minister for those that shall be Heirs of Salvation" (*PP* 158).

112. See Fish, *Self-consuming Artifacts,* 224–64, a chapter entitled "Progress in *The Pilgrim's Progress.*"

113. For some cogent disagreements with this Fishean reading, see especially Cunningham, "Glossing and Glazing," 21; as well as Vincent Newey, "Bunyan and the Confines of the Mind," and Philip Edwards, "The Journey in *The Pilgrim's Progress,*" both in Newey's *"Pilgrim's Progress,"* 21–48 and 111–17, respectively.

114. See Kaufmann, *"Pilgrim's Progress,"* 111–17.

115. See *J* 77. This image of the current of Creation is from the preface to chapter 4 of *Jerusalem,* entitled "To the Christians," in itself a miniature treatise on how to read the archetypes of Christian mythology and Christian process. The concept of the westerly "current of Creation" followed by Jesus, and the antithetical current set into motion by the Wheel of Religion, is voiced in the verses concluding the argument.

These verses seem appropriate to the present context in some respects, and even possibly directly allusive to it. See, for example, the closing lines of the plate where the speaker reverses the pessimism of Bunyan's observation at the end of the *Progress* about the implosive relations between heaven and hell, viz.: "For Hell is opend to Heaven; thine eyes beheld/The dungeons burst & the Prisoners set free."

116. The entire structure of the *Progress* relies on a system of typological parallels, as noted earlier. In this case, Bunyan draws an analogy between the malleability of experience in the Slough of Despond and in the River of Death. The slough has saving "steps" for those who would seek them, and the river has shallow areas for those who believe in the ease of crossing over. The second situation calls for a greater degree of consciousness but less doggedness and force of personal will. Thus Bunyan allows Christian to exhibit fortitude without awareness in the earlier episode, relegating the conscious exploration of the situation to the narrator/dreamer, who is there fully dissociated from Christian's personality.

117. M. H. Abrams, *Natural Supernaturalism*, 233, quoting Hegel. Although it is currently unfashionable to draw on Hegelian models, which have been red-flagged for their totalizing assumptions, or to cite the *Phenomenology* as any kind of exemplar of Romantic attitudes toward consciousness, recent critical work on Hegel (and on the Hegel/Blake match) seems to me to call for a new assessment of this state of affairs. For discussion of some of the issues, see David Punter, *Blake, Hegel and Dialectic* (Amsterdam: Rodophi, 1982); the exchange between Punter and Nelson Hilton on the merits of Punter's investigation in *Blake: An Illustrated Quarterly* 17 (Spring 1984) and 18 (Summer 1984); and Dan Miller, "Blake and the Deconstructive Interlude," 149–53. Also, for defenses of a more forgiving reading of Hegel (or a Hegelian reading of Derrida) among critics of continental philosophy, see Deborah Chaffin, "Hegel, Derrida, and the Sign," and Christina M. Howells, "Derrida and Sartre: Hegel's Death Knell," both in *Derrida and Deconstruction,* ed. Hugh J. Silverman (London: Routledge, 1989), 77–91 and 169–81, respectively.

118. Abrams, *Natural Supernaturalism*, 229.

119. Adams, "Synecdoche and Method," 48. As Adams conveys in this essay, Blake's idea of a telos paradoxically resists the supposedly concomitant idea of finalization or absolute closure. For Blake, teleology is, like interpretation, part of the troping process (the next room of the dream); and troping in turn is part of the generic rhetoric of the psyche. Indeed, troping as a visionary activity demands and generates the sort of psychological perspective that involves a special kind of suspension of (dis) belief: the kind that finds and explores the inexhaustible consonance—or tropic relation—between psychic and poetic faith.

120. Edinger, *Ego and Archetype,* 182, from his chapter entitled "The Trinity Archetype and the Dialectic of Development."

121. Despite the fact that Derrida goes to great lengths to distinguish his concept of *différance* from Hegel's absolutist notion of the *Aufhebung,* there are (*toujours déjà*) important, mutually subversive similarities between the two notions as well. Furthermore, I would argue that these similarities, like the differences that underlie them, are analogous to the kinds of comparisons that can be made between aspects of the visions

of Hegel and Blake. For more on the slipperiness of the Derrida/Hegel connection, see John Llewelyn, "A Point of Almost Absolute Proximity to Hegel," *Deconstruction and Philosophy: The Texts of Jacques Derrida,* ed. John Sallis (Chicago: University of Chicago Press, 1987), 87–95; Chaffin, "Hegel, Derrida, and the Sign"; and Howells, "Derrida and Sartre."

122. Cf. Edinger, *Ego and Archetype,* 193: "Since individuation is never truly complete, each temporary state of completion or wholeness must be submitted once again to the dialectic of the trinity in order for life to go on." Representing a similar situation in the individuation of the images of the dreamer's psyche, Blake ends his version of the *Progress* with reminders of the process-state.

123. Abrams, *Natural Supernaturalism,* 234, quoting Hegel's *Phenomenology.*

124. It is difficult to identify the figures that make up this heavenly host, but surely the one on the right is a woman. Blake follows in this the format of his illustrations to Job, where Job and Job's wife are raised equally into a heavenly perspective. Other precedents in Blake's visual work are his many pictures of the Last Judgment, which feature risen women as well as risen men: risen humanity is his goal. In this Blake goes beyond Bunyan, who never asked the question (until Part II of the *Progress*): where is woman in the scheme of imaginative redemption?

125. See Blake's letter to Trusler, August 23, 1799 (E702/K793). In this discussion of allegory I am relying heavily on the theoretical treatment accorded it by Maureen Quilligan in her *The Language of Allegory.* Also helpful to me were the essays in Stephen J. Greenblatt, ed., *Allegory and Representation* (Baltimore: Johns Hopkins University Press, 1981).

126. Quilligan, *Language of Allegory,* 226.

127. Ibid., 220.

128. Ibid.

129. Ibid., 64: "Perhaps language cannot redeem language, so that poetry cannot redeem society; fiction may only entertain. But all allegories do aim at redemption; and because they must work with language, they ultimately turn to the paradox at the heart of their own assumptions about words and make the final focus of their narratives not merely the social function of language, but, in particular, the slippery tensions between literalness and metaphor. They scrutinize language's own problematic polysemy."

130. Blake's model is clearly the final cut of the first illustrated edition of the *Progress,* the so-called fifth edition of 1682. This engraving, known as "The Pilgrims Riding the Clouds," was replaced in the fourteenth edition by a woodcut of the Flemish design no. 9, "Christian and Hopeful in the River," which in its turn became the iconographic source for Blake's Plate 27. See Figs. B14 and B30. It would appear that the issues of closure raised by Bunyan's text infect as well the illustrative convention, for we can observe a curious equivocation about the nature of the last design in the book's fourteenth edition, where the ambiguous quatrains explicating no. 14 of the fifth edition are retained even though they exist in a relation of radical disjunction with the changed subject of the illustration. The quatrain reads:

> Now, now look how the holy Pilgrims rise
> Clouds are their chariots, Angels are their Guide!

> Who would not here for him all Hazards run
> That doth provide for his when the World's done?

When Stothard fashioned his series of eight designs for the *Progress* in 1788, he played on the problematics of the closing illustration (Fig. B59) by amalgamating the motifs of both earlier final plates in his own composition, entitled "The Pilgrims Cross the River to Heaven's Gate." This was an amalgamation that Blake pointedly resisted, and indeed his reversion to the model of the earliest closing design was itself a statement about revision, original derivation, and the open-endedness of all "final" states.

131. Abrams, *Natural Supernaturalism*, 230–31.

WORKS CITED

Abrams, M. H. *Natural Supernaturalism: Tradition and Revolution in Romantic Literature.* New York: Norton, 1971.

Adams, Hazard. "Blake and the Philosophy of the Literary Symbol" (rev. version). In *Essential Articles for the Study of William Blake, 1970–1984,* edited by Nelson Hilton, 1–14. Hamden, Conn.: Archon Books, 1986.

———. "Revisiting Reynolds' *Discourses* and Blake's Annotations." In *Blake in His Time,* edited by Robert N. Essick and Donald Pearce, 128–44. Bloomington: Indiana University Press, 1978.

———. "Synecdoche and Method." In *Critical Paths: Blake and the Argument of Method,* edited by Dan Miller, Mark Bracher, and Donald Ault, 41–71. Durham, N.C.: Duke University Press, 1987.

Aers, David. "William Blake and the Dialectics of Sex." *ELH* 44 (1977): 500–514.

Arnheim, Rudolf. *Visual Thinking.* Berkeley and Los Angeles: University of California Press, 1971.

Ault, Donald. *Narrative Unbound: Revisioning Blake's "Four Zoas."* Barrytown, N.Y.: Station Hill Press, 1985.

———. "Re-Visioning *The Four Zoas.*" In *Unnam'd Forms: Blake and Textuality,* edited Nelson Hilton and Thomas A. Volger, 105–40. Berkeley and Los Angeles: University of California Press, 1987.

———. *Visionary Physics: Blake's Response to Newton.* Chicago: Chicago University Press, 1974.

Baker, C. H. Collins. "Some Illustrations of Milton's *Paradise Lost* (1688–1850)." *Library,* 5th ser., 3 (1948): 1–21, 101–19.

Barthes, Roland. *S/Z: An Essay.* Translated by Richard Miller. New York: Farrar, Straus & Giroux, 1974.

Behrendt, Stephen. *The Moment of Explosion: Blake and the Illustration of Milton.* Lincoln: University of Nebraska Press, 1983.

Bellin, Harvey F., ed. *Blake and Swedenborg: Opposition Is True Friendship. The Sources of William Blake's Art in the Writings of Emanuel Swedenborg.* New York: Swedenborg Foundation, 1985.

Bentley, G. E., Jr. *Blake Records.* Oxford: Clarendon Press, 1969.

———. "William Blake and 'Johnny of Norfolk.'" *Studies in Philology* 53 (1956): 60–74.

————, ed. *William Blake: "Vala or The Four Zoas": A Facsimile of the Manuscript. A transcript and a Study of Its Growth and Significance*. Oxford: Clarendon Press, 1963.

Bentley, G. E., Jr., Robert N. Essick, Shelley M. Bennet, Morton D. Paley, and Robert P. Wark. *Essays on the Blake Followers*. San Marino, Calif.: Huntington Library and Art Gallery, 1983.

Bindman, David. *The Complete Graphic Works of William Blake*. New York: Putnam, 1978.

————, ed. *Colour Versions of William Blake's Job Designs from the Circle of John Linnell*. London: William Blake Trust, 1987.

————, ed. *William Blake's "Illustrations of the Book of Job": The Engravings and Related Materials with Essays*. London: William Blake Trust, 1987.

Binyon, Laurence. *The Engraved Designs of William Blake*. London: Benn, 1926.

Binyon, Laurence, and Geoffrey Keynes, eds. *Illustrations to the Book of Job by William Blake*. New York: Pierpont Morgan Library, 1935.

Bishop, Morchard. *Blake's Hayley: The Life, Works, and Friendships of William Hayley*. London: Gollanez, 1951.

Blake, William. *Blake: Complete Writings with Variant Readings*. Edited by Geoffrey Keynes. London: Oxford University Press, 1966.

————. *Blake's Poetry and Designs*. Selected and edited by Mary Lynn Johnson and John E. Grant. New York: Norton, 1979.

————. *The Complete Poetry and Prose of William Blake*. New rev. ed. Edited by David V. Erdman, with commentary by Harold Bloom. New York: Anchor Books, 1982.

————. *The Gates of Paradise*. 3 vols. Edited by Geoffrey Keynes. London: Trianon Press Facsimile, 1968.

Bloom, Harold. *The Anxiety of Influence*. New York: Oxford University Press, 1973.

————. *A Map of Misreading*. New York: Oxford University Press, 1975.

————. *Poetry and Repression*. New Haven: Yale University Press, 1976.

Blunt, Anthony. *The Art of William Blake*. New York: Columbia University Press, 1959.

Bowie, Malcolm. *Freud, Proust, and Lacan: Theory as Fiction*. Cambridge: Cambridge University Press, 1987.

Bracher, Mark. *Being Form'd: Thinking Through Blake's "Milton."* Barrytown, N.Y.: Station Hill Press, 1985.

————. "Rouzing the Faculties: Lacanian Psychoanalysis and the Marriage of Heaven and Hell in the Reader." In *Critical Paths: Blake and the Argument of Method*, edited by Dan Miller, Mark Bracher, and Donald Ault, 159–203. Durham, N.C.: Duke University Press, 1987.

Brogan, Harold O. "Blake on Women: Oothoon to Jerusalem." *CEA Critic* 48 (1986): 125–36.

Brooks, Peter. *Reading for the Plot: Design and Invention in Narrative*. New York: Knopf, 1984.

Brown, John. *John Bunyan: His Life, Times, and Work*. Rev. ed. Edited by Frank Mott Harrison. London: Hulbert, 1928.

Buchanan, E. S., ed. *John Bunyan's "A Book for Boys and Girls: Country Rhymes for Children."* New York: American Tract Society, 1928.

Bunyan, John. *Grace Abounding to the Chief of Sinners (GA)*. Edited by Roger Sharrock. Oxford: Clarendon Press, 1962.

———. *"The Pilgrim's Progress" by John Bunyan, 1628–1688, Illustrated with 29 Watercolor Paintings by William Blake*. Edited by G. B. Harrison, with an introduction by Geoffrey Keynes. New York: Limited Editions Club, 1941.

———. *The Pilgrim's Progress from This World to That Which Is to Come (PP)*. Edited by James Blanton Wharey. 2d ed. revised by Roger Sharrock. Oxford: Clarendon Press, 1960.

Burke, Joseph. "The Eidetic and the Borrowed Image: An Interpretation of Blake's Theory and Practice of Art" (1964). In *The Visionary Hand: Essays for the Study of Blake's Art and Aesthetics,* edited by Robert N. Essick, 253–302. Los Angeles: Hennessey & Ingalls, 1973.

Butlin, Martin. "An Extra Illustration to *Pilgrim's Progress.*" *Blake Newsletter* 19 (Winter 1971–72): 213–14.

———. *The Paintings and Drawings of William Blake*. 2 vols. New Haven: Yale University Press, 1981.

Calamy, Edmund. *The Art of Divine Meditation*. London, 1680.

Carr, Stephen Leo. "Illuminated Printing: Toward a Logic of Difference." In *Unnam'd Forms: Blake and Textuality,* edited by Nelson Hilton and Thomas A. Vogler, 177–96. Berkeley and Los Angeles: University of California Press, 1986.

Case, Thomas. *Mount Pisgah; or, a Prospect of Heaven*. London, 1670.

Cecil, David. *The Stricken Deer; or, The Life of Cowper*. London: Constable, 1943.

———. *Visionary and Dreamer: Two Poetic Painters—Samuel Palmer and Edward Burne-Jones*. Princeton: Princeton University Press, 1969.

Chaffin, Deborah. "Hegel, Derrida, and the Sign." In *Derrida and Deconstruction,* edited by Hugh J. Silverman, 77–91. London: Routledge, 1989.

Chayes, Irene H. "Blake's Ways with Art Sources: Michelangelo's *The Last Judgment.*" *Colby Library Quarterly* 20 (1984): 60–89.

Coates, Robert M. "The Art Galleries: William Blake and the Frick." *New Yorker,* June 9, 1960, 69–70.

Coleridge, Samuel T. *Biographia Literaria*. 2 vols. Edited by James Engell and W. Jackson Bates. Vol. 7 of *The Collected Works of Samuel Taylor Coleridge,* edited by Kathleen Coburn. Princeton: Princeton University Press, 1983.

———. *Notes on English Divines*. 2 vols. Edited by Rev. Derwent Coleridge. London, 1853.

Culler, Jonathan. "The Mirror Stage." In *High Romantic Argument: Essays for M. H. Abrams,* edited by Lawrence Lipking, 149–63. Ithaca: Cornell University Press, 1981.

Cunningham, Valentine. "Glossing and Glozing: Bunyan and Allegory." In *John Bunyan Conventicle and Parnassus: Tercentenary Essays,* edited by N. H. Keeble, 217–40. Oxford: Clarendon Press, 1988.

Curran, Stuart, and Joseph Anthony Wittreich, Jr., eds. *Blake's Sublime Allegory: Essays* on *"The Four Zoas," "Milton," "Jerusalem."* Madison: University of Wisconsin Press, 1973.

Dallenbach, Lucien. *The Mirror in the Text.* Translated by Jeremy Whitely and Emma Hughes. Chicago: University of Chicago Press, 1989.

Damon, S. Foster. *A Blake Dictionary: The Ideas and Symbols of William Blake.* Providence, R.I.: Brown University Press, 1965; reprinted Boulder, Colo.: Shambhala, 1979.

———. *William Blake, His Philosophy and Symbols.* Gloucester, Mass.: Peter Smith, 1958.

Darton, F. J. Harvey. *Children's Books in England.* 3d ed. Revised by Brian Alderson. Cambridge: Cambridge University Press, 1982.

De Rola, Stanislas Klossowiski. *Alchemy: The Secret Art.* New York: Avon Books, 1974.

Dickstein, Morris. "The Price of Experience: Blake's Reading of Freud." In *The Literary Freud: Mechanisms of Defense and the Poetic Will,* edited by Joseph Smith, 67–111. New Haven: Yale University Press, 1980.

Dictionary of National Biography. 22 vols. Edited by Leslie Stephen and Sidney Lee. London: Oxford University Press, 1917.

Digby, George Wingfield. *Symbol and Image in William Blake.* Oxford: Clarendon Press, 1957.

Dunbar, Pamela. *William Blake's Illustrations to the Poetry of Milton.* Oxford: Clarendon Press, 1980.

Eaves, Morris. "Blake and the Artistic Machine: An Essay on Decorum and Technology." *PMLA* 92 (1977): 903–27. Reprinted in *Essential Articles for the Study of William Blake, 1970–1984,* edited by Nelson Hilton, 175–210. Hamden, Conn.: Archon Books, 1986.

———. "A Reading of Blake's *Marriage of Heaven and Hell,* Plates 17–20: On and Under the Estate of the West." *Blake Studies* 4 (Spring 1972): 81–117.

———. *William Blake's Theory of Art.* Princeton: Princeton University Press, 1982.

Edinger, Edward F. *Ego and Archetype: Individuation and the Religious Function of the Psyche.* New York: Putnam, 1972.

———. *Encounter with the Self: A Jungian Commentary on William Blake's "Illustrations of the Book of Job."* Toronto: Inner City Books, 1986.

Edwards, Gavin. "Repeating the Same Dull Round." In *Unnam'd Forms: Blake and Textuality,* edited by Nelson Hilton and Thomas A. Volger, 26–48. Berkeley and Los Angeles: University of California Press, 1987.

Edwards, Philip. "The Journey in *The Pilgrim's Progress.*" In *"The Pilgrim's Progress": Critical and Historical Views,* edited by Vincent Newey, 111–17. Liverpool: Liverpool University Press, 1980.

Erdman, David V. *Blake: Prophet Against Empire. A Poet's Interpretation of the History of His Own Time.* 3d ed. Princeton: Princeton University Press, 1977.

———. *A Concordance to the Writings of William Blake.* 2 vols. Ithaca: Cornell University Press, 1967.

———. "The Steps (of Dance and Stone) That Order Blake's *Milton.*" *Blake Studies* 6 (Fall 1973): 73–87.

———. "William Blake's Debt to James Gillray." *Art Quarterly* 12 (1949): 165–70.

————, ed. *The Illuminated Blake: All of Blake's Illuminated Works with a Plate by Plate Commentary.* New York: Doubleday, 1974.

Erdman, David V., with Tom Dargan and Marlene Deverell–Van Meter. "Reading the Illuminations of Blake's *Marriage of Heaven and Hell.*" In *William Blake: Essays in Honour of Sir Geoffrey Keynes,* edited by Morton D. Paley and Michael Phillips, 162–207. Oxford: Clarendon Press, 1973.

Erdman, David V., and John E. Grant, eds. *Blake's Visionary Forms Dramatic.* Princeton: Princeton University Press, 1970.

Erdman, David V., and Donald K. Moore, eds. *The Notebook of William Blake: A Photographic and Typographic Facsimile.* Rev. ed. New York: Readex Books, 1977.

Essick, Robert N. "Blake and the Traditions of Reproductive Engraving." *Blake Studies* 5 (Fall 1972): 59–104.

————. *The Separate Plates of William Blake.* Princeton: Princeton University Press, 1983.

————. *William Blake, Printmaker.* Princeton: Princeton University Press, 1980.

————, ed. *The Visionary Hand: Essays for the Study of William Blake's Art and Aesthetics.* Los Angeles: Hennessey & Ingalls, 1973.

Essick, Robert N., and Donald Pearce, eds. *Blake in his Time.* Bloomington: Indiana University Press, 1978.

Evans, G. Blakemore, Robert A. Pratt, Robert W. Rogers, Jack Stillinger, and Gardiner Stillwell, eds. *Milton Studies in Honour of Harris Francis Fletcher.* Urbana: Illinois University Press, 1961.

Fish, Stanley E. *Self-consuming Artifacts: The Experience of Seventeenth-Century Literature.* Berkeley and Los Angeles: University of California Press, 1972.

Fletcher, Angus. *Allegory: The Theory of a Symbolic Mode.* Ithaca: Cornell University Press, 1970.

Forrest, James K., and Richard L. Greaves, eds. *John Bunyan: A Reference Guide.* Boston: G. K. Hall, 1982.

Fox, Susan. "The Female Metaphor in William Blake's Poetry." *Critical Inquiry* 3 (Spring 1977): 507–19. Reprinted in *Essential Articles for the Study of William Blake, 1970–1984,* edited by Nelson Hilton, 75–90. Hamden, Conn.: Archon Books, 1986.

Franz, M.-L. von. "The Process of Individuation." In *Man and his Symbols,* edited by C. G. Jung and M.-L. von Franz, 158–229. New York: Doubleday, 1964.

Freccero, John. *Dante: A Collection of Essays.* Englewood Cliffs, N.J.: Prentice-Hall, 1965.

Freeman, Rosemary. *English Emblem Books.* London: Chatto & Windus, 1948; reprinted New York: Octagon Books, 1966.

Freud, Sigmund. *The Standard Edition of the Complete Psychological Works of Sigmund Freud.* 24 vols. Edited by James Strachey et al. London: Hogarth Press, 1953–74.

Frieling, Barbara. "Blake at the Rim of the World: A Jungian Consideration of *Jerusalem.*" *Journal of Evolutionary Psychology* 8 (1987): 211–18.

Frosch, Thomas R. *The Awakening of Albion: The Renovation of the Body in the Poetry of William Blake.* Ithaca: Cornell University Press, 1974.

Frye, Northrop. *Fearful Symmetry: A Study of William Blake.* Princeton: Princeton University Press, 1947.

———. "Poetry and Design in William Blake." *Journal of Aesthetics and Art Criticism* 10 (1951): 25–42.

———. "The Road of Excess." In *The Stubborn Structure: Essays on Criticism and Society,* 160–74. Ithaca: Cornell University Press, 1970.

———, ed. *Blake: A Collection of Essays.* Englewood Cliffs, N.J.: Prentice-Hall, 1966.

Frye, Roland Mushat. *God, Man, and Satan: Patterns of Christian Thought and Life in "Paradise Lost," "Pilgrim's Progress," and the Great Theologians.* Princeton: Princeton University Press, 1960.

Gadamer, Hans-Georg. *Truth and Method.* 2d rev. ed. Translated by Joel Weinsheimer and Donald G. Marshall. New York: Crossroad, 1990.

Gallant, Christine. *Blake and the Assimilation of Chaos.* Princeton: Princeton University Press, 1978.

George, Diana Hume. *Blake and Freud.* Ithaca: Cornell University Press, 1980.

Gilchrist, Alexander. *Life of William Blake.* Rev. ed. Edited by Ruthven Todd. London: Dent, 1942.

———. *Life of William Blake, Pictor Ignotus.* 2 vols. London: Macmillan, 1863.

Gillespie, Diane Filby. "A Key to Blake's *Job:* Design XX." *Colby Library Quarterly* 19 (June 1983): 59–68.

Gillray, James. *The Works of James Gillray, from the Original Plates.* London: Henry G. Bohn, 1851.

Glazer-Schotz, Myra, and Gerda Norvig. "Blake's Book of Changes: On Reading Three Copies of the *Songs of Innocence and of Experience*." *Blake Studies* 9 (1980): 100–121.

Gleckner, Robert. *Blake and Spenser.* Baltimore: Johns Hopkins University Press, 1985.

Glen, Heather. *Vision and Disenchantment: Blake's "Songs" and Wordsworth's "Lyrical Ballads."* Cambridge: Cambridge University Press, 1983.

Godard, Jerry Caris. *Mental Forms Creating: William Blake Anticipates Freud, Jung, and Rank.* Lanham, Md.: University Press of America, 1985.

Goldberg, Arnold, ed. *Advances in Self Psychology.* New York: International University Press, 1980.

Gottlieb, Gerald, ed. *Early Children's Books and Their Illustrations.* New York: Pierpont Morgan Library, 1975.

Grant, John E. "Interpreting Blake's 'The Fly.'" In *Blake: A Collection of Essays,* edited by Northrop Frye, 32–55. Englewood Cliffs, N.J.: Prentice-Hall, 1966.

Greenblatt, Stephen J., ed. *Allegory and Representation.* Baltimore: Johns Hopkins University Press, 1981.

Greenham, Richard. *The Workes.* London, 1599–1600.

Hagstrum, Jean H. "Blake and the Sister Arts Tradition." In *Blake's Visionary Forms Dramatic,* edited by David V. Erdman and John E. Grant, 82–91. Princeton: Princeton University Press, 1970.

———. "Christ's Body." In *William Blake: Essays in Honour of Geoffrey Keynes,* edited by Morton D. Paley and Michael Phillips, 129–56. Oxford: Clarendon Press, 1977.

———. *William Blake, Poet and Painter: An Introduction to the Illuminated Verse.* Chicago: University of Chicago Press, 1964.

Haller, William. *The Rise of Puritanism.* New York: Harper & Row, 1957.

Halloran, William F. "*The French Revolution:* Revelation's New Form." In *Blake's*

Visionary Forms Dramatic, edited by David V. Erdman and John E. Grant, 30–56. Princeton: Princeton University Press, 1970.

Harding, M. Esther. *Journey into Self.* London: Longman's Green, 1956.

Harrison, Frank Mott. *A Bibliography of the Works of John Bunyan.* London: Bibliographic Society Transactions, 1932.

———. "Some Illustrators of *The Pilgrim's Progress* (Part One): John Bunyan." *Library,* 4th ser., 3 (December 1936): 241–63.

Haskin, Dayton. "The Burden of Interpretation in *The Pilgrim's Progress.*" *Studies in Philology* 79 (1982): 256–78.

Hawkins, Henry. *The Devout Hart, 1634.* Edited by John Horden. London: Scolar Press, 1975.

Hayley, William. *Life of Cowper.* 2 vols. London: J. Johnson, 1802. 2d ed. 3 vols. London: J. Johnson, 1804.

Heidegger, Martin. *Being and Time.* Translated by John Macquarrie and Edward Robinson. New York: Harper & Row, 1962.

Hess, Eckhard H. "Attitude and Pupil Size." *Scientific American,* April 1965, 46–54.

———. "The Role of Pupil Size in Communication." *Scientific American,* November 1975, 110–19.

Hill, Draper, ed. *The Satirical Etchings of James Gillray.* New York: Dover, 1976.

Hillman, James. *Archetypal Psychology: A Brief Account.* Dallas: Spring Publications, 1985.

———. *Healing Fiction.* Barrytown, N.Y.: Station Hill Press, 1983.

———. *Revisioning Psychology.* New York: Harper & Row, 1975.

Hilton, Nelson. *Literal Imagination: Blake's Vision of Words.* Berkeley and Los Angeles: University of California Press, 1983.

———. Review of *Blake, Hegel, and Dialectic,* by David Punter. *Blake: An Illustrated Quarterly* 17 (Spring 1984): 164–69.

———. "Some Sexual Connotations." *Blake: An Illustrated Quarterly* 16 (1982–83): 166–71.

———. "Under the Hill." *Blake: An Illustrated Quarterly* 22 (Summer 1988): 16–17.

———, ed. *Essential Articles for the Study of William Blake, 1970–1984.* Hamden, Conn.: Archon Books, 1986.

Hilton, Nelson, and Thomas A. Volger, eds. *Unnam'd Forms: Blake and Textuality.* Berkeley and Los Angeles: University of California Press, 1986.

Hind, Arthur. *An Introduction to a History of Woodcut.* 2 vols. New York: Dover, 1963.

Horn, William Dennis. "Blake's Revisionism: Gnostic Interpretation and Critical Methodology." In *Critical Paths: Blake and the Argument of Method,* edited by Dan Miller, Mark Bracher, and Donald Ault, 72–98. Durham, N.C.: Duke University Press, 1987.

Howard, John. "An Audience for *The Marriage of Heaven and Hell.*" *Blake Studies* 3 (Fall 1970): 19–51.

Howells, Christina M. "Derrida and Sartre: Hegel's Death Knell." In *Derrida and Deconstruction,* edited by Hugh J. Silverman, 169–81. London: Routledge, 1989.

Hoy, David Couzens. *The Critical Circle: Literature, History, and Philosophical Hermeneutics.* Berkeley and Los Angeles: University of California Press, 1978.

Iser, Wolfgang. *The Implied Reader: Patterns of Communication in Prose Fiction from Bunyan to Beckett.* Baltimore: Johns Hopkins University Press, 1974.

Jacobi, Jolande, ed. *Paracelsus: Selected Writings.* 2d ed. Princeton: Princeton University Press, 1958.

Jaensch, E. R. *Eidetic Imagery and Typological Methods for Investigation.* Translated by Oscar Oeser. London: Kegan Paul, 1930.

Johnson, Mary Lynn. "Emblem and Symbol in Blake." *Huntington Library Quarterly* 37 (February 1974): 151–70.

Jung, Carl Gustav. *The Collected Works of C. G. Jung.* 20 vols. Bollingen Series, 2d ed. Translated by R. F. C. Hull. Princeton: Princeton University Press, 1960–78.

———. *Memories, Dreams, Reflections.* Edited by Aniela Jaffe. New York: Pantheon Books, 1961.

Jung, C. G., and M.-L. von Franz, eds. *Man and his Symbols.* New York: Doubleday, 1964.

Jung, C. G., and W. Pauli. *The Interpretation of Nature and the Psyche.* New York: Pantheon Books, 1955.

Kaufmann, U. Milo. *"The Pilgrim's Progress" and Traditions in Puritan Meditation.* New Haven: Yale University Press, 1966.

Keeble, N. H., ed. *John Bunyan Conventicle and Parnassus: Tercentenary Essays.* Oxford: Clarendon Press, 1988.

Kemtz, Gail. "A Reading of Blake's *The Gates of Paradise.*" *Blake Studies* 3 (Spring 1971): 171–85.

Keynes, Geoffrey. *Blake Studies: Essays on His Life and Work.* 2d ed. Oxford: Clarendon Press, 1971.

———. *Engravings by William Blake: The Separate Plates and a Catalogue Raisonée.* Dublin: Emery Walker, 1956.

———. Introduction to *"The Pilgrim's Progress" by John Bunyan (1628–1688), Illustrated with 29 Watercolor Paintings by William Blake,* edited by G. B. Harrison, vii–xxxii. New York: Limited Editions Club, 1941.

———. *William Blake's Engravings.* London: Faber & Faber, 1950.

———, ed. *The Letters of William Blake.* London: Rupert Hart-Davis, 1956.

King, James. *William Cowper: A Biography.* Durham, N.C.: Duke University Press, 1986.

Kiralis, Karl. "William Blake as an Intellectual and Spiritual Guide to Chaucer's *Canterbury Pilgrims.*" *Blake Studies* 1 (Spring 1969): 139–90.

Klonsky, Milton. *William Blake: The Seer and His Visions.* New York: Harmony Books, 1977.

Knapp, Steven. *Personification and the Sublime: Milton to Coleridge.* Cambridge, Mass.: Harvard University Press, 1985.

Kohut, Heinz, and Ernest S. Wolf. "The Disorders of the Self and Their Treatment: An Outline." *International Journal of Psychoanalysis* 59 (1978): 413–25.

Lacan, Jacques. "The Function and Field of Speech and Language in Psychoanalysis." In *Ecrits: A Selection,* 30–113. Translated by Alan Sheridan. New York: Norton, 1977.

———. *The Four Fundamental Concepts of Psycho-Analysis.* Edited by Jacques-Alain Miller; translated by Alan Sheridan. New York: Norton, 1978.

Langland, Elizabeth. "Blake's Feminist Revision of Literary Tradition in 'The Sick Rose.'" In *Critical Paths: Blake and the Argument of Method,* edited by Dan Miller, Mark Bracher, and Donald Ault, 225–43. Durham, N.C.: Duke University Press, 1987.

Larabee, Stephen A. *English Bards and Grecian Marbles.* New York: Columbia University Press, 1943.

Larrissy, Edward. *William Blake.* Oxford: Blackwell, 1985.

Leader, Zachary. *Reading Blake's "Songs."* London: Routledge & Kegan Paul, 1981.

Lichtenberg, Joseph, Melvin Bornstein, and Donald Silver, eds. *Empathy.* 2 vols. Hillsdale, N.J.: Analytic Press, 1984.

Lindberg, Bo. *William Blake's Illustrations to the Book of Job.* Åbo: Åbo Akademi, 1973.

Lipking, Lawrence. "Quick Poetic Eyes: Another Look at Literary Pictorialism." In *Articulate Images: The Sister Arts from Hogarth to Tennyson,* edited by Richard Wendorf, 3–25. Minneapolis: University of Minnesota Press, 1983.

———, ed. *High Romantic Argument: Essays for M. H. Abrams.* Ithaca: Cornell University Press, 1981.

Lister, Raymond. *Samuel Palmer and "The Ancients."* Cambridge: Cambridge University Press for the Fitzwilliam Museum, 1984.

———. "Two Blake Drawings and a Letter from Samuel Palmer." *Blake Newsletter* 22 (Fall 1972): 53–54.

Llewelyn, John. "A Point of Almost Absolute Proximity to Hegel." In *Deconstruction and Philosophy: The Texts of Jacques Derrida,* edited by John Sallis, 87–95. Chicago: University of Chicago Press, 1987.

Lukacher, Ned. *Primal Scenes: Literature, Philosophy, Psychoanalysis.* Ithaca: Cornell University Press, 1986.

McGann, Jerome J. *The Romantic Ideology: A Critical Investigation.* Chicago: Chicago University Prss, 1983.

Mariani, Valero. *Michelangelo the Painter.* New York: Abrams, 1964.

Martz, Louis L. *The Paradise Within: Studies in Vaughan, Traherne, and Milton.* New Haven: Yale University Press, 1964.

Mauquoy-Hendrickx, Marie, ed. *Les étampes des Wierixs conservées au cabinet de la Bibliothèque Royale Albert Premier: catalogue raisonné.* Brussels: Bibliotheque Royale Albert 1er, 1978.

Mellor, Anne K. *Blake's Human Form Divine.* Berkeley and Los Angeles: University of California Press, 1974.

———. "Blake's Portrayal of Women." *Blake: An Illustrated Quarterly* 16 (1982–83): 148–55.

———. "Blake's *Songs of Innocence and of Experience:* A Feminist Perspective." *Nineteenth-Century Studies* 2 (1988): 1–17.

Miller, Dan. "Blake and the Deconstructive Interlude." In *Critical Paths: Blake and the Argument of Method,* edited by Dan Miller, Mark Bracher, and Donald Ault, 139–67. Durham, N.C.: Duke University Press, 1987.

Miller, Dan, Mark Bracher, and Donald Ault, eds. *Critical Paths: Blake and the Argument of Method*. Durham, N.C.: Duke University Press, 1987.

Mills, David. "The Dreams of Bunyan and Langland." In *"The Pilgrim's Progress": Critical and Historical Views,* edited by Vincent Newey, 154–81. Liverpool: Liverpool University Press, 1980.

Mitchell, W. J. T. *Blake's Composite Art: A Study of the Illuminated Poetry*. Princeton: Princeton University Press, 1978.

———. "Blake's Visions of the Last Judgment: Some Problems of Interpretation." In *Blake's Visions of the Last Judgment,* a *Blake Newsletter* pamphlet for the MLA Blake seminar, December 1975.

———. "Style and Iconography in the Illustrations of Blake's *Milton*." *Blake Studies* 6 (1975): 47–71.

Muir, Percy. *English Children's Books, 1600–1900*. London: B. T. Batsford, 1954.

Natoli, Joseph. "A Study of Blake's Contraries with Reference to Jung's Theory of Individuation." Ph.D. diss., State University of New York at Albany, 1973.

Nellist, Brian. "*The Pilgrim's Progress* and Allegory." In *"The Pilgrim's Progress": Critical and Historical Views,* edited by Vincent Newey, 132–53. Liverpool: Liverpool University Press, 1980.

Nemerov, Howard. *The Next Room of the Dream*. Chicago: University of Chicago Press, 1962.

Newey, Vincent. "Bunyan and the Confines of the Mind." In *"The Pilgrim's Progress": Critical and Historical Views,* edited by Vincent Newey, 21–48. Liverpool: Liverpool University Press, 1980.

———. "'With the Eyes of My Understanding': Bunyan, Experience, and Acts of Interpretation." In *John Bunyan Conventicle and Parnassus: Tercentenary Essays,* edited by N. H. Keeble, 189–216. Oxford: Clarendon Press, 1988.

———, ed. *"The Pilgrim's Progress": Critical and Historical Views*. Liverpool: Liverpool University Press, 1980.

Norman, H. J. *Cowper and Blake*. Olney, Eng.: Thomas Wright, 1913.

Norvig, Gerda. "Critical Appraisal and the Dating Game: The Case of Blake's *Man Sweeping the Interpreter's Parlor*." *Blake: An Illustrated Quarterly* (forthcoming).

———. "Images of Wonder, Images of Truth: Blake's Illustrations to *The Pilgrim's Progress*." Ph.D. diss., Brandeis University, 1979.

Nurmi, Martin K. *Blake's "Marriage of Heaven and Hell": A Critical Study*. Kent, Ohio: Kent State University Press, 1957.

———. "Negative Sources in Blake." In *William Blake: Essays for S. Foster Damon,* edited by Alvin Rosenfeld, 303–18. Providence, R.I.: Brown University Press, 1969.

Ostriker, Alicia. "Desire Gratified and Ungratified: William Blake and Sexuality." *Blake: An Illustrated Quarterly* 16 (1982–83): 156–65. Reprinted in *Essential Articles for the Study of William Blake, 1970–1984,* edited by Nelson Hilton, 211–36. Hamden, Conn.: Archon Books, 1986.

Owen, John. *The Works*. 17 vols. Edited by Rev. William H. Goold and Rev. Charles W. Quick. Philadelphia: Leighton Publications, 1850.

Paglia, Camille. *Sexual Personae: Art and Decadence from Nefertiti to Emily Dickinson.* New Haven: Yale University Press, 1990.

Paley, Morton D. "The Art of 'The Ancients.' " *Huntington Library Quarterly* 52 (1989): 97–124.

———. *The Continuing City: William Blake's "Jerusalem."* Oxford: Clarendon Press, 1983.

———. "Cowper as Blake's Spectre." *Eighteenth-Century Studies* 1 (1968): 236–52.

———. *Energy and the Imagination: A Study of the Development of Blake's Thought.* Oxford: Clarendon Press, 1970.

———. "The Figure of the Garment in *The Four Zoas, Milton,* and *Jerusalem.*" In *Blake's Sublime Allegory: Essays on "The Four Zoas," "Milton," "Jerusalem,"* edited by Stuart Curran and Joseph Anthony Wittreich, Jr., 119–39. Madison: University of Wisconsin Press, 1973.

———. "William Blake, the Prince of the Hebrews, and the Woman Clothed with the Sun." In *Blake: Essays in Honour of Sir Geoffrey Keynes,* edited by Morton D. Paley and Michael Phillips, 260–93. Oxford: Clarendon Press, 1973.

———. " 'Wonderful Originals'—Blake and Ancient Sculpture." In *Blake in his Time,* edited by Robert N. Essick and Donald Pearce, 170–97. Bloomington: Indiana University Press, 1978.

Paley, Morton D., and Michael Phillips, eds. *Blake: Essays in Honour of Sir Geoffrey Keynes.* Oxford: Clarendon Press, 1973.

Palmer, A. H. *The Life and Letters of Samuel Palmer.* London, 1892.

Parisi, Frank M. "Emblems of Melancholy: *For Children: The Gates of Paradise.*" In *Interpreting Blake: Essays,* edited by Michael Phillips, 70–110. Cambridge: Cambridge University Press, 1978.

Patrick, J. Max, ed. *The Prose of John Milton.* New York: Doubleday, 1967.

Penfield, Wilder, and L. Roberts. *Speech and Brain Mechanisms.* Princeton: Princeton University Press, 1959.

Phillips, Michael, ed. *Interpreting Blake: Essays.* London: Cambridge University Press, 1978.

Pickering, Samuel F. *John Locke and Children's Books in the Eighteenth Century.* Knoxville: University of Tennessee Press, 1981.

Pointon, Marcia. *Milton and English Art.* Toronto: University of Toronto Press, 1970.

Praz, Mario. *Studies in Seventeenth-Century Imagery.* 2d ed. Rome: Edizione di Storia e Litteratura, 1964.

Priestly, Joseph. *Theological and Miscellaneous Works.* 22 vols. London, 1822.

Punter, David. "Blake/Hegel/Derrida: A Reply to Nelson Hilton's Review of *Blake, Hegel, and Dialectic.*" *Blake: An Illustrated Quarterly* 18 (Summer 1984): 58–63.

———. *Blake, Hegel, and Dialectic.* Amsterdam: Rodophi, 1982.

Quarles, Francis. *Hieroglyphikes of the Life of Man.* 8 vols. London: M. Flesher for John Marriot, 1638.

Quilligan, Maureen. *The Language of Allegory: Defining the Genre.* Ithaca: Cornell University Press, 1979.

Raysor, T. M., ed. *Coleridge's Miscellaneous Criticism.* London: Constable, 1936.

Reynolds, Joshua. *Discourses on Art*. New York: Collier Books, 1961.

Ricoeur, Paul. *Freud and Philosophy: An Essay on Interpretation*. Translated by Denis Savage. New Haven: Yale University Press, 1970.

Rose, Edward J. "Blake's Illustrations for *Paradise Lost, L'Allegro,* and *Il Penseroso:* A Thematic Reading." *Hartford Studies in Literature* 2 (1970): 40–67.

———. "Blake's Metaphorical States." *Blake Studies* 4 (Fall 1971): 9–31.

Rosenblum, Robert. "The International Style of 1800: A Study in Linear Abstraction." Ph.D. diss., New York University, 1956.

———. *Transformations in Late Eighteenth-Century Art*. Princeton: Princeton University Press, 1970.

Rosenfeld, Alvin, ed. *William Blake: Essays for S. Foster Damon*. Providence, R.I.: Brown University Press, 1969.

Rossetti, William Michael. "Annotated Catalogue of Blake's Pictures and Drawings." In *Life of William Blake, Pictor Ignotus,* by Alexander Gilchrist, 2:201–64. London: Macmillan, 1863.

Rudd, Margaret. *Organiz'd Innocence: The Story of Blake's Prophetic Books*. London: Routledge & Paul, 1956.

Russell, Archibald. *The Engravings of William Blake: A Critical Study Together with a Catalogue Raisonné*. London: Grant Richards, 1912.

Salemi, Joseph S. "Emblematic Tradition in Blake's *The Gates of Paradise.*" *Blake: An Illustrated Quarterly* 15 (Winter 1981–82): 108–24.

Sallis, John, ed. *Deconstruction and Philosophy: The Texts of Jacques Derrida*. Chicago: University of Chicago Press, 1987.

Schiller, Gertrud. *Iconography of Christian Art*. 2 vols. Translated by Janet Seligman. Greenwich, Conn.: New York Graphic Society, 1971.

Sharrock, Roger. "Bunyan and the English Emblem Writers." *Review of English Studies* 21 (1945): 105–16.

———. "Life and Story in *The Pilgrim's Progress.*" In *"The Pilgrim's Progress": Critical and Historical Views,* edited by Vincent Newey, 49–68. Liverpool: Liverpool University Press, 1980.

Shaviro, Steven. "'Striving with Systems': Blake and the Politics of Difference." *Boundary 2* 10 (1982): 229–50. Reprinted in *Essential Articles for the Study of William Blake, 1970–1984,* edited by Nelson Hilton, 271–300. Hamden, Conn.: Archon Books, 1986.

Sibbes, Richard. *A Glance of Heaven*. London, 1638.

Silverman, Hugh J. ed. *Derrida and Deconstruction*. London: Routledge, 1989.

Singer, June. *The Unholy Bible: A Psychological Interpretation of William Blake*. New York: Putnam, 1970.

Singleton, Charles. "In Exitu Israel de Aegypto." In *Dante: A Collection of Essays,* edited by John Freccero, 102–21. Englewood Cliffs, N.J.: Prentice-Hall, 1965.

Siskin, Clifford. *The Historicity of Romantic Discourse*. Oxford: Oxford University Press, 1988.

Slote, Bernice, ed. *Myth and Symbol: Critical Approaches and Applications*. Lincoln: University of Nebraska Press, 1963.

Smith, Joseph, ed. *The Literary Freud: Mechanisms of Defense and the Poetic Will.* New Haven: Yale University Press, 1980.

Stein, Kenneth. "Blake's Apocalyptic Poetry: A Study of the Genre of Blake's Prophetic Books." Ph.D. diss., Brandeis University, 1969.

Storch, Margaret. "Blake and Women: 'Nature's Cruel Holiness.'" *American Imago* 38 (Summer 1981): 221–46.

———. *Sons and Adversaries: Women in William Blake and D. H. Lawrence.* Knoxville, University of Tennessee Press, 1990.

———. "The 'Spectrous Fiend' Cast Out: Blake's Crisis at Felpham." *Modern Language Quarterly* 44 (1983): 115–35.

Sturrock, John, ed. *Structuralism and Since: From Lévi-Strauss to Derrida.* Oxford: Oxford University Press, 1979.

Svendson, Kvester. "Some Illustrators of Milton: The Expulsion from Paradise." In *Milton Studies in Honour of Harris Francis Fletcher,* edited by G. Blakemore Evans, Robert A. Pratt, Robert W. Rogers, Jack Stillinger, and Gardiner Stillwell. Urbana: University of Illinois Press, 1961.

Swedenborg, Emanuel. *Apocalypse Revealed.* 3 vols. Manchester: C. Wheeler, 1791.

———. *The Wisdom of Angels Concerning the Divine Providence.* Translated by N. Tucker. London: R. Hindmarsh, 1790.

Talon, Henri. *John Bunyan: The Man and His Works.* Translated by Barbara Wall. Cambridge, Mass.: Harvard University Press, 1951.

Tannenbaum, Leslie. *Biblical Tradition in Blake's Early Prophecies: The Great Code of Art.* Princeton: Princeton University Press, 1982.

Tayler, Irene. *Blake's Illustrations to the Poems of Gray.* Princeton: Princeton University Press, 1971.

———. "The Woman Scaly." *MMLA Bulletin* 6 (Spring 1973): 74–87. Reprinted in *Blake's Poetry and Designs,* edited by Mary Lynn Johnson and John E. Grant, 538–53. New York: Norton, 1981.

Taylor, Gary J. "The Structure of *The Marriage:* A Revolutionary Primer." *Studies in Romanticism* 13 (Spring 1974): 141–45.

Thorpe, James, ed. *Milton Criticism: Selections from Four Centuries.* New York: Collier Books, 1969.

Thwaite, Mary. *From Primer to Pleasure in Reading.* Boston: Horn Books, 1972.

Tindall, William York. *John Bunyan, Mechanick Preacher.* New York: Columbia University Press, 1934.

Toynbee, Paget, ed. *Dantis Alagherii Epistolae: The Letters of Dante.* Oxford: Clarendon Press, 1920.

Turner, James. "Bunyan's Sense of Place." In *"The Pilgrim's Progress": Critical and Historical Views,* edited by Vincent Newey, 91–110. Liverpool: Liverpool University Press, 1980.

Van Ghent, Dorothy. *The English Novel: Form and Function.* New York: Harper & Row, 1953.

Vaughan, Thomas. *The Works of Thomas Vaughan, Mystic and Alchemist.* Edited by Arthur Edward Waite. New Hyde Park, N.Y.: University Books, 1968.

Viscomi, Joseph. *Prints by William Blake and His Followers.* Ithaca: Herbert F. Johnson Museum of Art, Cornell University, 1983.

Wark, Robert. *Drawings by John Flaxman in the Huntington Collection.* San Marino, Calif.: Huntington Library and Art Gallery, 1970.

Warner, Janet E. *Blake and the Language of Art.* Kingston and Montreal: McGill-Queen's University Press, 1984.

————. "Blake's Use of Gesture." In *Blake's Visionary Forms Dramatic,* edited by David V. Erdman and John E. Grant, 174–95. Princeton: Princeton University Press, 1970.

Webster, Brenda. *Blake's Prophetic Psychology.* Athens: University of Georgia Press, 1983.

————. "Blake, Women, and Sexuality." In *Critical Paths: Blake and the Argument of Method,* edited by Dan Miller, Mark Bracher, and Donald Ault, 204–24. Durham, N.C.: Duke University Press, 1987.

Wendorf, Richard, ed. *Articulate Images: The Sister Arts from Hogarth to Tennyson.* Minneapolis: University of Minnesota Press, 1983.

Werner, Bette Charlene. *Blake's Vision of the Poetry of Milton.* Lewisburg, Pa.: Bucknell University Press, 1986.

Wharey, James Blanton. *A Study of the Sources of Bunyan's Allegories, with Special Reference to Deguilleville's "Pilgrimage of Man."* Baltimore: J. H. Furst, 1904.

Whitaker, William. *Disputation on Holy Scripture Against the Papists, Especially Bellarmine and Stapleton.* Translated by Rev. William Fitzpatrick. London: Cambridge University Press, 1849.

Wills, James T. "An Additional Drawing for Blake's Bunyan Series." *Blake Newsletter* 23 (Winter 1972–73): 63–67.

————. "William Blake's Designs for Bunyan's *Pilgrim's Progress.*" Ph.D. diss., University of Toronto, 1975.

Wilson, Mona. *The Life of William Blake.* Edited by Geoffrey Keynes. London: Oxford University Press, 1971.

Wittcut, W. P. *Blake: A Psychological Study.* London: Hollis & Carter, 1946. Reprinted Port Washington, N.Y.: Kennikat Press, 1966.

Wittreich, Joseph Anthony, Jr. *Angel of Apocalypse: Blake's Idea of Milton.* Madison: University of Wisconsin Press, 1975.

————. "Sublime Allegory: Blake's Epic Manifesto and the Milton Tradition." *Blake Studies* 4 (Spring 1972): 15–44.

————. *Visionary Poetics: Milton's Tradition and His Legacy.* San Marino, Calif.: Huntington Library and Art Gallery, 1979.

————, ed. *Calm of Mind: Tercentenary Essays on "Paradise Regained" and "Samson Agonistes."* Cleveland: Press of Case Western Reserve University, 1971.

————, ed. *The Romantics on Milton: Formal Essays and Critical Asides.* Cleveland: Press of Case Western Reserve University, 1970.

Wooden, Warren W. *Children's Literature of the Early Renaissance.* Edited by Jeanie Watson. Lexington: University Press of Kentucky, 1986.

Wordsworth, William. *The Prose Works of William Wordsworth.* 3 vols. Edited by W. J. B. Owen and Jane Worthington Smyser. Oxford: Clarendon Press, 1974.

Wright, Thomas. *The Life of William Blake.* 2 vols. Olney, Eng.: Thomas Wright, 1929.

Yeats, William Butler. "Blake's Illustrations to Dante." In *Essays and Introductions.* New York: Collier Books, 1968.

INDEX

244n.28, 253n.31, 263n.76, 264n.80. *See also* Puritan practice

Carr, Stephen, 241n.18, 259n.52

Cecil, David, 238n.1, 264n.80, 267n.98

Chaffin, Deborah, 297n.117, 298n.121

Chaucer, Geoffrey, 73, 107–9, 211; Blake's illustrations to, 107, 271n.119; and psychology of types, 108

Chayes, Irene H., 241n.16, 247n.1

Children's literature, 76, 78, 258n.49. *See also under* Blake, William: and children's literature

Christian Takes Leave of His Companions (*Warrior with Angels*), 181–82, 293n.91

Christopher, Saint, 282n.46

Coates, Robert M., 278n.17

Coleridge, Samuel Taylor, 13, 19–20, 237n.33, 279n.28

Corbin, Henry, xxvii

Cowper, William, 87–91, 93, 94, 264n.80, 265nn.81,83,84, 266n.92, 267n.98

Culler, Jonathan, 11

Cunningham, Valentine, 276n.7, 296n.113

Dallenbach, Lucien, 287n.70

Damon, S. Foster, 240n.11, 246n.40, 250n.11, 262n.73, 263n.76

Dante Alighieri, 73, 98, 268n.102; Blake's illustrations to, 7, 271n.119

Dargan, Tom, 262nn.73,76

Darton, F.J. Harvey, 258n.49

De Rola, Stanislas Klossowiski, 274n.141

Derrida, Jacques, 297nn.117,121

Descriptive Catalogue, A, 32, 49, 103, 107–9, 233n.5, 241n.17, 271n.124, 272n.127, 279n.25, 296n.107; Chaucer commentary in, 107–9, 235n.22, 272n.127

Dickstein, Morris, 237n.26

Digby, George Wingfield, 236n.26, 256n.40

Dissenting tradition. *See under* Blake, William: and dissenting tradition; Bunyan, John: and dissenting tradition; Puritan practice

Dreams, 18, 39, 105; Blake, role of, in, 96, 110–17, 126–27, 138, 149–50, 160, 179, 197, 207, 267n.100, 274n.138; Bunyan, role of, in, 103, 138, 160, 246n.45, 292n.85; rhetoric of, 112, 138, 197, 207,

292n.85. *See also* Dream-vision; *Illustrations to "The Pilgrim's Progress"* (Blake); *The Pilgrim's Progress*

Dream-vision: and allegory, 127–28; dreams-within-dreams in, 43, 112, 114–17, 164–65, 246n.45, 274n.138; *The Gates* as, 113, 114–17; *The Pilgrim's Progress* as, xxvi, 3, 17, 39, 96, 103, 126, 128–29, 138; symbolic transformations in, 68. *See also* Allegory; *The Gates of Paradise; Illustrations to "The Pilgrim's Progress"* (Blake)

Dryden, John, 73

Dunbar, Pamela, 276n.6

Dürer, Albrecht, 180, 280n.29

Eaves, Morris, 20, 233n.55, 237nn.29,35, 239n.7, 241n.17, 262n.76, 269n.11, 278n.21, 295n.101

Edinger, Edward F., 236n.26, 270n.118, 271n.121, 298n.122

Edwards, Gavin, 236n.22

Edwards, Philip, 276n.7, 296n.113

Empathy, 235n.32. *See also under* Blake, William: and empathy

Enthusiasm, 87–88; and evangelism, 88, 266n.92

Erdman, David V., 62, 69, 71, 82, 231n.2, 248n.3, 253n.26, 254nn.33, 34, 255n.37, 256nn.39,40, 258n.51, 259nn.52,56, 261n.67, 262nn.73,76, 268n.104, 271nn.121, 124, 272n.127, 273n.131, 274nn.136,137

Essick, Robert N., 248nn.2,4, 249n.5, 250nn.12,14, 295n.101

Europe, 59, 69–71, 255n.37, 267n.100, 295n.103

Everlasting Gospel, The, 274n.138

Extrinsic-devalorization. *See* Literary theory

Faerie Queene, The, 211

Farnese Hercules, the. See *Hercules Farnese*

Finch, Francis Oliver, 238n.1

Fish, Stanley, 203, 249n.8

Flaxman, John, 69, 93–94, 123–24, 243n.25, 255n.37, 265n.83, 276n.6, 295n.103

Flaxman, Nancy, 255n.37

Fletcher, Angus, 81, 261n.68, 276n.7

Forrest, James K., 277n.15

124–213, 218–19; allegory, critique of, 126–28; antithesis in, 141, 144–45, 147, 160, 190, 194, 204; architecture in, 144, 156–57, 161, 163, 176, 180, 192, 196, 198–99, 282n.40, 292n.87, 294n.96; Bible, image of, 143, 151, 281n.39; brotherhood in, 188, 203; Christian's burden in, 142, 146, 164, 167, 169–70, 196, 281n.38, 289n.75, 295n.106; conversion in, 167, 172, 173; criticism of, 124, 277n.10; doubling in, 122, 138, 139, 145, 148, 151–52, 154, 161, 171, 172, 176, 179, 180–81, 186, 188–89, 200–201, 277n.10, 289n.76; formal devices in, 17, 135–36, 140, 141, 143, 145, 146–47, 148–49, 151, 154, 155–57, 160, 162, 164, 167, 169–70, 171–72, 175, 177, 180–81, 183–84, 188–89, 190, 192, 194, 200, 202–4, 206–7, 285n.56; frontality in, 145, 148, 153, 164, 169, 175, 186, 188; garments in, 134, 135, 141–42, 144–45, 161–62, 164, 172–73, 178, 181, 187, 194, 198, 200, 286n.63, 290n.80, 292n.85, 294n.101; gender in, 172, 289n.77, 294n.100, 298n.124; homoeroticism in, 184–85; horizontality of, 143, 154, 160, 171, 200, 207; individuation motif in, 23, 129, 183, 201, 205–6, 207; initiation in, 172, 200; interpretation in, 128, 160–61, 186–87; keys in, 160, 196, 198; landscape in, 135–36, 141, 143–44, 146–47, 149–50, 151, 152, 153, 154, 156, 163, 165, 167, 168, 170, 177, 186, 188, 192; lions in, 134, 143, 146, 170, 178, 179, 280n.29, 289n.75, 293n.93; narration, theme of, 186–87; narrative structure of, 124–25, 155, 158, 160, 163–64, 166–68, 185, 194, 201, 207, 282n.42; narratological distortions of Bunyan's text in, 23, 163, 167–68, 185, 194; and *The Notebook,* 78, 82; nudity in, 161–62, 186, 194–95, 196; and *Progress* illustrations by others, 7, 23, 119, 122, 136–38, 146, 151, 167, 190, 218–19, 275n.1, 276n.10, 281n.39, 282n.42, 284n.52, 286n.59, 293n.92, 294n.100, 295n.103, 298n.130; psychological perspectives in, 17, 23, 126–27, 128–29, 139, 141–42, 146, 148, 152–54, 155–56, 161–63, 168–70, 173, 175, 177, 179, 180, 183, 186–88, 191–

93, 194, 196, 198, 201, 203–5, 206–9; quadrupling in, 129, 171, 181, 188, 200–202, 207; rainbow in, 134–36, 139, 141, 149, 156, 161, 170, 172, 177–78, 194, 199–200, 205, 240n.11; and reader/viewer response, 141, 149, 152–53, 163, 164, 166, 186, 192, 198, 209; Roll of eternal identity in, 173, 176, 178, 292n.89, 294n.96; scientific doubt in, 191–92; self-division in, 141–42, 144–45, 204; self-reflexivity in, 160–61, 162–63, 165–66, 187, 195; sequential groupings of, 140, 143–44, 149, 151, 153–55, 158, 160, 171, 175, 177–78, 180–82, 184–85, 188–89, 200–201, 205, 277n.10, 280n.35, 285n.54, 289n.75, 292n.89, 293n.91; sword in, 179, 180, 185, 292n.89, 294n.96; tripling in, 151, 154–55, 162, 171, 175, 180, 201, 277n.10, 280n.34, 289n.76; typological recurrence in, 135–36, 151–52, 158, 162, 165–66, 169–70, 186, 190, 191, 192, 195, 196, 200–201, 202–4, 209; verticality of, 141, 149, 154, 170, 177, 200. *See also* Blake, William; Dreams; Dream-vision; *The Pilgrim's Progress*

—characters in: Apollyon, 135, 181, 183–85, 186, 187, 188–89, 191, 192, 195, 293n.93; damsels of House Beautiful, 180–81; the dreamer (*see* the narrator/dreamer); Evangelist, 139, 143, 151–52, 153–54, 195, 281n.39; Faithful, 186–88, 191–95, 200, 201, 247n.46; Giant Despair, 194–97; Good-will, 78, 156–58, 162, 187, 205; Help, 148–49, 153, 169–70, 283n.48; Hopeful, 192–93, 196, 197–98, 200–202, 204, 206–7; the Interpreter, 160–61, 163, 187–88, 200, 201, 287n.46; Jesus, 168–70, 171, 173, 184–85, 208–9; Man in the Iron Cage, xxix, 78, 82, 161–63, 196; Man Who Dreamed of the Day of Judgment, 163–65, 168, 173, 196, 290n.80; the narrator/dreamer, 23, 43, 134–35, 141–42, 143, 146, 149, 152, 156, 160–63, 165–66, 168, 170, 175, 177–78, 184–85, 186–88, 190–91, 193, 194, 195–96, 198–210 passim, 212, 247n.46, 276–77n.10; Obstinate and Pliable, 144–47; porter of House Beautiful, 176, 181; Shepherds of the

Traveller in Repose, The (Blake), 287n.69
Turner, James, 231n.5, 276n.7

Urizen, The Book of, 246n.43, 267n.100

Valley of the Shadow of Death, The (Cowper), 264n.80
Valley of the Shadow of Death, The (Gillray), 253n.26
Van Ghent, Dorothy, 276n.7
Van Meter, Marlene Deverell, 262n.73, 262n.76
Varley, John, 243n.25
Vaughan, Henry, 245n.40
Vaughan, Thomas, 245n.40
Virgil, On (Blake), 282n.41
Viscomi, Joseph, 238n.1
Visionary hermeneutics: Blake's practice of, xxviii, xxix, xxx, 4–6, 20, 21, 26, 31, 33, 45, 74, 78, 84, 125, 129, 163, 238n.7; definition of, 4–5
Vision of the Last Judgment, A, 15, 21, 27–31, 43, 44, 53, 100–105, 109, 127, 139, 236nn.22,24, 240n.15, 252n.22, 269n.113, 271n.124, 272n.127; and heavenly meditation, 40; hermeneutics of, 27–31; Noah in, 31, 240nn.11,13; quoted, 16, 17, 32, 33, 45, 55, 68, 69, 199, 239n.10, 240n.12, 247n.50

Wark, Robert, 255n.37
Warner, Janet E., xxix, 278n.19
Webster, Brenda, 237n.26
Werner, Bette C., 276n.6
Wharey, James Blanton, 243n.26, 271n.119, 275n.27
White, Robert, 136
Wierix, Anton, 58–59, 68, 76, 252nn.19,20,21, 260n.58
Wills, James T., 233n.8, 234n.15, 281n.35, 293n.91
Wilson, Mona, 238n.1, 267n.96, 268n.101
Wittcut, W. P., 236n.26
Wittreich, Joseph Anthony, Jr., 233n.10, 252n.22, 256n.38
Wolf, Ernest S., 236n.23
Wooden, Warren W., 258n.49
Wordsworth, William, 13–14, 20, 237n.35, 249n.7
Wright, Thomas, 250n.14, 265n.80, 266nn.91,92, 293n.83

Yeats, William Butler, 32, 81, 232n.6, 242n.19

Compositor:	Keystone Typesetting, Inc.
Text:	10.5/13.5 Bembo
Display:	Bembo
Printer:	Thomson-Shore, Inc.
Binder:	Thomson-Shore, Inc.